T0369528

FAITH
OF THE AGES

The Hebraic Roots of the Christian Faith

RICHARD N. RHOADES
MA. DIV.

Faith of the Ages
The Hebraic Roots of the Christian Faith

iUniverse books may be ordered through booksellers or by contacting:

iUniverse LLC
1663 Liberty Drive
Bloomington, IN 47403
www.iuniverse.com
1-800-Authors (1-800-288-4677)

Because of the dynamic nature of the Internet, any web addresses or links contained in this book may have changed since publication and may no longer be valid. The views expressed in this work are solely those of the author and do not necessarily reflect the views of the publisher, and the publisher hereby disclaims any responsibility for them.

ISBN: 978-1-4759-3004-7 (sc)
ISBN: 978-1-4759-3006-1 (hc)
ISBN: 978-1-4759-3005-4 (e)

Printed in the United States of America

iUniverse rev. date: 08/21/2014

Photos and Art Illustrations
Art illustrations were done by Sharon Higgins, a Southwestern Artist who paints and lives in Albuquerque, New Mexico: Front Cover & pages 20, 21, 26, 30, 44, 47, 53, 96, 106, 108, 109, 111, 112, 114, 118, 134, 151, 154, 157, 159, 161, 162, 163.

Library of Congress: pages 45, 152, 158.

Map of Seven Churches of Revelation used by permission from the Holman Bible Atlas. Thomas Brisco © 1998, Broadman & Holman Publishers: page 136.

Wikimedia Commons: pages 38, 46, 48, 101, 135, 169, 170, 172, 179.

Scripture quotations marked AKJV are from the Authorized King James Version of the Bible.

Scripture quotations marked JPS are from the Tanakh, published by the Jewish Publication Society.

Scripture quotations marked The Scriptures are from the Messianic Institute for Scripture Research.

Scripture quotations marked NASV are from the American Standard Bible. Copyright © 1960, 1962, 1968, 1971, 1972, 1973, 1975, 1977, 1995, by the Lockman Foundation. Used by permission.

Scripture quotations marked NIV are from the Holy Bible, New International Version, NIV. Copyright © 1973, 1978, 1984 by Biblica, Inc. Used by permission. All rights reserved worldwide.

Contents

Other Works

by

Richard N. Rhoades

*

Lady Liberty

The Ancient Goddess

Of America

*

The Babylon Code

Is AMERICA In Prophecy?

*www.ladylibertybooks.net

To God goes all the honor and glory for the inception and completion of this book. Thank you for restoring my health and sparing my life.

> "You O LORD are mighty forever. You raised the dead. You are mighty to save. You sustain the living with grace, resurrect the dead with abundant mercy, uphold the falling, heal the sick, set free those in bondage, and keep faith with those that sleep in the dust. Who is like You, King, who causes death and restores life, and makes salvation sprout?" [The Geebore Adonai—the Might of God portion of the Amida.]

Acknowledgements

So many people deserve credit for their contributions to the completion of this book. My dear wife, Judith, has been a treasure. Without her loving support and understanding this book would never have been possible. The advice of the sisters Marion Lynch and Marjorie Down on the writing of the manuscript has been invaluable. Patricia Lane's help was critical to my securing out-of-print books for research. The art work of the gifted Southwestern Artist Sharon Higgins cannot be measured. Sharon paints in oils, watercolors and acrylics on canvas, paper and on unusual surfaces such as slate, and lives in Albuquerque, New Mexico. Her unique style of art can be viewed at several locations in New Mexico, including the Natural Resources Building at the New Mexico State Fair. Dean Wheelock and Rick Lastrapes have made a significant contribution to this book by proof-reading the manuscript and offering helpful suggestions.

Finally, I must not forget to acknowledge all the wonderful people at *Adat Yeshua Messianic Jewish Synagogue* in Albuquerque, New Mexico. I especially want to thank Rick Lastrapes, who was the spiritual leader of *Adat Yeshua* at the time I was introduced to my Hebraic roots.

May the LORD bless each of you.

Preface

WHAT IS THIS BOOK ABOUT?

Primarily, this book is about two walks of faith, which explains Sharon Higgins' front cover illustration of the aged cultivated olive tree and the stunted wild olive bush. Although the cultivated olive tree and the wild olive bush belong to the same tree family they are uniquely different. The cultivated olive tree is one of the hardest trees on the planet and produces mature olives that can be used in a variety of ways. Because of an extensive root system the cultivated olive tree can tolerate drought well, live up to several centuries, and remain productive throughout its life-time. The wild olive bush is much different. When left alone in its natural state the wild olive bush produces olives, but they are small and worthless.[1] Regardless of how much attention is given to the wild olive bush in its natural state it can only produce mature fruit when grafted onto the good rootstock of a cultivated olive tree.[2]

Paul, who was a native of the Mediterranean region, where cultivated olive trees and wild olive bushes grew in abundance, would have been well-acquainted with the unique characteristics of the "wild olive bush". Not surprisingly, when Paul wrote to the predominately Gentile Believers in Rome he masterfully referred to them as "wild olive branches" (Rom. 11:17).

For centuries, most Christians believed that because the New Testament was written in Greek the study of its Greek roots should take priority over the study of the Hebrew Scriptures. Today that conception is changing. Christian scholars are now beginning to examine the Hebraic origins of Scripture with renewed interest. For example, the Bible language scholars Roy Blizzard Jr., and David Blivin, co-authors of the book entitled

Understanding the Difficult Words of Jesus, point out that 78 percent of the biblical text was written in Hebrew and only 22 percent in Greek.[3] It can also be established that Matthew, Mark, Luke, and Acts 1-15 are highly Hebraic, which accounts for another 43 percent of the New Testament,[4] making the origins of the Holy Scriptures more than 90 percent Hebraic.

In 1965, Dr. Merrill Tenney, former Dean of the Graduate School of Wheaton College, wrote a book entitled *New Testament Times,* pointing Christians to the need to understand the Jewish context in which the New Testament was written, saying:

> The revelation of God in the New Testament was imparted through men who lived in a definite locale of time and space, and who spoke in the imagery and circumstances of their own era. While the truth and application of the message are unquestionably eternal and unchanging, the correct interpretation depends largely upon a proper comprehension of its historical setting. Because the authors lived within the milieu they described, they took for granted that their contemporaries would understand it too, and consequently did not attempt to explain many details which would be quite patent to their readers. To us of the twentieth century the facts which they assumed to be obvious and hence unnecessary to explain are obscure. We can comprehend the historical context of these writings only by careful research and reconstruction of the environment from which they emanated.[5]

With this aim in mind, we shall explore the origins of those first century followers of the young Rabbi from Nazareth, represented by the cultivated "Olive Tree," and the origins of the Christian Church, which are represented by the wild olive bush. We will also look at the anti-*Semitism* of the Greek and Latin Church Fathers, the Roman Emperor Constantine, Roman Catholic Church authorities, and leaders of the Reformation, who all played a major role in moving Christianity away from its Hebraic roots. In addition, we will look at several passages of Scripture that were added to and subtracted from the ancient Greek manuscripts.

One of the most interesting aspects of this book are the many comments of Christian, Jewish, and Messianic scholars. In our research, we have found some of Christianity's most distinguished scholars making statements that directly oppose modern day Christian thought.

Hopefully, this book will answer some of your questions about the first century community of Believers, the roots of your own Christian faith, and the rich Hebrew heritage you have in *Yeshua* (Jesus). Please be aware that anything printed in this book can be personally researched and verified. In fact, we strongly encourage you to research these subjects for yourself. In doing so, you will have your own facts on which to base your own conclusions on the *Faith of the Ages*.

Richard Rhoades

Foreword

The history of Christianity is remarkable, not only for its impact on the history of mankind, but also because it reveals that the Christian drama is still unfolding in amazing–almost unimaginable–ways. Since the death and resurrection of Yeshua (Jesus) this history has been marked by three great events–one political, one technological and one supernatural.

The first of these was the formation of the Roman Catholic Church during the reign of Emperor Constantine the Great. In 313 C.E. (A.D.) Constantine issued the Edict of Milan, which paved the way for Christianity to become the official religion of the Roman Empire. In fact, even as the Empire collapsed into the dust, the Roman Catholic Church was prospering and growing into a monolith so great that even the mighty kings of Europe stood in her shadow. But the often forgotten footnote is that while she towered above the greatest kingdoms of mankind, her roots were not in the rich soil from which she had first taken hold. In other words, she had severed herself from the Jewish stock of Yeshua and the authors of Scripture, and she had formulated a doctrine which has many names, but can simply be called "Replacement Theology," the idea that the Roman Catholic Church has replaced the Jewish people in God's economy because they were "Christ killers" and therefore under a curse. And so everything Jewish was either stricken from her or otherwise mutated and reformatted. For example, the Pontiff wears a yarmulke (a Jewish skull cap) and holds a staff reminiscent of the one that graced the hand of Moses as he led the children of God though the Red Sea toward the Land of Promise. And those who serve him are called priests, not unlike those who kept the mighty fires of promise before the majestic Temple in Jerusalem.

Such might have been the end of this Christian drama had a German goldsmith named Johannes Gutenberg not invented the printing press in 1440. A seemingly insignificant event at the time, the Gutenberg press opened the door for the ordinary parishioner to possess his or her own Bible. No longer was the priest king over his subjects, for everyone was free to see for himself or herself exactly what the Word of God said. We now know that this spiritual upheaval could not be stopped. From the moment a young monk named Martin Luther nailed his Ninety-five Theses to the door of Castle Church in Whittenberg, Germany, in 1517, until today, the Protestant Reformation of the Roman Catholic Church has remained a challenge to the authority of the Pope as the great mediator between man and God. But this was reformation–not transformation–and the basic tenant that the Church had supplanted Israel in God's plan of redemption was so fundamental to Protestant thinking as to be beyond dispute. After all, hadn't the Jews roamed as nomads over the face of the earth, homeless and helpless, since the glorious resurrection of Christ? Didn't nearly 2,000 years of history settle the issue?

But the God of miracles was not finished. On May 14, 1948, His hand touched the heart of mankind in a way no one could have foreseen beforehand nor ignore afterwards. For on that day, the nation of Israel was reborn out of the dust of the Promised Land. Through the words of the prophet Isaiah–uttered centuries before the birth of Yeshua and preserved in caves overlooking the Dead Sea waiting to be rediscovered in the spring of 1947–God had foretold of His plans for His people: *7"Before she went into labor, she gave birth; Before her pain came, she bore a son. 8 Who has ever heard such a thing? Who has ever seen such things? Can a country be born in one day? Can a nation be born all at once? For as soon as Zion went into labor, she brought forth her children. 9Shall I bring to the moment of birth and not give delivery?" says the Lord. "Shall I who causes birth shut the womb?" says your God. 10 "Rejoice with Jerusalem and be glad with her, all you who love her! Rejoice greatly with her, all you who mourned for her, 11 so that you may nurse and be satisfied by her comforting breast, so you may drink deeply and delight in her abundance of glory." Isaiah 66:7-11.*

Richard Rhoades is a man who has been caught by the flow of God's Word and been moved to unravel the truth of the Message of hope and salvation through Messiah Yeshua. This is a personal journey, an unfinished journey whose ultimate destination is the very bosom of God. If you are a seeker of truth, I encourage you to investigate this book, which should challenge and provoke you to a deeper understanding of "the mystery that has been hidden from the ages and from the generations, but has now been revealed to His saints." Colossians 1:26.

Rick Lastrapes
Former Congregational Leader
Adat Yeshua Messianic Jewish Congregation

Introduction

Oddly enough, this story begins with a prayer. It was the shortest prayer I have ever prayed. But it changed my life in a way I could never have imagined.

My life changing experience began on a beautiful summer day in 2003. That particular morning I was taking a walk around Ellis Lake, located at the heart of my hometown Marysville, in northern California. At that particular time I had been a Christian for about forty years, of which seven years were devoted to preparing for the ministry, receiving a B.A. degree, with a major in religion, from Pasadena Nazarene College, and a Master of Divinity degree at Asbury Theological Seminary, in Wilmore, Kentucky. Shortly afterward, I was invited to work with the Billy Graham Evangelistic Team. As a Crusade Coordinator, I would travel across the country by plane from city to city, organizing and training Christians for city-wide evangelistic campaigns that were scheduled months in advance. During that time I was privileged to study and work with some of the great Christian men and women of the twentieth century. Yet, with all of those rich experiences and training something was missing. I still had unanswered questions about my Christian faith. And I didn't know where to go to find the answers.

That morning as I walked around the lake, my thoughts turned to the Scriptures. As a Christian, I had been taught that the Old Testament was no longer relevant to my life as a Believer in Christ. Consequently, for most of those forty years as a Christian I had little, if any, interest in the Old Testament Scriptures.

During my years in college and seminary I was taught that the Holy Bible was the inspired, unchanging Word of God. At the same time, I was taught that the Old Testament was done away with the coming of Christ.

"Why." I thought, "were the Hebrew Scriptures no longer relevant to Christians?" How could I ever hope to understand the faith of Abraham, whom Paul addressed in his Epistle to the Gentile Believers in Rome as 'our father Abraham' (Rom. 4:1, 12), if I did not understand the Hebrew Scriptures? And how is it that the Jewish people, whose Bible is the Hebrew Scriptures, also hold Abraham to be the "father of their faith"?

That morning as I walked around the lake I knew that I had hit a wall and could go no further in my quest for the truth unless the LORD helped me. I prayed a brief but simple prayer, saying: "Father, help me to see the Scriptures through Jewish eyes."

In a matter of a few weeks I found myself loading some clothes and office equipment in my Ford Bronco, and saying goodby to my wife, family, and friends. My destination was Albuquerque, New Mexico. Five years earlier, my wife and I had lived in Albuquerque and operated a small advertising business. This time I would return by myself. My wife had to stay in California and take care of her elderly parents. Little did I know that my simple prayer would take me a thousand miles away from home, returning only for brief visits every four to five months over the next four years.

At that particular time my wife had a cousin living in Albuquerque. She called him by phone and asked if he would mail me a copy of the *Albuquerque Journal* classified ad section. A few days later, I received the ad section in the mail and quickly began scanning the ads in the office rental section.

My attention was immediately drawn to an ad at the very bottom of the listings. I called the listed number and inquired about the office for rent. After the rental agent informed me about the particulars I said: "I'll take it!" She replied, "Don't you want to see it first?" I said: "No. Just hold it for me. I'm driving from California. I'll be there in three days!"

Three days later, I arrived in Albuquerque and drove over to see my new office. When I climbed out of my Bronco, I noticed a large church complex directly across the street. After checking out my office, I drove by what I believed to be a church. Only this time, I glanced at the marquee and saw the word "Synagogue." My first thought was that of a Jewish synagogue.

The next day I drove to my office and looked at the marquee again. This time I saw the name *Adat Yeshua Messianic Synagogue*. At that moment my thoughts flashed back to the morning I was walking around Ellis Lake and prayed that brief prayer, asking the LORD to help me see the Scriptures through Jewish eyes. His answer to that simple prayer now stood before me as a bold reality!

That following Saturday morning my thousand mile journey to see the Scriptures through Jewish eyes began at *Adat Yeshua Messianic Synagogue.* I shall never forget my first Shabbat service on August 18, 2003, just prior to the Fall festivals of Rosh HaShanah, Yom Kippur, and Sukkot. At that time I knew absolutely nothing about the appointed holy days of the LORD, or the significance they had for me as a Christian. But that was about to change!

That morning for the first time in my life, I heard the Scriptures read aloud in Hebrew. For the first time in my life I saw both Jews and Gentiles coming together to worship the LORD, study the Scriptures, and sing songs of praise to the God of Israel and Messiah *Yeshua.*

That morning, as I joined the congregation and sang songs about the eternal majesty of *Elohim,* the Messiah *Yeshua,* and the holy city of Jerusalem, I choked as tears came to my eyes. As a Christian, I had been in hundreds of worship services that affirmed my Christian heritage. This was the first time I had ever been in a worship service that affirmed my Hebraic heritage.

As the service continued, I found myself comparing the Christian practice of teaching Scripture with the Jewish practice. Most Christian sermons always began with a reading from a selected passage of Scripture. The minister would then place his Bible on the pulpit or held it in one hand, rarely looking at it again as he spoke "off-the-cuff" for the remainder of the service.

That morning at *Adat Yeshua,* the Scripture reading began with a selected passage from the Hebrew Scriptures. When it came time for the morning teaching, Rick Lastrapes, the spiritual leader, began by explaining the historical background of his text. Rick then explained the text precept by precept and line by line, pointing out the meaning of certain words as they were understood by the people of that day.

I couldn't help but think that this must have been how it was with those first century community of Believers.

When Rick concluded his teaching and gave the Aaronic Blessing in Hebrew and then in English, I knew that the brief prayer I had prayed just a few weeks earlier had been answered. Although I was a thousand miles from my wife, family, and friends, I felt that I had found a new home, new friends, and a new family. But most important, I knew I had finally found what I had been searching for as a Christian -- my Hebrew roots.

Before attending *Adat Yeshua* I felt as though I had been living out my Christian experience in a dimly lit room. I could see, but my vision was distorted. Now I felt as if someone had turned on the lights, slowly at first and then brighter and brighter. As I sat under Rick's teachings, passages of Scripture which were once difficult to understand began to take on a whole new meaning. For the first time, I was now seeing the Scriptures through Jewish eyes.

One of the most enjoyable experiences was the Oneg Shabbat ('the pleasure of Shabbat'), which followed the morning service. Everyone would meet in an adjoining building for a simple meal and fellowship. I'll never forget that first Oneg. As I sat at a table eating and making friends with other like-minded Believers, Rick came over and welcomed me to *Adat Yeshua*. From that point on Rick and I became the best of friends, and the people at *Adat Yeshua* became my extended family.

As I left the Oneg that afternoon I couldn't help but reflect on the many years I had attended church. Making personal friendships in church did not come easy, especially in large churches. Most of the time, once the service concluded people made a hurried dash for their cars. About the only opportunity people had for fellowship was when attending a church social. Even then, there was little time for fellowship on a personal level. For most of my forty years as a Christian, I found myself going in-and-out the doors of the church a stranger to what should have been one of the richest experiences of being a Believer – fellowship with other Believers.

Perhaps the most troubling part of this story is that its your story too! If so, let me assure you that you too can know the real Jewish Messiah of Israel, not as He is portrayed by the Western Church -- void of everything Jewish. You too can know the Hebrew context in which the Believers of the first century lived and died; not as it is taught by the Western Church -- void of everything Jewish. You too can know the faith of Abraham and those first century followers the young Rabbi from Nazareth, not as it is taught by the Western Church -- void of its Hebraic roots.

In the Book of Matthew, we are told that the young Rabbi taught a parable which likened the discovery of the Kingdom of Heaven to a man finding a *hidden treasure* in a field. When the man finally found that *hidden treasure* he sold all that he had and bought the field (Matt. 13:44).

By simply reading this book with an open mind you too will understand the reason the young Rabbi from Nazareth likened the discovery of the rule of the Kingdom of Heaven to a *hidden treasure.* You too will understand why this certain man refused to quit searching until he found that *hidden treasure.* You too will understand why this man sold everything he had when he found that *hidden treasure,* and bought the field. And its my prayer that when you find this *hidden treasure* you too will sell everything you have and *buy the field.*

Shalom Alechem [Peace be unto you.]
Richard Rhoades

Chapter 1

THE GREAT MISCONCEPTION OF MATTHEW 5:17

Do not think that I came to abolish the Law or the Prophets;
I did not come to abolish but to fulfill (Matt. 5:17).

In the Hollywood movie *Foxfire* the celebrated actor Clint Eastwood is smuggled into Russia for the purpose of stealing Russia's most advanced fighter jet and flying it safely back to the U.S. Once Eastwood is smuggled into Russia he is taken to the home of two dissident Jewish engineers, a man and his wife, who have been involved in the development of the fastest plane in the world. Its highly technical 'brain' center was made with a thought-guided, thought-controlled weapons system that accepts human commands only in Russian. The pilot's thoughts are literally transmitted through his helmet to the computer.

Before Eastwood's character leaves for the Russian air base, he is briefed by the husband on how to operate the aircraft. After the briefing, he looks Eastwood straight in the eyes and says, "This is very important. When using your weapons you *must* think in Russian! You cannot think in English and transpose. You *must* think in Russian!"

In much the same manner, when seeking to understand the most important Book ever written, you *must* think as a Jew. You cannot think in English and transpose. You *must* think as a Jew!

How important is this concept to the understanding of the Scriptures? Karl Barth, one of Christianity's most respected theologians, says: "The Bible

1

is a Jewish book. It cannot be properly read, understood, or expounded unless we are to become Jews."[1]

Did Dr. Barth mean that we are to literally become Jews? Of course not! But his statement clearly emphasizes the importance of understanding *Yeshua,* the first century community of Believers, and the Scriptures from a Jewish perspective. The reasons can easily be summarized as follows:

* *Yeshua* was sent to earth as a Jew, a member of the House of Judah.
* *Yeshua* was reared by His Jewish parents to be *Torah* observant.
* *Yeshua* was a Jewish Rabbi who taught His disciples to be committed to the correct interpretation of the *Torah.*
* For the first forty years after the death and resurrection of *Yeshua* the community of Believers were predominately *Torah* observant Jews.
* All sixty-six books of the Bible were written by Jews, who employed Hebraic concepts that Greek speaking Believers understood.

Many will argue against the need for a Jewish understanding of the Scriptures. Today, however, several Christian scholars are beginning to acknowledge the replacement of Jewish Messianic leadership by the growing Gentile Christian community shortly after the destruction of the Temple, in 70 C.E. (A.D.). By the second century the faith of those first century followers of the young Rabbi from Nazareth was well on its way to being viewed by the people of that day as a Gentile faith -- void of its Hebraic roots.

Gnosticism's Influence on Christianity

When this writer became a Christian, much to the surprise of family and friends, he was told by his pastor: "Now that you're a Believer, a sinner saved by grace, God views you through the imputed righteousness of Jesus Christ, and His love is upon you. Christ not only died for your sins, He fulfilled the Law by obeying it for you. So when God looks at you, He only sees the imputed righteousness of His Son."

Although I was convinced that Christ had indeed died for my sins, I became confused when I read passages like Matthew 5:17, where *Yeshua* said: "Do not think that I came to abolish the Law and the Prophets; I did not come to abolish but to fulfill."

It wasn't until years later that I learned those very words of Jesus had been changed by second and third century Gnostic Christians, making them mean exactly the opposite of what the young Rabbi from Nazareth had said. It was equally troubling to learn that Gnostic Christians had made a profound impact on early Christian doctrine.

Marcion (85-160 C.E.), the son of a bishop, who was also a wealthy shipbuilder, became a student of the Gnostic Christian Cerdo, who taught that there was a profound difference between the God of the Old Testament and the God of the New Testament. Like Cerdo, Marcion believed that Christianity was the only true religion. Like Cerdo, Marcion rejected everything Jewish in Scripture. And like Cerdo, Marcion believed that the God of the Old Testament was a harsh and lesser God than the "good God" revealed in the New Testament.[2]

Marcion was so convinced that Paul's message of grace was in opposition to the *Torah* ['Law'] that he kept only edited portions of Paul's writings that agreed with his own theology. For Marcion, Paul was the only true Apostle. Marcion held that all the other Apostles had corrupted the teachings of *Yeshua* by mixing them with Jewish customs.

Marcion rejected the books written by Matthew, Mark, and John, because of Jewish influences. While he accepted the Book of Acts, he removed everything Jewish. Marcion also excluded 1st and 2nd Timothy, Titus, and Hebrews because of their Jewishness.[3] It is said that Marcion's misrepresentation of the Scriptures was so contrary to their true meaning that Polycarp, who was a student of John, called him the "firstborn of Satan."[4]

For Marcion, Matthew 5:17 was proof that the *Torah* ['Law'] had been *done away* with the coming of *Yeshua* and replaced by grace. According to Marcion's interpretation of Matthew 5:17, Jesus said: "Think not that I have come to fulfill the Law, I have not come to fulfill but to abolish it."

Today, most theologians agree that Marcion was a Heretic, who changed the original meaning of Scripture. The British scholar E. C. Blackman tells us that Marcion changed the meaning of Matthew 5:17 by "inverting the order of the clauses so as to give exactly an opposite sense."[5]

Yet, most theologians continue to hold some of Marcion's same Gnostic views as sound biblical doctrine. Addressing Matthew 5:17, the Scottish theologian William Barclay writes:

What ... did Jesus mean by the Law? He said that He had not come to destroy the Law, but to *fulfill* the Law. That is to say, He came really to bring out the real meaning of the Law. What was the real meaning of the Law?

When we look at the Ten Commandments, which are the essence and foundation of all law, we can see that their whole meaning can be summed in one word—*respect,* or even better, *reverence.* Reverence for God and for the name of God, reverence for God's day, respect for parents, respect for life, respect for property, respect for personality, respect for truth, respect for another person's good name, respect for oneself so that wrong desires may never master us—these are the fundamental principles of the Ten Commandments.

It is that reverence and respect which Jesus came to fulfill. He came to show men in actual life what reverence for God and respect for men is like.

... That reverence and that respect did not consist in obeying a multitude of petty rules and regulations. It consisted not in sacrifice, but in mercy; not in legalism but in love; not in prohibitions which demanded that men should not do things, but in commandments which made them mould (sic) their lives on the positive commandment of love.[6]

Notice that Dr. Barclay informs his audience that the Ten Commandments can be summed up on one word, "respect," which Christ came to fulfill for all men. While this teaching is highly popular within Christianity it, nevertheless, is the same argument made by Marcion in the second century. Two hundred years later, Marcion's "gospel"of love and reverence was championed by the "holy father" Augustine (354-430 C.E.), who said the Christian life could be summed up in one simple phrase: "Love God, and do what you like".[7]

Since that time, one of Christianity's main tenants has been that the God of the Old Testament is a different [*i. e.,* 'harsher'] God than the "good God" revealed in the New Testament. But for those who understand that *Yeshua* of the New Testament and *Elohim* of the Old Testament are One in the same, nothing could be further from the truth.

The Torah Observant Faith of Abraham

For most Christians, the giving of the *Torah* by God began with Moses at Mount Sinai. But for those who know the Hebrew Scriptures, the giving of the *Torah* by God can be traced all the way back to Abraham.

Contrary to the misconception of many, the Scriptures teach that long before Moses received the *Torah* at Mount Sinai, Abraham was given the *Torah* hundreds of years earlier. For example, the Scriptures teach that on one occasion God spoke to Isaac, Abraham's son, saying: "[Abraham] obeyed My voice and guarded My charge, My commands, My laws, and My *torahs*" (Gen. 26:5; *The Scriptures*).

It is significant for us to understand that the Hebrew word *"torahs"* (v. 5) is the very same Hebrew word employed by Moses in Exodus 24:12, when God spoke to Moses, saying: "Come up to Me on the mountain and be there, while I give you tablets of stone and the <u>torah</u> and the command which I have written, to teach them."

The Christian theologian H. C. Leupold, professor of Old Testament Exegesis in the Capital University of Columbus, Ohio, writes:

> Though, indeed, the promise originally given to Abraham was a promise of pure grace, without any merit or worthiness on his part, yet God's mercy deigned to note with delight the one thing that Abraham did, which kept him from making himself unworthy of the divine promises: Abraham obeyed every divine injunction. Therefore, these manifold blessings, Isaac is told, come upon him for Abraham his father's sake, or rather because of Abraham's faithful obedience. Remarkable is the scope of divine blessings that are mediated through faithful Abraham. In order to make prominent the thought that Abraham conscientiously did all that God asked, the various forms of divine commandments are enumerated; sometimes, of course, a divine word would fall under several of these categories. They are a "charge" or "observance" if they are to be observed (*mishmereth* from *shamar,* ("observe"). They are "commandments" (*mitswoth*) when regarded from the angle of having been directly *commanded.* They are "statutes" (*chuqqoth*) when thought of as immutable, and "laws" (*toroth*) insofar as they involve divine instruction or teaching.... By the use of these

terms Moses, who purposes to use them all very frequently in his later books, indicates that "laws, commandments, charges, and statutes" are nothing new but were involved already in patriarchal religion.[8]

The Torah Observant Faith of Yeshua

Although most theologians continue to view *Yeshua* from a Western Christian perspective – void of His Hebraic roots – some are now beginning to acknowledge His Judaic faith. For example, one scholar of the Kittel *Theological Dictionary of the New Testament* writes:

> It is not surprising that according to the Synoptic account Jesus Himself keeps the Law.... Jesus recognizes the Law to be God's good will not only for Himself but also for others. To the question of right conduct He gives the answer: *tas evtolas oidas* (Mk. 10:19). He does not accept as good any other will than the will of God revealed in the Law. Apart from this He does not champion any other goodness (Mk. 10:18, cf., also Lk. 10:25 ff.).[9]

The Christian language scholar David Bivin writes: "Perhaps the most convincing proof that Jesus was a sage was his style of teaching, because he used the same methods of Scripture interpretation and instruction as other Jewish teachers of his day."[10]

And the orthodox Rabbi Harvey Falk says of the young Rabbi from Nazareth:

> It is therefore worthy of note that the only statement of Jesus of Nazareth to be found in the Talmud is "I come not to destroy the Law of Moses nor to add to the Law of Moses" (Shabbat 116B). This question is introduced to the text in order to ascertain Jesus' view of the binding character of the Torah for all time, and is identifiable with his exhortation in the Sermon on the Mount (Matthew 5:17), "Do not suppose that I have come to abolish the Torah. I did not come to abolish, but to fulfill. I tell you this: So long as heaven and earth endure, not

a letter, not a stroke, will disappear from the Torah until it is achieved. If any man therefore sets aside even the least of the Torah's demands, and teaches others to do the same, he will have the lowest place in the Kingdom of Heaven, whereas anyone who keeps the Torah, and teaches others so, will stand high in the Kingdom of Heaven." These words–which he surely considered as central to his message of salvation–are followed almost immediately by "For I say unto you, that except your righteousness shall exceed the righteousness of the Scribes and Pharisees, ye shall in no case enter into the Kingdom of Heaven."[11]

The Torah Observant Faith of Paul

For the Heretic Marcion, as well as many Christians, Paul was the only true Apostle of Gentile Christianity. Because among the Apostles, although Paul was a Jew, the content of his writings were the least Jewish.

According to Luke, however, Paul was a *Torah* observant Pharisee *before* and *after* his conversion experience on the road to Damascus. Luke records that several years *after* Paul's conversion he told a Jewish Sanhedrin: "Men, brothers, I am a Pharisee, the son of a Pharisee..." (Acts 23:6).

It is significant for us to understand that in the Greek text Paul's use of the verb "I am" is written in the Present Active tense. The Christian Greek scholars H. E. Dana and Julius R. Mantey write: "The progressive force of the present tense should always be considered as primary....... (1) *The Progressive Present.* This use is manifestly nearest the root idea of the tense. It signifies action in progress, or state in persistence, and may be represented by the graph (--------------)."[12]

In other words, Paul's use of the verb "I am" means that his action as a practicing Pharisee was *continuous* [*lit.,* 'without interruption'].

What was the understanding of a Pharisee among the people of that day? The Christian scholars of the *Unger's Bible Dictionary* tell us that "the Pharisees united themselves more closely into an association that made a duty of the law's punctilious observance."[13]

Here we see that Paul was not only *Torah* observant, he belonged to a sect of Judaism that was very precise, and even went to extremes in the observance of *Torah.* Yet, most theologians argue that Paul could never have

been a Pharisee because *Yeshua* condemned the Pharisees, saying, "woe...
to you, scribes and Pharisees, hypocrites!" (Matt. 23:13).

So here is the great question: Was *Yeshua's* scathing remarks directed
at all Pharisees, or just to a certain group of Pharisees? The scholars of the
Encyclopedia Judaica write:

> While the Pharisees, as a whole, set a high ethical standard
> for themselves, not all lived up to it. It is mistakenly held that
> New Testament references to them as "hypocrites" or "offspring
> of vipers" (Matt. 3:7; Luke 18:9ff., etc.) are applicable to the
> entire group. However, the leaders were well aware of the
> presence of the insincere among their numbers, described by the
> Pharisees themselves in the Talmud as "sore spots" or "plagues
> of the Pharisaic party" (Sot. 3:4 and 22b). The apostle Paul
> himself had been a Pharisee, was a son of a Pharisee, and was
> taught by one of the sect's most eminent scholars Gamaliel
> of Jerusalem. Pharisaic doctrines have more in common with
> those of Christianity than is supposed, having prepared the
> ground for Christianity with such concepts as Messianism,
> the popularization of monotheism and apocalypticism, and
> with such beliefs as life after death, resurrection of the dead,
> immortality, and angels.[14]

Also, there is the account of Acts 21:17-26, where James, the half-
brother of *Yeshua* and leader of the Jerusalem community of Believers,
asks Paul to take four Jewish Believers with him to the Temple and "purify
yourself along with them, and pay their expenses ... and all will know ...
that you yourself also walk orderly, keeping the Law" (v. 21; NASV).

The significance of this event is that it occurred some thirty years
after the death and resurrection of *Yeshua*.[15] That's well over a quarter of a
century! Luke writes:

> 26 Then Sha'ul took the men on the next day, and having
> been cleansed with them, went into the Set-apart Place (the
> Temple) to announce the completion of the days of separation –
> until the offering should be presented for each one of them
> (Acts 21:26; *The Scriptures*).

The Torah Observant Faith of Jewish Believers

For most Christians, little, if anything, is ever said about the Judaic orthodoxy of those first three thousand Jewish Believers, who accepted *Yeshua* as the Messiah of Israel. Scholars agree, however, that they were all *Torah* observant Jews, who were in the Temple at Jerusalem to observe the Divine appointed festival of Shavuot/Pentecost (Acts 2:1-13). For example, the Church historian Philip Schaff tells us that "it was the 'feast of harvest,' or 'of the first fruits,' the anniversary celebration of the Sinaitic legislation, which was suppose to have taken place on the fiftieth day after the Exodus from the land of bondage."[16]

Luke records that Peter was in the Temple on that appointed day and spoke to the thousands who were gathered in the crowded courtyard, telling them about the signs, wonders, death and resurrection of the young Rabbi from Nazareth (Acts 2:14-40). "Then they that gladly received his word were baptized: and the same day there were added *unto them* three thousand souls," Luke said (v. 41).

Equally significant, the Hebrew scholar Joseph Good tells us that when those first Jewish Believers returned to their homes they carried Peter's message back to their family and friends, and their numbers multiplied by the tens of thousands.[17]

Thirty years later, Luke recorded that James said to Paul: "Thou seest brother, how many thousands of Jews there are which believe; and they are all zealous of the law" (Acts 21:20; AKJV).

The Torah Observant Faith of Gentile Believers

According to most theologians, Paul's missionary work among Gentile Believers is viewed as the beginning of Christianity. For example, Dr. Herbert Lockyer tells us that Paul was "the chief missionary and builder of Christianity."[18] But for those who understand the Hebraic faith of those first century Gentile Believers, nothing could be further from the truth.

About 52 C.E., Paul, who admitted that he was a Pharisee (Acts 23:6), wrote a letter to the Gentile Believers in Corinth, saying:

16 Therefore, I appeal to you to become imitators of me.

> 17 For this reason I have sent Timothy to you, who is my beloved and trustworthy son in the Master, who shall remind you of my ways in Messiah, as I teach everywhere in every assembly (1 Cor. 4:16-17; *The Scriptures*).

> ... **11** Become imitators of me, as I also am of Messiah (1 Cor. 11:1).

It is significant for us to understand that in Jewish thought the ultimate goal of a rabbi for his disciples is that they attain the status of *yechudit*, meaning "oneness". This oneness takes place when the disciple becomes one with his rabbi, especially in the observance of his teaching of *Torah*. Interestingly, this is the very same desire the young Rabbi from Nazareth expressed when He prayed to the Father for His own talmidim ['disciples'], saying: "... that they might be one as We are one" (Jhn. 17:22).

Another common misconception of Pauline thought is found in a passage that most scholars agree is one of the most important passages in the New Testament, Romans 7:1-14. In Romans 7:1-6, Paul speaks of being released from the *Torah* ['Law'] having died to what we were held by, so that we should serve in newness of the Spirit and not in oldness of the letter.

According to most theologians, Paul was speaking about the death of the *Torah* and its lack of relevance to the life of the Believer. However, when this passage is understood from a Jewish perspective it becomes evident that Paul was using a well-known concept in *halakhah* ['Jewish law'] which refers to the *death of the flesh* (*Bab. Niddah* 61b and parallels).

In Jewish thought, when a person is living in sin he is in bondage to the law against that sin until such time as death of the flesh frees him from that law. The point that Paul made in Romans 7 is that the Believer is to die to the carnal desires of the flesh, *not* to the *Torah*, which Paul plainly said is "holy, just, and good" (Rom. 7:12; AKJV).

In much the same manner, most theologians interpret Paul's use of the phrase "under the law" and "works of the law" as found in Romans, 1 Corinthians, and Galatians as being directed to those who believe in *Yeshua* and observe the *Torah* ['Law'] of Moses. But if this were the case, why would Paul say in one breath that Believers who observe the Law are "under the Law," and then say the Law is "holy, just, and good"?

The Christian scholar C. E. B. Cranfield sheds some light on this very important question in his masterful commentary on Romans, saying:

> ... the Greek language of Paul's day possessed no word group corresponding to our "legalism," "legalist," and "legalistic." This means that he lacked a convenient terminology for expressing a vital distinction, and so was seriously hampered in the work of clarifying the Christian position with regard to the law. In view of this, we should always, we think, be ready to reckon with the possibility that **Pauline statements, which at first sight seems to disparage the law, were really directed not against the law itself but against that misunderstanding and misuse of it for which we now have a convenient terminology. In this very difficult terrain Paul was pioneering.**[19] (Emphasis added.)

John Wesley (1703-1791), who was a minister of the Anglican Church and whose teachings had to be in keeping with Christian orthodoxy, recognized the vital role the *Torah* had in the life of the Believer. As one of the most influential leaders of Christianity, Wesley's teachings were often much better than the religion he served. In Wesley's sermon entiitled *"The Original Nature, Property, and Use of the Law,"* he says:

> I cannot spare the law one moment, no more than I can spare Christ: see I now want it as much, to keep me to Christ, as I ever wanted it to bring me to him. Otherwise, this 'evil heart of unbelief' would immediately 'depart from the living God.' Indeed each is continually sending me to the other,–the law to Christ, and Christ to the law. On the one hand, the height and depth of the law constrains me to fly to the love of God in Christ; on the other, the love of God in Christ endears the law to me "above gold or precious stones;" which I know every part of it is a gracious promise, which my Lord will fulfill in its season.
>
> Who art thou then, O man, that 'judgest the law, and speakest evil of the law?'–that rankest it with sin, Satan, and death, and sendest them all to hell together? The Apostle James esteemed judging or 'speaking evil of the law' so enormous a piece of wickedness, that he knew not how to aggravate the guilt

of judging our brethren more, than by showing it included this. "So now," says he, 'thou are not a doer of the law, but a judge!' A judge of that which God hath ordained to judge thee! So thou hast set up thyself in the judgment-seat of Christ, and cast down the rule whereby He will judge the world! O take knowledge what advantage Satan hath gained over thee; and, for the time to come, never think or speak lightly of, much less dress up as a scarecrow, this blessed instrument of the grace of God. Yea, love and value it for the sake of him from whom it came, and of Him to whom it leads. Let it be thy glory and joy, next to the cross of Christ. Declare its praise, and make it honourable (sic) before all men.[20]

The First Century Meaning of the term "Law"

Among the many recorded teaching of the young Rabbi from Nazareth, none are more Jewish than this following statement: "Think now that I am come to destroy the <u>law</u> [Gk. *nomas*] or the prophets: I am not come to destroy, but to fulfill" (Matt. 5:17; AKJV).

For centuries theologians have maintained that the Greek term *nomas* ['law'] is pregnant with Jewish overtones, such as "legalistic," "Old Testament," and "Old Dispensation". However, according to a growing number of Christian scholars the Greek term *nomas* is a Hebrew parallelism that is filled with Hebraic meaning. For example, one scholars of Kittel's *Theological Dictionary of the New Testament* writes:

> In the LXX [Heb. *torah*] is in the vast majority of cases translated *vomos* (some 200 times out of 220). *vomos,* however, is even more common than [*torah*] (some 240 times). There is an inner shift due to the fact that the LXX *vomos* renders the [Heb. *torah*] of the latter state of development, and the latter meaning establishes itself in other cases too. Thus in Is. 8:16, what the prophet passes on to his disciples is in the LXX immediately identified with the Torah in the latter sense; it is the epitome of divine teaching and the divine Law.[21]

It is worthy to note that Matthew employs the Greek term *nomos* a total of eight times (Matt. 5:17, 18; 7:12; 11:13; 12:5; 22:36, 40; & 23:23). Each time the Greek word *nomas* is employed it is preceded by a *definite article,* such as <u>ton</u> *nomon* (5:17), <u>tou</u> *nomou* (v. 18; 23:23), <u>o</u> *nomos* (7:12; 11:13; 12:40), and <u>to</u> *nomo* (12:5; 22:26), meaning "<u>the</u> law".

The Greek scholars Dana and Mantey tell us that the basic function of the Greek *definite article* is to point out the "individual identity" of a person or thing.[22] Thus, with Matthew's employment of the *definite article* before the term *nomos,* it is clear that he is not addressing rabbinic law. Rather, he is marking the identity of <u>the</u> Law [*Torah*], which he assumes will be known by his audience.

Equally significant, the Christian Greek scholars William F. Arndt and F. Wilbur Gingrich inform us that the Greek word *nomos* not only means law but "especially the Mosaic Law... in a strict sense *the law* = the Pentateuch, the work of Moses the lawgiver."[23]

During the first century, the need for including the *definite article* before the Greek term *nomos* was crucial to the understanding of what the writer was saying. Because it made a clear distinction between rabbinic law and the *Written Torah.* Over a period of three hundred years the Pharisees had built "hedges" [*i.e.,* man-made rules] around the *Torah* for the purpose of keeping people from breaking the commandments of God.

According to tradition, the *Oral Torah* was implicitly contained within the Hebrew Scriptures. The expansion of the *Oral Torah* came about by searching in the Scriptures for a principle, an implied provision, or a precedent, by which a new question could be answered or new actual conditions or emergencies could be met.[24]

For example, the *Written Torah* states that the Sabbath day is to be kept holy; that on the Sabbath no work is to be done. One rabbinic definition of work was "to carry a burden" on the Sabbath. From that definition of work came the definition that a burden is food equal in weight to a dried fig, enough wine for mixing in a goblet, milk enough for one to moisten eye-salve, paper enough to write a customs house notice upon, ink enough to write two letters of the alphabet, reed enough to make a pen.[25]

To *heal* a person on the Sabbath also came under the definition of work. *Healing* on the Sabbath was allowed only when a person's life was threatened. Even then, a remedy could be used only to keep a physical illness from becoming worse; no remedy could be used to make a physical illness better. A plain bandage could be put on a wound, but with no ointment. Likewise, a plain wadding could be put into a sore ear, but with no ointment.[26]

By employing the *definite article* before the Greek word *nomos* Matthew makes it perfectly clear that he was not addressing rabbinic law. Rather, the people of that day would have understood that Matthew's use of the *definite article* before the word *nomos* indicated that he was addressing the great *Written Torah* [*i.e.,* the first five books of Moses].

Why was this understanding important to the people of that day? The Christian Judaic scholar George Foote Moore (1851-1931), chairman the History of Religion in Harvard University, writes:

> [The Law] is a source of manifold misconceptions that the word is customarily translated "Law," though it is not easy to suggest any one English word by what it would be better rendered. 'Law' must, however, not be understood in the restricted sense of legislation, but must be taken to include the whole revelation– all that God has made known of his nature, character, and purpose, and what he would have man be and do. The prophets call their own utterances 'Torah'; and the Psalms deserved the name as well.... In a word, Torah in one aspect is the vehicle, in another and deeper view it is the whole content of revelation.[27]

The First Century Meaning of the term "Destroy"

For most Christians, Christ came to "destroy" the *Torah* ['Law']. Arndt and Gingrich inform us that the Greek word for "destroy," *kataluo* means "to do away with, abolish, annul, make invalid, or repeal the law Mt. 5:17a."[28]

According to the best Greek mansuscripts available, Matthew employs the *absolute negative* Greek word *"ouk"* not once but twice, saying: "Think *ouk* ['not'] that I am come to destroy the law or the prophets: I am *ouk* ['not'] come to destroy but to fulfill" (v. 17; AKJV).

Here we see that the young Rabbi told the people of His day in the strongest terms possible that He had <u>not then or at any time</u> come "to *do away* with, abolish, annul, make invalid, or repeal" the *Torah* and the Prophets.

This should be highly troubling to every Christian. Because with *Yeshua's* use of the double *absolute negative* Greek word *"ouk"* ['not'], He made His position on the validity of the *Torah* so clear that the most common people of His day – the uneducated and illiterate – could understand what He meant.

The First Century Meaning of the term "Fulfill"

Perhaps the most misunderstood word *Yeshua* used in Matthew 5:17 is the Greek word *pleroo* ['fulfill'], which most theologians interpret as meaning "to supersede or replace". According to Arndt and Gingrich, however, the Greek word *pleroo* means "to bring to completion, finish what had already begun."[29]

With this understanding, here is the great question: What work of redemption had God begun with Adam and Eve, Noah, Moses, David and Solomon that pointed to its "completion"/"fulfillment" with the coming of the promised Messiah?

Addressing this very same Hebraic concept, the Christian scholars of *The Complete Word Study New Testament* tell us that Jesus meant that "He had come not only to fulfill their types and prophecies by His works and sufferings, but that He had also come to demonstrate His perfect obedience to the Law of God and fully explain it in His teachings."[30]

Equally significant, in the Gospel of Matthew the Greek word *pleroo* is employed twelve times. Each time, it is used in respect to the fulfillment of the ancient prophesies that identified certain characteristics of the promised Messiah of Israel. For example, the term *pleroo* is used in the prophetic fulfillment of *Yeshua's* birth (Matt. 1:22-23; Isa. 7:14); His visit to Egypt (Matt. 2:15; Hos. 11:1); the weeping of the women in Bethlehem after the murder of their children because of His birth (Matt. 2:17-18; Jer. 31:15); His identity as a Nazarene (Matt. 2:23; Jud. 13:5; 1 Sam. 1:11); the location of His ministry (Matt. 4:14-16; Isa. 9:1-2); the nature of His ministry (Matt. 8:17; Isa. 53:4); His mission as the Servant of God, whose Name the Gentiles would trust (Matt. 12:17-21; Isa. 42:1); His use of parables (Matt. 13:14, 35; Isa. 6:9); His kingly entrance into Jerusalem (Matt. 21:4-5; Zech. 9:9); His arrest (Matt. 26:54-56; Isa. 53:7); and the purchase price of His betrayal (Matt. 27:9-10; Zech. 11:12-13).

Nowhere is the meaning of the prophetic word *pleroo* more evident than in Matthew's account of Rabbi *Yeshua's* perfect fulfillment of the Divine appointed Spring festivals, as found in the Hebrew Scriptures. For example, the Feast of Passover points to the shed blood of *Yeshua,* who became the sacrificial Lamb of God (Num. 28:16-25; Matt. 26:26-30). Likewise, the festival of Unleavened Bread points to the body of *Yeshua,* which was without sin, pierced, and broken for our redemption, just as the Matza bread that is eaten during the festival of Unleavened Bread is pierced and broken (Num. 28:17-25s; Matt. 27:26). The festival of First Fruits points to the resurrected Messiah *Yeshua,* who became the First Fruit of the harvest (Lev. 23:9-11; Matt. 28:1-10). And Leviticus 23:15-21 points to Messiah *Yeshua's* perfect fulfillment of the festival of Shavuot/Pentecost in Acts 2:1-5.

In the Hebrew Scriptures the most symbolic event that points to *Yeshua's* sacrificial death is the account of Abraham offering up his only son, Isaac, on Mount Moriah (Gen. 22).

In Exodus, the LORD commanded the children of Israel to take a lamb "without blemish" (Ex. 12:9), slay it and put its shed blood on the door posts of their dwellings prior to their deliverance in Egypt, pointing to the great Passover Lamb of God – the promised Messiah of Israel -- *Yeshua HaMashiach.*

In Leviticus, the LORD established the sacrificial system for man's sin, which points to the shedding of *Yeshua's* sacrificial death for the sins of mankind (Lev. 1-6:7; 6:8-8:36; 9:1-4).

In Numbers, the children of Israel are commanded to take a red heifer "without spot" and bring it before the High Priest to be examined. Once the red heifer was examined by the High Priest it was taken outside the camp ['Jerusalem'] where it was slain for the sins of the people, pointing to the sacrificial death of *Yeshua,* Who was brought before the High Priest Caiaphas to be examined and then taken outside the city to be executed (Num. 19:2-3; Matt. 26:57-68; 27:1-2).

About 1,000 years before the birth of *Yeshua,* David was inspired to write the following Messianic passage, saying:

> 1 My El, My El, why have you forsaken Me –
> ... 7 All those who seek Me mock Me, they shoot out the
> lip, they shake the head *saying,*
> 8 "He trusted in [YHVH], let Him rescue Him;

Let Him deliver Him, seeing He has delighted in Him!"
… 12 Many bulls have surrounded Me, strong ones of
Bashan have encircled Me.

13 They have opened their mouths against Me, as a raging
and roaring lion.

14 I have been poured out like water, and all My bones
have been spread apart; My heart has become like wax; it has
has melted in the midst of My inward parts.

15 My strength is dried like a potsherd, and My tongue
is cleaving to My jaws; and to the dust of death You are
appointing Me.

16 For dogs have surrounded Me, a crowd of evil ones have
encircled Me, piercing My hands and My feet;

17 I count all My bones. They look, they stare at Me.

18 They divide My garments among them, and for My
raiment they cast lots (Ps. 22: 1, 7-8, 12-18; *The Scriptures*).

What are the odds that someone would come on the scene of history
hundreds of years after these passages were written and become the perfect
fulfillment of every Messianic *Torah* type and prophetic word? The odds
are astronomical. Yet, this is precisely what happened in the life and death
of the young Rabbi from Nazareth.

Clearly, Matthew had no problem understanding the significance of
Yeshua's coming on the scene of Jewish history. No other Gospel account
links *Yeshua's* perfect fulfillment of the *Torah* and Prophets as does Matthew.

Most certainly, Luke had no problem understanding that *Yeshua's* life,
ministry, death, and resurrection represented the fulfillment of the *Torah*
and Prophets (Lk. 4:18-21; 10:23-24; 24:25-26, 44-47). Nor did Mark
have a problem understanding that *Yeshua* was the perfect fulfillment of
the *Torah* and Prophets (Mk. 1:2-3, 40-44; 12:10; 14:49, 61; 15:24, 28-
29, 34, 36).

John also establishes that he understood that *Yeshua's* life, death, and
resurrection to be the perfect fulfillment of the *Torah* and Prophets (Jhn.
1:2, 29, 45; 2:22; 3:14; 5:39, 46-47; 6:32-35, 45, 49-51, 58; 7:38-42;
8:17-18; 11:51-52; 12:16, 34-36, 38-41; 15:25; 17:12; 18:9; 19:24, 28,
36-37; 20:9, 30-31).

The same can be said for Peter, who affirmed to thousands of his Jewish brethren, on Pentecost day in the Temple, that the young Rabbi from Nazareth perfectly fulfilled the *Torah* and the Prophets (Acts 3:18-25).

All of these men were first century witnesses to the life, death and resurrection of the young Rabbi from Nazareth. Yet, in spite of this overwhelming evidence, since the time of the Greek and Latin Church Fathers, and fourth century Catholic Church authorities, Christian theologians have continued to hold to Marcion's interpretation of Matthew 5:17; that the Greek term *pleroo* ['fulfill'] means the *Torah* ['Law'] was *done away* with the coming of *Yeshua* and superseded by grace.

By the way, one of the most misunderstood topics in Scripture is the concept that the *Torah* was *done away* and superseded by grace with the coming of *Yeshua*. Like Marcion, most theologians hold to the notion that grace did not exist *until* the day Peter preached to the thousands gathered in Jerusalem on the great day of Shavuot/Pentecost, when three thousand souls were converted and added to the Kingdom of Heaven.

According to the Hebrew Scriptures, however, "Noah found *hen* [Heb.'grace'] in the eyes of the LORD" before the great deluge destroyed all living things from the face of the earth. As a result, Noah and his family were spared (Gen. 6;8).

Lot and his family experienced God's *hen* and were saved from the great destruction of Sodom (Gen. 19:19). It was *hen* alone that spared the children of Israel from complete annihilation after they broke the Sinai Covenant (Ex. 34:6, 7). David was an obvious recipient of *hen* time and again, affirming that the LORD was "good and ready to forgive" (Ps. 86:5; 103:3). Isaiah exalted the LORD as the One who will "abundantly pardon" (Isa. 55:7).

Contrary to the misconception of many, the Hebrew word *hen* ['grace'] appears over five times more often in the *Torah* than it does in the writings of Paul.

The Perpetuity of Torah

If there were any doubts in the minds of the Jewish people as to how the young Rabbi from Nazareth viewed the validity of the *Torah*, those doubts were dispelled when *Yeshua* said: "For verily I say unto you, Till heaven and earth pass, one jot or one title shall in no wise pass from the law, till all be fulfilled" (Matt. 5:18; AKJV).

In Jewish thought, the *iota* is regarded as the smallest letter. In form, it is like an apostrophe — ' —. But the young Rabbi didn't stop with the *iota*. He went on to include the *tittle*, which is the smallest part of a letter, the little line at each side of the foot [bottom] of a letter, such as with the letter I.

Yet for many, these words of *Yeshua* are merely the words of an over-zealous scribe. For example, the Christian theologian Alexander Bruce says in *The Expositor's Greek Testament:* "These verses were on first view a Judaistic look, and have been regarded as an interpolation, or set down to the credit of an over-conservative evangelist."[31]

This, my friend, is precisely the reason we need a comprehensive understanding of the Hebraic roots of the first century community of Believers. Because history concurs that the *Torah* observant faith of those first followers of the young Rabbi from Nazareth has been revised again and again, making it appear that the *Written Torah* [*i.e.,* the first five books of Moses] was *done away* with the coming of *Yeshua* and replaced with a New Dispensation of grace.

Chapter 2

THE ROOTS OF REPLACEMENT THEOLOGY

Bible scholars have long agreed that neither *Yeshua* or Paul ever renounced their Judaic faith, or attempted to start a new religion. But even more important, some Christian scholars are now acknowledging that the early Church did indeed renounce its Hebraic roots and start out on a course of its own making.

Dean Merrill Tenney tells us that after the destruction of the Temple, in 70 C.E., "Gentile adherents chose to abandon the Law and to steer a separate course.... By the year A.D. 85 the church was launched on an independent course. Having survived its first conflict with Roman authority in the person of Nero, it sought to confirm its position theologically and politically."[1]

By the fourth century Church authorities had developed doctrines that literally did away with the Jewishness of the Scriptures. The most fundamental change was the idea that the *Torah* of the Hebrew Scriptures/Old Testament was in direct opposition to the doctrine of grace in the Apostolic Writings/New Testament. Apologists defended Church doctrine, insisting that the *Torah* ['Law'] of the Old Testament had been *done away* with the coming of *Yeshua* and superseded by grace.

New doctrines opposing the *Torah* began springing up *as* early as 120-160 C.E. (AD)

Eusebius

20

among the African communities represented by Tertullian and were later promoted by Church leaders, such as Bishop Eusebius in Caesarea (260-340 C.E.), and Bishop John Chrysostom (349-400 C.E.) at Antioch in Syria. Eusebius, known as the "Father of Church History," wrote eulogies in praise of the Roman Emperor Constantine, who was a devout sun-worshiper for many years after his questionable conversion to Christ.

Chrysostom

During Chrysostom's first two years as a bishop in Antioch he preached a series of eight sermons in which he denounced both Jews and Judaizing Christians who were taking part in Jewish festivals and other Jewish observances.[2] It is said that the aim of Chrysostom's eight anti-Jewish sermons, entitled *Against Judaizing Christians,* was to stop Christians from participating in Jewish customs and prevent the erosion of his flock.

Chrysostom claimed that on the Shabbats and Jewish festivals synagogues were full of Christians, especially women who loved the solemnity of the Jewish liturgy, enjoyed listening to the blowing of the shofar on holy days, and applauded preachers who were in accordance with Jewish customs.[3] Chrysostom described the synagogue as a place "worse than a brothel and a drinking shop; it was a den of scoundrels, the repair of wild beasts, a temple of demons, the refuge of brigands and debauchees, and the cavern of devils, a criminal assembly of the assassins of Christ."[4]

Centuries later, Chrysostom's anti-*Semitism* was used to persecute the Jewish people and attack their Judaic faith. During Hitler's reign of terror the Nazi Party in Germany quoted and reprinted Chrysostom's works to legitimize the persecution of Jews and the Holocaust in the eyes of the German and Austrian Christians.[5]

Origin, who is hailed by theologians as one of the great minds of the early Church, took Paul's phrase "the letter of the Law" and developed a whole new teaching on legalism, making a distinction between the term "legalism" to be synonymous with Judaism, which he both condemned. The coined term "legalism" caught on in the Christian community, and since that time it has been used by theologians and Church leaders to brand *Torah* observant men and women as being "legalistic" and "under the Law".

For many, Paul's use of the phrase "the letter of the Law" was a phrase meant to identify those who taught that obedience to the *Torah* was the means whereby one attained salvation. But a close examination of Paul's use of the phrase "the letter of the Law" reveals that Paul never once condemned the *Torah* or those who observed it as being "legalistic" (2 Cor. 3:1-18).

Nevertheless, shortly after the First Council of Nicea, in 325 C.E., which was convened by the sun-worshiping Emperor Constantine (280-337 C.E.), in Bithynia [present day Turkey], Church authorities declared all things Jewish to be heretical.

The Universal Sabbath Principle

Interestingly enough, Roman Catholic scholars agree that the seventh day is indeed the biblical Sabbath. Moreover, Catholic authorities base their belief in the seventh day Sabbath on the following passage: "And Elohim blessed the seventh day and set it apart, because He rested [Heb. *shabbath,* 'sabbathed'] from all His work which Elohim in creating had made" (Gen. 2:3; *The Scriptures*).

Yet, since the fourth century, Catholic scholars, then later Protestant theologians, have maintained that the Mosaic injunction to set aside a specific day of the week, such as Saturday, should be viewed as a *"universal Sabbath principle"*.

Ironically, the very passage Catholic and Protestant theologians use to support the idea of a *"universal Sabbath principle"* is based on the Fourth Commandment of the Decalogue, which plainly states: "Remember the Sabbath day, to set it apart. Six days you labour, and shall do all your work, but the seventh day is a Sabbath of [YHVH] your Elohim" (Ex. 20:8-11; *The Scriptures*).

In Christian thought, since the Ten Commandments are universal moral principles that are binding upon all men the Sabbath is as much a moral principle as any of the other commandments. The Christian theologian Benjamin Field says in his book entitled *The Handbook of Christian Theology:*

> The essence of Sabbath law is that one day in seven, the
> seventh day after six days of labor should be appropriated to

sacred uses. Accordingly we find that, in the original institution (Gen. 2:3) it is stated in general terms that God blessed and sanctified the seventh day, which must, undoubtedly, imply the sanctity of every seventh day, at whatever given time the cycle may commence. In the Decalogue it is also mentioned in the same indefinite manner with respect to time. Nothing more being expressedly required than to observe a day of sacred rest after six days of toil. The seventh day is to be kept holy, but not a word is said as to what epoch the commandment of the series is to be referred. It is the seventh day in reference to the six before mentioned.[6]

From a Christian perspective, Dr. Field's argument sounds well and good *until* we understand that the Julian calendar, instituted in 45 B.C.E. by Julius Caesar, is the calendar which is used for reckoning time regarding the events of ancient history before 1582. At that time, the Gregorian calendar was instituted to rectify the miscalculation of leap year inherent in the Julian system. Pope Gregory XIII added ten days to the calendar at midnight on Thursday, October 4, which then became Friday, October 15. By making this adjustment, the days in the year and the days of the month changed, but *not* the days of the week. The seven day week and seventh day Sabbath have continued uninterrupted from the Julian and Gregorian reckoning of time to this present date.

Scholars have astronomically and mathematically verified that the Sabbath the young Rabbi from Nazareth kept is the same day of the week it is now. They have found that the astronomical proofs are precise to one-millionth of a second, and the mathematical calculations are accurate to within one ten-millionth of a day.

Even more important, however, the biblical account affirms that *Yeshua* did *not* change the seventh day Sabbath. Rather, He affirmed the Divine origin and sanctity of the seventh day Sabbath by declaring Himself to be "LORD of the Sabbath" (Matt. 12:1-8).

The Sabbath: "For Jews Only"

Since the time of the Greek and Latin Church Fathers, one of Christianity's most popular arguments is that the seventh day Sabbath is for Jews only. The Christian theologian D. Shelby Corlett says in his book entitled *The Christian Sabbath:*

> The principle of the Sabbath, a sacred day of rest after six days of toil, is universal; but the Sabbath as a memorial to Israel, the seventh day of Israel's week, the cycle of which began with their deliverance from Egypt, specifically with the giving of the manna, was not universal. It was definitely related to Israel alone and not to other peoples or nations, for God positively stated the Israel memorial Sabbath "is a sign between me and the children of Israel forever."[7]

Dr. Corlett's argument sounds well and good *until* we learn that during biblical times the seventh day Sabbath was also observed by non-Jews, such as the Kenizzite Caleb, the Canaanite prostitute Rahab, and the Moabite woman Ruth, who chose to remain with Naomi, saying: "… thy people shall be my people, and thy God my God" (Ruth 1:16; AKJV).

At Mount Sinai, the LORD told Moses: "There is <u>one Torah</u> for the native-born and for the <u>stranger</u> [Heb. *ger,* 'foreigner, alien'] who sojourns among you" (Ex. 12:49; *The Scriptures*).

Hundreds of years later God spoke to Isaiah, saying: "… the sons of the stranger who join themselves to [YHVH]… to be His servants, all who guard the Sabbath, and not profane it, and hold fast to My covenant – them shall I bring to My set-apart mountain, and let them rejoice in my house of prayer… for My house is called a house of prayer for all the peoples" (Isa. 56:6, 7).

Neverthless, most theologians view the above passages as belonging to the Old Testament and, therefore, no longer relevant to New Testament Believers. But for those who understand the *Torah* observant faith of those first century followers of the young Rabbi from Nazareth, nothing could be further from the truth.

For example, in Acts 13:13-15 Luke states that when Paul and his company came to the region of Antioch in Pisidia, they went into the synagogue on the Sabbath day, and listened to the reading of the *Torah* and Prophets. Then Paul stood up and taught the people; both Jews and Gentiles. When Paul finished his teaching the Gentiles asked him to return to the synagogue on the following Sabbath and teach to them the Scriptures, which at that time would have been the *Torah* (vs.42-44).

In Acts 15:14-21, James affirms the Gentile practice of attending synagogues every Sabbath to hear the reading and teaching on the *Torah* of Moses. And in Acts 17:2, Luke writes that when Paul came to Thessalonica, he entered the local synagogue "as his manner was," and went unto them three Sabbaths and taught the Scriptures.

Equally significant, the great scholars of antiquity affirm that the seventh day was the day of rest kept by *all* the peoples of the Roman Empire. Philo (20 B.C.E. – 50 C.E.), the Hellenistic Jewish scholar of Alexandria, writes:

> And in short, it is very nearly an universal rule, from the rising of the sun to its extreme west, that every country, and nation, and city, is alienated from the laws and customs of foreign nations and states, and that they think that they are adding to the estimation in which they hold their own laws by despising those in use among other nations. But this is not the case with our laws which Moses has given to us; for they lead after them the inhabitants of continents, and islands, the eastern nations and the western, Europe and Asia, in short, the whole inhabitable world from one extremity to the other. For what man is there who does not honor that sacred seventh day, granting in consequence a relief and relaxation from labor, for himself and for all those who are near to him, and that not to free men only, but are to slaves, and even to beasts of burden.[8]

The first century Jewish historian Flavius Josephus (37 C.E. — sometime after 100 C.E.) writes:

> ...among the mass of the people there has for a long time been a great amount of zeal for our worship; nor is there a single town among the Greeks or barbarians or anywhere else, not a single nation to which observance of the Sabbath as it exists among ourselves has not penetrated; while fasting and burning of lights, and many of our laws with regard to meats, are also observed.[9]

Contrary to the arguments of many, these ancient accounts hardly sound as though the Gentile peoples of the first century believed the seventh day Sabbath was *done away* with the coming of the young Rabbi from Nazareth. Nor does it sound as though they believed the seventh day Sabbath belonged to the Jews only. Nevertheless, by the second century the Divine model of the seventh day Sabbath was well on its way to being replaced with the Sun-Day Sabbath.

Justin Martyr

Ignatius (50-107 C.E.), the first bishop of Antioch to call himself a Christian, was the first who contrasted the Sun-Day Sabbath with the Jewish Sabbath as something as something *done away* with.[10]

Irenaeus

Justin Martyr (100-165 C.E.), in controversy with a Jew, is recorded as saying, "the pious before Moses pleased God without circumcision and the Sabbath, and that Christianity requires not one particular Sabbath, but a perpetual Sabbath."[11] Justin *reasoned* that the selection of the first day of the week for the purposes of Christian worship was "because on that day God dispelled the darkness and the chaos, and because Jesus rose from the dead and appeared to his disciples."[12]

Irenaeus of Lyons, (140-210 C.E.), regarded the Jewish Sabbath as a *symbol* and typical Jewish ordinance.[13] Irenaeus also interpreted Israel as the Christian Church, the spiritual seed of Abraham (Irenaeus, *Against Heresies,* Book 5, Chapter 32).

Tertullian, (about 150-240 C.E.), viewed the Sun-Day Sabbath as *figurative* of rest from sin and typical of man's final rest, saying, "We have nothing to do with Sabbaths, new moons of Jewish festivals, much less with those of the heathen. We have our own solemnities, the Lord's day, for instance, and Pentecost."[14] The Alexandrian fathers held the same view, "with some fancies of their own concerning the allegorical meaning of the Jewish Sabbath," says Philip Schaff.[15]

Eusebius (about 260-about 340 C.E.), refused to call Sun-Day the Sabbath. Rather, he referred to it as "the first and chief of days and day of salvation."[16] A strong supporter of the sun-worshiper Constantine, Eusebius commended the emperor for commanding "all to assemble together every week to keep the LORD's day."[17]

Athanasius (296-373 C.E.) spoke of the keeping of the LORD's Day on Sun-Day as "the perpetual memorial of the resurrection" and held that the "old Sabbath had deceased."[18] Macarius, a presbyter of Upper Egypt (about 300-391 C.E.), *spiritualized* the seventh day Sabbath as a "type and shadow of the true Sabbath, which is freedom from sin."[19] Hilary of Poitiers (300-368 C.E.) viewed the whole of life as a preparation for the "eternal Sabbath" of the next life.[20] Epiphanius (about 320-403 C.E.) maintained that the keeping of Sun-Day as the LORD's Day was an "institution of the Apostles."[21] Ambrose (340-397 C.E.) regarded Sun-Day as an "evangelical festival, and contrasted it with the irrelevant "legal Sabbath."[22]

Jerome made the same distinction.[23] Augustine (354-430 C.E.) also derived the keeping of Sun-Day from the resurrection, and not from the Fourth Commandment.[24]

The Preamble of Christian Faith

The Christian scholar Paul J. Glenn informs us that the Greek Church Fathers taught that Greek philosophy had prepared the way for the Christian Revelation.[25] For the Greeks, philosophy was the *praeambula fidei,* or "preamble of the Faith," which made it an apt instrument for setting forth Christian Revelation in a scientific order.[26]

By the fourth century, the Fourth Commandment had been *theorized, hypothesized, spiritualized, allegorized* and *figuratively* explained away by the Greek and Latin Church Fathers in such a manner as to make the Christian Sun-Day Sabbath a sacred institution of the Roman Catholic Church. Thus when Constantine gave his Sun-Day Edict, in 321 C.E., it is said that he was merely acknowledging the prevailing practice of Sun-Day worship that had grown within Christian congregations from the time of the Church Fathers.

Constantine's Sun-Day Edict

On the 7th of March, 321 C.E., Constantine decreed that under penalty of death, all government officials, tradesmen and merchants throughout the empire were to cease work on the *"venerable day of the Sun-god Mithras,"* Sun-Day. In translation from Latin, Constantine's Sun-Day Edict reads in part as follows:

> Let all the judges and townspeople and the occupations of all trades rest upon the venerable day of the Sun. But let those who are situated in the country, freely and at full liberty attend to the business of agriculture. Because it often happens that no other day is so fit for the sowing of corn or the planting of vines, lest the critical moment being let slip, *m*en should lose the commodities of heaven. Given this 7th day of March, Crispus and Constantine being consuls each of them for the second time.[27]

Since that infamous day in Church history, Constantine has been hailed by Catholic and Protestant Christians as the great champion of the Christian Sabbath. In reality, however, Constantine's Sun-Day Edict had nothing to do with honoring the Christian Sabbath.

When Constantine made his Sun-Day Edict he employed the old astrological and pagan titles *Dies Solis,* which was familiar to all his sun-worshiping subjects. By doing this, Constantine made certain that his Sun-Day Edict would be as applicable to the pagan worshipers of Hercules, Apollo, and Mithra, as to Sun-Day worshiping Christians.

Scholars agree that it wasn't until *after* Constantine's reign that the biblical term "Sabbath" and the pagan name "Sun-Day" were used by Roman Catholic Church authorities to refer to Sun-Day as the LORD's day.[28]

To Constantine's credit, he did bestow many important favors upon Christians, such as the abolishment of death and cruel punishment. But were these acts of benevolence based upon Constantine's personal convictions? Or, were they made out of imperial expedience? According to the historian Will Durant, Constantine acted purely from political motives.[29]

Constantine seldom adhered to the Church's requirements of worship, and his letters to bishops made it clear that he cared little for their theological differences. It is said that when Constantine presided over Church councils he treated bishops as his political subjects. The Christian historian W. T. Jones writes:

> The Christian's, who claimed Constantine as their own and lavished their praises upon him, believed that he had been converted at the battle which won him his throne, when the cross appeared to him in a vision with the convenient and instructive motto: "In this sign conquer!" Constantine probably found it useful to pray to all sorts of gods for assistance, and if he thought that the Christian God helped him gain the crown he may have felt some gratitude. Political considerations also, almost certainly, influenced Constantine's policy of encouraging and supporting Christianity. It was certainly to his advantage to be allied with the tough, fast-growing sect which had managed to build up an elaborate and far-flung organization while withstanding a series of persecutions. In any case, whatever Constantine obtained from Christianity, imperial favor greatly assisted the rise of orthodoxy. For the emperors did not like ecclesiastical squabbling and found it desirable to encourage "uniformity." Thus it was Constantine who convoked the Council of Nicea, lent it the prestige of his presence, and, though he must have been indifferent to the whole question being debated, lent his valuable support to the Athanasian party (advocates of the Trinity doctrine).[30]

Even the scholars of *The Catholic Encyclopedia* acknowledge Constantine's politically motivated interest in the Church, saying:

> Some bishops, blinded by the splendor of the court, even went so far as to laud the emperor as an angel of God, as a sacred being, and to prophesy that he would, like the Son of God, reign in heaven. It has consequently been asserted that Constantine favored Christianity merely from political motives, and that he has been regarded as an enlightened despot who made use of religion to advance his policy.[31]

The First Christian Emperor

Perhaps the strongest evidence that contradicts the claim that Constantine was the first Christian Emperor comes from Constantine himself. During the time of Constantine's reign he maintained the title "Pontifus Maximus," meaning "the high priest of the Mysteries" [a title inherited by the Roman Catholic popes from the Pagan emperors of Rome, beginning with Caesars in 63 B.C.E.]. Philip Schaff says:

Constantine

> Constantine reverenced all the gods as mysterious powers: especially Apollo, the god of the sun, to whom in the year 308 he presented munificent (sic) gifts. Nay, so late as the year 321 he enjoined regular consultation of sooth sayers in public misfortunes, according to ancient heathen sage; even later, he placed his new residence, Bysantium, under the protection of the God of the Martyrs and the heathen goddess of Fortune; and down to the end of his life he retained the title and dignity of a *Pontifex Maximus,* or high priest of the heathen hierarchy. His coins bore on one side the letters of the name of Christ, on the other the figure of the Sun god, and the inscription 'Sol invictus' [Committed to the Invincible Sun].[32]

Expanding on Constantine's love for the pagan dieties of Rome, Edward Gibbon writes:

> Whatever symptoms of Christian piety might transpire in the discourses or actions of Constantine, he preserved till he was near forty years of age in the practice of the established religion; and the same conduct which in the court of Nicomedia might be imputed to his fear could be ascribed to the inclination or policy of the sovereign of God. His liberality restored and enriched the temples of the gods; the medals which issued from his Imperial mint are impressed with the figures and attributes of Jupiter and Apollo, of Mars and Hercules; and his filial piety increased the council of Olympus by the solemn apotheosis of

his father Constantius. But the devotion of Constantine was more peculairly (sic) directed to the genius of the Sun, the Apollo of Greek and Roman mythology; and he was pleased to be represented with the symbols of the God of Light and Poetry.... The altars of Apollo were crowned with the votive offerings of Constantine; and the credulous multitude were taught to believe that the emperor was permitted to behold with mortal eyes the visible majesty of their tutelar deity; and that, either walking or in a vision, he was blessed with the auspicious omens of a long and victorious reign. The Sun was universally celebrated as the invisible guide and protector of Constantine.[33]

In 326 C.E., the year following the great Council of Nicea, Constantine had his son Crispus put to death and his wife Fausta was suffocated to death in an overheated bath. About this same time Constantine had his sister's son flogged to death and her husband strangled – even though he had promised to spare his life.[34] Constantine then had a bronze statue of himself set atop a tall column as Apollo, the Sun-god.

In an attempt to put Constantine's cold-blooded murder of family members in the best possible light, the scholars of *The Catholic Encyclopedia* write: "Even after his conversion he caused the execution of his brother-in-law Licintus, and of the latter's son, as well as of Crispus his own son by his first marriage, and of his wife Fausta.... After reading these cruelties it is hard to believe that the same emperor could at times have mild and tender impulses; but human nature is full of contradictions."[35]

As to Constantine's questionable conversion, Edward Gibbon writes:

> The eloquent Lactantius, in the midst of his court, seems impatient to proclaim to the world the glorious example of the sovereign of Gaul; who (A.D. 306), in the first moments of his reign, acknowledged and the majesty of the true and only God. The learned Eusebius has ascribed the faith of Constantine to the miraculous sign which was displayed in the heavens while he mediated and prepared the Italian expedition (A.D. 312).–Euseb. in Vit. Const. 1. i. c. 27. The historian Zosimus maliciously asserts that the emperor had imbrued his hands in the blood of his eldest son, before he (A.D. 326) publically renounced the gods of Rome and of his ancestors (Zos. 1. ii.

104.). The perplexity produced by these discordant authorities is derived from the behavior of Constantine himself. According to the strictness of ecclesiastical language, the first of the *Christian* emperors was unworthy of that name till the moment of his death; since it was only during his last illness (A.D. 337) that he received, as a catechumen, the imposition of hands, and was afterward admitted, by the initiatory rites of baptism, into the number of the faithful.[36]

Sun-Day: *"the Divine positive law"*

When Constantine decreed *the venerable day of the Sun-god Mithra* to be the official day of rest for all his subjects there was little resistance from pagans, as well as the Christian community. For all practical purposes the "New Dispensation" of grace ushered in by Constantine had effectively replaced the "Old Dispensation" of *Torah* ['Law'] in the minds of fourth century Christians.

Oddly enough, in replacing the "old" Law of Moses, Christianity became a "new law" unto itself. Professor George Foote Moore writes:

> Even Christianity, in spite of its Pauline antinomianism and its actual emancipation from the Old Testament law, had hardly got fairly started in the Greek and Roman world when it began to think of itself and talk of itself as a 'new law,' and develop this idea not only in the sphere of ritual, where it made large borrowings from the Levitical priesthood, but with much more serious consequences in the realm of doctrine. Eventually, recondite dogmas derived from alien philosophies were defined not only as revealed truth to guide man in his search for God, but as a divinely prescribed norm of opinion and belief upon intellectual conformity to which the issues of eternal life depended.[37]

In the latter part of the fourth century the Divine model seventh day of rest was repudiated by the Catholic Cardinal Jerome. Some one hundred years later, in 538 C.E., the seventh day Sabbath was condemned by the Council of Orleans as belonging strictly to the Jews and, therefore, non-Christian.

In 789 C.E., the Roman Emperor Charlemagne decreed that all labor on Sun-Day was a violation of the Third Commandment. For obvious reasons Roman Catholic Church authorities abolished the Second Commandment: "Thou shalt not make unto thee any graven images, or any likeness *of anything* that *is* in heaven above, or that *is* in the earth beneath, or that *is* in the water under the earth" (Ex. 20:4; AKJV). The Fourth Commandment, "Remember the Sabbath day, to keep it holy" became the Third Commandment in Roman Catholicism.

From that point on the idea of replacing the Divine model seventh day of rest with Sun-Day was adopted by Christian congregations as an institution of *"divine positive law"*.[38]

The first recorded ratification of Constantine's Sun-Day Law took place thirty-eight years after the Council of Nicea, in 363 C.E. The Synod of Laodecia decreed that Christians should not worship on the seventh day Sabbath but, instead, observe Sun-Day as the official Christian Sabbath. The decree states in part:

> Here the Fathers order that no one of the faithful shall work on the Sabbath as do the Jews, but that they should honor the Lord's day; on account of the Lord's resurrection, and that on that day they should abstain from manual labor and go to church. But this abstaining from work on Sunday they do not lay down as a necessity, but they add, "if they can." For if through need or any other necessity any one worked on the Lord's day this was not reckoned against him (Canon 29).[39]

The Replacement of Hanukkah

Shortly after Constantine became Emperor of the Roman Empire, in 310 C.E.,tradition holds that the first recorded Christmas was held in December 311 C.E. Ten years later, after Constantine's victory at the Council of Nicea, it is said that Church authorities ratified December 25 as the day to celebrate *Yeshua's* birth.

According to the scholars of *The Encyclopedia Americana* the first mention of December 25 as the birth date of *Yeshua* occurred in A.D.

336, in an early Roman calendar. The scholars of *World Book* tell us that by A.D. 336 all the Christian churches except the Armenian Church observed the birth of *Yeshua* on December 25; that this date was not set in the West until about the middle of the fourth century and in the East until about a century later.[40]

Contrary to the misconception of many, the Church's decision to celebrate December 25 as *Yeshua's* birth-date had nothing to do with honoring His birth. Nor was it meant to counter the pagan influence of the Sun-god Mithra. Rather, the Christian scholars of the *Expository Dictionary of New Testament Words* tell us that December 25 was chosen as the day to celebrate *Yeshua's* birth because Church authorities wanted to increase the influence of the Church and make Christianity more acceptable to pagan "converts," who continued to celebrate the rebirth of the sun on December 25.[41]

At that particular time December 25 was the birth date pagans celebrated their chief deities throughout the Roman Empire, which included the Roman Sun-god Mithra, the Babylonian Sun-god Nimrod, the Egyptian Sun-god Ra, the Greek Sun-god Apollo, and the chief god of the Greek pantheon, Zeus.

Thus it was no coincidence that the blending of *Yeshua's* birth with the birth of the Sun-god Mithra originated at a time when the cult of the sun was particularly strong in Rome. Nor was it a coincidence that at the beginning of the third century the title "Sun of Justice" appeared as a title of Christ.[42] The Scottish theologian Alexander Hislop writes:

> *Within the Christian Church* no such festival as Christmas was ever heard of *till the third* century, and that not till the *fourth* century was far advanced did it gain much observance. How, then, did the Romish Church fix on December 25th as Christmas-day? Why, thus: Long before the fourth century, as long before the Christian era itself, a festival was celebrated among the *heathen,* at that precise time of the year, in honour (sic) of the birth of the son of the Babylonian queen of heaven; and it may fairly be presumed that, in order to conciliate the heathen, and to swell the number of the nominal adherents of Christianity, the same festival was adopted by the Roman Church, giving it only the name of Christ.[43]

As to the secular record of the pagan influence on the selection of the December 25 date for *Yeshua's* birth there is ample evidence. The scholars of *Collier's Encyclopedia* write:

> During the first three centuries of the Christian Era there was considerable opposition in the Church to the pagan custom of church at Rome assigned December 25 as the date for the celebration of the feast (Christmas), possibly about A.D. 320 or 353. By the end of the fourth century the whole Christian world was celebratings Christmas on that day, with the exception of the Eastern churches, where it was celebrated on January 6. The choice of December 25 was probably influenced by the fact that on this day the Romans celebrated the Mithraic feast of the Sun-god (natalis solis invicti), and that Saturnalia also came at this time.[44]

Expanding on the significance of December 25, the scholars of the *Encyclopedia Britannica* state:

> The traditional customs connected with Christmas have developed from several sources as a result of the coincidence of the celebration of the birth of Christ with the pagan agricultural and solar observations at midwinter. In the Roman world the Saturnalia (December 17-25) was a time of merrymaking and exchange of gifts. December 25 was also regarded as the birth of the Iranian mystery god Mithra, the Sun or Righteousness.[45]

And the scholars of the *Encyclopedia Americana* write:

> The celebration of this day (December 25) as Jesus' birth date was probably influenced by *pagan* (unchristian) festivals held at that time. The ancient Romans held year-end celebrations to honor Saturn, their harvest god; and Mithras, the god of light. Various peoples in northern Europe held festivals in mid-December to celebrate the end of the harvest season. As part of all these cele- brations, the people prepared special foods, decorated their homes with greenery, and joined in singing and gift giving. These customs gradually became part of the Christmas celebration.[46]

By the mid-fourth century the practice of celebrating *Yeshua's* birth on December 25 with Christ's Mass was a well established tradition among congregations identified with the Roman Catholic Church. And by the beginning of the twelfth century, the celebration of "Christ's Mass" ['Christmas'] on December 25 had become the most important religious festival in Europe.

Yeshua's Observance of Hanukkah

Although the Festival of Dedication [Hanukkah] is not one of the appointed festivals of Leviticus 23, it is in the New Testament and was a festival celebrated by *Yeshua*. Some would argue that *Yeshua* never observed this festival; that He just happened to be in the Temple on that particular day. But the facts simply do not support this argument.

Those who make such a claim fail to take into account the fact that *Yeshua* was a *Torah* observant Jewish Rabbi, who would never have risked the rejection of His own people simply because the Festival of Dedication was not an appointed festival of Leviticus 23. They also fail to take into account the fact that *Yeshua* was reared by *Torah* observant parents, especially by Mary, who "found favor with God".

But most important, John made it a point to record *Yeshua's* presence at the Festival of Dedication. As the last living witness of the life, death, and resurrection of the young Rabbi from Nazareth, John never wrote anything about his beloved Master that was coincidental. Every word, letter, and tense had a meaning and purpose.

There can be little doubt that John wanted his Jewish brethren to know that the Messiah of Israel did indeed honor the Feast of Dedication. John writes: "And it was at Jerusalem the feast of dedication, and it was winter. And Jesus walked in the temple in Solomon's porch" (Jhn. 10:22-23; AKJV).

The Origin of Hanukkah

Today, most Christians who read John 10:22-23 tend to overlook this particular festival and do not understand what is being commemorated. The New International Version Study Bible (NIV) notes that this event was "the commemoration of the dedication...of the temple by Judas Maccabeus in December in December 165 B.C., after it had been profaned by Antiochus Epiphanes. This was the last great deliverance the Jews had experienced."[47]

Prior to 168 B.C.E., the ruthless Syrian ruler Antiochus invaded Israel and instituted a religious persecution, outlawing the *Torah* and commanding all Jews to conform to his own religion, which was rooted in Syrian-Greek mythology.

Although several Jews resisted Antiochus' rule and were killed, many had already blended the worship of God with the pagan festivals of people living around them. Thus it was relatively easy for Antiochus to establish religious reforms, making Sabbath observance, the study of the *Torah*, and the practice of circumcision forbidden under the penalty of death.

But Antiochus' hatred for the Jewish people and their Judaic faith didn't stop there. He forced them to work on the Sabbath. Amd most abominable for a Jew, Antiochus made them sacrifice swine on the holy Altar and eat it. His ultimate act of contempt was to institute prostitution in the holy Temple. He then placed an image of Zeus in the Temple and renamed it "Olympus".

While many Jews adopted this new form of religion, Mattathias ben Johanan, a Levite priest who was advanced in years, refused to comply with Antiochus' demands. It is said that when one Judean came forward to offer a sacrifice on a pagan altar Mattathias not only killed the Judean, he also slew the royal officer who ordered the act. Mattathias then overthrew the altar and, with his five sons, fled into the Gophna Hills, an area of heavily forested ridges and valleys. Word of the revolt soon spread, and Mattahias' small band was joined by others.

Shortly afterwards, Mattathias and his small band of warriors began overthrowing pagan altars, and re-established Jewish customs and worship among the people. Unfortunately, Mattathias did not live to realize his dream of setting his people free. He died in 166 B.C.E.

The following year, in 165 B.C.E., Matthathias' third son, Judah, became the leader of the revolt. Early in the revolt, Judah was given the name Maccabee, meaning "hammer" or "sledgehammer," in recognition of his ferociousness in battle. From that point on Judah's band of warriors were known as the "Maccabees".

Mindful of the superiority of the Seleucid forces, Judah avoided direct engagement with the main army. Instead, he used the element of surprise attack on smaller enemy forces. The strategy worked. Judah was able to win a series of victories. As the word spread of Judah's victories, men from the surrounding villages joined the Maccabee cause.

Judah "Maccabee"

Shortly afterwards, Judah won a major victory at the Battle of Emmaus, causing the Seleucid commander to withdraw his forces to the coast. After several more months of fighting, Judah drove out the Seleucid forces from Jerusalem. It is said that on the day Judah and his valiant warriors marched into a liberated Jerusalem there was great celebration and rejoicing.

Judah purified the defiled Temple on the 25th of Kislev (December 14, 165 B.C.E.), and restored the Temple services. The rededication of the Temple became a permanent Jewish holiday and is still celebrated annually as Hanukkah.

The ancient historian Charles Foster Kent, professor of Biblical Literature at Yale University, writes:

> After two years of almost constant fighting, Judas and his associates, by their courage and zealous devotion, had won their religious freedom by which they had sacrificed all else. With mingled feelings of sadness and joy, they turned to the sacred city to restore the interrupted service of the temple. Renegade Jews and hated Syrians still insulted them from the battlements of the citadel of Acra, which Judas was unable to capture. While his soldiers guarded against attack from the Syrian garrison, and the sanctuary, "blameless priests cleansed the holy place and bore out the stones of defilement" (I. Mac. iv. 46). Then a new altar was built, the temple repaired and furnished anew. On the twenty-fifth day of the ninth month, December, 165, B.C., just three years after it had been defiled by Antiochus, the temple was rededicated, and its service reinstated. Universal joy filled all hearts, and found expression in solemn sacrifices and loud songs of praise. For eight days, they celebrated the great event, and decreed that every after it should be commemorated by a yearly feast (I. Mac. iv. 47-59).[48]

According to tradition, during the rededication of the Temple the priests made a temporary Menorah and made plans to relight it. As they searched for the ritually pure olive oil that was needed to relight the Menorah they discovered that the Greeks had defiled all the oil except for one cruse, which contained enough oil to keep the Menorah burning for only one day.

Levitical priests decided to use the only cruse of oil available to relight the Menorah; also called the "Eternal Light". Tradition holds that the oil of this one cruse of ritually pure olive oil continued to burn for eight straight days, giving the people time to go out into the olive groves and produce more pure olive oil, which took precisely eight days.

Although there is no biblical basis for the celebration of Hanukkah, after 165 B.C.E., the Festival of Dedication was celebrated annually by the Jewish people, then later by *Yeshua* Himself, as well as those first century followers of the young Rabbi from Nazareth.

For orthodox Jews, Hanukkah is still celebrated as a commemoration of the restoration of Israel, the rededication of the Temple, and the eight day miracle of the "Eternal Light".

For the first century followers of *Yeshua,* Hanukkah was a festival which pointed to the promised Messiah of Israel as the "Eternal Light of the nations".

Affirming this first century understanding, about 95 C.E., John began his Gospel prologue about *Yeshua* -- the "Eternal Light of the nations," saying:

> 1 In the beginning was the Word, and the Word was with Elohim, and the Word was Elohim.
>
> 2 He was in the beginning with Elohim.
>
> 3 All came to be through Him, and without Him not even one came to be that came to be.
>
> 4 In Him was life, and the life was the light of men.
>
> 5 And the light shines in darkness, and the darkness has not overcome it.
>
> 6 There was a man sent from Elohim, whose name was Yohanan [John].
>
> 7 This one came for a witness, to bear witness of the Light, that all might believe through him.
>
> 8 He was not that Light, but that he might bear witness of that Light.

9 He was the true Light, which enlightens every man, coming into the world (Jhn. 1:1-9; *The Scriptures).*

In 336 C.E., Church authorities began replacing the celebration of *Yeshua* as the "Eternal Light" with Christ's Mass ['Christmas'] by blending it with the Roman celebration of Saturnalia, which began on December 17 and ended on the birth day of the pagan Sun-god Mithra, December 25.

Although Christ's Mass specifically replaced the winter festival of Hanukkah its institution as one of the most holy days in the Christian calendar had much broader implications -- the replacement of the biblically appointed Fall festivals.

How do we know this to be the caswe? In the Hebrew Scriptures there is a direct link between Rosh HaShanah, Yom Kippur, and Sukkot, which are linked to Hanukkah in the Second Book of Maccabees, stating in part as follows:

> They celebrated it for eight days with rejoicing in the manner of the Feast of Tabernacles, mindful of how but a little while before at the festival of Tabernacles they had been wandering about like wild beasts in the mountain caves. That is why, bearing thyrsi and graceful branches and also plam leaves, they offered up hymns to Him.... (2 Macc. 10:6-7).

Thus it was that by the fourth century Christ's Mass ['Christmas'] was adopted by Roman Catholic Church authorities and became the replacement for not only the "Eternal Light" Festival of Dedication ['Hanukkah'], but also for the biblically appointed festivals of Rosh HaShanah, Yom Kippur and Sukkot ['the Feast of Tabernacles'].

From that point on Christ's Mass ['Christmas'] became one of the most celebrated festivals of the Church. But for most Christians, few knew the origins of the mass they were celebrating. The Messianic researcher Lew White writes:

> **Missa,** Latin for *depart,* was the last word spoken at a Catholic *"Mass",* and so the word for the liturgical procedure **seems** to be from that. It was tacked-on to the word "Christ" because the Mass on December 25th was called *Christ's Mass.* But even the "Mass" existed before Catholicism. It was what

the Pagan priest of Mithraism and Mandaeanism called their *Mass of the Dead,* which was a ghastly "sacramental" ritual of animal and human sacrifice–on an indoor "altar", with Pagan worshipers assembled in two rows of benches with a center aisle. The Pagan priest would be at one end of the room, mumbling obscurely, leading the service to Mithras. At the spring equinox, new "initiates" into the mysteries of the cult were "baptized" (sprinkled) in blood, under a bull being hacked to death. This was the time which the earth's orbit "crossed" over the celestial equator. These sun-worshipers interpreted this as "**Mithras slaying the bull**"–the sun had "crossed" over the celestial equator, overcoming the "bull", which they called the constellation of **Tarsus** (Latin for "bull").[49]

Ashtoreth Worship

Accompanying this blending of Christ's birth with the festival of Mithra, on December 25, was the pagan custom of honoring the Canaanite goddess Ashtoreth with a decorated cut-down tree called "the Asherah tree". Among the ancient Canaanites the Asherah tree was used in the worship of the goddess Ashtoreth, the consort of Baal. The sacred image of Asherah was a tree that was cut down, nailed in place by a hammer, and then decorated with silver and gold ornaments. Sound familiar?

During King Solomon's reign the Israelites adopted this pagan rite and blended it with the worship of the LORD. The Hebrew Scriptures tell us that Solomon "went after Ashtoreth the goddess" (1 Kings 11:5).

After Solomon's death, about 926 B.C.E., the kingdom was divided into two kingdoms, with ten tribes in the north called Israel, and Judah and Benjamin in the south. As to the reason, the Scriptures state: "...because that they have forsaken Me, and have worshiped Ashtoreth the goddess of the Sidonians..." (1 Kings 11:33; NASV).

The Israelite's worship of Ashtoreth with the Asherah tree was only the beginning of the their apostasy. In the northern kingdom, beginning with Jeroboam's reign (931-901 B.C.E.), the people blended their worship of God with the pagan worship of neighboring peoples. By the time of King Ahab's reign (874-853 B.C.E.), who married Jezebel the daughter of Ethbaal, king of the Sidonians, the religion of the northern tribes had become so corrupted that they were building temples for the worship of Baal and his consort Ashtoreth (1 Kings 16:29-33).

In 745 B.C.E., Tiglath-Pileser III ascended the throne of Assyria and marched his army through the Mediterranean countries, forcing them to become provinces of the Assyrian Empire. Resentment soon turned to revolt, and from that point on the northern tribes were marked for ruin and captivity. Vowing to bring the northern territories into submission, Tiglath-Pileser marched his army against the ten tribes of Israel and neighboring peoples, destroying their towns and villages, taking them captive, and deporting their men, women and children to Assyria.

With the exception of Samaria, all the towns and villages of northern Israel were annexed and divided into provinces over which Assyrian governors ruled. All that was left of Israel was a small token of statehood, the mountain of Ephraim, where Hoshea, who had become king by killing his predecessor, Pekah, was allowed to reign as king (2 Kings 15:30).

After the death of Tiglath-Pileser, Hoshea made a pact with Egypt, and refused to pay the annual tribute to the new Assyrian ruler, Shalmaneser V. When Shalmaneser learned of Hoshea's pact with Egypt he dispatched his soldiers against Hoshea, ending the northern kingdom (2 Kings 17:6). From Assyria, the ten tribes of the northern kingdom were dispersed among the nations of the world, where their descendents remain to this present day.

As a result of the Assyrian invasion and conquest of the northern kingdom large numbers of Israelites from the north fled to Judah, carrying with them their idolatrous customs of Ashtoreth worship. In time, the worship of Ashtoreth was gradually adopted by the people of Judah, who gave the goddess a new name – "Queen of Heaven" (Jer. 7:14-18).

By the beginning of 627 B.C.E., the people of Judah were blending their worship of the God of Israel with the goddess Ashtoreth, now called "the Queen of Heaven". Decrying this pagan custom, Jeremiah said: "Learn not the way of the heathen... for their customs *are* vain: for *one* cutteth a tree out of the forest, the work of the hands of the workman, with the axe. They deck it with silver and gold; they fasten it with nails and hammers, that it move not. They are upright as the palm tree, but they speak not..." (Jer. 10:2-5; AKJV).

Jeremiah's admonition fell on deaf ears. In 586 B.C.E., Nebuchadnezzar led his war-hardened troops to Judah, invading the land and destroying its walled cities and villiages, including Jerusalem and the holy Temple. The elite of Judah were carried away to Babylon, and the kingdom of Judah ended.

During the course of time, as pagan deities were adopted by different civilizations names were changed. However, many of the pagan customs remained the same, such as with Mithra, whose cult worship was identified with the worship of the great Mother goddess. The scholars of *Hastings Encyclopedia of Religion and Ethics* inform us that the Mithra cult was associated with "a female goddess of an easily recognized Semitic type" that goes all the way back to the Babylonian cult of the great Mother goddess, saying:

> Mithraism lent itself readily to alliances with other worship, especially those of female divinities, which supplied what it was unable to offer to women, and it seems to have been specially associated with the cult of the Magna Mater (Great Mother).[50]

While there is no evidence that the Ashtoreth cult of Israel was directly connected to the Mithra cult of Rome, there is evidence that certain customs and secret rites practiced by her devotees were identical to those practiced by the cult of Mithra.

For those initiated into the secrets of Mithraism the symbol of the Ashreah tree had specific meanings. The erect-pointed Asherah tree symbolized a "phallus," the male reproductive member. The little balls which were hung on its branches symbolized "testicles," and the tinsel represented the "semen" of the male deity Baal. The wreath represented the "womb" of a woman, and the green ivy and holly were symbols of the Roman deity "Saturn."[51] The Roman custom was to give presents during Saturnalia. Whereas the yule-log are remnants of the old Teutonic nature worship.[52]

America's First "Christmas Tree"

Today, Christian scholars agree that one of the primary reasons the cult of Mithraism became popular among the peoples in the West was because of its celebration of the Asherah tree. Dean Merrill Tenney writes: "Through the returning veterans and the Oriental travelers and businessmen who visited the West it became a popular faith, particularly in the army."[53]

Before long the celebration of Saturnalia, with the custom of exchanging gifts placed under the Asherah tree, became an annual tradition among the peoples of Europe, especially with the German peoples. "Mithraic shrines abounded in the Rineland of Germany," Professor Tenney said.[54]

The "Christmas tree"

Centuries later the first recorded "Christmas tree" in America was found in the camp of the Hessian soldiers at the famous Battle of Trenton, during the War of Independence. About 30,000 Hessian soldiers from northern Germany hired themselves out to Great Britain to fight against the American revolutionaries, and brought with them the European custom of celebrating Christmas with the "Christmas tree," on December 25.

On Christmas night, in 1776, General George Washington's crumbling Continental Army crossed the ice-packed Delaware River on crudely made river-boats and carried out a successful attack against the Hessian soldiers. During most of the nine hours it took for Washington's army to cross the Delaware River the Hessian soldiers were celebrating Christmas with holiday foods, spirits, songs, merrymaking, and the traditional "Christmas tree".

Early the following morning the Hessian soldiers, who were still tired from the previous night's festivities, were caught off-guard and quickly defeated by Washington's spirited military charge. Out of 1,400 Hessian soldiers 900 were captured.

Historians agree that the miraculous Trenton victory marked the turning point for Washington's depleting Continental Army, and the eventual defeat of the British Army in the War of Independence.

General Washington leading his troops at the Battle of Trenton.

Later, when German settlers came to Pennsylvania in the early nineteenth century they brought with them the popular tradition of celebrating Christ's birth with the "Christmas tree". In 1856, President Franklin Pierce set up the first "Christmas tree" inside the White House. In 1870, Congress made Christmas a national holiday. By 1877, the American custom of setting up the "Christmas tree" was well established. And in 1923, President Calvin Coolidge began the custom of lighting the National "Christmas tree" on the White House grounds.[55]

The Blending Mithraism with Christianity

Historians agree that Mithraism was the chief rival of Christianity during the third and fourth centuries. Unknown to most Christians, Catholic Church authorities made dramatic changes in order to transform pagans into "converts".

By the fourth century the Church's adoption of Mithraic practices was so complete that pagan sun-worshipers felt perfectly comfortable worshiping in Christian churches. One historian put it well when he said: "Christianity didn't conquer Mithraic Paganism. Mithraism blended in, and changed names."[56]

Today, no other inner sanctuary of Christianity represents the influence of Mithraic sun-worship as does the interior of St. Peter's Basilica.

The inner Basilica's radiant sunburst *Sun images above St. Peter's Altar*

Notice that the above photo to the left shows a huge golden image of a radiant sunburst, which is located on the wall directly above the altar inside St. Peter's Basilica. On the photo to the right is St. Peter's Altar [*i.e.*, 'the Pope's Altar'] and a ninety-five foot canopy which is supported by four huge columns, twisted and slightly covered with branches. At the top of each of the four columns high above the altar is an image of the sun.

Addressing the pagan origins of sun-worship and its influence on Christianity, Alexander Hislop writes:

Egypt, the *disk* of the Sun was represented in the temples, and the sovereign and his wife and children were represented as adoring it.... In the great temple of Babylon, the golden image of the Sun was exhibited for the

King Akhenatom (1365-1347 B.C.E.) and Queen Nefertiti make offerings to the Sun-god Aton.

Apostate Israelite sun-worshipers.

worship of the Babylonians. ... In the worship of Baal, as practised (sic) by the idolatrous Israelites in the days of their apostacy, the worship of the sun's image was equally observed; and it is striking to find that the image of the sun, which apostate Israel worshipped (sic), was erected *above the altar.* From all this, it is manifest that the image of the sun above, or on the altar, was one of the recognized symbols of those who worshipped (sic) Baal or the Sun. And here in a so-called Christian Church, a brilliant plate of silver, "in the form of a Sun," is so placed on the altar, that every one who adores at that altar must bow down in lowly reverence before that image of the *"Sun."*[57]

With this understanding, here is the great question: How was the cult of Mithra able to blend itself into Christianity by merely changing names? W. T. Jones tells us that a cardinal belief of Mithraism was a savior-deity whose worship promised eternal life, and held that there were basically two primary forces at work in the world: the powers of good and evil, which became a battleground for a struggle between these two forces, much like two opposing armies locked in combat.[58]

Like the spiritual warfare of Christians, in Mithraism the soul's earthly existence was a testing ground for the soul. If the soul conquered the force of evil, it would return to the deity from which it came. If the soul succumbed to the force of evil, it would be sentenced to suffer eternally in hell with demons, who are the agents of the evil force.

Like Christianity's concept of a Savior and Judge, Mithra was both mankind's savior and judge, who would judge men after death on the merits of their good and bad deeds. Like Christianity's concept of Divine protection for persevering Christians, the same held true for the followers of Mithra. For those who fought the evil force, Mithra was always present to protect and help them overcome evil. And like Christianity's teaching on overcoming evil through Christ, it was through Mithra that his faithful devotees could overcome evil and be triumphant in the end.

Since Mithra was identified with the sun, which represented the good, in contrast to darkness, representing evil, like the special holidays of Christianity, many of Mithra's festivals were celebrated at special times of the solar year. And like the Church's observance of Christ's birth-date, on December 25, the high festival of Mithra fell on December 25, the day of the sun's rebirth after the winter solstice.

Mithra slaughtering a bull, Rome (200-300 C.E.).

The Sacred Rites of Membership

In the cult of Mithraism, candidates were admitted only after they had performed the seven rites of initiation. Passing from one initiation rite to another corresponded to the heavenly journey of the soul. Promotion was obtained through the initiates submission to a religious ritual ['kneeling'], casting off the old life ['nakedness'], and liberation from bondage through the "Mysteries" of Mithraism ['compliance'].

The initiation process required the initiate to symbolically climb a ceremonial ladder with seven rungs, which represented the seven known celestial bodies. By symbolically ascending the ceremonial ladder through successive initiations, the candidate could proceed through the seven levels of heaven, which were called *Corax* ['Raven'], *Nymphus* ['Male Bride'], *Miles* ['Soldier'], *Leo* ['Lion'], *Peres* ['Persian'], *Heliodromus* ['Sun-Runner'], and *Pater* ['Father']. Each level was protected by one of the seven celestial bodies: Mercury, Venus, Mars, Jupiter, the Moon, the Sun, and Saturn.

The lowest rung of initiation into the grade of *Corax* symbolized the death of the new initiate, from which he would arise reborn as a new man. The rung represented the end of his old life as an unbeliever and cancelled out previous beliefs that were unacceptable to the Mithraic cult.

Passing from one rung ['grade'] to another was accompanied by the clashing of cymbals, the beating of drums, and the unveiling of a statue of Mithras. The initiate drank wine from a cup and ate a sun-shaped piece of bread to signify his acceptance of Mithra. Before the Mithraic "Mystery" Mass began the sun-shaped pieces of bread were exposed to the rays of the sun. So by eating the sun-shaped pieces of bread the initiates believed they were partaking of the essence of the Sun-god Mithra.[59]

When the initiate reached the grade of the *Miles* ['Soldier'], he was given a crown, which he had to reject by saying, "Only Mithra is my crown". At that point a priest, who was called *Patre Sacrorum,* "Father of the Sacred Mysteries," would place the sign of Mithra, a cross, on the forehead of the initiate to symbolize his ownership by Mithra. From that point on the initiate belonged to the *Invincible Sun-god Mithra.*

Absolute loyalty to authority became the cardinal virtue of the Mithraic religion and the vehicle for fraternal obedience. The male-only cult of Mithra, which in the third and fourth centuries became particularly popular with the Roman soldiers, compared the practice of their religion to their training for warfare in the military.

Since Mithra was a chaste and celibate deity, his male devotees were taught to reverence celibacy. Equally important, all the male cult members considered themselves sons of the same Mithra Father, owing to one another a brother's affection.

For the followers of Mithra, Sun-Day was not only the day of the Sun-god Mithra, whom the Romans called *"Domini"* [Latin: 'Lord'], it was "the Lord's Day". Sound familiar?

The Replacement of Passover

Of all the festivals God gave to His covenant people Israel, none represents His eternal love and redeeming mercy as does the Feast of Passover. For the Jewish people, *pesach* ['Passover'] is an appointed feast to be observed as a memorial of their Divine intervention and deliverance from four hundred years of slavery in Egypt:

> 14 'And this day shall become to you a remembrance. And you shall observe it as a festival to [YHVH] throughout your generations – observe it as a festival, an everlasting law (Ex. 12:14; *The Scriptures*).

For the *Torah* observant first century followers of the young Rabbi from Nazareth the Feast of Passover was much more than just a memorial of Israel's deliverance from the bondage of Egypt. As a result of the young Rabbi's sacrificial death, the Feast of Passover was now observed as a memorial of their own deliverance from the bondage of sin. Just as *Yeshua* commanded, when He told His disciples:

> 13...do this in remembrance of Me (Lk. 22:19).

During the second and early third centuries, despite the Church's rejection of observing Passover, many Christians continued to observe the Passover Seder with Jewish congregations on the 14th of Aviv. But this would soon change.

At the Council of Nicea, in 325 C.E., Church authorities agreed to abolish the Divine appointed Passover festival and replace it with what Constantine called "the more legitimate festival of Easter". From that point on Christians were forbidden to observe Passover.

Church historians agree that the anti-*Semitic,* sun-worshiper Constantine was at the center of the great Nicean debate. Philip Schaff informs us that it was Constantine who invited the Christian bishops to the Council, and paid their expenses both to and from Nicea.[60] Of the estimated eighteen hundred bishops scattered through the empire, only three hundred and eighteen attended the Council. It is said that when the bishops arrived in Nicea, Constantine hosted a great banquet for them in his palace.

Eusebius describes Constantine as a "figure of the reign of Christ on earth," saying: "he remunerated the bishops lavishly, and dismissed them with a suitable valedictory, and with letters of commendation to the authorities of all the provinces on their homeward way."[61]

Over the centuries, scholars have debated whether or not Constantine acted on his own in calling for the Council. The *Catholic Encyclopedia* simply states that it is not known whether Constantine acted solely in his own name or worked with Pope Sylvester I.

Although the facts are uncertain, it is unlikely that Constantine acted on his own. It is believed that if Constantine did not consult with Pope Sylvester it is highly likely that he consulted with a trusted bishop, such as Eusebius of Caesarea.

Eusebius later wrote about Constantine's presence in the Council in glowing terms, saying, "himself proceeded through the midst of the assembly like some heavenly messenger of God, clothed in raiment which glittered as it were with rays of light, reflecting the glowing radiance of a purple robe, and adorned with the brilliant splendor of gold and precious stones" (Eusebius, *The Life of the Blessed Emperor Constantine,"* Book III, Chapter X).

Perhaps the most significant event of the Nicea Council was its absence of Jewish bishops, who were not invited. Shortly after the conference Constantine wrote a letter to all the non-Jewish bishops who had not attended, appealing to them in the name of "Christian unity" to reject everything Jewish. Recorded in the writings of Eusebius, Constantine's letter shows his contempt for the Jews, saying in part:

> It was... declared improper to follow the custom of the Jews in the celebration of this holy festival [Easter], because, their hands having been stained with crime, the minds of these wretched men are necessarily blinded. ... Let us, then, have nothing in common with the Jews, who are our adversaries. ... avoiding all contact with that evil way. ... who after having compassed the death of the Lord, being out of their minds, are guided not by sound reason, but by unrestrained passion,

wherever their innate madness carries them.... a people so utterly depraved.... Therefore, this irregularity must be corrected, in order that we may no more have anything in common with those parricides and murders of our Lord.... no single point in common with the perjury of the Jews.[62]

Constantine's Influence on the Church

Constantine's personal involvement in the Council of Nicea marked the first time a head of State became involved in theological matters of the Church. But it would not be his last. Encouraged by his success at Nicea, Constantine moved the forty days of "weeping for Tammuz" [*i.e.,* the Babylonian Sun-god: the reincarnated Nimrod who was born on December 25 and died in the fourth month called "Tammuz" on the Jewish Calendar] on the Christian Calendar to be the forty days preceding Easter. The "fast of Tammuz" was then renamed "Lent," which was preceded by a gluttonous, drunken sex orgy that later became known as "Mardi Gras".

Sixteen years after the Council of Nicea, in 341 C.E., the Synod of Antioch ratified the Nicean decision, decreeing excommunication from the Church for observing Easter at the same time as the Jewish Passover. The decree states in part:

> Whosoever shall presume to set aside the decree of the holy and great Synod which was assembled at Nice in the presence of the pious Emperor Constantine, beloved of God, concerning the holy and salutary feast of Easter; if they shall obstinately persist in opposing what [then] rightly ordained, let them be excommunicated and cast out of the Church; this is said concerning the laity. But if anyone of those who preside in the Church whether he be bishop, presbyter, or deacon, shall presume, after this decree, to exercise his own private judgment to the subversion of the people and to the disturbance of the churches, by observing Easter [at the same time] with the Jews, the holy Synod decrees that he shall thenceforth be an alien from the Church, as one who not only heaps sins upon himself, but who is also the cause of destruction and subversion to many; and it disposes not only such persons themselves from

their ministry, but those also who after their disposition shall presume to communicate with them. And the deposed shall be deprived even of that external honour, of which the holy Canon and God's priesthood partake (Canon 1).[63]

In response, Catholic Church authorities decreed that "the more legitimate festival of Easter" should replace the Divine appointed festival of Passover, and that Easter be celebrated on the first Sun-Day after the full moon, on or after the vernal equinox.[64]

With the arrival of the vernal Equinox, sun-worshiping pagans believed the Mother Earth was impregnated by the sun and the cycle of life began anew. Accompanying this belief, the spring festival of Easter was celebrated with a ritual of sexual acts, and used fertility symbols like rabbits and eggs.

In time, the pagan rites of Easter were adopted and became an integral part of the Church's celebration of Christ's resurrection. The Christian researcher Susan Richardson says in her book entitled *Holidays and Holy Days:*

> There are several reasons for the rabbit, or hare, to be associated with Easter, all of which come through pagan celebrations or beliefs. The most obvious is the hare's fertility. Easter comes during spring and celebrates new life.... The hare or rabbit's burrow help the animal's adoption as part of Easter celebrations. Believers saw the rabbit coming out of its underground home as a symbol of Jesus coming out of the tomb.[65]

Addressing Christianity's adoption of the pagan symbolism of the Easter Egg, Lillian Eichler says in her book entitled *The Customs of Mankind:*

Easter Rabbit

The Christians borrowed the egg and made it part of their Easter festivities, but they made it emblematic of the Resurrection. To them the egg was regarded somewhat in the light of a prison or tomb, from which future life escaped. Thus, a writer in the *Gentleman's Magazine* for July, 1783, remarks that the egg at Easter is "an emblem of the rising up out of the grave, in the same manner as the chick, entombed, as it were in the egg, in due time is brought to life."'

It would seem that the original purpose of colouring (sic) eggs was to imitate the new colours (sic) of the earth, induced by the coming of spring and the blossoming of the flowers. But when the original custom was taken over by the Christian Church the eggs were decorated principally in red, to denote the blood of Christ.

... The rabbit's part in Easter festivities originated with an old superstition that rabbits lay eggs on Easter Eve. This superstition is possibly Teutonic in origin, but no one knows precisely when it started or what was the original meaning or purpose behind it.[66]

The *Original Webster's Unabridged Dictionary* (1901) says of the pagan origins of Easter:

Easter, sax. *easter;* Gem. *ostern;* suppose to be from e*ostre,* the goddess of love, or Venus of the north, in honor of whom a festival was celebrated by our pagan ancestors, in April; whence this month was called *Eastermonth. Easter is* supposed, by Beda and others, to be the *Astarte* of the Sidonians.[67]

And the scholars of the *Encyclopedia Britannica* (1934) write:

Easter (es'ter). Ostra, or Eastre, was the goddess of Spring in the religion of the ancient Anglos and Saxons. Every April a festival was celebrated in her honor. With the beginnings of Christianity, the old gods were put aside. From then on the festival was celebrated in honor of the resurrection of Christ, but was still known as Easter after the old goddess.

Each Spring, to insure a productive harvest season, devotees of the goddess would conduct a fertility rite by rolling eggs decorated with the bright colors of Spring across their fields, believing it would make their land fertile. They would then hide these same eggs in a rabbit's nest to keep them from "evil spirits". Sound familiar?

By the early seventeenth century the Easter Egg was recognized by Catholic Church authorities as a sacred symbol of the resurrection of Christ. In honor of that resurrection symbol, Pope Paul V. (1605-1621) pontificated the following "Sacred Egg" prayer to be prayed by Christians on Easter Sun-Day, which states in part:

> Bless O Lord, we beseech thee, this thy creature of *eggs,* that it may become wholesome sustenance unto thy servants, *e*ating it in remembrance of our Lord Jesus Christ.[68]

During this same period, the Sun-Day Protestant translators of the 1611 Authorized King James Bible replaced the Greek term *"pascha"* ['Passover'], as found in the ancient Greek manuscripts, with the pagan term "Easter," stating:

> 4 And when he [Herod] had apprehended him [Peter], he put *him* in prison, and delivered *him* to four quaternions of soldiers to keep him; intending after <u>Easter</u> [Gk. *pascha*] to bring him forth to the people (Acts 12:4; AKJV).

The "LORD's Supper"

As early as the second century new Church doctrines began to replace the first century *Torah* observant faith of those first followers of the young Rabbi from Nazareth. Greek and Latin Church Fathers began to redefine the appointed Feast of Passover by figuratively explaining away *Yeshua's* words about the sacrament of bread and wine, saying: "This is My body which is given for you ... this cup which is poured out for you is the new covenant in My blood" (Lk. 22:19-20; NASV).

Addressing the Church's interpretation of the Scriptures, the British language scholar E. W. Bullinger says: "It may be truly said that most of the gigantic errors of Rome, as well as the erroneous and conflicting views of the Lord's People, have their root and source, either in figuratively explaining away passages which should be taken literally, or in taking literally what has been thrown into a peculiar form or Figure of language...."[69]

For most Greek and Latin Church Fathers, *Yeshua's* words about the bread and wine were meant to be taken literally. For example, Ignatius referred to the sacrament of the bread and wine as "the flesh of our crucified and risen Lord Jesus Christ," and "the consecrated bread a medicine of immortality and an antidote of spiritual death."[70]

Justin Martyr held to the same interpretation; that the bread and wine of sacrament was the actual flesh and blood of Christ.[71] Irenaeus taught that the bread and wine in the sacrament became the "Word of God," and that through the power of the Holy Spirit, by taking of the elements "one is strengthened in both soul and body unto eternal life."[72] Tertullian made the words *Hoc est corpus meum* [*lit.*, "This is My body"] to be equivalent to the words *figura corporis mei* [*lit.*, "My bodily figure"].[73] Clement referred to the wine as being symbolic of the blood of Christ, saying: "the believer receives not the physical, but the spiritual blood, the life, of Christ."[74] Origin viewed the sacrament as an allegory, making the bread represent the Old Testament, and the wine the New Testament, and the breaking of the bread the multiplication of the Word of God, which feeds the soul.[75]

Thomas Aquinas held the sacrament to be a "*sacrifice* because it repeats Christ's oblation on the cross ... a *communion* because it presents the uniy of the Church ... a *viaticum* because it is heavenly manna for pilgrims on their way to haven."[76]

Aquinas also used a term of John Damascus, the *assumption,* "because the sacrament lifts us up into the Deity of Christ," and calls it *hostia* "because it contains Christ himself, who is the oblation of our salvation."[77]

Scholars agree that the consecration rite of the Mass, which is suppose to transform the sun-disk wafer and wine into the actual body and blood of *Yeshua,* is one of the oldest ceremonies of *primitive* religion.[78] For example, in the classic work entitled *Hastings' Encyclopedia of Religion and Ethics* there are several pages devoted to many nations, tribes, and religions "Eating the god".[79] Justin Martyr states that bread and a cup of water were set forth with certain words of blessing in the sacred Mithric rites.[80] Tertullian wrote that Mithra signs the cross on soldier's foreheads, celebrates an oblation of bread, and introduces a symbol of the resurrection.[81]

Even the scholars of the *Catholic Encyclopedia* (1911) admit the following: "Mithraism had a Eucharist, but the idea of a sacred banquet is as old as the human race and existed at all ages and amongst all peoples."[82]

Once the Divine appointed Feast of Passover was abolished by the Nicean Council, in 325 B.C.E., the blending of the Mass of Mithra with

Christianity's revision of the "Last Supper" was only a step away. The Messianic researcher Lew White writes:

> Every "Mass" is truly a Black Mass. The Pagan mind 'mixed' this up with the Passover Seder known as "the Last Supper", and *POOF!* The "magic' became our Sun-Day **morning** "supper". You have just broken the *Truth Barrier*, as I call it. The word *abracadabra* was used during the Mithraic mystery Mass, when they *transubstan- tiated* a sun-shaped disc of bread into the sun, and ate it. You can find this out by digging it up in a library or the internet. The Catholic priest is believed to be endowed with the power to **transubstantiate** any bread into Yahushua simply by saying the words, *HOC EST CORPUS MEUM*, "THIS IS MY BODY". This produced the phrase, **hocus-pocus, a** euphemism for any type of sleight-of-hand. The Mandaeans also had *"7 sacraments"*, among which were *Holy Matrimony,* the *Eucharist"* sun-disc bread wafer, *"Confession", Holy Orders,* and the *Mass of the Dead* itself. They were sun-worshipers, from which a "Church Father", Augustine had come from.[83]

The "New Covenant"

By the fourth century the one covenant *Yeshua* said would never be destroyed was, nevertheless, abolished by Roman Catholic Church authorities and replaced with what is commonly called "the New Covenant". The essence of Christianity's New Covenant Theology can be summerized in part as follows:

> ... that God has maintained an eternal purpose in Christ, which has been expressed through a multiplicity of distinct historical covenants; that prominent among these are those designated Old Covenant and the New Covenant; that the former, confined to the people of Israel alone, was established while the nation was assembled before Mt. Sinai and was made obsolete through its fulfillment by the life and death of Jesus the Messiah; that it was comprised largely of shadows pointing to Jesus and His body, the Church; and that, therefore, the age in

which it remained operative was at all times a period of maturity as compared to the age of fulfillment, which was inaugurated with Christ's first coming.[84]

While a vast majority of Catholic and Protestant theologians hold to the above statement of faith, some Christian scholars are now beginning to acknowledge the flawed premise of Christianity's New Covenant Theology. Dr. Ron Moseley, a pastor who has studied the Jewish roots of Christianity at Princeton Theology Seminary and the Jerusalem and Hebrew Universities in Jerusalem, writes:

> The fact that the terms "Old Covenant" and "New Covenant" are only found a total of four times in the biblical text indicates that both contain the same basics, and we are to fulfill the Old by obeying the New. In the New Covenant, nothing has been replaced, except the blood of Jesus. The difference, as well as the advantage is that Christ has opened the floodgates of the kingdom for all mankind.
> Hebrews 8:13 speaks of a new covenant which has made the first covenant *"old"* and *"ready to vanish."* To understand this, we must realize that the subject of this letter was the old priesthood and sacrificial system which was about to change for two reasons: first, because the Temple, along with its sacrifices, was about to be destroyed (or was already destroyed, depending upon when this letter was written); and, second, because Christ had come as a different manifestation of the sacrifice and high priesthood. Under no circumstances did Paul or any Jewish Christian writer suppose that God's unchanging nature, which stands behind the Old Covenant, was about to vanish.[85]

The Two Meanings of the term "New"

According to *The Original Webster's Unabridged Dictionary,* the English word "new" means: "lately made, invented, produced, or come into being; that has existed in short time only; recent in origin."[86]

In Greek, however, there are two different words for the term "new" that express two different ideas. The Christian scholars of *The Complete*

Word Study New Testament inform us that the Greek word *kainos* means "to renew qualitatively, to renew, to dedicate, concecrate into a qualitatively new use" as contrasted with *neos,* which means "numerically new".[87]

Arndt and Gingrich tell us that *neos* means: *"new, fresh–a.* of things such as *new dough* with no yeast, *new wine* as compared to *old, aged wine... young* as in *completely young"...* new in relation to time, as that which has recently come into being... numerically distinct."[88]

Here we see a distinct difference when comparing the English definition of the word "new" with the Greek definition of the word *kainos.* When thinking in English and transposing, the real meaning of the Greek words *kaine diathnkn* [*lit.,* 'renewed covenant'] is lost. For most theologians, the English term "new" is understood as "numerically new," as in a "new" Covenant of grace that has made the "old" Mount Sinai Covenant *vanish.*

According to the best Greek manuscripts available, the writer employs the qualitative Greek word *kaivnv,* meaning "renewed," not once but twice, saying: "'See the days are coming,' says [YHVH], 'when I shall conclude with the house of Yisra'el and with the house of Yehudah a renewed [Gk. *kaivnv*] covenant....' By saying 'renewed' [Gk. *kaivnv*], He has made the first old. Now what becomes old and growing aged is near disappearing" (Heb. 8:8, 13; *The Scriptures*).

Although the Apostolic Jewish writers used the common Greek language of that day to express their thoughts, those thoughts were still expressed as Hebraic concepts. And when we bypass those Hebraic concepts when transposing them into English, or any other language, we often lose the express teaching those ancient Jewish writers were communicating to the people of their day. This has been especially true of the Greek term *kainos,* in Hebrews 8:13, where the writer points out that the change made in the Covenant was *qualitative,* not *quanitative,* as in "numerically new".

Qulatative Changes of the Covenant

For those who argue for a "new" covenant that was instituted by the young Rabbi from Nazareth, logic dictates that they explain the many changes in the Covenant recorded in Scripture preceding Christ's coming. For example, in the Adam and Eve narriative, although the term "covenant" is never mentioned the idea of a covenant relationship existed between Adam and Eve and God, who said: "Of every tree of the garden thou mayest freely eat: but of the tree of knowledge of good and evil, thou shalt not eat of it; for in the day that thou eatest thereof thou shalt surely die" (Gen. 2:16-17; AKJV).

After the Adam and Eve "Disobedience Event," we see a *qualitative* change or admendment, added to the Covenant in the form of a promise: that a woman would bring forth a child Deliverer, who would destroy the works of the serpent/Satan (3:15).

In Genesis 6:18, God promised to establish His covenant with Noah and his "seed". Adding a *qualitative* change/amendment to the Covenant after the Great Flood, the LORD said: "… neither shall all flesh be cut off any more by the waters of a flood: neither shall there any more be a flood to destroy the earth" (9:11).

In Genesis 12, God added a *qualitative* change to the Covenant with Abram, saying: "… I will make of thee a great nation, and I will bless thee, and curse him that curseth thee: and in thee shall all families of the earth be blessed" (vs. 1-3).

Several years later, God added a *qualitative* change to the Covenant, telling Abram that he would have a son (15:3), and inherit the land from Beersheba (21:33) to Dan (14:14). About fourteen years later, God added another *qualitative* change to the Covenant by changing the name of Abram to Abraham, which included the covenant sign of circumcision (17).

Hundreds of years later, on Mount Sinai, God added another *qualitative* change to the Covenant by establishing it with Moses and the children of Israel in the form of written words, which are called by the Sages *aseret ha devarim* [*i.e.,* 'Ten Words'] on stone tablets (Ex. 34:28).

Still later, God added another *qualitative* change to the Covenant by promising that the royal seed was from then on to be in the house of David (2 Sam. 7:12).

Finally, in the Gospel of Mark, we are told that the young Rabbi from Nazareth made another *qualitative* change in the Covenant when He "… took bread, having blessed, broke it, gave it to them and said, 'Take eat, this is My body.' And taking the cup, giving thanks, He gave it to them, and they all drank from. And He said to them, 'This is My blood, that of <u>the covenant</u> [Gk. *tns diathnkns*], which is shed for many'" (Mk. 14:22-24).

Notice the *definite article* before the word "covenant". Why did Mark employ the words "*tns diathnkns,*" meaning "the Covenant"? Because *Yeshua* was talking about "the one and only Covenant," which

He and His disciples, as well as the people of that day, were well acquainted with.

Nevertheless, by adding the word "new" to the word "covenant," over the centuries Catholic and Protestant theologians have been successful in making the case for a numerical "New Covenant Theology".

The Origin of the terms
"Old Testament" and "New Testament"

Among the many new concepts of Western Civilization, none have had a more profound impact on Western thought than the terms "Old Testament" and "New Testament". Simply because it is from these two concepts that the boundaries between the East and West, the Old World and the New World, Judaism and Christianity have been established in the minds and hearts of the peoples of the world.

The Original Webster's Unabridged Dictionary informs us that the term "testament" means: "1. A solemn, authentic instrument in writing, by which a person declares his will as to the disposal of his estate and effects after his death. A *testament,* to be valid, must be made when the testator is of sound mind, and it must be subscribed, witnessed, and published in such a manner as the law prescribes."[89]

According to the translators of the Authorized King James Version, *Yeshua* not only used the term "new," but also the term "testament" in His last words to His disciples, saying: "... this is my blood of the new testament, which is shed for many for the remission of sins" (Matt. 26:28; Mk. 14:24; and Lk. 22:20; AKJV).

Before the term "testament" was used in the 1611 Authorized King James Version, it was employed in the old Latin Vulgate and continued to be used by Jerome, in 382 C.E., in his revised Latin Vulgate. From that point on Jerome's new Latin Vulgate became the standard Bible used by all Christians for the next 1,000 years. By the time the King James Version was published, in 1611, the term "testament" was well-established within the Christian community and, therefore, left in the King James text by English Protestant translators.

The problem with the use of the term "testament" is that it does not exist in the best extant Greek manuscripts. The Bible language scholar Dr. E. W. Bullinger writes:

The word "Testament," as a translation of the Greek word *diatheke* (which means 'covenant'), has been nothing less than a great calamity; for, but its use, truth has been effectively veiled all through the centuries; causing a wrong turning to be taken... by which the errors of tradition have usurped the place of important truth.

The word "Testament" as a name for a collection of books is unknown to Scripture. It comes to us through the Latin Vulgate. This was the rendering in the older Latin Versions before Jerome's time; but Jerome, while using *foedus* or p*ractum* for the Hebrew *berith* in the O.T., unfortunately reverted to *testamentum* in his version of his N.T. translation (A.D. 382-405). Some of the Latin Fathers preferred *instrumentum* much in the sense of our legal use of the word. Rufinus uses the expression *novum et vetus instrumentum,* and Augustine uses both words *instrumentum* and *testamentum.* From the Vulgate, the word testament passed both into the English Bibles and the German.[90]

By the end of the fourth century the main tenants of the Christian faith were firmly established by Catholic Church authorities, replacing the *Torah* observant faith of those first century followers of the young Rabbi from Nazareth with a numerical "Old Testament" and "New Testament" religion, which exists in both Catholic and Protestant Christianity to this present date.

Chapter 3

THE SECT OF THE NAZARENES

"After five days the high priest Ananias came down with some
elders, with an attorney named Tertullus, and they brought charges
to the governor against Paul," saying, "... we have found this man
to be a real pest... and a ringleader of the sect of the Nazarenes"
Acts 24:1, 5; NASV

For most theologians, Christianity began with the descent of the Holy
Spirit on the one-hundred-and-twenty Jewish followers of the young
Rabbi from Nazareth gathered together in an upper room at Jerusalem on
Pentecost day.

According to the Christianity's own account, however, there are several
problems with this claim. For example, the Christian scholars of *The
Illustrated Bible Dictionary* tell us that it wasn't until about 59 C.E., some
thirty years *after* the death and resurrection of *Yeshua*, when the name
Christian was first coined by the pagan community of Antioch, in Syria.[1]

Another problem is the lack of biblical evidence to support the claim that
the first century community of Believers were Christians. Even Christian
scholars admit that the name "Christian" was not consistently used as a
self-designation until the *Didache*.[2] Nor was the name "Christian" used
by Ignatius, the bishop of Antioch, until late first century or early second
century.[3] With the exception of 1 Peter 4:16, there is no evidence that first
century Believers addressed themselves as Christians. There is, however,
abundant evidence that first century Believers referred to themselves as

"brothers," "saints," "faithful," "disciples," "children," "beloved," "servants," "slaves," etc.

Another problem is Luke's account of the events of Acts 2:47. According to most New Testament versions, Acts 2:47 says: "And the LORD added to the church daily such as should be saved." Search the Greek text! Nowhere can the term "church" be found. Translators have substituted the word "church" for the Greek word *ekklesia,* meaning *"assemblage, gathering, meeting."*[4]

Some would argue that *ekklesia* is correctly translated "church" because it refers to the *assembly, gathering, meeting* of Believers. Arndt and Gingrich, however, inform us that the Greek term *ekklesia* is much more than an *assembly, gathering,* and *meeting* of Believers. Rather, *ekklesia* is a Hebrew parallelism employed in the *Septuagint* "for the *congregation* of the Israelites, especially when gathered for religious purposes (Deut. 31:30; Judges 20:2) to hear the law (Deut. 4:10; 9:10; 18:16)."[5]

Another problem is the lack of biblical evidence to support the claim that Paul himself was a Christian. Search the Scriptures! Nowhere can evidence be found to support the claim that Paul was a Christian. But there is evidence that Paul was a *Torah* observant Pharisee some thirty years *after* his conversion experience on the road to Damascus (Acts 23:6).

Finally, in this writer's opinion, the most troubling problem is the lack of evidence to support the claim that the young Rabbi from Nazareth and His disciples were the founders of Christianity. Search the Scriptures! Nowhere can there be found any evidence to support such a claim.

Yet today, distinguished theologians continue to claim that Acts 2 is proof of the beginning of Christianity and the Church. For example, professors Dr. Ralph Earl, Harvey J. S. Blaney, and Carl Hanson agree with the following statement of faith found the reference book entitled *Exploring the New Testament:* "The Book of Acts is the first church history. It gives us the high lights in the story of Christianity from about A.D. 30-60; that is, during the first generation. Hence it is one of the most important documents of all literature. For the spread of Christianity has been the most significant movement in the last two thousand years."[6]

Williston Walker, the former Yale professor of Church history refers to those early first century Believers as "the first Christians."[7] And the Bible expositor A. C. Hervey of the *Pulpit Commentary* refers to those first Believers as "Christian Jews [8] ... who would not admit that they were Christians."[9]

The problem with each of these claims is that they are essentially the same as made by the anti-Jewish Greek and Latin Church Fathers, the sun-worshiping Roman Emperor Constantine, and the anti-Jewish Catholic Church authorities of the fourth century.

This, my friend, is precisely the reason we need a better understanding of the Jewish origins of the young Rabbi from the village of Nazareth, as well as the Hebraic roots of those first century Believers called "Nazarenes".

"He Shall Be Called A Nazarene"

Scholars agree that when *Yeshua* began His ministry both He and His disciples were viewed by the religious establishment as being little more than a band of religious radicals from the northern part of Galilee, and whose young Rabbi was from the infamous village of Nazareth.

According to the biblical record, many of the religious leaders of that day belonged to the sect of the Pharisees. As we have seen, even Paul was a Pharisee (Acts 23:6). So here is the great question: What religious sect did the young Rabbi from Nazareth identify with?

Although the facts are uncertain, scholars agree that the teachings of *Yeshua* had more in common with the teachings of the Hillel Pharisees than any other group of that day. For example, the great Rabbi Hillel made the following popular summation of the *Torah,* saying: "What you would not have done to you, do not to another; that is the whole Law, the rest is commentary."

Now compare Hillel's statement with that of the young Rabbi, Who said: "Whatever you wish men to do to you, do also to them, for this is the Torah and the Prophets" (Matt. 7:12; *The Scriptures*). The rabbis Jacob Emden, Samuel Edels, Harvy Falk, and the Tosafists all agree that Hillel would have permitted prayer for the sick on the Sabbath, and the strict Shammai Pharisees would not.[10]

Affirming the existence of these two prominent schools of first century Jewish thought, Mark records that *Yeshua* did indeed heal on the Sabbath and was criticized by a certain group of Pharisees (Mk. 3:1-6). Matthew records that the "scribes and Pharisees" complained to the young Rabbi that His disciples did not wash their hands before eating (Matt. 15:1-2). And Luke records that when a "certain Pharisee" saw that the young Rabbi did not wash before eating (Lk. 11:37-38), *Yeshua* cited a familiar

Hillel teaching on cleansing the outside of the cup (vs. 39-44), making a distinction between the teaching of Hillel and the ritual washings demanded by the strict Shammai Pharisees. While the facts are uncertain as to the young Rabbi's religious affilation, the evidence indicates that *Yeshua* often sided with the teachings of the Hillel Pharisees.

For some, however, the teachings of *Yeshua* are rooted in the prophetic words "He shall be called a Nazarene". The scholars of *Unger's Bible Dictionary* write:

> At first it was applied to Jesus naturally and properly, as defining His residence.... its dialect rough, provincial, and strange, and its people seditious, so that they were held in little consideration. "The name of Nazarene was but another word for *despised one.* Hence, although no prophet has ever said anything of the word Nazarene, yet all those prophecies describing the Messiah as a *despised one* are fulfilled in His being a *Nazarene.* But we are convinced that something more than this is intended. The Heb. word for Nazareth was Netzer, a *branch,* or rather *germ....* Nazareth is called a germ from its insignificance, yet it shall through Him, fill the earth with its importance.[11]

It is significant for us to understand that in Hebraic thought the term "Nazarite" was often referred to by the ancient prophets as the "Branch" (*neser*) that would come from the root of Jesse (Isa. 11:1), and similar passages, or to the "Nazirite" (*nazir,* Judg. 13:7; 1 Sam. 1:11).[12]

The scholars of *Unger's Bible Dictionary* inform us that the Hebrew term *nazir,* and *nezir elohim,* meaning "Nazarite of God," is a term that comes from *nazar,* meaning "to separate," distinguishing one as being separated from other persons and things consecrated to God (cf. Gen. 49:26; Deut. 33:16).[13] According to others, the Hebrew word *nezer,* meaning a "diadem," contains the original idea of *nazar,* which means "to crown." In Hebraic thought, the "hair" of a person is regarded as a crown.[14]

Thus in Scripture the "Nazarite of God" is viewed as a "crowned one," because his mark of "separation to God is on his head" (Num. 6:7), which is obviously a reference to the mass of *uncut hair* on his head, as with Samson and Samuel (Judg. 13:7; 1 Sam. 1:11). Commenting on Matthew's use of the term Nazarite or *nazir,* the scholars of the *Illustrated*

Bible Dictionary state: "... all the different quotation formula in Mat. 2:23 from that in, *e.g.,* Mt. 1:22; 2:15, 17, suggest that a prophetic *theme,* not a prediction is in mind."[15]

Why is this prophetic *theme* important to our understanding of the young Rabbi from Nazareth? Because this same prophetic *theme* is used as an allegory in the Hebrew Scriptures for the Messiah. For example, the Hebrew word *"nazir"* is applied to the *vine* of the grape vineyards of Israel, in Leviticus 25:5, 11, which was not to be pruned during the seventh Sabbatical year [*lit.,* 'year of rest'] and left to grow on its own.[16] And the scholars of *Strong's Exhaustive Concordance* write: "**nazir,** *separate,* i.e., consecrated (as *prince,* a *Nazarite*); hence (fig. from the latter) an *unpruned* vine (like an unshorn Nazarite)."[17]

In Jewish thought the word *nazir* is highly significant. Because the command of Leviticus 25 *not* to prune "the vine" every seventh year has Messianic significance. Its provisions called for regular land redistribution, the end of slavery, and a perpetual "Sabbath rest" for both the land and people. In the Jewish calendar, years were to be divided into groups of seven, with the seventh year designated as the Sabbatical year [*lit.,* 'year of rest'].

In the seventh year no farming was to be done (Lev. 25:3-5), debts were to be canceled (Deut. 15:2), and slaves were to be set free (Deut. 15:12). The fiftieth year was set aside and celebrated as the Year of Jubilee (Lev. 25:8-9). The commands for the year of Jubilee were the same as those for the seven year Sabbatical rest, except that within walled cities, property automatically reverted to the family to which it had been originally assigned (Lev. 25:13).

Luke records that when *Yeshua* began His ministry, He returned to His home of Nazareth and, as His custom was, He went into the synagogue on the Sabbath and stood up to read the Book of Isaiah (Lk. 4:16-17), saying:

> 18 The Spirit of the LORD is upon me, because he has anointed me to preach the gospel to the poor; he hath sent me to heal the brokenhearted, to preach deliverance to the captives, and recovering the sight of the blind, to set at liberty them that are bruised.
>
> 19 To preach the acceptable year of the LORD (vs. 18-19; Isa. 61:1-2; AKJV).

What was the "acceptable year of the LORD" in the minds of the Jewish people of that day? Arndt and Gingrich tell us that the Greek word for "acceptable" (v. 19), *dektos* means *"acceptable, welcome; of prophets, and of God: Sabbaths... sacrifices... fasting."*[18] Moreover, the Greek word *dektos* is a Hebraic parallelism of the Hebrew word *ratsown*, derived from *ratsah* ['acceptable'], meaning *"delight* (especially as shown): favor, (good) pleasure."[19]

Why is this Hebraic parallelism significant? Because it means that the young Rabbi's announcement of "the acceptable year of the LORD" was the prophetic fulfillment of the "seventh year Sabbath" and "fiftieth year of Jubilee," when all debts were to be canceled, slaves were to be set free, property restored to the original owners, and the vine [*'nazir'*] in the vineyards of Israel were to be left unpruned.

Now take a look at John's account of the young Rabbi's use of the *vine* as a *metaphor* to *represent* Himself as the fulfillment of the seventh year Sabbath, the fiftieth year of Jubilee, and the unpruned *vine* [*'nazir'*] of the vineyards of Israel. Quoting the young Rabbi, John writes:

> **15** <u>I am the true vine, and my Father is the husbandman.</u>
>
> 2 Every branch in me that beareth not fruit he taketh away: and every *branch* that beareth fruit, he purgeth it, that it may bring forth more fruit.
>
> 3 Now ye are clean through the word which I have spoken unto you.
>
> 4 <u>Abide in me, and I in you. As the branch cannot bear fruit of itself, except it abide in the vine, no more can ye, except ye abide in me.</u>
>
> 5 <u>I am the vine, ye *are* the branches: He that abideth in me, and I in him, the same bringeth forth much fruit: for without me ye can do nothing.</u>
>
> 6 If a man abide not in me, he is cast forth as a branch, and is withered; and men gather them, and cast *them* into the fire, and they are burned.
>
> 7 If ye abide in me, and my words abide in you, ye shall ask what ye will, and it shall be done unto you.
>
> 8 Herein is my Father glorified, that ye bear much fruit; so shall ye be my disciples (Jhn. 15:1-8; AKJV).

"For My Name's Sake"

Continuing His discourse, *Yeshua* told His disciples:

> 20 Remember the word that I said unto you, The servant is not greater than his lord. If they have persecuted me, they will also persecute you; if they have kept my saying, they will keep yours also.
> 21 But all these things will they do unto you **for my name's sake,** because they know not him that sent me (Jhn. 15:20-21; AKJV).

For most theologians, *Yeshua's* employment of the term "name's sake" was a direct reference to Christians. According to Arndt and Gingrich, however, the Greek word for "name's sake" (v. 21), *ovoma* means *"to obtain the same name."*[20] *The Original Webster's Unabridged Dictionary* defines the term "namesake" as follows: "One that has the same name as another."[21]

As earlier noted, even Christian scholars agree that the name Christian did not exist until some thirty years later, about 59 C.E. This being the case, how could *Yeshua* be referring to a religious group called "Christians" that had not yet been named?

On the other hand, there is abundant evidence that for most of the first century the young Rabbi's namesake was *"Yeshua* [Jesus] of Nazareth" (Matt. 21:11; 26:71; Mk. 1:9, 24; 10:47; 14:67; 16:6; Lk. 4:34; 18:37; 24:9; Jhn. 1:45; 18:5, 7; 19:19; Acts 2:22; 3:6; 4:10; 6:14; 10:38; 22:8; 26:9).

Why was this particular namesake of the young Rabbi significant? Because at that time it was a serious matter to be identified with the young Rabbi from Nazareth. Even the Christian scholars of the *Expositor's Greek Testament* admit that the name "Nazarene" was "... applied as a term of contempt to the followers of Jesus, as it had been to Jesus Himself, Who was stamped in the eyes of the Jews as a false Messiah by His reputed origin from Nazareth."[22] And the scholars of *The International Standard Bible Encyclopedia* write:

> In the name "Nazarene," the Jews, who opposed and rejected Christ, poured out all the vials of their antagonism, and the word became a Jewish heritage of bitterness. It is hard

to tell whether the appellation, on the lips of evil spirits, signifies dread or hatred (Mk 1, 24; Lk 4, 34). With the gatekeepers of the house of the high priest the case is clear. There it signifies unadulterated scorn (Mt 26, 71; Mk 14, 67). Even in His death the bitter hatred of the priests caused this name to accompany Jesus, for it was at their dictation written above His cross by Pilate (Jn 19, 19).... If, on the one hand, therefore, the name stands for devotion and love, it is equally certain that on the other side it represented the bitter and underlying hatred of His enemies.[23]

The Nazarenes

Today, little, if anything, is ever said or written about those first followers of *Yeshua* called Nazarenes. Nevertheless, there is ample evidence of their existence. For example, the scholars of *The Illustrated Bible Dictionary* inform us that those first disciples of *Yeshua* were *Torah* observant, attended synagogues, and healed and spoke in the name of *Yeshua*.[24] The Church historian Philip Schaff writes:

> They united the observance of the Mosaic law with their belief in the Messiahship and divinity of Jesus, used the Gospel of Matthew in Hebrew, deeply mourned the unbelief of their brethren, and hoped for their future conversion in a body, and for the millennial reign of Christ.[25]

The early nineteenth century English scholar Charles Buck says of the Nazarenes in his work entitled *A Theological Dictionary:*

> The fathers frequently mentioned the gospel of the Nazarenes, which differs nothing from that of St. Matthew, which was either Hebrew or Syriac, for the use of the first converts, but afterwards corrupted by the Edomites. These Nazarenes perceived their first gospel in its primitive purity. Some of them were still in being in the time of Jerome, who does not reproach them with any gross errors. They were very

zealous observers of the Law of Moses, but held the traditions of the Pharisees in very great contempt.[26]

And Professor George Foote Moore writes about the growing influence of the Nazarenes on Judaism, saying:

> The chief book of the Nazarenes was their 'gospel,' for which they evidently claimed the character of sacred Scripture. The holy spirit might have departed from Israel centuries ago, but it had come back again and rested upon their apostles and prophets; inspired books were again possible. The vehemence with which the leading rabbis of the first generation of the second century express their hostility to the gospel and other book of the heretics, and to their conventicles, is the best evidence that they were growing in numbers and influence; and even among the teachers of the Law were suspected of leanings toward the new doctrine. The war under Hadrian brought about complete separation of the Nazarenes from the body of Judaism, and after the war the animosity diminished with the danger of the spread of infection within the synagogue.[27]

In the fourth century, Jerome wrote about the Nazarenes, saying: "they believe that Messiah, the son of God, was born of the Virgin Mary" (Jerome, *Letter 75, Jerome to Augustine*). Epiphanius, the only Jewish convert to become a bishop in Salamis, Cyprus, said of the Nazarenes: "They come from the north country, and Trans-Jordania. They keep the Law, but could not believe in astrology. They do not believe in animal sacrifices and they eat no living thing. They do not accept as genuine the parts of the Bible referring to such practices. They have the Gospel according to Matthew in its entirety in Hebrew. For it is clear that they still preserve this, in the Hebrew alphabet, as it was originally written" (Epiphanius, *Panarion 29.9.4*).

Eusebius said of the Nazarenes: "And he [Heggesippus the Nazarene] quotes some passages from the Gospel according to the Hebrews and from the Syriac [the Aramaic], and some particulars from the Hebrew tongue, showing that he was a convert from the Hebrews, and he mentions other matters as taken from the oral tradition of the Jews" (Eusebius of Caesarea, *Ecclesiastical History 4.22*).

The most important account, however, is Luke's account of how Paul was perceived by the people of his day: "a ringleader of the sect of the Nazarenes" (Acts 24:5). Why is this designation important to our understanding of Paul and his ministry among Gentile Believers? Because the term "ringleader" in Greek, *protostates* is a military term meaning "one standing first in the ranks,"[28] such as a captian leading his troops in battle.

Yet, since Christianity became a prominent movement in the second century little, if anything, has been said or written about those *Torah* observant followers of the young Rabbi from Nazareth called "Nazarenes". As you shall see, there was good reason Catholic Church authorities wanted them to disappear from the pages of history.

Condemned as Heretics

Scholars agree that the Edict of Milan gave to each individual of the Roman world the right to choose his own religion. But for Constantine and the Catholic Church authorities that right had certain limitations. Edward Gibbon writes:

> With the knowledge of truth, the emperor imbibed the maxims of persecution; and the sects which dissented from the Catholic church were afflicted and oppressed by the triumph of Christianity. Constantine easily believed that the Heretics, who presumed to dispute *his* opinions, or to oppose *his* commands, were guilty of the most absurd and criminal obstinacy; and that a seasonable application of moderate severities might save those unhappy men from the danger of an everlasting condemnation. Not a moment was lost in excluding the ministers and teachers of the separated congregations from any share of the rewards and immunities which the emperor had so liberally bestowed on the orthodox clergy. But as the sectaries might still exist under the cloud of royal disgrace, the conquest of the East was immediately followed by an edict which announced their total destruction. – Euseb. Vit. Const. 1. iii. c. 63, 66. After a preamble filled with passion and reproach, Constantine absolutely prohibits the assemblies of the Heretics, and confiscates their public property to use either of the revenue or of the Catholic church.[29]

On February 27, 380 C.E., the Roman Emperor Theodosius, who was born into a Catholic family, declared the Catholic Church to be the only legitimate Imperial religion. Three years later, in 383 C.E., Theodosius issued the following decree, stating in part:

> It is our pleasure that all the nations which are governed by our clemency and moderation should steadfastly adhere to the religion which was taught by St. Peter to the Romans; which faithful tradition has preserved; and which is now professed by the pontiff Damasus, and by Peter, bishop of Alexandria, a man of apostolic holiness. According to the discipline of the apostles, and the doctrine of the Gospel, let us believe in the sole deity of the Father, the Son, and the Holy Ghost; under an equal majesty, and pious Trinity. We authorize the followers of this doctrine to assume the title of Catholic Christians; and as we judge that all others are extravagant madmen, we brand them the infamous name of Heretics; and declare that their conventicles shall no longer usurp the respectable appellation of churches. Besides the condemnation of Divine justice, they must expect to suffer the severe penalties which our authority, guided by heavenly wisdom, shall think proper to inflict upon them.[30]

About six weeks after making Christianity the State Religion of Rome, on January 10, 381 C.E., Theodosius began to forcefully expel all bishops, clergy, assemblies, and individuals who refused to become Catholic Christians. Over a period of fifteen years (380-394 C.E.), Theodosius issued some fifteen edicts against "Heretics" that deprived them of any legal hope of escaping punishment.

Adding to the anti-Jewish phobia of that day, in 386 C.E., the great Catholic orator John Chrysostom, bishop at Antioch in Syria, delivered eight sermons *Adversus Judaeos* [*lit.*, Against the Judaizers].

Thus it was that those belonging to the sect of the Nazarenes were forced to go underground. Many had to hide in caves and deep forests to avoid capture, torture, and death. As they fled for their lives, their homes and places of worship were burned to the ground, and their property confiscated, often in the name of Christ and the Church. When caught, they were tortured in the basements of Catholic churches until they renounced their faith and pledged to accept Christianity, or were often put to death.

At that particular time anyone who claimed to be a follower of *Yeshua* and was not a Catholic Christian was looked upon as a Heretic, being a direct threat to the teachings of Catholicism. Although the Nazarenes continued to hold to the validity of both the Hebrew Scriptures and the Apostolic Writings/New Testament the only documentation which now remains is to be found in the archives of the Roman Catholic Church. For obvious reasons all of their original hand written documents were destroyed by Catholic authorities so the rewriting of Church history could remain uncontested.

The "Heretic's" Profession of Faith

Although many records of the torture of Jews and Nazarenes in the basements of Catholic churches were erased or hidden by Church officials, history concurs that there were many who converted to the Christian faith. But before they could be accepted into the Catholic Church and receive baptism they had to appear before a Catholic court and make a confession of Christian faith, renounce their Hebraic faith, and declare their desire to be accepted into the Christian Church. One following "Profession of Faith" of uncertain Eastern origin, attached to the *Clementine Recognitions,* states in part:

> ... I renounce the whole worship of the Hebrews, circumcision, all its legalisms, unleavened bread, Passover, the sacrificing of lambs, the feasts of Weeks, Jubilees Trumpets, Atonement, Tabernacles, and all the other Hebrew feasts, their sacrifices, prayers, aspersions, purifications, expiations, fasts, Sabbaths, new moons, foods and drink. And I absolutely renounce every custom and institution of the Jewish laws.... if I make this statement falsely and deceitfully... may there come upon me all the curses which Moses wrote in Deuteronomy... and may I be without any hope of pardon, and in the age to come... may my soul be set down with Satan and his demons.[31]

Unfortunately, this recorded profession of faith is but one of many that were required by Catholic authorities. For more information on this subject check out the book written by James Parkes entitled *The Conflict of the Church and the Synagogue.*

The Great "Falling Away"

By the fourth century the worst fear of the Apostle Paul had finally happened. The great falling away from the *Torah* observant faith of those first century followers of the young Rabbi from Nazareth had taken place exactly as Paul had stated in his farewell address to the Nazarene Believers in Ephesus, saying:

> 29 For I know this, that after my departure savage wolves shall come in among you, not sparing the flock.
> 30 Also from among yourselves men shall arise, speaking distorted *teachings,* to draw away the taught ones after themselves (Acts 20:29-30; *The Scriptures*).

Later, expressing that same concern from a prison cell in Rome, about 66 C.E., Paul wrote to Timothy, saying:

> 4 For there shall be a time when they shall not bear sound teaching, but according to their own desires, they shall heap up for themselves teachers tickling the ear,
> 5 and they shall indeed turn their ears away from the truth, and be turned aside to myths (2 Tim. 4:3-4; *The Scriptures*).

For many, the above passages are addressing the great falling away from the Christian faith just before the return of Christ. But not according to a growing number of Christian scholars who have discovered that the modern day misconception of a great latter day apostasy is largely due to the incorrect English translation of the Greek word *apostasia* found in 2 Thessalonians 2:3.

In Kenneth Wuest's work entitled *Word Study in the Greek New Testament,* the former chairman of New Testament Greek at Moody Bible

Institute informs us that the phrase "falling away" is a misrepresentation of the Greek word *apostasia* and should rather be translated "departure". Dr. Wuest says, "The root verb *aphistemi* is found fifteen times in the New Testament. It is translated 'depart' eleven times." Although it is often found translated with similar meanings, "the predominant meaning of this verb in the New Testament... is that of the act of a person departing from a place.... Liddell and Scott in their classical lexicon give as the second meaning of *apstasis.* 'a departure, a disappearance.' Dr. E. Schuyler English, to whom the author is deeply indebted for calling his attention to the word 'departure' as the correct rendering of *apostasia* in this context, is authority for the fact that... the Greek word (means) 'a departure' in this context: Tyndale (1534), Coverdale (1535), the Geneva Bible (1537), Cranmer (1539), and Beza (1565), and so used it in their translations."[32]

Professor Wuest goes on to say that *apostasia* was at times used to denote a defection or revolt; however, this meaning "should not be imposed upon the word where the context does not qualify the word by these meanings."[33] For additional information on this fascinating subject see Kenneth Wuest's Third Volume of his *Word Study in the Greek New Testament,* as well as the scholarly *Liddell & Scott's Greek-English Lexicon.*

Equally significant is the writing of Jude, the brother of James and half-brother of *Yeshua,* who was concerned about the increasing shift away from the *Torah* observant faith of those first followers of *Yeshua.* Sometime before the destruction of Jerusalem, in 70 C.E., false teachers were being accepted into the Nazarene community at an alarming rate. Thus Jude wrote to the Nazarene Believers in Asia Minor, saying:

> 3 Beloved, when I gave all diligence to write to you of the common salvation, it was needful for me to write unto you, and exhort *you* that *ye* should earnestly contend for the faith which was once delivered unto the saints.
>
> 4 For there are certain men crept in unawares, who were before of old ordained to this condemnation, ungodly men, turning the grace of our God into lasciviousness, and denying the only Lord God, and our Lord Jesus Christ (Jude 1:3-4; AKJV).

Why is this passage important to our understanding of what was really happening among the *Torah* observant Believers of that day? Arndt and Gingrich inform us that the Greek word for "lasciviousness" (v. 4), *aselgela* means "wantonness, readiness for all pleasure, one who does whatever his desires dictates."[34] Sound familiar?

By the second and third centuries the *Torah* observant faith of those first century followers of the young Rabbi from Nazareth was being redefined by the Heretic Marcion and Church Fathers as merely another sect of Judaism.

By the fourth century the heretical doctrine of Replacement Theology had become a cardinal doctrine of the Roman Catholic Church. Apologists were claiming that the *Torah* of Moses had been *done away* with the coming of *Yeshua* and, therefore, was no longer revelant to New Testament Believers.

The same held true for the leaders of the Reformation, in the early 1500s. While breaking with the Church on the matters of salvation by works and supremacy of the Pope, Catholic reformers continued to cling to many of the man-made doctrines, holidays, and traditions of the Mother Church.

By the early 1600s, King James authorized the new 1611 King James Bible. Translators interpreted the Greek word *apostasia* in 2 Thessalonians 2:3 as meaning a latter day "falling away," stating: "Let no man deceive you by any means: *for that day shall not come,* except there come a falling away [Gk. *apostasia*] first, and that man of sin be revealed, the son of perdition."[35]

From that point on later versions of the Bible included that same interpretation of the Greek word *apostasia*. And from that time to this present date unsuspecting Christians have been taught to believe in an end time "falling away" from the Christian faith when, in fact, the great apostacy began with the Heretic Marcion, the anti-Jewish Greek and Latin Church Fathers, the sun worshiping Roman Emperor Constantine, and the anti-Jewish Catholic Church authorities of the fourth century.

Remarkably, after some nineteen hundred years the *Torah* observant faith of those first century followers of the young Rabbi from Nazareth is now quietly being re-discovered by thousands of diligent seekers of truth. Today, Catholics, Protestants and Jews are discovering the rich Hebrew heritage that belongs to them as Believers in *Yeshua HaMashiach*. As this quiet work of the *Rauch HaKodesh* continues to spread throughout the world, Believers of every race, tongue, and religious affiliation are now beginning to understand that their rich Hebraic heritage in the Jewish Messiah of Israel is rooted to the *Torah* observant faith of the Hebrew patriarchs and first Commonwealth of Israel, thereby giving each person all the rights, privileges, and responsibilities belonging to that citizenship.

Chapter 4

THE GRAFTING-IN TO THE "OLIVE TREE"

13 But I am speaking to you who are Gentiles ... 16 if the first piece of dough is holy, the lump is also; and if the root is holy, the branches are too. 17 But if some off the branches were broken off, and you, being a wild olive tree, were grafted in among them and became partaker with them of the rich root of the olive tree, 18 do not be arrogant toward the branches, remember that it is not you who supports the root, but the root supports you.
Romans 11:13, 16-18; NASV

For many, the above words of Paul merely affirm the Christian doctrine that the Jewish people have been replaced by the Church. But for those who understand the Hebraic concept Paul is communicating, nothing could be further from the truth.

As you shall see, a close examination of the Greek text reveals that Paul is addressing a much greater issue: the important role the cultivated olive tree [*i.e.*, representing the first Commonwealth of Israel] plays in the husbandry of wild olive branches [*i.e.*, representing Gentile converts]. The Christian Bible expositor J. Barmby put it well when he likened Paul's illustration of the olive tree and the wild olive branch to the union of a child-bearing marriage, saying:

"... to marry
A gentile scion of the wildest stock,

79

And make conceive a bark of baser kind,
By bud of nobler race."[1]

In Hebraic thought, the importance of the cultivated olive tree cannot be overstated. In biblical times the olive tree was a symbol of righteousness. Its prolific fruitfulness was compared to a righteous man (Ps. 52:8; Hos. 14:6), whose offspring are described as 'olive branches' (Ps. 128:3). The olive tree was also called the king of the trees (Jdg. 9:8), and at coronations its oil was used as a symbol of sovereignty (1 Sam. 16:13). Its wood was used during the Festival of Tabernacles to construct booths (Neh. 8:15). In Zechariah 4:3, the two olive trees are symbols of fruitfulness, illustrating the abundance with which God had provided for the people's needs. In Job 15:33, the shed blossoms of the olive tree are likened to an unrighteous man, who "casts off his blossom, like the olive tree." When a cultivated olive tree is cut down, new shoots spring up, so that as many as five new trunks come forth from the old trunk of the tree.

In contrast, the fruit of the wild olive bush in its natural state is small and worthless.[2] Unlike the cultivated olive tree, the wild olive bush lacks a good root system. In order for the wild olive branch to produce mature fruit it has to be grafted-in to the rich root system of the cultivated olive tree.

Affirming the rich Hebraic symbolism the cultivated olive tree represents, Dr. Barmby aptly says: "By the *firstfruit* and the *root* is signified the original stock of Israel, the patriarchs; by the *lump* and the *branches,* the subsequent nation throughout all time."[3]

The Rich Root of the "Olive Tree"

For many, the rich root of the cultivated olive tree represents Christ. But there are problems with this claim that give rise to the following questions: If *Yeshua* is indeed the root of the cultivated olive tree, why did God tell Abraham "... you shall become a father of many nations" (Gen. 17:5)? If *Yeshua* is the root of the cultivated olive tree, why did God say to Abraham: "I shall make you bear fruit exceedingly, and make nations of you" (v. 6)? And if *Yeshua* is the root of the cultivated olive tree, why did God promise Abraham that He would establish His covenant "between

Me and you and your seed after you in their generations, for an everlasting covenant" (v. 7)?

Today, Bible scholars are taking a fresh look at these passages and coming to new conclusions. For example, C. B. Cranfield says: "While some take *e riza* (Greek: 'the root'), to refer to Christ, and some take it to refer to the Jewish Christians, there is a very widespread agreement among commentators that it must refer to the patriarchs...."[4]

The Messianic Jewish scholar David Stern writes: "The olive tree which God cultivated is Israel. Its root is the Patriarchs – Abraham, Isaac, and Jacob.... That the root is the Patriarchs is confirmed by Romans 4:16 ('Abraham the father of us all') and Galatians 3:7, 29. Also compare the Book of Enoch 93:5: 'And his [*sc.* Abraham's] posterity shall become the plant of righteousness for evermore.'"[5]

And the Christian language scholar David Bivin says in his book entitled *New Light on the Difficult Words of Jesus:*

> Paul spoke about Israel as a "cultivated olive tree" whose rootage was in the Patriarchs, particularly Abraham. Some Bible commentators, however, interpreted the root of the olive tree as Christ or his messianic program. When making that claim, they came dangerously close to endorsing an old, rotten idea: the root represents the New Israel, that is, the Church.[6]

Even more important, however, are the words of Paul, who wrote to the new Gentile converts of Galatia, about 55 or 56 C.E., saying:

> 7 Know ye therefore that they which are of faith, the same are the children of Abraham.
>
> 8 And the Scripture foreseeing that God would justify the heathen through faith, preached before the gospel unto Abraham, *saying,* In thee shall all nations be blessed.
>
> 9 So then they which be of faith are blessed with faithful Abraham.
>
> ... 29 And if ye *be* Christ's, then are *ye* Abraham's seed, and heirs according to the promise (Gal. 3:7-9, 29; AKJV).

Nevertheless, by the fourth century Roman Catholic Church authorities had revised that first century *Torah* observant faith in such a way that it made Christ to be the root of the olive tree, the Pope to be Christ's representative on earth, and the Church to be the *new Israel.*

The "New Israel" Deception

For many, the term anti-*Semitism* brings to mind the late nineteenth century pogroms of Russia, as well as the concentration camps and death furnaces of Hitler's anti-Jewish campaigns of the 1930s-'40s. Although these atrocities against the Jewish people are condemned by most Western nations, today there is a subtle form of anti-*Semitism* that is largely ignored by most Church leaders. It is the heretical doctrine that the Church has replaced the physical children of Israel as the *new Israel.*

While anti-*Semitism* has taken many different forms of expression over the centuries, scholars agree that its roots go all the way back to the anti-Jewish writings of the Greek and Latin Church Fathers. One such example is Justin Martyr (100-165 C.E.), who boasted: "For the true spiritual Israel are we who have been led of God through this crucified Christ." [Justin Martyr's *Dialogue with Trypho,* Chapter XI.]

By the fourth century the Replacement Theology of the Church Fathers had become a cornerstone of the Christian faith. From that point on Catholic Church authorities, and later Protestant theologians taught that the *spiritual* Church had replaced the physical children of Israel as the *new Israel.*

Unfortunately, during the past nineteen hundred years little has changed. Today, this same replacement doctrine is being taught to unsuspecting Christians by prominent Christian leaders. For example, the author Steve Wohlberg says in his book entitled *Exploding the Israel Deception,* whose "Foreword" is written by Doug Batchelor, the popular radio and TV host, and director of *Amazing Facts* ministries:

> It is true that "all Israel shall be saved." But, as we studied in Chapter 3 of this book, the big question is "Which Israel?" Remember, "they are not all Israel, which are of Israel" (Rom. 9:6). There is a natural Israel according to the flesh, and there is an Israel in the Spirit made up of Jews and Gentiles who believe in Jesus Christ. To apply the "all Israel" which "shall be saved" to

a group of Jews who are separate from the Church is to rebuild the wall that Jesus Christ died to abolish![7]

Echoing the same *new Israel* sentiment, the celebrated theologian Karl Barth says in his widely read book entitled *The Christian Life: Church Dogmatics:*

> The first Israel, constituted on the basis of physical descent from Abraham, has fulfilled its mission now that the Saviour of the world has sprung from it and its Messiah has appeared. Its members can only accept this fact with gratitude, and in confirmation of its own deepest election and calling attach themselves to the people of this Saviour, their own King, whose members the Gentiles are now called to be as well. Israel's mission as a natural community has now run its course and cannot be continued or repeated.[8]

Equally significant is the propagation of the *new Israel* replacement doctrine by the Mother Catholic Church, which goes all the way back to the fourth century. For example, the expression "People of God [Latin: *populis Dei*] is found in the writings of Augustine's (354-430 C.E.) *De civitate Dei* ['The City of God'], and Pope Leo's I (400-461 C.E.) *Lenten Sermon.* The expression "People of God" continued to be used by Church officials up to and including Pope John's letter *Signutari studio* of July 1960.

During the Second Vatican Council (1962-1965), Catholic authorities officially declared the Church to be the "People of God" [*Lumengentian,* Chapter II]. The written declaration spoke of "the people to whom the testament and promises were given" as among those who "are related in various ways to the "People of God".[9]

From that point on Popes have used the expression "The People of God" when referring to the Church. Pope Paul VI used it with regard to his profession of faith known as the *Credo of the People of God.* Pope John Paul II used it in his catechetical instructions, teaching that the Church is the *new People of God.* And Pope Benedict XVI has spoken of the Church as "the people of God throughout the world, united in faith, love, and empowered by the Spirit to bear witness to the risen Christ to the ends of the earth."[10]

Unlike Protestant *new Israelites,* however, the Vatican has sought to physically replace the Jewish people's control of the sacred city Jerusalem. For example, in 1095, Pope Urban II proclaimed the First Crusade with the goal of restoring the Church's control of Jerusalem and access to holy sites in and near the city. Following the first crusade there were six major crusades and several minor ones during the next 200 years that struggled to liberate and control the Holy Land. But they all ended in failure.

On January 5, 1964, Pope Paul VI made, for the first time in the history of the Papacy, a Papal visit to Israel. Upon entering Israel in Megiddo the Pope exclaimed: "We are coming as pilgrims, we come to venerate the Holy Places, we come to pray."[11]

During the Pope's visit he only spent eleven hours in Israel. He avoided Israeli-controlled West Jerusalem, refusing to meet there with then Sepharadic Chief Rabbi Yitzhak Nissim. Pope Paul VI never once called Israel by name, and went out of his way to avoid using the word "Jew". He avoided all sites of Jewish significance, including Israel's national Holocaust museum and memorial. The Pope did, however, use the occasion to praise his mentor, Pope Pius XII, defending his silence during the Holocaust.[12]

The Vatican only recognized the State of Israel in 1994, forty-six years *after* its creation. But this was only *after* the Vatican and Israel signed the "Fundamental Agreement," on December 30, 1993, that deals with the property rights [which are vast] of the Roman Catholic Church within the State of Israel.[13] And this was only *after* a secret deal the Vatican signed with Israel via Deputy Foreign Minister Yossi Beilin and Shimon Peres [without the approval of the Knesset], in 1992, that gives the Catholic Church not only "extrateritoral status" to their properties but also control over the entire city of Old Jerusalem as "custodians" under UN presence.[14] To this present date, the Vatican does not recognize Israeli sovereignty over the Old City of Jerusalem. Yet, when the terrorist organization PLO was formed by Yasser Arafat, in 1964, the Vatican was one of the first to recognize it.[15] And since that time, the Vatican has increasingly supported the Palestinian's cause and ignored the radical Islamic acts of violence, murder, and terror against the Israeli people.

More recently, on January 5, 2014, the Vatican announced that another Pope, Francis, would visit the Holy Land to celebrate the 50th anniversary of Pope Paul VI's visit in 1964. The Vatican announced that Pope Francis' three-day visit would be a "pilgrimage of prayer".

Upon arriving at the Amman airport in Jordan, on May 24, Pope Francis was driven to a city stadium where he conducted an afternoon mass in front of a large altar. He was then carried by helicopter across the Jordan River, bypassing Israel proper, to the Palestinian Authority (PA) controlled Bethlehem, where he was met by Mahmoud Abbas [head of the terrost Fatah group], who accused Israel of "Judaizing" Jerusalem. Earlier, Pope Francis addressed what he called "the Palestine State," calling for a two-state solution, and called Abbas "a man of peace".[16]

While in Bethlehem, Pope Francis conducted an open-air mass and delivered his message, facing an image of a giant baby Jesus wrapped in a keffiyeh, the very symbol of Palestinian anti-Christianity/anti-*Semitism.* From there, the Pope was escorted in a car caravan to Manger Square that just happened to stop at the Israeli security wall that separates Jerusalem from the Hamas controlled Bethlehem.

Although Pope Francis' visit was billed by the Vatican as a "pilgrimage of prayer," it soon became evident that his visit was much more. On Sun-Day, May 25, the Pope's itinerary, which was planned by the PA, called for a "drive-by" of the Israeli security wall located near an Israeli military watchtower.[17] Complying with the PA's wishes, when the caravan stopped the Pope got out of his car and walked over to the wall to pray.

On the wall in front of a bold spray-painted graffiti display, declaring: "Free Palestine," "Apartheid Wall," and "Bethlehem looks like Warsaw Ghetto," comparing the Palestinians' plight with that of the Jews under the Nazis, Pope Francis bowed his head and prayed, with his head resting on the wall. Shortly afterwards, a picture of the Pope praying at the the wall circulated the globe. The *Telegraph* reported that Pope Francis' gesture "delighted Palestinians".[18]

Shortly afterwards, when the open-air mass at Manger Square concluded, Pope Francis extended an invitation to Abbas and Israeli President Shimon Peres to join him at the Vatican to pray for "Peace," saying: "I offer my home in the Vatican as a place for this encounter of prayer."[19]

During the Pope's visit he struck the right tone for the Palestinians, as well as the Israelis. In the wake of the "Wall Event," Israeli officials invited the Pope to visit Israel's national memorial for terror victims. Pope Francis not only accepted the invitation, but went on national Israeli TV news and made a brief but forceful rejection of terrorism.

Both Peres and Abbas accepted Pope Francis' invitation to meet with him at the Holy See in Rome.

Although the Vatican billed the meeting at the Holy See as nothing more than a desire to "pray for peace," Pope Francis told Peres and Abbas that he hoped the summit would mark "a new journey" toward peace. "Peacemaking calls for courage, much more so than warfare," the Pope said. "It calls for the courage to say yes to encounter and no to conflict."[20]

Afterwards, a Vatican analyst for the National Catholic Reporter said: "In the Middle East, symbolic gestures and incremental steps are important. And who knows what conversations can occur behind closed doors in the Vatican."[21]

Thus it was that the Holy See's centuries old struggel to control the Old City of Jerusalem was renewed, with the aim of shaping events in such a way that the latter day promises of God to the physical descendants of Abraham, Isaac, and Jacob will eventually be applied to "the Church," the *new People of God.*

The Flawed "New Israel" Premise

When God made His covenant with to the people of Israel, He said: "… **if** you diligently obey My voice, and shall guard My covenant, **then** you shall be My treasured possession above all the peoples… and you shall be to Me a reign of priests and a set-apart nation" (Ex. 19:5-6).

Over the centuries, Israel rebelled against the LORD and were judged harshly. For example, in 722 B.C.E., the northern tribes of Israel were carried away into captivity by the Assyrians because of idolatry. And in 586 B.C.E., Jerusalem and the Temple were destroyed and the people of Judah were taken captive by Nebuchadnezzar and carried away to Babylon, ending the kingdoms of Israel and Judah.

For many, God's final break with the Jewish people came with the destruction of Jerusalem and the Temple by the Romans in 70 C.E., and the Jewish people were, once again, dispersed among the nations of the earth. According to Steve Wohlberg, God's final rejection of the Jewish people took place when *Yeshua* [Jesus] wept over Jerusalem (Matt. 23:37-38). Wohlberg writes: "This time God was not saying: 'You blew it. Let's try again.' Israel's decision to crucify Christ would have permanent consequences. The result was a searing separation – a painful divine divorce."[22]

But is this what really happened? Not according to Paul, who addressed the same *new Israel* argument, saying: "Hath God cast away his people? God forbid! For I am also an Israelite, of the seed of Abraham of the tribe of Benjamin. God hath not cast away his people which he foreknew." (Rom. 11:1-2; AKJV).

Perhaps the greatest flaw in the *new Israel* argument is the failure to take into account the unchanging nature of God Himself. Matthew records that when Peter came to the young Rabbi and asked how many times he should forgive a person, saying: "till seven times?" *Yeshua* replied: "I do not say to you, up to seven times, but up to seventy times seven" (Matt. 18:22).

Did Paul understand this biblical concept about the boundless love and forgiveness of God? Indeed he did! Addressing God's forgiveness and restoration of the Jewish people, Paul told the Gentile Believers in Rome: "And they also, if they abide not still in unbelief, shall be grafted in: for God is able to graft them in again" (Rom. 11:23).

Did Jeremiah understand this biblical concept about God's forgiveness and restoration of the Jewish people? Indeed he did! Writing to the latter day descendants of Abraham, Isaac, and Jacob, Jeremiah says:

> 31 "See, the days are coming" declares [YHVH], "when I shall make a new covenant with the house of Yisra'el and with the house of Yehudah,
>
> 32 not like the covenant I made with their fathers in the day when I took them by the hand to bring them out of the land of Mitsrayim (Egypt). My covenant which they broke, though I was a husband to them," declares [YHVH].
>
> 33 "For this is the covenant I shall make with the house of Yisra'el after those days, declares [YHVH]: I shall put My Torah in their inward parts, and write it on their hearts. And I shall be their Elohim, and they shall be My people.
>
> 34 "And no longer shall they teach, each one his neighbour, and each one his brother, saying, 'Know [YHVH],' for they shall all know Me, from the least of them to the greatest of them," declares [YHVH]. "For I shall forgive their crookedness, and remember their sin no more" (Jer. 31:31-34; *The Scriptures*).

According to the Christian scholars of *Strong's Exhaustive Concordance* the Hebrew word for "new" (v. 31) is *chadash,* meaning "to rebuild:– renew."[23] As earlier noted, the writer of the Book of Hebrews addresses this very same passage in Hebrews 8:8-9, employing the Greek word *kainos,* meaning "to renew in a qualitative sense, as contrasted with 'new' in a numerical sense."[24]

Affirming this qualitative sense of the Greek word *kainos* from a Jewish perspective, the Bible language scholar Rick Lastrapes writes:

> Hebrews 8:8 says "But God found fault with the people, saying: 'The days are coming,' says the Lord, 'when I will make a new covenant with the house of Israel and with the house of Judah.'" This is not like when someone renews their wedding vows. It is more like when someone has a child, and they say: "I'm not abolishing those rules we have, like brushing your teeth, but I'm adding something to it. I'm giving you your own key to the house, and I am going to treat you according to your age." It's not replacement, but addition. What the writer of Hebrews is saying is that way, way back in the days of Jeremiah, when the children of Israel went into captivity, God said through His prophet, "You've demonstrated that you can't keep Torah unless something changes."
>
> The writer of Hebrews builds off this by arguing that since God said way, way back in the days of Jeremiah that He would give to Israel a new covenant because Torah wasn't enough, no one should be surprised if God brought the Messiah to change Israel, not to defeat their enemies as even today the Messiah is viewed by Israel. But the writer of Hebrews is careful to make it clear that the "new covenant" in Jeremiah 31:31-34, which includes statements that show the covenant in Jeremiah 31 is NOT the "new covenant" through Yeshua. That is why he quotes Jeremiah 31:31-34, which includes statements that show the covenant that Jeremiah spoke about hasn't occurred yet. It will happen, but it hasn't happened yet. But the fact that God said it would happen means that Torah by itself isn't enough because the Jewish nation cannot keep Torah and won't be able to without God doing something.[25]

"In Those Days" and "At That Time"

With this understanding, here is the great question: Did the Hebrew prophets tell us when this great restoration of the physical children of Israel and Judah will take place? Indeed they did!

In Jeremiah 31:33 and Hebrews 8:10, both writers use the latter day Hebraic concept "...**those days**...." Why is this latter day concept important? Because in Jewish thought the Hebraic concept "**those days**" is often used to address a specific time period called "Day of the LORD".

Emil G. Hirsch, chief Rabbi of the Har Sinai Congregation of Chicago for forty-two years (1880-1923), as well as editor of the Bible for the *Jewish Encyclopedia,* informs us that the Day of the LORD is "an essential factor in the prophetic doctrine of divine judgment at the end of time, generally, though not always, involving both punishment and blessing. It is identical with 'that day' (Isa. xvii. 7, xxx. 23, xxxviii. 5; Hos. ii. 18; Micah ii. 4, v. 10; Zech. ix. 16; xiv. 4, 6, 9), 'those days' (Joel iii. 1), 'that time' (Jer. xxxi. 1, R.V.; xxx. 25. Hebr.; Zeph. iii. 19, 20), or simply 'the day' (Ezek. vii. 10), or 'the time.'"[26]

Affirming this use of the latter day Hebrew concept "**those days**," Jeremiah says:

> 14 "See, the days are coming,' declares [YHVH], 'when I shall establish the good word which I have promised to the house of Yisra'el and to the house Yehudah:
> 15 '**In those days and at that time** I cause a Branch of righteousness to spring forth for Dawid (sic). And He shall do right-ruling and righteousness in the earth.
> 16 '**In those days** Yehudah shall be saved, and Yerushalayim dwell in safety. And this is that which shall be proclaimed to her: [YHVH] our Righteousness' (Jer. 33:14-16; *The Scriptures*).

Again, written in the context of the last days, Jeremiah says:

> 4 "**In those days and at that time**," declares [YHVH], "the children of Yisra'el shall come, they and the children of Yehudah together, weeping as they come, and see [YHVH] their Elohim.

5 "They shall ask the way to Tsiyon, their faces toward it, 'Come and let us join ourselves to [YHVH], in an everlasting covenant, never to be forgotten"

... 20 "**In those days and at that time,**" declares [YHVH], "the crookedness of Yisra'el shall be searched for, but there shall be none; and the sin of Yehudah, but none shall be found. For I will pardon those whom I leave as a remnant" (Jer. 50:4-5, 20; *The Scriptures*).

Addressing this same latter day restoration of the Jewish people, the prophet Amos says:

11 **In that day** will I raise up the tabernacle of David that is fallen, and close up the breaches thereof, and I will raise up his ruins, and I will build it as in the days of old....

... 14 And I will bring again the captivity of my people Israel, and they shall build the waste cities, and inhabit *them;* and they shall plant vineyards, and drink the wine thereof, they shall also make gardens, and eat of the fruit of them.

15 And I will plant them upon their land, and they shall no more be pulled up out of their land which I have given them, sayeth the Lord thy God (Amos 9:11-15; AKJV).

Did Paul, who was schooled under Gamaliel, the grandson of the great Hillel, and himself a Pharisee and celebrated doctor of the *Torah,* understand this future *qualitative* change in the Covenant? Indeed he did!

About 58 or 59 C.E., Paul wrote to the Gentile Believers in Rome, saying:

25 For I would not, brethren, that ye should be ignorant of this mystery, lest ye should be wise in your own conceits; that blindness in part is happened to Israel, until the fulness of the Gentiles be come in.

26 <u>And so all Israel shall be saved</u>: as it is written, There shall come out of Zion the Deliverer, and shall turn away ungodliness from Jacob;

27 For *this* is my covenant unto them, when I shall take away their sins.

28 As concerning the gospel, *they are* enemies for your sakes: but as touching the election, *they are* beloved for the fathers' sakes.

29 <u>For the gifts and calling of God</u> *are* without repentance (Rom. 11:1-2, 25-29).

Notice Paul's use of the nominative predicate "beloved" (v. 28), which in Greek is *agapetoi,* and comes from the verb *agape,* meaning "the divine love of God". Why is this understanding important to Paul's argument about the Jewish people? *Agape* is the same word used in John 3:16: "For God so <u>loved</u> [Gk. *egapesen*] the world that He gave His only begotten Son." The significance of Paul's employment of the term *agape* cannot be overstated. Because it means "benevolent love," *not* in doing what the person loved desires. Rather, it is the doing of what the One who loves *deems to be needed.*

Unlike the Gentile Believers in Rome, Paul understood that even though the Jewish people rejected *Yeshua* as God's fulfillment of the promised Messiah of Israel, "*they are* <u>beloved</u> [Gk. *agapetoi*] of God for their fathers sakes" (v. 28).

In Greek, the nominative predicate is usually that part of a sentence which follows a form of the verb *"to be"* [Gk. *eimi*], which is often omitted. In other words, Paul is affirming that the *agape* love *Yeshua* had for the Jewish people when "He came to His own and His own received Him not" (Jhn. 1:11) ... *continues to this present day.*

This hardly sounds as though Paul believed the *new Israelite* replacement doctrine; that God rejected the Jewish people because they rejected His Son, *Yeshua HaMashiach.* Nor does it sound as though Paul believed God replaced the Jewish people with the so-called *spiritual Israel* – the Church.

Nevertheless, by the second century the anti-Jewish Greek and Latin Church Fathers were teaching that the *spiritual* Church was the *new Israel.* By the fourth century, Roman Catholic Church authorities declared the tenets and observances of the holy Mother Church to be ordained of God, and began purging everything Jewish from the Christian faith.

Richard N. Rhoades

The Master Plan of Grafting

For those who have learned the art of grafting one branch to another it is common knowledge that a graft will not work unless the cut branch is compatible with the host tree, such as the grafting of one variety of peach with another variety of peach, or one variety of plum with another variety of plum, or one variety of almond with another variety of almond, etc. The cut branch and host tree can be different as to variety, but both must be of the same species.

Also, the cuttings for both the grafted branch and host tree branch must be such that it will allow both branches to fit snugly together so that the two branches can grow together to become _one_ branch. This is achieved by making cuts in the two branches that will allow them to fit snugly together and then taping them until the cut parts are firmly pressed together and sealed, to protect them from any outside diseases. If this step is not done correctly the graft will not take hold and the "grafted branch" will soon wither and die.

Most important, the tree to which the branch is being grafted must be of good rootstock. Because once the graft takes place the grafted branch is totally dependant on the host tree's root system for its nourishment, maturity and, eventually its fruit bearing capacity. If the host tree is not of good rootstock, the roots will be susceptible to a bacterial canker, which can kill both the grafted branch and the tree, or severely damage its fruit producing capacity.

The successful grafting of one branch to another is also dependent on the season of the year and climate. For example, experienced grafters know that the best time to graft is between mid-February and early March, just before the climate begins to change. The tempature begins to warm the rich nutrients that flow from the roots up into the host tree and to the branches, and the miracle of the two branches becoming _one_ takes place.

Remarkably, we are now witnessing a nineteen hundred year old climate change between Jew and Gentile Believers. What began in the 1960s and '70s as a handful of Messianic worshipers has now become a full blown movement that is identified with the _Torah_ observant faith of those first century Jew and Gentile followers of the young Rabbi from Nazareth.

For example, from 2003 to 2007 the Messianic movement grew from 150 Messianic houses of worship in the United States to as many as 438, with over 100 in Israel and more worldwide.[27] In 2008, the Messianic movement was reported to have between 6,000 and 15,000 Messianic members in Israel,[28] and 250,000 in the United States.[29] According to the *Jerusalem Post,* as of June 2006, there were an estimated 12,000 Messianic Jews living in Israel, most of whom made Aliya under the Law of Return. Today, it is estimated that there is now approximately 15,000 to 20,000 Messianic Jewish Believers in Israel. And despite the ongoing persecution of Messianic Believers, the body of Messiah is growing each day as more and more Israelis are accepting *Yeshua* as the Messiah of Israel.

As predicted by Paul, the times of the Gentiles are now being fulfilled. The foundations of long standing Judaic and Christian institutions are now beginning to crack. As a result, people are beginning to question some of the doctrines and traditions on which their faith has been built.

At the same time, a new spiritual order is emerging. Jews and Gentiles are now being grafted into the rich root of the cultivated "Olive Tree" [*i.e.,* the first Commonwealth of Israel].

This, my friend, is precisely the reason Paul wrote about the need for the "wild branches" and "natural branches" to be grafted into the rich root of the cultivated "Olive Tree". And this is precisely the reason Paul's message to the Believers at Rome is as relevant today as it was some two thousand years ago.

Chapter 5

THE REPLACEMENT OF THE "OLIVE TREE"

About 139 C.E., the Christian theologian Marcion went to Rome and made a generous gift to the congregation, hoping his anti-Jewish views of the Apostolic Writings would be accepted. But after carefully examining them the congregation returned his money and excommunicated him. Not to be denied, Marcion started his own church, merging the anti-Jewish tenents of Gnosticism with Christianity.

Because Marcion was haunted with the problem of evil and the suffering of mankind he developed a dualistic concept of God, which contrasted the god of this world with the God of mercy revealed in Christ. As a student of the Gnostic Christian Cerdo, Marcion modified his position by maintaining that the Creator-God in the Old Testament was weak and unjust, and therefore, was to be rejected by Christians. Christ, on the other hand, was the revelation of the unknown God of mercy, and Man's only knowledge of the "good God". Thus for Marcion, as with Cerdo, the authority of the *Torah* of Moses was *done away* with the coming of Christ, and the "just God" became unjust because of Christ's revelation of the "good God".[1]

During this same period the Greek and Latin Church Fathers sought to advance their allegorical interpretation of Scripture. A number of the Church Fathers devoted much of their writings to denigrate the Jews because they rejected Christ and refused to convert to Christianity.

For example, Clement of Alexandria, who believed in three grades of knowledge with respect to the religious truths, maintained that the first grade is philosophy, the second grade is faith in the Christian revelation, and the third grade is the scientific systematization of dogmatic truths, which is the true *Gnosis,* the *Christian Gnosis,* and its possessor is the perfect Christian philosopher who adheres to truth by faith and understanding, by will and intellect.[2] Clement wrote that Christians looked upon themselves as a separated people, "a new race, the true Israel" (1 *Clem.* 61).

Origin adopted from Philo the opinion that Greek philosophy comes from "Revelation".[3] While Origin believed himself to be a Christian, scholars agree that his doctrinal errors can be traced to his love of Platonic philosophy.[4]

In Origin's *Symposion,* he describes the Church as "the garden of God in the beauty of eternal spring, shining in the richest splendor of immortalizing fruits and flowers;" and as the "virginal, unspotted, every young and beautiful royal bride of the divine Logos." And Hermas of Rome (115-140 C.E.) wrote that Christians are the Church "which was created before the sun and moon, and for her sake the world was framed" (Hermas, *Vis.,* 2:4).

Addressing the pagan influence of Gnosticism and Manicheanism on the second century Christian apologists of Alexandria, Msgr. Paul J. Glenn writes:

> The precise time of the founding of the Alexandrian School is not known, but it enjoyed some fame as early as the middle of the 2nd century. It was then under the leadership of Pantaenus, who had been a Stoic before his conversion, and whose renown rests largely upon the fact that Origin and Clement were his pupils. The Alexandrian School was inaugurated to teach Gentiles the Christian Religion and to prepare them for Baptism; hence it is often mentioned in history as "The Alexandrian School of Catechetics." But it was soon apparent that something more was needed by the pupils of this School than a simple statement of the truths of the Christian Religion. Alexandria was at this time a great intellectual centre (sic); noted pagan philosophers lived there, as well as leading Gnostics and Manichees. Many pupils of the School of Catachetics had philosophical difficulties to overcome, especially those who had been under Gnostic or Manichean influence. Hence the teachers of the School studied philosophy with great earnestness; their work grew more and more scientific in method; they directed their best efforts against pagan philosophy in general and against Gnosticism and Manicheism in particular.

It must be mentioned that some of the teachers in Alexandrian School, Fathers thought they were, did not always succeed in avoiding Gnostic and Manichean errors in their expositions of doctrine. This does not mean that they were not full-fledged Christians; it merely means that they were fallible men, and that they made mistakes in their explanations of some of the dogmas of the Faith in which they believed with all sincerity.[5]

History concurs that down through time many of these second century replacement doctrines have had a profound impact on the schools of Christianity. Beginning with King Charlemagne's "Palatine" or "Palace School," which became the center of Christian learning in the eighth century, to the Christian "Scholastic Schools" of the thirteenth century, which used the Greek Aristotelean philosophies of reason alone for the investigation of the truth, to the Catholic and Protestant schools of the sixteenth century, Christian learning centers have continued to train unsuspecting Christians to adopt the same anti-Jewish replacement doctrines of the second and third century Gnostic Christians.

Augustine

One of the champions of the anti-Jewish replacement doctrines was Augustine (354-430 C.E.), who was a Manichaean before becoming a Christian convert. A. Berkeley Mickelsen, former professor of the New Testament Interpretation at Bethel Theological Seminary in St. Paul, Minnesota, says of the Manichaean influence on Augustine:

The Manichaean religious movement (which began in the third century A.D.) pointed with scorn at the anthropomorphisms in the Old Testament. "Look how literal interpretation results in absurdity," the adherents to Manichaeanism exclaimed. All this was meant to discredit the Old Testament and Christianity. Such

Augustine

objections kept Augustine, for a while, from embracing Christianity. Then came Ambrose who took Paul's statement that "the letter kills but the spirit makes alive" as a slogan for allegorical interpretation. In this approach Augustine found a way to overcome the objections of the Manichaeans to the Old Testament. Through allegorizing traditional Christianity became tenable for Augustine. Augustine was an incisive theologian and a clear thinker. He knew that sound principles are important for interpretation. Yet he himself allegorized extensively.... We see that with Augustine the tradition of the church is beginning to play a prominent role in controlling interpretation. Although Augustine's theological tractates have freshness and vigor, his biblical exegesis often fails to set forth with forcefulness and freshness what the original writer wanted to say. Allegorization soon was to take over the methodology of biblical scholars for a thousand years.[6]

As the Roman Catholic bishop of Hippo, Augustine embraced Marcion's ideas about grace, as opposed to the Law [*Torah*]. Like Marcion, Augustine opposed the Jewishness of the Scriptures and rejected the harsh and lesser Deity of the Old Testament.[7]

Once the idea was accepted that the God of the Old Testament was a lesser God than the God of the New Testament, the next step was to accept the idea that Israel was a lesser People. Because of the Roman destruction of Jerusalem and the Temple, in 70 C.E., Augustine regarded Israel has having been cast aside by God and replaced by the Church.

Over the centuries, Augustine's belief that the Church had replaced Israel dominated the theology of the Roman Catholic Church. In time, Augustine's Replacement Theology was adopted by the Protestant churches of Eruope.

For Augustine, the Messiah of the New Testament was always one of personal connection with a being in whom man's only real satisfaction or good is to be found. In philosophical terms, Professor Williston Walker informs us that Augustine's "concept of God was borrowed from Neo-Platonism."[8]

For Plato, the ideal is not the dominion of law, but rather the rule of a just king who possesses true knowledge (Pol., 294a/b; cf. Plat. Leg., IX 875c/d).[9] Thus for Augustine, the "good God" was no longer bound by the

Law of Moses. Not only was the "good God" of the New Testament over the Law, He Himself was the Law both for Himself and others.

How influential was Augustine on Western Christian thought? Bernard Ramm, the Christian scholar and author of the widely read work entitled *Christian Apologetics,* writes:

> Outside of the apostolic circle it is difficult to find a man with a greater stature than that of Augustine, bishop of Hippo. He was a mystic, saint, preacher, administrator, scholar, theologian, controversialist, philosopher, historian, letter writer, commentator, teacher, and author. This great genius created the philosophy of history with his *City of God* and introspective religious literature with his *Confessions.* The roots of our modern university curriculum stem from his work, *On Christian Doctrine.* He is the chief parent of medieval mysticism, monasticism, and scholasticism. He dominated the theology of the Middle Ages as its greatest authority. The Reformers claimed that they were doing nothing more or less than returning to Augustine. In fact, Calvin said he could write his theology out of Augustine!
>
> ... However, Augustine was not without his critics. He has been accused of sponsoring the type of artificial thought which became so characteristic of medieval scholasticism. Because Augustine had such a turbulent problem with sex in his own life he is accused of giving it a morbid interpretation and thus adversely influencing Christian thought.... In his Platonism which put such a high value on thought and concept and so little on sense and experience he is judged as retarding the growth of the sciences. In his debates with the various heretics he is charged with creating a spirit of ecclesiastical dogmatism within Christendom. And to others his views of ecclesiology were far to Romish and authoritarian.
>
> Although Augustine was a man with a mighty intellect he nevertheless was also a mystic. Confessions, prayers, and adorations were his daily spiritual fare.
>
> ... He was influenced little by Aristotle and much by Plato. He remarks that Plato apparently worshipped (sic) the true God and says it "is evident that none [of the philosophers]

come nearer to us than the Platonists" (*City of God*, VIII, 5). He also asserts that they are "the noblest of the philosophers" (*City of God*, X, 1). Furthermore the Christian has every right to the use of the correct conclusions of the Platonists because they "have unlawful possession" of the truth (*On Christian Doctrine*, II, 40).[10]

Scholars agree that Plato approached religion as a function of the state, not as a matter of individual faith and conviction.[11] Equally troubling is Augustine's statement that Christians have every right to use the "correct conclusions" of the Platonists. Because history concurs that the Church's most renowned theologians have relied heavily on Augustine's theology in the shaping of Christian dogma.

For Augustine, being a good Platonist meant that the truth could only be found *in the realm of the inner world*. "Do not go outside, come back into your very own self, truth dwells in the inner man," wrote Augustine (*The True Religion*, XXXIX, 72). Again, speaking to sinners Augustine asks them to seek God, saying: "He is within the very heart.... Return to your heart, O ye transgressors!" (*Confessions*, IV, 12). For this reason Augustine's philosophy has rightly been called *"the metaphysics of subjectivity"*.[12]

This too is troubling. Bernard Ramm says: "It is generally granted that Augustine was also weakened in his thought by neo-Platonic elements. His doctrine of sin as negation or lace or privation is neo-Platonic and not Scriptural."[13] William Walker writes: "It is evident that, clear as was the system of Augustine in many respects, it contained profound contradictions, due to the intermingling of deep religious and Neo-Platonic thoughts and popular ecclesiastical traditionalism."[14] For Augustine, Msgr. Glenn says: "Sin is a moral evil, being the privation of that conformity which should exist between man's free act and the Norm of Morality which is Conscience, and, ultimately, the Eternal Law [Divine Reason]."[15]

Here we see that Augustine's doctrinal position on Law and grace was rooted in the Platonian concept of God. What was Plato's concept of God? In Plato's acclaimed *Republic,* he writes: "God is not the author of all things, but of good only."[16]

Equally troubling, scholars agree that Augustine was a devout Manichaean for nine years. Manichaeism taught that there are two *supreme* principles of all things. The one is good; it is spirit, light, *God*. The other is evil; it is matter, darkness, *Satan*.[17] Each of these independent principles and powers make up the universe. Man, like everything else, is such a mixture of both principles; he is made of two parts, one rational and pure [soul], the other irrational and sensual [body].[18] In man, as in the world, the principles of good and evil are in constant conflict. If the good part of man [the soul] conquers the evil part [the body], it will go, after death, into happiness and light. If the evil part of man [the body] conquers, the soul will suffer until it achieves victory over its body.[19]

For third and fourth century Manichaeans, Christ was the spirit of light, who took on a human body and came to teach man how to deliver himself from the evil part of his body.[20] This was the meaning of redemption; liberation of the soul from the control of the "evil" body.[21] The responsibility for the soul's liberation from the body was based entirely on the man who perfectly practiced "inner-reflection" and "bodily denial".[22]

Now we understand Augustine's rationale for championing the Heretic Marcion's teaching that the God of the Old Testament was a harsh and lesser God; that the young Rabbi from Nazareth was a human manifestation of the good God; and that with the coming of *Yeshua* the *Torah* was *done away* and superseded by grace. Now we know why Augustine believed that truth could only be found *in the realm of the inner world.* Now we know how the doctrine of continual inward *penance* became a cardinal Roman Catholic doctrine of salvation by "works," which expressed itself in *various carnis mortificationes,* [*lit.,* 'various mortifications of the flesh'].

The Reformers

During the period leading up to the Reformation, distinguished men such as the English theologian John Wycliffe (1320-1384), the first to translate the Scriptures into English, and Miles Coverdale (1488-1568), the translator of the first printed English Bible, were heavily influenced by Augustine. In 1514, Miles Coverdale was ordained a priest and later entered the Augustine Monastery at Cambridge. John Wycliffe was such a close follower of Augustine's theology that he was called "John of Augustine" by his pupils.[23]

In the sixteenth century the notion that grace was in direct opposition to Law was strengthened when the French theologian John Calvin

(1509-1546) endorsed Augustine's position in his treaties entitled *Institutes of Christian Religion,* which became the theological guide for the reformed churches of Protestantism.

On July 17, 1505, Martin Luther (1483-1546) entered the Augustinian friary in Erfurt, where he too was heavily influenced by Augustine's anti-Jewish/anti-*Torah* theology. In 1507, Luther was ordained into the Catholic priesthood, and in 1508 he began teaching at the University of Wittenberg. Although Luther was a giant among those of the Reformation, he was unable to break free of his anti-Jewish training as an Augustinian priest. In the latter years of life he wrote voluminous numbers of tracts against the Pope, Jews, etc. Two years before his death, Martin Luther wrote a treaties entitled *"Concerning the Jews and Their Lies,"* saying in part:

Martin Luther

Let me give you my advice.

First, their synagogues or churches should be set on fire. And whatever does not burn up should be covered or spread over with dirt so that no one may ever be able to see a cinder of it. And this ought to be one for the honor of God and of Christianity in order that God may see that we are Christians.... Secondly, their homes should be broken down and destroyed. Thirdly, they should be deprived of their prayer books and the Talmud in which such idolatry, lies, cursing, and blaspheme are taught. Fourthly, their rabbis must be forbidden under the threat of death to teach anymore....

Fifthly, passport and traveling privileges should be absolutely forbidden to Jews. Let them stay at home. Sixthly, they ought to be stopped for usury. For this reason, as said before, everything they possess they stole and robbed us through their usury, for they have no other means of support. Seventhly, let the young and strong Jews and Jewesses be given the flail, the axe, the hoe, the spade, the distaff, and spindle, and let them earn their bread by the sweat of their noses as is enjoined upon

Adam's children. We ought to drive the lazy bones out of our system.

If, however, we are afraid that they might harm us personally, or our wives, children, servants, cattle, et cetera... then let us apply the same cleverness (expulsion) as the other nations, such as France, Spain, Bohemia, et cetera...and settle with them for that which they have extorted from us, and after having it divided up fairly, let us drive them out of the country for all time.

To sum up, dear princes and notables who have Jews in your domains, if this advice of mine does not suit you, then find a better one so that you and we may all be free from this inseparable Jewish burden... the Jews.[24]

Today, many find it hard to believe that this great Reformer had such contempt for the Jewish people of his homeland, especially in the latter years of his life. According to the historian Robert Michael, however, Luther was concerned with the Jewish question all his life, despite his devoting only a small portion of his work to it.[25]

Like other Catholic Christians, Luther wanted the Jewish people to accept the Christian Jesus, whose Jewishness had been sanitized by fourth century Roman Catholic Church authorities. In rejecting the Christian Jesus the Jews became the "quintessential *other*,"[26] a perfect model of opposition to the Augustinian view of Gentile Christianity.

In one of Luther's earlier works entitled *"That Jesus Christ was Born a Jew,"* he writes about the Church showing kindness toward Jews, but only with the aim of converting them to Christianity and the Church; what was called *Judenmission.*[27]

When Luther's efforts to convert the Jewish people of Germany to Gentile Christianity failed he became increasingly hostile toward them.[28]

Luther's main works on the Jews were his treaties entitled *Von den Juden und Ihren Lugen* ['On the Jews and Their Lies'], and *Vom Schem Hamphoras und vom Geschlecht Christi* ['On the Holy Name and the Lineage of Christ'], both written in 1543, just three years before his death.[29] In both of these works, Luther argued that the Jews were no longer the chosen people of God, but were "the devil's people." The Jews are "base, whoring people," said Luther, "that is, no people of God, and their boasts of lineage, circumcision, and law must be accounted as filth."[30] Attacking the Judaic Faith, Luther wrote that the synagogue was a "defiled bride, yes, an incorrigible whore and an evil slut...."[31] Finally, Luther said that the Jews were full of the "devil's feces... which they wallow in like swine."[32]

For Luther, stirring up anti-*Semitism* among the German people against the Jews of Germany, and, if necessary, expelling them from the fatherland, was the work of LORD. History concurs that this is exactly what happened. Throughout the 1580s anti-*Semitic* riots caused the expulsion of thousands of Jews from several German Lutheran provinces.[33]

The Nazi's Use of Christian Anti-Semitism

Unfortunately, Luther's campaign against the Jews did not end in the sixteenth century. Robert Michael tells us that just about every anti-Jewish book printed during the reign of the Nazi regime contained references to and quotations from Luther's anti-Jewish works.[34]

One of Hitler's top henchmen, Heinrich Himmler, wrote admiringly of Luther's sermons and writings on the Jews in 1940.[35] When the city of Nuremberg presented a first edition of Luther's treaties, *"On the Jews and their Lies,* to Julius Streicher, editor of the Nazi newspaper *Der Sturmer,* on his birthday in 1937, the newspaper described it as the most radically anti-*Semitic* tract ever published.[36]

On December 17, 1941, seven Protestant regional church confederations issued a statement agreeing with the Nazi policy of forcing Jews to wear the yellow badge, stating: "since after his bitter experience Luther had already suggested preventive measures against the Jews and their expulsion from German territory."[37]

The most troubling use of Luther's anti-*Semitic* writings came from the Satanic driven Chancellor of Germany, Adolf Hitler. Echoing Luther's words in his book entitled *Mein Kampf* ['My Struggle'], Hitler said: "Hence today, I believe that I am acting in accordance with the will of the Almighty Creator: by defending myself against the Jew, I am fighting for the work of the Lord."[38]

By 1934, the anti-*Semitism* of Hitler and his Nazi regime inflamed anti-*Semitic* sentiments throughout Germany. It is said that one Christian teacher taught her school children to recite the following poem: "Jews are sinners. They slaughter Christian children. They cut their throats. They are damn Jewish filth."[39] The teacher threatened to punish the children if they did not learn the poem by heart to recite in the classroom the following day.

On September 15, 1935, in a national speech to the German people, Hitler addressed what he called "The Jewish Problem". From that point on Jews were no longer German citizens. Marriage between Jews and Germans was outlawed. Even the act of sexual intercourse between a German and Jew was outlawed.[40]

In the fall of 1938, 1,200 synagogues were set to the torch and allowed by city officials to burn to the ground, just as Luther had advocated. Shortly afterwards, 30,000 Jews were arrested and sent to concentration camps.[41] This, however, was only a foretaste of what was to come. The thousands of Jews who left Germany were forced to leave behind 90 percent of their assets.[42] Those who could not afford to leave Germany lost everything, including their lives. Before long there were thousands of concentration camps scattered throughout Europe, which were just like the death camps of **DACHU**, **AUSCHWITZ**, and **BUCHENWALD**.[43]

The real tragedy of this story is that the anti-*Semitism* of Hitler's Third Reich didn't begin with Martin Luther. Nor did it begin with Augustine. The earliest records show that anti-*Semitism* began with the Gnostic Christian Marcion and the second century Greek and Latin Church Fathers, who went to great lengths to establish that both the Jewish people and their Judaic faith belonged to an "Old Testament" that had been replaced by the "New Testament" Church.

The Converting of Christianity to Paganism

By the fourth century the replacement doctrines of the Roman Catholic Church had become such a radical departure from those of the second and third centuries that priests, philosophers, and historians were compelled to record their observations. One contemporary Catholic priest, Faustus, who lived during the reign of Diocletian, wrote a letter to Augustine, saying:

> You have substituted your love feasts for the sacrifices of
> the Pagans; for their idols, your martyrs, whom you serve with
> the same honors. You appease the shades of the dead with wine

and feasts; **you celebrate the solemn festivals of the Gentiles, their calends, and their solstices; and as to their manners, those you have retained without any alteration. Nothing distinguishes you from the Pagans, except that you hold your assemblies apart from them.**[44] (Emphasis added.)

Again, in the fourth century the learned M. Turretin recorded the changes he witnessed, saying:

It was not so much the (Roman) Empire that was brought over to the faith, as the faith that was brought over to the Empire; not the Pagans who were converted to Christianity, but Christianity that was converted to Paganism.[45] (Emphasis added.)

Then in the year 439, the Greek philosopher Socrates wrote:

Although most all assemblies throughout the world celebrate the sacred mysteries on the Sabbath every week, yet **the Christians of Alexandria and Rome, on account of some ancient tradition, have ceased to do this.**[46] (Emphasis added.)

The following year, in 440, the Greek historian of the Church, Sozomen, noted:

The people of Constantinople and almost everywhere, assemble together on the Sabbath, **as well as on the first day of the week.**[47] (Emphasis added.)

Thus it was, by the fourth century the heretical doctrine of Replacement Theology was firmly established as a cardinal doctrine of the Church. In time, those who had been faithful to the doctrines and traditions of the Mother Church were elevated to the level of sainthood, bestowing on them titles such as "St." Irenaeus, "St." Ignatius, "St." Justin Martyr, "St." Dionysius, "St." Chrysostom, "St." Clement, "St." Eusebius, and the "holy father" Augustine.

By the way, in both the Hebrew and Apostolic Writings the term "saint" is always used in the context of a living, not a dead person. The term "saint" was never employed as a title of a person after death, such as with the Roman Catholic Church's canonization of dead "saints." Nor was it the practice of first century Believers of *Yeshua* to portray their dead with "halos" to symbolize their holiness.

The practice came from pagans, who used yellow nimbuses and floating gold hoops in stone carvings, paintings, and stained-glassed windows, as well as statues; to identify their deities and founders as beings indwelt by the Sun-god.[48]

St. Augustine

Nevertheless, by the fourth century the *Torah* observant faith of those first century followers of the young Rabbi from Nazareth was well on its way to becoming little more than a faint memory of the past. In its place would be a new religion called Christianity, which would be built upon a much revised account of the Jewisness of the young Rabbi from Nazareth, the Jewishness of the Apostles, the Jewishness of the first century Believers, and the Jewishness of the Apostolic Writings. The Christian historian W. T. Jones writes:

It is an anachronism, of course, to talk about "Christianity" until many years after Jesus' death. What we have now to trace, indeed, is the gradual development of Christianity—a body of theological beliefs and complicated dogmas—out of the simple teachings of Jesus. Though the product (we cannot say *final* product, for Christianity, even today, after twenty centuries, is still evolving) was something radically different from the Jewish Yahweh worship which Jesus himself practiced, the views of Jesus remain at the core of Christianity. The intellectual life of the early Church was indeed largely determined by the struggle to make Jesus' Judaism and Oriental mystery cultism and late Greek philosophy fit together peacefully into one philosophy of religion. And this body of doctrine had to be accompanied to the administrative needs of an ever-growing and complex institution. Neither of these closely associated and reciprocally effective enterprises was in any sense planned. Doctrines and institutions grew – the work of many hands; and as they grew they created problems which were left unsolved for the vexation of future generations.[49]

Chapter 6

ADMISSIONS ABOUT THE SABBATH

By the beginning of the second century the controversy over the observance of the seventh day Sabbath had ceased to be the major issue it was in the first century. The Church had become predominately Gentile in membership and almost exclusively in leadership. Justin refers to a few Gentile Christians who still observed the *Torah,* but states that the majority of Christians would not associate with such persons.[1]

From this point on the debate over the observance of the *Torah* was no longer an issue within Gentile Christianity. When the Synod of Laodecia ratified Constantine's Sun-Day Edict in 363 C.E., Sun-Day was already a well established institution of the Catholic Church.

Even at the hottest point of the great Reformation debate the Church's changing of the seventh day Sabbath to Sun-Day remained uncontested. Luther and Calvin endorsed the Mother Church's practice of public worship on Sun-Day, maintaining that the Law [*Torah*] had ended with the coming of Christ.

Thus it is not surprising most modern day Christians believe that the observance of the Sun-Day Sabbath goes all the way back to the Apostles. This belief, however, was not shared by earlier Christian leaders. Between the sixteenth and twentieth centuries there were several prominent Christian leaders, as well as denominational statements of faith, that affirmed the validity of the seventh day Sabbath.

Even Catholic Church authorities admit that the seventh day is indeed the Sabbath. In fact, many Catholic leaders openly boast that it was the Catholic Church that changed the observance of the seventh day Sabbath to Sun-Day.

Perhaps you've heard about the seventh day Sabbath admissions of these earlier Christian leaders. If not, you can now read for yourself what many of them really thought about the seventh day Sabbath. As you read these admissions, note the many comments from the wide spectrum of Protestant Church leaders and denominations, as well as those from historians, agnostics, and Catholic Church authorities, who are quite candid about the fact that there is no biblical authority for observing Sun-Day as the Christian day of worship.

The Congregational Church

R. W. Dale

"It is quite clear that however rigidly or devotedly we may spend Sunday we are not keeping the Sabbath. The Sabbath was founded on a specific divine command. We can plead no such command for the observance of Sunday. There is not a single line in the New Testament to suggest that we incur any penalty by violating the supposed sanctity of Sunday." R. W. Dale, (1829-1895), *The Ten Commandments,* p. 106-107.

Lyman Abbot

"The current notion that Christ and His apostles authoritatively substituted the first day for the seventh, is absolutely without any authority in the New Testament." Layman Abbot (1835-1922), in the *Christian Union,* June 26, 1890.

"The Christian Sabbath is not in the Scriptures, and was not by the Primitive Church called the Sabbath." Timothy Dwight (president of Yale College from 1795 to 1817), *Theology: Explained and Defended* (1823), Sermon 107, Vol. 3, p. 258.

Timothy Dwight

The Lutheran Church

"They (Roman Catholics) refer to the Sabbath Day, as having been changed into the Lord's Day, contrary to the Decalogue, as it seems. Neither is there any example more boasted of than the changing of the Sabbath Day. Great, say they, is the power of the Church, since it has dispensed with one of the Ten Commandments!" The *Augsburg Confession of Faith*, art. 28, as published in *The Book of Concord of the Evangelical Lutheran Church*, Henry Jacobs, ed. (1911), p. 63.

"But they err in teaching that Sunday has taken the place of the Old Testament Sabbath and therefore must be kept as the seventh day had to be kept by the children of Israel. In other words, they insist that Sunday is the divinely appointed observance of Sunday by so called blue laws.... These churches err in their teaching, for the Scripture has in no way ordained the first day of the week in place of the Sabbath. There is simply no law in the New Testament to that effect." John Theodore Mueller (1885-1967), *Sabbath or Sunday*, pp. 15, 16.

The Presbyterian Church

"There is no word, no hint, in the New Testament about abstaining from work on Sunday.... Into the rest of Sunday no divine law enters.... The observance of Ash Wednesday or Lent stands exactly on the same footing as the observance of Sunday." Canon Eyton, *The Ten Commandments*, pp. 52, 63, 65.

"The Sabbath is part of the Decalogue – the Ten Commandments. This alone forever settles the question as to the perpetuity of the institution.... Until, therefore, it can be shown that the whole moral law has been repealed, the Sabbath will stand.... The teaching of Christ confirms the perpetuity of the Sabbath." T. C. Blake, *Theology Condensed,* pp. 474, 475.

The Anglican Church

"And where are we told in the Scriptures that we are to keep the first day at all? We are commanded to keep the seventh; but we are nowhere commanded to keep the first day.... The reason we keep the first day of the week holy instead of the seventh day is for the same reason that we observe many other things, not because the Bible, but because the church has enjoined it." Isaac Williams (1802-1865), *Plain Sermons on the Catechism,* Vol. 1, pp. 334, 336.

The Church of Christ

"I do not believe that the Lord's day came in the room of the Jewish Sabbath, or that the Sabbath was changed from the seventh to the first day, for this plain reason, where there is no testimony, there can be no faith. Now there is no testimony in all the oracles of heaven that the Sabbath was changed, or that the Lord's day came in the room of it." Alexander Campbell, *Washington Reporter,* October 8, 1821.

"'But,' some say, 'it was changed from the seventh to the first day.' Where? When? And by whom? No man can tell. No: it never was changed, not could it be, unless creation was to be gone through again; for the reason assigned must be changed before the observance, or respect to the reason, can be changed! It is all old wives' fables to talk of the change of the Sabbath from the seventh to the first day. If it be changed, it was that august personage who changed it, who changes times and laws

EX OFFICIO–I think his name is DOCTOR ANTICHRIST."
Alexander Campbell, *"The Christian Baptist,"* February 2, 1842,
Vol. 1, no. 7, p. 164.

"There is no direct Scriptural authority for designating the first
day the Lord's day." D. H. Lucas, *"Christian Oracle,"* January
23, 1890.

The Moody Bible Institute

"The Sabbath was binding in Eden, and
it has been in force ever since. This fourth
commandment begins with the word
'remember,' showing that the Sabbath
already existed when God wrote the law
on the tables of stone at Sinai. How can
men claim that this one commandment
has been done away with when they
will admit that the other nine are still
binding? ... I honestly believe that this
commandment is just as binding today
as it ever was. I have talked with men who have said that it has
been abrogated, but they have never been able to point to any
place in the Bible where God repealed it. When Christ was on
earth, He did nothing to set it aside; He freed it from the traces
under which Scribes and Pharisees had put it, and gave it its
true place. 'The Sabbath was made for man, and not man for
the Sabbath.' It is just as practicable and as necessary for men
today as it ever was – in fact, more than ever, because we live in
such an intense age." D. L. Moody (1837-1899), *Weighed and
Wanting,* pp. 7, 47, 48.

D. L. Moody

"This Fourth Commandment is not a commandment for one
place, or one time, but for all places and times." D. L. Moody,
at San Francisco, January 1, 1881.

The Methodist Church

"But, the Moral Law contained in the Ten Commandments, and enforced by the prophets, he [Christ] did not take away. It was not the design of His coming to revoke any part of this. This is a law which never can be broken.... For every part of this law must remain in force upon all mankind, and in all ages; as not depending either on time or place, or any other circumstances liable to change, but on the nature of God and the nature of  God and the nature of man, and their unchangeable relation to each other." John Wesley (1703-1791), *The Works of the Reverend John Wesley,* John Emory, ed., Vol. 1, Sermon 25, p. 221.

John Wesley

"No Christian whatsoever is free from obedience of the commandments which are called moral.... The Sabbath was made for MAN; not for the Hebrews, but for all men." *Methodist Church Discipline* (1904), p. 23.

The Baptist Church

"There was and is a commandment to keep holy the Sabbath day, but the Sabbath day was not Sunday.... It will be said, however, and with some show of triumph, that the Sabbath was transferred from the seventh day to the first day of the week.... Where can the record of such a transaction be found? Not in the New Testament – absolutely not. There is no scriptural evidence of the change of the Sabbath institution from the seventh to the first day of the week.... To me it seems unaccountable that Jesus, during three years intercourse with His disciples, often conversing with them upon the Sabbath question, never alluded to any transference of the day; also, that during forty days of His resurrection life, no such thing was intimated.... Of course, I quite well know that Sunday did come into use in early Christian history as a religious day, as we learn from the Christian Fathers and other sources. But what a pity that it comes branded with the mark of paganism, and christened with the name of the sun god, when adopted and sanctioned by papal apostasy, and bequeathed as a sacred legacy to Protestantism." Edward T. Hiscox, author of the *Baptist Manual,* in a paper read before the New York minister's conference held November 13, 1893.

"The first four commandments set forth man's obligation directly toward God.... But when we keep the first four commandments, we are likely to keep the other six.... The fourth commandment sets forth God's claim on man's time and thought.... The six days of labor and the rest on the Sabbath are to be maintained as a witness to God's toil and rest in the creation.... Not one of the ten words is of merely racial significance.... The Sabbath was established originally in no special connection with the Hebrews, but as an institution for all of mankind, in commemoration of God's rest after the six days of creation. It was designed for all the descendants of Adam." *Adult Quarterly, Southern Baptist Convention Series,* August 15, 1937.

"The sacred name of the seventh day is Sabbath. This fact is too clear to require argument (Exodus 20:10 quoted)... on this point the plain teaching of the Word has been admitted in all ages.... Not once did the disciples apply the Sabbath law to the first day of the week, – that folly was left for a later age, nor did they pretend that the first day supplanted the seventh. Joseph Hudson Taylor, *The Sabbath Question,* pp. 14-17, 44.

"We believe that the law of God is the eternal and unchangeable rule of His moral government." *Baptist Church Manual,* Art. 12.

The Church of England

"The Lord's day did not succeed in the place of the Sabbath.... The Lord's day was merely an ecclesiastical institution. It was not introduced by virtue of the fourth commandment, because for almost three hundred years together they kept that day which was in that commandment.... The primitive Christians did all manner of works upon the Lord's day even in times of persecution when they are the strictest observers of all the divine

Jeremy Taylor

commandments; but in this they knew there was none." Bishop Jeremy Taylor (1613-1677), *Ductor Dubitantium*, Part 1, Book II, Chap. 2, Rule 6, Sec. 51, 59.

"Merely to denounce the tendency to secularize Sunday is as futile as it is easy. What we want is to find some principle, to which as Christians we can appeal, and on which we can base both our conduct and our advice. We turn to the New Testament, and we look in vain for any authoritative rule. There is no recorded word of Christ, there is no word of any of the apostles, which tells how we should keep Sunday, or indeed that we should keep it at all. It is disappointing, for it would make our task much easier if we could point to a definite rule, which left us no option but simple obedience or disobedience.... There is no rule for Sunday observance, either in Scripture or history." Dr. Stephen, Bishop of Newcastle, N.S.W., in an address reported in the *Newcastle Morning Herald*, May 14, 1942.

The Christian Church

"It [the Church] has reversed the fourth commandment by doing away with the Sabbath of God's Word, and instituting Sunday as a holiday." N. Summerbell, *History of the Christian Church*, Third Edition, p. 415.

Historians

Eusebius, the fourth century bishop of Caesarea and Father of Church History, states: "All things, whatsoever that it was duty to do on the Sabbath, these we have transferred to the Lord's day (Sunday)." *Commentary on the Psalms.*

The German Church historian Augustus Neander (1789-1850): "Opposition to Judaism introduced the particular festival of Sunday very early, indeed, into the place of the Sabbath.... The festival of Sunday, like all other festivals, was always only a human ordinance, and it was far from the intentions of the apostles to establish a divine command in this respect, far from them, and from the early apostolic church, to transfer the laws of the Sabbath to Sunday. Perhaps, at the end of the second century a false application of this kind had begun to take place; for men appear by that time to have considered laboring on Sunday as a sin." Augustus Neander, *General History of the Christian Religion and Church*, Vol. 1, p. 186.

Encyclopedias

"Sunday was a name given by the heathens to the first day of the week, because it was the day they worshipped (sic) the sun,... the seventh day was blessed and hallowed by God Himself, and... He requires His creatures to keep it holy to Him. This commandment is universal and a perpetual obligation.... The Creator 'blessed the seventh day'–declared it to be a day above all days, a day–on which His favour (sic) should assuredly rest.... It is not the Jewish Sabbath, properly so-called, which is ordained in the fourth commandment. In the fifth commandment, or the sixth whole injunction there is no Jewish element, any more than there is in the third command-." *Eadie's Biblical Cyclopedia,* 1872 Edition, p. 561.

"Thus we learn from Socrates (HE., vi.c.8) that in his time public worship was held in the churches of Constantinople on both days. The view that the Christian's Lord's day or Sunday is but the Christian Sabbath deliberately transferred, from the seventh to the first day of the week does not indeed, find categorical expression till a much later period.... The earliest recognition of the observance of Sunday as a legal duty is a constitution of Constantine in A.D. 321, enacting that all courts of justice, inhabitants of towns, and workshops were to be at rest on Sunday, with an exception in favor of those engaged in agricultural labor.... The Council of Laodecia (363)... forbids Christians from Judaizing and resting on the Sabbath day, preferring the Lord's day, and so far as possible resting as Christians." *Encyclopedia Britannica,* 1899 Edition, Vol. 23, p. 654.

Agnostics

The nineteenth century agnostic Henry M. Taber writes: "Probably very few Christians are aware of the fact that what they call "Christian Sabbath" (Sunday) is of pagan origin. The first observance of Sunday that history records is in the fourth century, when Constantine issued an edict reading 'let all the judges and people of the town rest and all the various trades be suspended on the venerable day of the sun.' At the time of the issue of this edict, Constantine was a sun-worshipper (sic); therefore it could have had no relation whatever to Christianity.... I challenge any priest or minister of the Christian religion to show me the slightest authority for the religious observance of Sunday. And, if such cannot be shown by them, why is it that they are constantly preaching about Sunday as a holy day?... The claim that Sunday takes the place of Saturday, and that because the Jews were supposed to be commanded to keep the seventh day of the week holy, therefore the first day of the week should be kept by Christians, is so utterly absurd as to be hardly worth considering.... That Paul habitually observed and preached on the seventh day of the week is shown in Acts 18:4– 'And he reasoned in the synagogue every Sabbath' (Saturday)." Henry

M. Taber, *Faith or Fact,* ("Preface" written by the renowned agnostic Robert G. Ingersol), pp. 112, 114, 116.

The Catholic Church

"It is well to remind the Presbyterians, Baptists, Methodists, and all other Christians, that the Bible does not support them anywhere in their observance of Sunday. Sunday is an institution of the Roman Catholic Church, and those who observe the day (Sunday) observe a commandment of the Catholic Church." Catholic Priest Brady, in an address, reported in the *Elizabeth, NJ News,* on March 8, 1903.

"The sun was a foremost god with heathen-dom.... The sun has worshippers (sic) at this hour in Persia and other lands.... There is, in truth, something royal, kingly about the sun, making it a fit emblem of Jesus, the Sun of Justice. Hence the church in these countries would seem to have said, to 'Keep that old pagan name (Sunday). It shall remain consecrated, sanctified.' And thus the pagan Sunday, dedicated to Balder, became the Christian Sunday, sacred to Jesus." Catholic Priest William Gildea, *The Catholic World,* March 1894, p. 809.

"Of course the Catholic Church claims that the change was her act. And the act is a mark of her ecclesiastical power and authority in religious matters." C. F. Thomas, Chancellor of *Cardinal Gibbons,* in answer to a letter regarding the change of the Sabbath, November 11, 1895.

"I have repeatedly offered $1000 to anyone who can prove to me from the Bible alone that I am bound to keep Sunday holy. There is no such law in the Bible. It is a law of the holy Catholic Church alone. The Catholic Church says, 'No. By my divine power I abolished the Sabbath and commanded you to keep holy the first day of the week.' And lo! The entire civilized world bows down in reverent obedience to the command of the Holy Catholic Church." Catholic Priest Thomas Enright, C.S.S.R.,

February 1884. Printed in the *American Sentinel,* a New York
Roman Catholic journal, in June 1893, p. 173.

"If Protestants would follow the Bible, they would worship God
on the Sabbath Day. In keeping Sunday they are following a law
of the Catholic Church." Albert Smith, Chancellor of the
Archdiocese of Baltimore, replying for the Cardinal, in a letter
dated February 10, 1920.

"The Pope is of so great authority and power that he can modify,
explain, or interpret even divine law. The Pope can modify
divine law, since his power is not of man, but of God, and he
acts as viceregent of God upon earth." Lucius Ferraris, Prompta
Bibliotheca, art. Papa, II, Vol. VI, p. 29

"The leader of the Catholic Church is
defined by the faith as the Vicar of Jesus
Christ. The Pope is considered the man on
earth who 'takes the place' of the Second
Person of the omnipotent God of the
Trinity." Pope John Paul II, *Crossing the
Threshold of Hope,* p. 3, 1994.

Pope John Paul II

America's Sun-Day Law

Despite the religious guarantees of the First Amendment, in 1863,
representatives of eleven Protestant denominations met together and
established an interchurch organization called the *National Reform
Movement,* whose mission was to secure the legislation of a mandatory
National Sunday Law for all of Amerca. By 1882, "Blue laws" were passed
by state and local governments, mandating criminal arrests, fines, and
imprisonment for violating America's new "Sunday law".

In 1883, John Shea, a high ranking Catholic priest, responded to the
passage of the "Blue laws," saying:

"Strange as it may seem, the State, in passing laws for the
due sanctification of Sunday, is unwittingly acknowledging the

authority of the Catholic Church, and carrying out more or less faithfully its prescriptions.

"... The Sunday, as a day of the week set apart for the obligatory worship of Almighty God, to be sanctified by a suspension of all servile labor, trade, and worldly avocations and by exercise of devotion,–is purely a creation of the Catholic Church.

"It is not the Jewish Sabbath; it is, in fact, entirely distinct from it, and not governed by the enactments of the Mosaic law. It is part and parcel of the system of the Catholic Church as absolutely as is any other of her sacraments, her festivals and feasts, her days of joy and mourning, her indulgences, and her jubilees.

"The Catholic Church created the Sunday Sabbath and made the very regulations which have come down on the statute-books, and she still constantly, from her pulpits, her catechists' chairs, and the confessional, calls on her faithful to obey them, to sanctify the day, and refrain from all that desecrates it....

"Protestantism, in discarding the authority of the Church (Catholic), has no good reason for its Sunday theory, and ought logically, to keep Saturday as the Sabbath.... For their present practice Protestants in general have no authority but that of a Church which they disown, and there cannot be a greater incon- sistency than theirs in asking the state to enforce the Sunday Laws."[2]

The Convert's Catechism of Catholic Doctrine

SECTION II. WHAT THE CATHOLIC CHURCH ORDAINS:
Chapter II
The Law of God
3. The Third Commandment.

Q. What is the Third Commandment?
A. The Third Commandment is: Remember that thou keep holy the Sabbath day.

Q. Which is the Sabbath Day?
A. Saturday is the Sabbath day.
Q. Why do we observe Sunday instead of Saturday?
A. The Church substituted Sunday for Saturday, because Christ rose from the dead on a Sunday, and the Holy Ghost descended upon the Apostles on a Sunday.
Q. By what authority did the Church substitute Sunday for Saturday?
A. The Church substituted Sunday for Saturday by the plenitude of that divine power which Jesus Christ bestowed upon her.
Q. What does the Third Commandment command?
A. The Third Commandment commands us to sanctify Sunday as the Lord's Day.
Q. What does the Third Commandment forbid?
A. The Third Commandment forbids (1) The omission of prayer and divine worship; (2) All unnecessary servile work; (3) Whatever hinders the keeping of the Lord's Day holy.
Q. Is the desecration of the Lord's Day a grievous matter?
A. The desecration of the Lord's Day is a grievous matter in itself, though it admits of light matter."[3]

"Upon this Rock"

Notice that in the above Catholic statement of faith the authority cited for changing the seventh day Sabbath to Sun-Day is the claim of the "divine power which Jesus Christ bestowed upon the Church." The significance of this claim can not be overstated. Because it was in the early third century that Catholic Church authorities proclaimed the Pope to be the earthly head of the Mother Church as the successor of Peter.[4]

The passage of Scripture Church authorities used to support this claim is found in Matthew 16:18, where *Yeshua* said to Peter: "I also say to you that you are Peter, and upon this rock I will build my church; and the gates of Hades will not overpower it" (NASV).

According to Catholic authorities, this passage is proof that Peter is the rock upon which *Yeshua* said His Church would be built. But according to the Scriptures, nothing could be further from the truth. Speaking of Himself in the third person, *Yeshua* said to the people of His day: "... he who falls on this stone..." (Matt. 21:44; AKJV).

In a letter to the Corinth Nazarenes, Paul said: "Moreover, brethren, I would that ye should be ignorant, how that all our fathers were under the cloud, and all passed through the sea; and were all baptized unto Moses in the cloud and in the sea; and did all eat the same spiritual meat; and did all drink the same spiritual drink; <u>for they drank of that spiritual Rock that followed them: and that Rock was Christ</u> (1 Corin. 10:1-4).

Hundreds of years earlier, Isaiah foretold the coming of the Messiah, saying: "Therefore thus saith the LORD God, Behold, I lay in Zion for a foundation a stone, a tried stone, a precious corner *stone,* a sure foundation..." (Isa. 28:16). Indeed, throughout the Scriptures, the LORD Himself is called a "Rock" (2 Sam. 22:32; Ps. 18:2, 31, 46; 28:1; 31:3; 42:9; 63:2, etc.).

Even Peter understood *Yeshua* to be the "Rock" of Ages, telling the Believers in Asia Minor that He is "a living stone... the chief cornerstone, chosen, precious... a stone of stumbling, and a rock that makes for falling..." (1 Pet. 2:4-8).

Yet, in spite of this clear evidence, the *Catholic Encyclopedia* (article: 'Peter') informs us that it was during the time of Calixtus, who was bishop of Rome, from 218 to 223 C.E., that Matthew 16:18 was used to support the Catholic claim that Peter was the *rock* upon which the Church was founded, and that the bishop of Rome was Peter's successor.

To support this claim, Catholic scholars maintain that as early as the third century tradition held that Peter was bishop of Rome from 42 C.E. until 67 C.E. But this claim too has a problem. Luke records that Peter, who had been set free from jail "went down from Judah to Caesarea, and there he abode" (Acts 12:19). This was about 44 C.E., about the time of Herod's death.

So here is the great question: If Peter was indeed the bishop of Rome from 42-67 C.E., how was it that when Paul wrote to the congregation in Rome, about 56 C.E., he sent greetings to some twenty-seven people but never mentioned Peter (Rom. 16:3-15)? The noted theologian J. B. Lightfoot maintains that the absence of Paul's greeting to Peter suggests that Peter was not in Rome. Rather, it is more probable that Peter went to Antioch (*Commentary on Acts,* Vol. 8, pp. 273, 289).

Nevertheless, sometime between 218 and 223 C.E., Catholic Church authorities claimed Matthew 16:18 as the biblical authority for the Pope's temporal authority over the Church as the successor of Peter.

From that point on, Catholic authorities began to replace the seventh day Sabbath, the appointed Spring and Fall festivals, and the Jewishness of the Apostolic Writings with the ordinances, doctrines and traditions of the Mother Church – *the new People of God.*

Chapter 7

THE APOSTOLIC/
CHURCH TIMELINES

Church history is the most extensive, and, including the
sacred history of the Old and New Testaments, the most important
branch of theology. It is the backbone of theology on which it
rests, and the storehouse from which it derives its supplies. It is the
best commentary of Christianity itself, under all its bearings. The
fullness of the stream is the glory of the fountain from which it flows.

Philip Schaff

For most Christians the Church's historical view of the first century
Apostolic Era has indeed been the backbone on which Christianity rests, as
well as the storehouse from which it derives its theology. This is especially
true in regards to the birth of the Church.

According to most theologians, Pentecost day was the birthday of the
Church and the beginning of the Christian Era. But when this claim is
examined in the light of the biblical record there are several problems that
arise.

The most important is the lack of biblical support. For example, Luke
records that just before the *Yeshua* ascended into heaven He told His Jewish
disciples not to leave Jerusalem "but to wait for the promise of the Father"
(Acts 1:4).

What promise was *Yeshua* addressing? Although there are many
promises in Scripture, to the Jewish people of that day "the promise of
the Father" was unlike any other promise in Scripture. The Jewish people

knew it well. It had been declared hundreds of years earlier by the prophet Isaiah, saying:

> 44 "But now listen, O Jacob, My servant, and Israel, whom I have chosen:
>
> 2 Thus says the LORD who made you and formed you from the womb, who will help you, 'Do not fear, O Jacob My servant; and you Jeshurun whom I have chosen.
>
> 3 'For I will pour out water on the thirsty *land* and streams on the dry ground; I will pour out My Spirit on your offspring and My blessing will be upon your descendants;
>
> 4 and they will spring up among the grass like poplars by streams of water'" (Isa. 44:1-4; NASV).

Clearly, this passage is a promise to the physical descendants of Jacob -- the people of Israel. Moreover, it is clear from the text that *Yeshua's* disciples knew about this particular promise. Luke records that the disciples asked *Yeshua* about its fulfillment, saying: "LORD, is it at this time You are restoring the kingdom to Israel?" (Acts 1:6; NASV).

Yet, in spite of the Jewishness of this passage, theologians claim that this particular promise had nothing to do with the Jewish people. Rather, it marked the birthday of the Christian Church.

At the same time, most theologians agree that the one hundred-and-twenty men and women gathered together in the "upper room" on Pentecost day, waiting for the fulfillment of that great promise, were all Jewish followers of *Yeshua*. Indeed, most theologians agree that the three thousand who accepted *Yeshua* as the Messiah on that historic day were all *Torah* observant Jews. In fact, most Christian scholars agree that the name Christian did not appear on the scene until 59 C.E., some thirty years after that historic Pentecost day. And most theologians agree that the name "Christian" was not consistently used among Believers until the early second century.

So what is the truth? Was that historic Pentecost day, in Acts 2, the long awaited fulfillment of the great promise of the Father to the people of Israel? Or, was it the birthday of the Christian Church?

As you shall soon see, when the events of the those first followers of *Yeshua* are viewed from a chronological timeline they make a compelling case for a Messianic faith that is based on the *Torah* observant faith of the young Rabbi from Nazareth, the Apostles, and first century community of Believers.

On the other hand, when the events of the Church are viewed from a chronological timeline they make a compelling case for a Christian faith that is not only void of its Hebraic roots, but is, in fact, hostile to the faith of *Yeshua*, the Apostles, and first century community of Believers.

The Apostolic Timeline

About 30 C.E. According to Luke, *Yeshua* began His public ministry when He was about thirty years of age (Lk. 3:23), which was some time after John the Baptist's mission, about 28 C.E. (Lk. 3:1f.). The length of *Yeshua's* ministry was about three years. This would place His death at about 30 C.E. According to *Yeshua's* own words, He was in the grave "three days and three nights" (Matt. 12:40). The Gospel account that *Yeshua* was executed on "the day of preparation" (Mk. 15:42; Lk. 23:52-54) does not prove He died on a Friday. John states that it happened on a "high" Sabbath (Jhn. 19:31), which was the High Sabbath of Unleavened Bread that follows Passover.

Fifty days from the festival of First Fruits [representing *Yeshua's* resurrection from the Tomb] Peter preached at the Temple site to thousands of *Torah* observant Jews gathered in Jerusalem for the appointed High Sabbath of Shavuot/Pentecost. The Messianic researcher Dean Wheelock says of this event: "It was only at the Temple where an audience of thousands could have heard these disciples proclaiming the good news of the gospel. It was only at the southern entrance to the Temple where there were an adequate number of *mikvaot* [Heb. 'baptismal pools'] to accommodate the immersion of 3,000 new Believers in one day."[1]

From this point on Believers continued to worship in the Temple (Acts 2:44-46). Even the Church historian Williston Walker agrees that these first followers of *Yeshua* practiced Temple worship, saying: "The early Jerusalem company were faithfully in attendance at the temple, and in obedience to Jewish law, but, in addition, they had their own special services among themselves, with prayer, mutual exhortation, and 'breaking of bread' daily in private houses."[2]

According to the Christian work titled *Halley's Bible Handbook,* as well as other Christian sources, Pentecost was the "Birthday of the Church".[3] Indeed, many Christian theologians mark Pentecost as the day the spiritual Church replaced the physical children of Israel as the *new Israel.*

About 32 C.E.   Some two years after the death and resurrection of *Yeshua,* Paul became a Believer while traveling on the road to Damascus (Acts 9:3).

40-45 C.E.   Matthew wrote his gospel primarily to a Jewish audience for the purpose of showing the Jewish people that the acceptance of *Yeshua* as the promised Jewish Messiah was not a rejection of the Hebrew Scriptures.[4]

46 C.E.   Paul and Barnabas begin their first missionary journey to the Gentiles in early 46 C.E., going to the cities of Antioch, Salamis and Paphos on the Isle of Cyprus, Perga, Antioch in Pisidia, Lystra, Iconium, and Attalia.

Luke records that when Paul and Barnabas went to the peoples in Asia Minor, they went to the synagogues and taught on the Sabbath, saying:

> But passing through from Perga, they came to Antioch in Pisidia, and went into the congregation on the Sabbath day and sat down. And after the reading of the Torah and the Prophets, the rulers of the congregation sent to them, saying, 'Men, brothers, if you have any word of encouragement for the people, speak.' And Sha'ul, standing up and motioning with his hand said, 'Men, Yisra'elites and those fearing Elohim, listen... to you the word of this

deliverance has been sent... and by Him everyone who believes is declared right from all *sins* from which you were not able to be declared right by the Torah of Mosheh.'... And when the Yehudim went out of the congregation, <u>the gentiles begged to have these words spoken to them the next Sabbath</u>. ... **And on the next Sabbath almost all the city came together to hear the Word of Elohim** (Acts 13:14-16, 26, 39, 42-44; *The Scriptures*).

Addressing the Jewish context in which Paul and Barnabas went to the synagogues on the Sabbath, the Hebrew scholar Joseph Good writes:

> The Gentile believers of the first century are seldom understood by today's Bible scholars. They belonged to a group known as the 'sebomenoi,' or G-d fearers. These were Gentiles who had left paganism and were already attending synagogues. They observed the Sabbath, as well as the Jewish festivals, and had incorporated into their own life-style many of the Jewish customs. Laws within the Torah defined how they were to be treated as well as how they were to live. It should be pointed out that observance of the Torah had nothing to do with the salvation of an individual, which could only be obtained by faith in the Messiah. For these 'sebomenoi' believers, as well as the Jewish believers, the Torah defined their faith and their walk with G-d. Within the Sabbath, festivals, and customs, these two groups understood the working of the Messiah (Colossians 2:16-17).[5]

48 C.E. Early in 48 C.E., the Jerusalem Council met to establish the rules for Gentile Believers acceptance into the Nazarene fellowship. The Council ruled that Gentile Believers should "abstain from the defilement of idols, and from what is strangled, and from blood" (Acts 15:20). "For from ancient

127

generations Mosheh has, in every city, those proclaiming him – being read in the congregations every Sabbath" (v. 21).

In the Spring of 48 C.E., Paul made his second missionary journey to the cities of Damascus, Antioch in Syria, Issus, Tarsus, Derbe, Lystra, Iconium, Antioch in Pisidia, Troas, Neapolis, Philippi, Amphipolis, Berea, Athens, Corinth, Ephesus, Caesarea, and Jerusalem.

At the Areopagus, or Mars' Hill, overlooking Athens, Paul "... **reasoned in the synagogues with the Jews, and with the devout persons** [Gentile God-fearers], and in the market daily with them that met with him ... and they took him to the Areopagus ..." where Paul found an altar "TO THE UNKNOWN God" and made his famous address of Acts 17.

52 C.E.   Paul made his third and final missionary journey to the Greek cities of Antioch, Issus, Tarsus, Derbe, Lystra, Iconium, Antioch in Pisidia, Laodicea, Ephesus, Perganum, Troas, Neapolis, Philippi, Amphipolis, Apollonia, Thessalonica, Berea, Corinth, Assos, Mitylene, Miletus, Paara, Tyre, Ptolemais, Caesarea, and Jerusalem.

In Corinth, Paul met Aquila and Pricilla, who themselves had recently moved to Corinth from Rome. Perhaps for as many as eighteen months (Acts 18:11 cf.), Paul was their house guest and fellow-tentmaker, or leather worker. During this time Paul "... **reasoned in the synagogue every Sabbath, and persuaded Jews and Greeks ... then he left there and went to the house of a man named Titius Justus, a worshiper of God, whose house was next to the synagogue**" (Acts 18:4, 7).

54 C.E.   Paul wrote his first letter to the Gentile Believers in Corinth from Ephesus, saying:

> 19 For though I am free from all, I made myself a servant to all, in order to win more,

20 and to the Yehudim [Jews] I became as a Yehudite, that I might win Yehudim; to those who are under Torah, as under Torah, so as to win those who are under Torah; 21 to those without Torah, as without Torah –**not being without Torah toward Elohim, but under Torah of Messiah** – so as to win those who are without Torah (1 Cor. 9:19-21; *The Scriptures*).

The Christian scholar James Denny says of this passage in the *Expositor's Greek New Testament:* "In relation to Gentiles also he [Paul] takes an attitude open to misunderstanding and which he wishes to guard: 'to those out-of-<u>law</u> [Gk. **t. avomois**] as out-of-law—though I am not out-of-law in respect of God, but in-<u>law</u> [Gk. **evvomos**] in respect of Christ."[6]

55. C.E.   Paul wrote his second letter to the Gentile Believers in Corinth, warning them not to place their confidence in false teachers, saying: "For we do not presume to count ourselves or compare ourselves with those who commend themselves. **But they, measuring themselves by themselves, and comparing themselves among themselves are not wise**" (2 Cor. 10:12).

56 C.E.   Paul wrote his letter to the Gentile Believers in Galatia. "Galatians" is the book most Christian theologians hail as the "Magna Charta of Christian Liberty". When making this claim, however, they fail to point out that Paul was dealing with a group identified with the "Shammai Pharisees". These were Jewish Believers who made circumcision and *Torah* observance required as prerequisites for salvation.

About 56 C.E., Paul also wrote his letter to the Believers in Rome, who were predominately Gentiles (Rom. 1:13). For most Christians, Paul's letter to the Gentile Believers in Rome was meant to instruct them in the biblical doctrine of salvation, especially the teaching on justification by faith (4:1-25). While the doctrine of justification by faith alone is indeed one of the major themes of Romans, in chapter two, Paul also addresses the relevance of the *Torah* in the life of the Believer, saying:

11 For there is no partiality with Elohim.

12 For as many as have sinned without Torah shall also perish without Torah, and as many as sinned in the Torah shall be judged by the Torah.

13 For not the hearers of the Torah are righteous in the sight of Elohim, but the doers of the law shall be declared right (Rom. 2:11-13; *The Scriptures*).

57 C.E. When Paul arrived at Miletus, near the end of his third missionary journey, he sent for the elders of Ephesus and warned them that "... savage wolves shall come in among you, not sparing the flock. Also from among yourselves men shall arise, speaking distorted teachings, to draw away the taught ones after themselves" (Acts 20:29-30).

59 C.E. Sometime during 59 C.E., or shortly thereafter the name Christian was first coined by pagans as a name to designate the Antioch Gentile Believers of Syria (Acts 11:26). This was almost thirty years *after* the death and resurrection of *Yeshua*. For the remainder of the first century the name Christian does not occur in the New Testament as a name used by Believers.[7] Instead, first century Believers continued to refer to themselves as "disciples," "brothers," "faithful," saints," "servants," "slaves," etc.

Approximately 59 C.E., Paul was taken into custody in Jerusalem by the Romans. Paul's arrest took place during the time of the Procurator Felix, who held that office from 52-60. This puts the dating of Paul's last visit to Jerusalem almost 30 years *after* the death and resurrection of *Yeshua*. During this time the Jewish Believers in Jerusalem were still practicing Temple worship (Acts 21)

It was in Caesarea on the Mediterranean, where Paul was commanded to be kept in Herod's judgment hall, where charges were brought against him before the governor Felix by a speaker for the high priest, Tertullus, saying: "For we have found this man a pestilent fellow, and a mover of sedition among all the Jews throughout the world and **a ringleader of the sect of the Nazarenes"** (Acts 24:5).

60 C.E.   Paul wrote his letter to the Gentile Believers in Colossi to refute the teachings of Jewish Believers who taught the necessity of observing the rules of the *Oral Torah* (Col. 2:20-23). Paul refutes these false teachers by saying: "… why, as if you were living in the world, do you submit yourself to decrees … in accordance with the commandments of men?" (vs. 20; NASV).

61 C.E.   The Book of Acts was written by Luke who, most likely, was a Hellenistic Jew. At the time of the writing of Acts, which was about thirty years after the death and resurrection of *Yeshua,* both the Jew and Gentile Believers in Jerusalem were still observing Temple worship (Acts 2:46).

62 C.E.   Paul wrote his letter to the Gentile Believers in Philippi during his first Roman imprisonment. Philippi was the city where Paul met Lydia, a Gentile God-fearer, and a number of other proselyte women on the bank of the river "… **on the Sabbath day … a place of prayer.** And having sat down … spoke to the women who met there" (Acts 16:13), since there was no synagogue in Philippi.

63 C.E.   Paul wrote his first letter to Timothy to encourage him in the work of the ministry and to oppose false teaching, saying:

> 8 And we know that the Torah is good if one uses it legitimately,
> 9 knowing this: that Torah is not laid down for a righteous being, but for the *lawless* and unruly, for the wicked and for sinners, for the wrong-doers and profane, for those who kill their fathers and mothers, for murderers,

10 for those who whore, for sodomites, for kidnappers, for liars, for perjurers, and for whatever else that is contrary to sound teaching,

11 according to the esteemed Good News of the blessed Elohim which was entrusted to me (1 Tim. 8-11; *The Scriptures*).

Arndt and Gingrich inform us that the Greek word for "lawless," **avomois** means "*lawless,* with regard to the Mosaic Law."[8]

64 C.E. Paul wrote a letter to Titus who, most likely, was a Gentile Believer from Macedonia (Gal. 2:3). While Paul addressed several subjects, one of the most important was that *Yeshua* "gave Himself for us, to redeem us from all *lawlessness* and to cleanse for Himself a people, *His* own possession, ardent for good works" (Titus 2:14). Again, Arndt and Gingrich inform us that the Greek word for "lawlessness," **avomias** means "*lawless,* with regard to the Mosaic Law."[9]

About this same time, 64-67 C.E., Paul wrote his second letter to Timothy, warning him of the coming rejection of the *Torah* observant faith of those first followers of the young Rabbi from Nazareth, saying:

3 For there shall be a time when they shall not bear sound teaching, but according to their own desires, they shall heap up for themselves teachers tickling the ear,

4 and they shall indeed turn their ears away from the truth, and be turned aside to myths (2 Tim. 4:3-4; *The Scriptures*).

66 C.E. Peter wrote his second letter to the Gentile Believers in Asia Minor, which was directed against the Gnostic and Antinomian teachings of that day. Gnosticism taught that in addition to believing in Christ, one must also receive a special *gnosis* or esoteric knowledge. Antinomians taught that since salvation was by grace alone, the observance of the *Torah* of Moses was no longer relevant. Peter compares those who live a lawless [Gk. *avomois*][10] lifestyle to those who lived in Sodom and Gomorrah (2 Pet. 2-8).

By 66 C.E., false teachers were being accepted into the community of Believers at such an alarming rate that Jude was compelled to warn the Gentile Believers in Asia Minor, saying:

> 3 Beloved when I gave all diligence to write unto you of the common salvation, it was needful for me to write unto you, and exhort *you* that ye should earnestly contend for the faith which was once delivered unto the saints.
>
> 4 For there are certain men crept in unawares, who were before of old ordained to this condemnation, ungodly men, turning the grace of our God into lasciviousness, and denying the only Lord God, and our Lord Jesus Christ (Jude 3-4; AKJV).

About this same time, Paul was executed by the Romans.

67 C.E. The Roman commander Vespasian was dispatched to Judea by the Emperor Nero to put down a Jewish revolt, which began in the spring of 66 C.E., under the cruel procurator Gessius Florus, who demanded a heavy tribute of gold from the Temple treasury. With three infantry legions, a siege train, calvary, and a corps of engineers, Vespasian made his first target Galilee and methodically put down revolts in the cities of Japhia, Mount Gerizim to the south, Taricheae, Gamala, Mount Tabor and Gischala to the north, and Joppa, Jamnia and Azotus on the coast.

68 C.E. Vespasian launched a campaign to isolate Jerusalem. He first conquered the district east of the Jordan. In the west, Emmaus was taken and a legion garrisoned there marched down the Jordan valley from the north and took Jericho. Upon the overthrow and death of the Emperor Nero, Vespasian brought a temporary halt to his operations in Judea. Eventually he was declared emperor of Rome.

70 C.E. I

n the spring of 70 C.E., Vespasian sailed for Rome And left his son, Titus, in charge of the campaign against Jerusalem. On May 25, Titus succeeded in hammering a breach in the west outer wall of Jerusalem. The infantry poured through and took control of the northern quarter known as Bezetha ['New City']. Five days later the Romans made another breach in the second wall. Again

Titus

the Roman infantry rushed forward; only this time they found themselves being attacked by Jewish defenders in the narrow streets and alleyways, and were forced to retreat. In June the second wall was breached again, this time for good. The walls enclosing the Temple and the upper and lower cities were the most formidable barrier of all. Titus turned to starvation to overcome his last obstacle. Then the Romans sealed off Jerusalem completely with a wall of their own, made of earth which surrounded the city for some five miles. The Temple was burned and plundered by the Romans on the 10th of August, the same day of the year, according to tradition, the first Temple was destroyed by Nebuchadnezzar. Josephus writes:

> No one can conceive a louder more terrible shriek than arose from all sides during the burning of the Temple. The shout of victory and the jubilee of the legions sounded through the wailings of the people, now surrounded with fire and sword, upon the mountains around, even to Peraea, increased the deafening roar. Yet the misery itself was more terrible than this disorder. The hill on which the Temple stood was seething hot, and seemed enveloped to its

base in one sheet of flame. The blood was larger in quantity than the fire, and those that were slain more in number than those that slew them. The ground was nowhere visible. All was covered with corpses; over these heaps the soldiers pursued the fugitives.[11]

Roman soldiers plundering the Temple.

Philip Schaff tells us that the Believers of Jerusalem, remembering *Yeshua's* somber prediction (Matt. 24:2), "forsook the doomed city in good time and fled to the town of Pella in the Decapolis, beyond Jordan, in the north of Peraea, where king Agrippa II., before whom Paul once stood, opened to them a safe asylum. An old tradition says that a divine voice or angel revealed to their leaders the duty of flight. There, in the midst of a population chiefly Gentile, the church of the circumcision was restructured."[12]

85 C.E.   By 85 C.E., the destruction of the Temple was being viewed by the Gentile camp as a sign that God was *doing away* with the Old Dispensation and establishing a New Dispensation. Dr. Merrill Tenney writes: "Gentile adherents chose to abandon the Law and to steer a separate course.... By the year A.D. 85 the church was launched on an independent course. Having survived its first conflict with Roman authority in the person of Nero, it sought to confirm its position theologically and politically."[13]

95 C.E.   By 95 C.E., the great debate over the relevance of the *Torah* in the life of the Gentile Believer was just about over. Christianity was emerging as a *Torahless* religion, with a *Torahless* gospel. About this time, the LORD commissioned John to write a letter to the seven congregations of Asia Minor, calling them to return to their "first works" of faith.

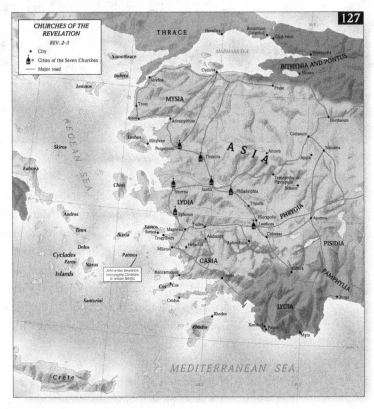

Map of the seven churches of Revelation.

To the congregation in Ephesus, the LORD said: **"I know your works, and your labour, and your endurance, and that you are not able to bear evil ones... and have laboured for My name's sake and have not become weary. But I hold this**

136

against you, that you have left your first love. So remember from where you have fallen and do the first works..." (Rev. 2:2-5; *The Scriptures*).

To the congregation in Smyrna, the LORD said: **"I know your works, and pressure, and poverty – yet you are rich – and the blasphemy of those who say they are Yehudim**[*] **and are not, but are a congregation of Satan"** (v. 9).

To the congregation in Pergamos, the LORD said: **"I know your works... and you hold fast My Name, and did not deny the belief in Me... but I hold a few matters against you, because you have those who adhere to the teaching of Balaam** [*i.e.,* Balaam was the soothsayer in the narrative in Numbers 22, who was involved with several gods and goddesses, and in the Apostolic Writings his name is identified with those 'having left the right way' – 2 Pet. 2:15; Jude 11],... **you also have those who adhere to the teaching of the Nikolaites** [*i.e.,* Nikolaites were a group within the congregation which clung to their pagan practices and sought to work out a compromise with paganism, to enable Believers to take part without embarrassment in some of those pagan and religious activities [14]], **which I hate. Repent..."** (Rev. 2:13-16).

To the congregation in Thyatira, the LORD said: **"I know your works, and love, and service, and belief, and your endurance.... But I hold against you that you allow that woman Izebel, who calls herself a prophetess** [*i.e.,* either an individual or group within the congregation who encouraged participation in pagan practices under the cloak of professing to be a Believer in *Yeshua* [15]], **to teach and lead My servants astray to commit whoring and to eat food offered to idols. And I gave her time to repent of her whoring, and she did not repent. See, I am throwing her into a sickbed, and those who commit adultery with her into great affliction, unless they repent of their works.... And all the assemblies**

---

*   See Glossary of Terms: Yehudim.

shall know that I am the One searching the kidneys and hearts. And I shall give to each one of you according to your works" (vs. 19-23).

To the congregation in Sardis, the LORD said: "**I know your works, that you have a name that you are alive, but you are dead. Wake up, and strengthen what remains and is about to die, for I have not found your works complete before Elohim**" (Rev. 3:1-2; *The Scriptures*).

To the congregation in Philadelphia, the LORD said: "**I know your works – see, I have set before you an open door, and no one is able to shut it – that you have a little power, yet have guarded My Word, and have not denied My Name. See, I am giving up those of the congregation of Satan, who say they are Yehudim**[*] **and are not, but lie.... Because you have guarded My Word of endurance, I also shall guard you from the hour of trial which shall come upon all the world...**" (vs. 8-11).

To the congregation in Laodecia, the LORD said: "**I know your works, that you are neither cold nor hot.... So, because you are lukewarm, and neither cold or hot, I am going to vomit you out of My mouth. Because you say, 'Rich I am, and I am made rich, and need none at all,' and do not know that you are wretched, and pitable, and poor, and blind, and naked. I advise you to buy from Me gold refined in the fire, so that you become rich; and white garments, so that you become dressed, so that the shame of your nakedness might not be shown; and anoint your eyes with oint-ment, so that you see**" (vs. 15-19).

According to most theologians, the "work" the LORD was addressing in the above passages was the work of being a "faithful witness" to Christ and zeal in His service. But for those who understand the Judaic faith of those first century Believers, it was much more.

---

* See Glossary of Terms: Yehudim.

History concurs that by the end of the first century the bright light of that first century faith was growing dim. By the fourth century the observance of the seventh day Sabbath, the appointed festival, and dietary laws had been *done away* and replaced by the doctrines and traditions of Catholic authorities.

How do we know this to be the case? In 363 C.E., the **Synod of Laodecia** – steming from the **Laodecia congregation** of Revelation 3:14-19 -- ratified Constantine's replacement of the appointed seventh day Sabbath with his Sun-Day Edict, as well as the Council of Nicea's replacement of the appointed festival of Passover for the "more legitimate festival of Easter".[16]

The Anti-Semitism of the Church Fathers

Scholars agree that with the exception of the Maccabean period, when Jews insisted on maintaining a strong wall of religious opposition to the encroachments of Hellenism and other religious practices, the Gentile attitude toward Jews was one of benevolent toleration.

The first of the Ptolemies and the Seleucidae conferred important political privileges upon the Jews who lived within their kingdoms. For example, Josephus records that Ptolemy III went so far as to offer sacrifice in Jerusalem (*Against Apion*, ii. 4-5). And one of the foremost friends of the Jews was Ptolemy VI, who sanctioned the building of a Jewish temple in Egypt.[17]

In the much the same manner, the Roman Senate legislated to the Jews the free exercise of their own religion, and even extended its protection to them when hostile attempts were made to suppress Rome's sanction of their Judaic faith.[18] Ironically, it was the pagan emperors Julius Caesar and Augustus who were chiefly responsible for giving the Jews formal recognition within the boundaries of the Roman Empire. Josephus records a large number of public enactments, partly decrees of the Roman Senate, partly edicts of Caesar and Augustus, and partly of Roman officials or municipal authorities of that period – all of which were enacted for the purpose of securing and confirming the rights of Jews within the empire to freely practice their Judaic faith (*Jewish Antiquities*, XIV. 10, XVI. 6).

Four of those enactments are said to have been enacted by Caesar and were complied with throughout the empire as follows: (1) a communication from the authorities of Laodicea to a Roman official, in which they assure Caesar that, in conformity with his instructions, they would not interfere with the Jews in the observance of the Sabbath and the practice of their religious rites; (2) a communication from the proconsul of Asia to the authorities of Jews in their observance of the Sabbath and the practice of their religious rites, and allow them to dispose of their earnings in the way they have been accustomed; (3) a public decree of the city of Halicarnassus, in which the Jews were to be allowed to observe their Sabbath and practice their religious rites; and (4) a public decree of the town of Sardes, in which the Jews were to be allowed to meet on the days appointed by them for the celebration of their religious observances, and further, the officials of the town were to assign them a place of their own "on which to build and in which to reside" (*Jewish Antiquities*, XIV. 10. 20-40).

After the death of Caesar, two contending ruling parties actually vied with each other over maintaining special privileges for Jews. For example, Dolabella, who took possession of Asia Minor, ratified the privilege of exemption of Jews from military service, as well as the right to observe their Judaic faith, which was conferred by previous governors, and sent communications to the officials of Ephesus to apprise them of this continuation of special Jewish privileges (Josephus, *Antiquities*, V. 247-250).

The Jews living in the city of Rome, which was the seat of a large Jewish community that numbered in the thousands,[19] shared in these special Jewish enactments. The Jewish historian Emil Schurer tells us that even after Rome's destruction of Jerusalem and the Temple, in 70 C.E., the Jews living in Rome were still at liberty to observe the Sabbath and appointed rites and festivals down to the second century.[20]

History concurs, however, that all of the benevolent Jewish tolerance of that period was reversed with the rise of Gentile Christianity. By the second century Christian apologists were making arguments that the destruction of the Temple was God's way of *doing away* with the "old" Mosaic order, and replacing it with a "new" order – the Christian Church. From that point on apologists and Catholic authorities attacked the Jews, their Judaic faith, and the Jewishness of the Scriptures. The Hebrew scholar Joseph Good writes:

> As the Jewish voice died, the anti-Semitic Gentiles ripped
> out every trace of the Jewish people that could be found.

Substitution of Biblical festivals by pagan beliefs was rampant. By the time of the Council of Nicea (325 C.E.), Constantine, who was very anti-Semitic, had taken over the church. Laws were issued forbidding Jewish believers to circumcise their children. Pesach was replaced with Easter (the Babylonian fertility goddess). Sukkot was replaced by Christmas (the Roman birthday of the sun god), and so on. Even the Gospels and the Epistles were gentilized when they were translated into other languages and were given common Gentile names and idomatic thoughts, causing people to miss the intended Jewishness of those Scriptures.[21]

Today, one of the primary arguments made for the Sun-Day Sabbath is that churches were already observing Sun-Day as the Christian Sabbath when Constantine made his Sun-Day Edict, in 321 C.E., and convened the Council of Nicea, in 325 C.E.

While this claim cannot be denied, it should hardly be taken as an Apostolic endorsement. Because the anti-*Semitism* of the Greek and Latin Church Fathers had already "poisoned the well" with their contempt of everything Jewish, including the Jewish people.

In the process of formulating a new theology they not only redefined the *Torah* observant faith of those first century followers of the young Rabbi from Nazareth, they severed Christian Believers from their Hebraic roots. Of this fact, there is ample evidence:

100 C.E. Ignatius, the first Gentile bishop of Antioch and the first bishop to refer to himself as a Christian, held Sun-Day to be the Christian Sabbath and the seventh day to be the Jewish Sabbath, which had been *done away* with the coming of Christ.[22] For Ignatius, the Jews, in rejecting Christ, were disinherited from the promises of their own sacred books. "Judaism," said Ignatius, "is nothing but funeral monuments and tombstones of the dead" (Ignatius, *To the Philadelphians,* VI. 1).

About 150 C.E. An unknown Christian apologist wrote a letter to Diognetus [also unknown] and stated that "in so far as they [Jews] are monotheists, they are better than the "heathen," and then added "their sacrifices are absurd... their scruples about the Sabbath ridiculous, their vaunting of circumcision nonsense, and their festivals of folly."[23]

160 C.E.   Justin Martyr taught there was no particular seventh day Sabbath. Rather the Sabbath was a "perpetual Sabbath."[24] Justin later wrote to the Jewish apologist Trypho, saying, "circumcision was given to you as a sign, that you may be separated from other nations, and from us [Christians], and that you alone may suffer that which you now justly suffer, and that your land may be desolate, and your cities burnt with fire. These things have happened to you in fairness and justice" (*Dialogue with Trypho*, Chapter XVI). Again, Justine said to Trypho of the Bible, "your Scriptures, or rather not yours but ours, for you, though you read them, do not catch the spirit that is in them" (*Trypho*, XXIX).

170 C.E.   Irenaeus, who was said to be a disciple of Polycarp, held that the seventh day Sabbath was merely a *symbol* and belonged to the Jews.[25] Irenaeus later wrote: "the Jews, had they been cognisant (sic) of our [Christian] future existence, and that we should use these proofs from the Scriptures which declare that all other nations will inherit eternal life, but they who boast themselves as being the house of Jacob are disinherited from the grace of God, would never have hesitated themselves to burn their own Scriptures" (Irenaeus, *Contra Haereses*, III, XXI; P.G., VII, p. 946).

181 C.E.   Theophilus, bishop of Antioch from 168 to 181 C.E., in his letters to Autolycus, after addressing the story of creation and the flood, and after pointing out pagan ignorance of these events, adds, "and therefore it is proved that all others have been in error, and that **we Christians alone have possessed the truth**."[26] (Emphasis added.)

200 C.E.   Clement of Alexandria held that everything Jewish was old and presented the doctrines of Christianity as the only true religion.[27]

235 C.E.   Hippolytus left no doubt about his contempt for Jews, saying: "And surely you [Jews] have been darkened in the eyes of your soul with utter darkness and everlasting servitude.... Furthermore, hear this yet more serious word: 'And their back do you bend always.' This means in order that they may be slaves to the nations, not for four hundred and thirty years, as in Egypt, not seventy as in Babylon, bend them to servitude, he says, 'always'" (Hippolytus, *Treaties Against the Jews*).

240 C.E.   Tertullian taught that the seventh day Sabbath, the new moons, and appointed festivals belonged to the Jews; that the LORD's Day, Sun- Day, was *symbolic* of a *figurative* rest from sin and typical of man's final rest.[28] Tertullian maintained that it was the Jews who stirred up the pagan persecution of Christians, saying, "the synagogues were the seed- plot of all the calumny against Christians" (Tertullian, *de Spectaculis,* XXX; P.L., I, p. 662).

245 C.E.   Origin viewed the seventh day Sabbath, the appointed festivals, and Jewish customs as legalistic and belonging to the Jews only. For Origin, Christianity was the pure religion of God.[29] Origin, like Tertullian, held that it was the Jews who stirred up the persecution of Christians, saying that Celsus has acted "like the Jews, who when Christianity first began to be preached, scattered abroad false reports of the Gospel, such as that Christians offered up an infant in sacrifice, and partook of its flesh, and again that the professors of Christianity wishing to do the works of darkness used to extinguish the lights, and each one to have sexual intercourse with any woman he chanced to meet" (Tertullian *de Spectaculis,* xxx; P.L., I, p. 622). Commenting on the 37th Psalm, Origin later wrote: "the Jews do not vent their wrath on the Gentiles who worship idols and blaspheme God, and they neither hate them nor rage against them. But against Christians they rage with an insatiable fury" (Origin, *On Psalm XXXVI;* P.G., XII, p. 1322).

300 C.E. Eusebius, bishop of Caesarea ['Father of Church History'], who was a loyal supporter of the sun-worshiper Constantine, had no love for the Jews. In citing the historical relationship between the patriarchs Abraham, Isaac, and Jacob and Christians, Eusebius made a sharp distinction between Hebrews and Jews. He maintained that though they themselves were not Jews, neither were they Gentiles. Rather, says Eusebius, "from the beginning they were Christians, and led a Christian life."[30]

325 C.E. Lactantius, a pupil of Arnobius, wrote instructions in the Christian faith and refuted the seventh day Sabbath, new moons, and appointed festivals as defunct and belonging to the Jews. He defended the Christian faith in such elegant Latin that he was called "The Christian Cicero."[31]

340 C.E. Ambrose, the bishop of Milan and regarded as a Christian statesman by his peers, admitted to leading a group of Christians in the burning of a synagogue in Milan. In a letter to the Emperor Theodosius, he gave the reason, saying: "so that there might be no place where Christ is denied."[32]

345 C.E. John Chrysostom, the gifted bishop and orator of the Church in Antioch, who was no lover of the Jews or their Judaic faith, said: "I hate the Jews. For they have the Law and they insult it."[33] Chrysostom later added: "the fact that the Holy Books of the Law are to be found in the synagugues makes them more destable, for the Jews have simply introduced these Books, not to honour them, but to insult them, and dishonor them"; "the Jews do not worship God but devils, so that all their feasts are unclean"; "God hates them [Jews], and indeed has always hated them. But since the murder of Jesus He allows them no time for repentance"; "It was of set purpose that He concentrated all their worship in Jerusalem that He might more easily destroy it"; "It was not by their [Jews] power that the Caesars did what they did to you: it was done by the wrath of God, and His absolute rejection of you"; "It is childish in the face of this absolute rejection to imagine that God will ever allow the Jews to rebuild their Temple or to return to Jerusalem"; "When it is clear that God hates them, it is the duty of Christians to hate them too" (Chrysostom, *Against Judaizing Christians,* Ser. I, III, IV, V, VI).

350 C.E.   Macarius, a presbyter of Upper Egypt, spiritualized the seventh day Sabbath as a type and shadow of the true and eternal Sabbath, which is freedom from sin.[34]

360 C.E.   Hilary, the bishop of Poitiers, so disliked Jews that he would not even answer their greetings in the streets.[35] Hilary refers to the Jewish people as "that people which has always persisted in iniquity, and out of its abundance of evil has gloried in wickedness."[36]

365 C.E.   Athanasius held that the seventh day Sabbath and appointed festivals were Jewish and outdated. Among the Christians of his day, he was known as the champion of Christian truth.[37]

385 C.E.   Augustine, who championed the anti-Jewish teachings of the Heretic Marcion, believed that the Law was *done away* with the coming of Christ and maintained that the Christian Sabbath, Sun-Day, was derived from the resurrection of Christ, not from the Fourth Commandment.[38]

395 C.E.   Epiphanius, the only Jewish Christian bishop of the early Church, taught that the Christian Sabbath was an institution of the Apostles.[39]

400 C.E.   Jerome hated everything Jewish. "The Jews," he sneered, "run to the synagogue every day to study the Law, in their desire to know what Abraham, Isaac and Jacob and the rest of the holy men did, and to learn by heart the books of Moses and the prophets. I could not tell you how many Pharisaic traditions there are today, told by the Talmudists, and I do not know their old 'wives' tales. Many of them are so disgusting that I blush to mention them."[40]

The Anti-Semitism of the Christian Councils

By the beginning of the fourth century Catholic Church authorities had begun to convert their hatred for Jews into canon law. For example, at the Spanish pre-Constantinian council meeting at Elvira four of its canons stated: (1) intermarriage between Jews and Christian girls was prohibited, unless a Jew was willing to be converted; (2) adultery with Jewish women was prohibited; (3) neither cleric nor layman was to accept Jewish hospitality; and (4), Christians were forbidden to have their fields blessed by Jews. The penalty for disobedience was five years' abstinence from communion.[41] The Council of Antioch ruled that any cleric who celebrated Passover with Jews would be excommunicated.[42] Twenty years later the same ruling was made by the Council of Laodicea.

In addition, in the *"Apostolic Canons,"* which are a Syrian compilation, are found the following four edicts: (1) no bishop, presbyter or deacon, or any other member of the clergy is to share in a Jewish fast or feast, or to receive from them unleavened bread or other material for a feast; (2) no cleric or layman is to go into a synagogue of Jews to pray; (3) no Christian is to tend the lamps of Jewish synagogues on the feast days; and (4), if any cleric through fear of Jews, denies the name of Christ he is to be expelled: if it be his own rank which he denies and repents, he is to be received back as a layman.[43]

The Anti-Semitism of the Western Kingdoms

In the fifth and sixth centuries the Catholic Visigoths and Franks legislated the following anti-Jewish laws: (1) Christian doctrine is not to be criticized; (2) Passover and Jewish feasts are not to be observed; (3) Circumcision is prohibited; (4) Distinctions of meats and foods are prohibited; (5) Practice of Jewish customs are to be punished; (6) Jews are not to work on Sun-Day; (7) Jewish books and teaching is to be suppressed; (8) Jews are not to mix with Christians between Holy Thursday and Easter; (9) Jews, heathen and heretics are to be allowed into the church up to the missa catechumenorum; and (10) Children of Jews are to be brought up by Christians.[44]

The Anti-Semitism of the Antioch Christians

Within early Christianity, Antioch of Syria was celebrated as the first Gentile city Paul and Barnabas visited when they began their first missionary journey to the Gentiles, in 46 C.E. As earlier noted, Antioch was where Believers were first called Christians, in 59 C.E. Antioch was also the ancient city of two of Christianity's most celebrated Church Fathers, Ignatius (50-107 C.E.) and John Chrysostom (349-400 C.E.), who were elevated to "sainthood" by the Catholic Church.

Thus it was that Antioch became the center of Gentile Christianity, a city destined to take the Christian gospel to the peoples of the Orient and Western Asia. Yet, by the fifth century there was a strong hatred among the Antioch Christians against Antioch's Jewish inhabitants. Antioch Jews, who had already lost their synagogues during the reign of the Emperor Theodosius (378-395 C.E.), lost the synagogue of Daphne in an anti-Jewish riot of Christians, in 489 or 490 C.E.[45]

When the Christian Emperor Flavius Zeno (425-491 C.E.) heard that Christians had burned the bones of dead Jews, it is said that he scoffed at the thought, saying that burning the bones of dead Jews was a waste of time when there were so many Jews living in Antioch that could have better burned.[46]

Apparently, the synagogue of Daphne was rebuilt. Because it was destroyed twenty years later by Antioch Christians in another anti-Jewish riot.[47] This time the synagogue was lost to the Jewish people permanently. Christians took possession of their property and built a church over its ruins, and then dedicated it to the Christian martyr Leontius.[48]

During this same period, the Emperor Zeno persecuted both Jews and *Torah* observant Samaritians. According to Samaritian sources, Zeno went to Sichem, in Samaria, gathered the elders, and asked them to convert to Christianity. When they refused, Zeno had many of them killed, and rebuilt their synagogue as a church. He then built several Christian edifices on Mount Gerizim, the sacred mountain where Samaritians worshiped God, on which he put a cross.[49]

In 484 C.E., the Samaritans revolted. They attacked Sichem, and burned the five Christian edifices Zeno had built on Samaritian holy places. Zeno personally went to Samaria to quell the rebellion. Shortly afterward he died, on April 9, 491 C.E.[50] According to popular legend, Zeno was buried alive after becoming insensible from either drinking or an illiness. It is said that his sarcophagus was not allowed to be opened as he cried out for help.[51]

The Church Timeline

100 C.E. By the second century the Church had become predominately Gentile in membership and almost exclusively so in leadership. Justin refers to a few Gentile Christians who, from weakness, still observed the Law, but he states that other Christians would not have intercourse whatever with such individuals (Justin, *Trypho,* Ch. xlvii). By 100 C.E., the compromise in Acts 15 had no further validity, as Jerome and Augustine later agree.[52]

110 C.E. Early historical records inform us that the first antinomians ['against the Law'] were Marcionites. The ringleader, Marcion, was a Gnostic Christian who hated everything Jewish. In the report of Irenaeus, Polycarp is said to have met Marcion in Rome, and being asked by him: "Dost thou know me?" Polycarp answered: "I know the first-born of Satan."[53]

139 C.E. Marcion went to Rome and presented his anti-Jewish gospel to the congregation. He gave the congregation 200,000 sesterces. After reading Marcion's revision of the Apostolic Writings the congregation gave back the money and excommunicated him from their fellowship, ruling Marcion to be a Heretic. Shortly after 139 C.E., due to the listing of "acceptable" writings according to Marcion, the Church was forced to begin the selection of which writings, circulating among congregations, would be authorized as holy Scripture.

160 C.E. Gentile congregations began to flourish and the doctrine of Replacement Theology began to take root, giving credibility to the notion that the Gentile Church had replaced the Jews as God's chosen people and that the *Torah* had been *done away* with the coming of Christ.

160-190 C.E. By the latter part of the second century independent congregations were uniting and calling themselves the Catholic ['Universal'] Church. Loosely organized congregations now became a closely knit corporate body with recognized leaders capable of defining faith and excommunicating all who did not accept Catholic dogma, Catholic traditions, and Catholic authority.

160-200 C.E. Under the leadership of Tertullian, new ideas opposing the *Torah* in the African congregations began springing up and were promoted by popular speakers, such as Bishop John Chrysostom, in Antioch of Syria.

185 C.E. Irenaeus of Lyons, writing in 185 C.E., represented the general Western feeling, portrayed the Roman church [the largest single Catholic church] as founded by Peter and Paul. Irenaeus further said: "It is a matter of necessity that every church should agree with this church."[54]

200 C.E. Most of the official canon of what came to be known as the New Testament was finalized by Church authorities

By 200 C.E., the Roman Church became the most influential center of the Western congregations – a position of which the Roman bishops made full use.

Those congregations which refused to accept the Roman Church's new role of leadership were excommunicated as rebellious assemblies.

250-257 C.E.   Church buildings began to be erected, when Roman persecution began to ease.[55]

300 C.E.   Baptism by immersion was changed to affusion [the act of pouring water upon or sprinkling]. Prayers for the dead became an established doctrine of the Roman Catholic Church.

306 C.E.   Constantine became the emperor of the Western provinces when his father Constantius died and his army proclaimed Constantine emperor.

312 C.E.   Constantine attacked and defeated his major rival in the West, Maxentius. The night before *Pontifex Maximus* Constantine was to face what is known as the Battle of Milvian Bridge he had a vision, or a dream, in which there appeared the Mithraic cross of light to him and the words "In this sign conquer".

The next day, October 28, 312 C.E., Constantine advanced behind a standard portraying the Mithraic cross of light. He was victorious in that battle, defeated his rival Maxentius, and united his subjects under the sign of the Mithraic cross of light, which had already decorated Roman battle standards for over one hundred years. The historian Durant says, "... to the worshiper of Mithra in Constantine's forces, the cross could give no offense, for they had long fought under a standard bearing a Mithraic cross of light."[56]

As a result of Constantine's victory, he became a strong supporter of Christianity and the Mithraic cross was adopted as a sacred symbol of the Roman Catholic Church, and later the Protestant churches.

Constantine's vision of the Mithraic cross of light at the Battle of Milvain Bridge.

Addressing the pagan origins of the cross the scholars of the *Encyclopedia Americana* (1945) write:

> The symbol of the cross was used throughout the world since the later Stone Age; Greek pre-Christian crosses were the tau and swastika; the cross first became a symbol of Christianity during the reign of Constantine.

The Arch of Constantine in Rome, located along the Via Triumphalis, erected to commemorate Constantine's victory over Maxentius at the Battle of Milvain Bridge.

313 C.E.   Constantine arranged a partnership with the Emperor Licinius, ruler of the Eastern provinces. They met in Milan and gave freedom of worship and equal rights to all religious groups. Constantine recognized the Church as a legal body with rights to hold property.

321 C.E.   Constantine abolished the Divine model of the seventh day of rest and decreed that all subjects of the Empire set aside Sun-Day, *"the venerable day of the Sun-god Mithra,"* as the official day of public rest and worship.

324 C.E.   Constantine defeated Licinius and became the sole ruler of the Roman Empire.

325 C.E.   The Council of Nicea convened, presided by Constantine, decreed under the penalty of death to anyone who adds or changes the creed of Nicea, which included the abolishment of Passover for "the more legitimate festival of Easter".

336 C.E.   The first mention of December 25 as the birth-date of Christ was recorded in an early Roman calendar. Williston Walker writes: "the date was influenced by the fact that December 25 was a great pagan festival, that of *Sol Invictus,* which celebrated the victory of light over darkness and the lengthening of the sun's rays at the winter solstice. The assimilation of Christ to the Sun god, as Sun of Righteousness, was wide spread in the fourth century and was furthered by Constantine's legislation on Sunday."[57]

339 C.E.   Pope Julius I proclaimed December 25 as the day to celebrate the birth of Jesus Christ.

341 C.E.   The Catholic Synod of Antioch ratified the Creed of Nicea.

354-430 C.E.   The Catholic Monk Augustine, who after his return to the Church became one of the four principle Latin Doctors of the Church, the others being Ambrose, Gregory the Great, and Jerome, championed the anti-*Torah* ideas of Marcion. Philip Schaff says: "Augustine struggled from the Manichaean heresy into catholic orthodoxy.... Augustine put the church above the Word, and established the principle of catholic tradition."[58]

363 C.E.   The Catholic Synod of Laodecia ratified Constantine's Sun-Day Edict.

375 C.E.   The veneration of angels and dead saints is instituted.

378 C.E.   Demasus, bishop of Rome, was elected *"Pontifex Maximus"* or "Supreme Pontiff"– the high priest of the mysteries. This title gained recognition for Demasus from the pagans and, again, there was opportunity to blend Christianity with the mysteries of Mithraism.

382 C.E. Jerome was commissioned by Pope Damasus I to make a revision of old Latin translations. Jerome's Latin Vulgate Bible became the definitive and officially promulgated Latin version of the Bible of the Roman Catholic Church. Repudiating the Jewishness

Jerome

of the Scriptures, Jerome wrote: "For the grace of the Law which hath passed away we have received the abiding grace of the Gospel; for the shadows and figures of the Old Testament we have the Truth of Jesus Christ" (Jerome, *Adv. Pelog.* I. 31, P.L. XXIII).

383 C.E. The Roman Emperor Theodosius made Christianity the State religion of the empire, and Church membership compulsory.[59]

Shortly afterwards, Civil and Church authorities joined together to stamp out everything Jewish from Christianity, thereby, making anyone who observed the Sabbath and appointed festivals enemies of the church. Philip Schaff writes: "Before the union of church and state ecclesiastical excommunications was an extreme penalty. Now banishment and afterwards even death were added, because all offenses against the church were regarded as at the same time crimes against the state and civil society.[60]

394 C.E. The "Sacrament of the Mass" is instituted.

431 C.E. The worship of Mary is instituted. Mary is given the title "Queen of Heaven," which is the very same title of the pagan goddess worshiped by the ancient Israelites (Jer. 7:18). Mary is worshiped as the "ever virgin" and the "Mediatrix".

The Pope proclaimed that he possessed the keys of authority given to the Apostle Peter (Matt. 16:19). During that same year, crosses were introduced in churches.

432 C.E.   Pope Sixtus III proclaimed December 25 the official date for Christ's Mass ['Christmas'].

500 C.E.   Catholic priests began to dress in priestly garb.

526 C.E.   The Sacrament of Extreme Unction is instituted.

538 C.E.   The seventh day Sabbath is decreed by the Council of Orleans as belonging strictly to the Jews.

586 C.E.   The crucifix image was sanctioned by the church of Rome.

593 C.E.   The doctrine of Purgatory is instituted by Pope Gregory the Great.

600 C.E.   The Latin language is the only language permitted by the Catholic Church for prayer.

700 C.E.   Kissing the feet of the Pope is ordered.

750 C.E.   The Temporal Power of the Pope is proclaimed.

754 C.E.   The Council of Constantinople ordered removal of all images and abolished image worship.

785 C.E.   Mary co-Redemptrix is instituted.

788 C.E.   Worship of the cross, relics, and images are re-authorized.

789 C.E.   Charlemagne decreed that all labor on Sun-Day was a violation of the Third Commandment.

790 C.E.	The idea of *replacing* the Divine model seventh day Sabbath with Sun- Day began to be viewed by local congregations as an "institution of *"divine positive law"*.
835 C.E.	After the *All Hallows Festival* was moved to November 1, Pope Gregory IV officially authorized it to coincide with the pagan Feast of the Dead, which began on October 31.
850 C.E.	The sacrament of Holy Water is instituted.
890 C.E.	The veneration of Joseph, the husband of Mary, is proclaimed.
965 C.E.	Baptism of the bells is instituted.
995 C.E.	The canonization of the dead is instituted.
998 C.E.	Fasting on Friday and during Lent is instituted.
1079 C.E.	The celibacy of the priesthood is declared.
1190 C.E.	Rosary Prayer Beads are instituted. During this same year the sale of Indulgences is instituted.
1198 C.E.	Pope Innocent III issued a decree that all who read the Bible should be put to death.
1215 C.E.	The doctrine of Trans-substantiation is instituted.
1220 C.E.	The adoration of the Wafer Host is instituted.
1229 C.E.	The Council of Tolouse passed a decree forbidding either the possession or reading of the Bible, as did also the Council of Trent.
1302 C.E.	Pope Boniface VIII issued his famous bull *Unam sanctam*, the claim to supremacy over civil powers. It affirmed that

temporal powers are subject to the spiritual authority, which is judged by the Pope alone.

1309 C.E. Pope Clement V canceled Boniface's *Unam sanctam* decree to please King Philip IV, of France.

1380 C.E. John Wycliffe was the first person to translate the Bible into English, which was based on Jerome's Latin Vulgate Bible. Although Wycliffe's ideas stressed the Church's incompatibility with the teachings of Christ and the Apostles, he nevertheless, was heavily influenced by Augustine's anti-*Torah* theology.

John Wycliffe

1450 C.E. The Jubilee Year was adapted by Church authorities for the purpose of binding the European nations closely to Rome and stir up a renewed sense of devotion to the Mother Church, which had grown cold during the ecclesiastical disputes of nearly a century.

1505 C.E. In 1505, Martin Luther joined the monastic order of the Augustinian emites, where he was heavily influenced by Augustine's anti-*Torah* theology. Like Augustine, Luther believed that the *Torah* had been *done away* with the coming Christ.

Martin Luther+

1506 C.E. Pope Julius II demolished the Old St. Peter's Basilica and began the work of rebuilding the church. It was completed in 1626. The court yard is designed as a circular chariot wheel, with the obelisk of Caligula standing erect in the center as its axel. Drawn on the cement floor of the court yard are actual spokes protruding from the obelisk ['axel'] to the rim of the wheel. The circular sun-image of a chariot wheel is often designed as a stained glass window that is placed above the altar, or is a very *common* design above the entrances of Catholic churches.

St. Peter's Basilica

1508 C.E.   The doctrine of Mary "Mother of God" is proclaimed.

1514 C.E.   Miles Coverdale the first man to print the Scriptures in English, was ordained a Catholic priest and later entered the Augustine Monastery at Cambridge where he was heavily influenced by Augustine's anti- *Torah* theology. Like Augustine, Coverdale believed that the *Torah* had been *done away* with the coming of Christ, and Israel had been replaced by the Church as the *new Israel*.

1517 C.E.   Martin Luther nailed his Ninety-Five Theses on the doors of the castle-church at Wittenberg, at twelve o'clock on

October 31, 1517. As the Father of the ultimate division between Protestant and Roman Catholics, Luther's most celebrated contribution was his elaboration on the doctrine of justification by faith alone.

Luther's Ninety-Five Theses attacked the abuses within the Roman Catholic Church – notably the loose life of the clergy, their excessive wealth, neglect of their spiritual duties, and the sale of indulgences – which intensified after Luther's protest in 1517 and his subsequent attacks on the supremacy of the Pope.

Luther retained the weekly communion as the conclusion of the regular service on the Lord's Day.[61] As for the Eucharist sacrament, Luther insisted on the real presence of Christ's body, "corporally existed in space," in the visible bread.[62] Yet, he held that the bread and wine was not "changed" into the body and blood of Christ. He reduced the number of church festivals and kept those of the Catholic Church which commemorated Christ's birth, death, and resurrection, such as the Incarnation [Christ's Mass/Christmas], Palm Sun-Day, Good Friday, Easter, and Pentecost. Luther held that church festivals, and even the Christian Sabbath, were abolished in principle, and observed only on account of the requirements of public worship and the weakness of the laity.[63] For Luther, the righteous [*i.e.,* justified] need no laws and ceremonies. For the justified, all the time is holy, every day is a day of rest, and every day a day of good work.[64]

1536 C.E.   The French Roman Catholic theologian John Calvin endorsed Augustine's anti-*Torah* theology in his comprehensive statement of Protestant beliefs, *The Institutes of Christian Religion.* While Calvin believed that the standard set before

John Calvin

the Christian is the Law of God, as contained in the Hebrew Scriptures,[65] he was, nevertheless, true to many of the Augustinian doctrines of the Catholic Church. Calvin held that the Church, comprised of Jews and Gentiles, had replaced the physical children of Israel as *"spiritual Israel,"* in Romans 11:26.[66] At one point in his writings, Calvin says: "I have had much conversation with many Jews: I have never seen either a drop of piety or a grain of truth or ingenuousness–nay, I have never found common sense in any Jew" (*Institutes* II. 11. 10)..

Philip Schaff says of Calvin: "Calvin's moral power extended over all the Reformed Churches, and over several nationalities – Swiss, French, German, Polish, Bohemian, Hungarian, Dutch, English, Scotch, and American. His religious influence upon the Anglo-Saxon race in both continents is greater than that of any native Englishman, and continues to this day."[67] Schaff concludes by saying: "Luther and Calvin learned much from Augustine, and esteemed him higher than any human teacher since the Apostles."[68]

1545 C.E.   The Roman Catholic Church convened the Council of Trent in the Austrian Tyrol and proclaimed that "the worship of sacrifice was not to cease in the Church, and that in the Eucharist or Mass a true and proper sacrifice is offered to God."[69] A curse was pronounced by the Council on any who believed otherwise, stating: "If any one saith that in the Mass a true and proper sacrifice is not offered to God... let him be anathema."[70]

In 1545, Church tradition is proclaimed to be equal with Scripture.

1580 C.E.   The Pope is proclaimed "Lord God".

1586 C.E.   Caligula's obelisk, which was brought from Egypt to Rome in 34- 41 C.E., was moved to its present location in St. Peter's court yard by the order of Pope Sixtus V.

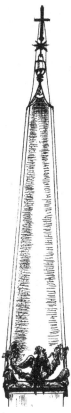

St. Peter's Obelisk in front of St. Peter's Basilica

In ancient times, for *pillars* to carry out their intended symbolism they were placed upright – *erect* – pointing upward to the hot Asian circular sun. The Christian Bible scholar C. I. Scofield says that these erected pillars were a symbol of those "given over to phallic cults."[71] The Christian author Sanger Brown says, "The usual explanation of the obelisk is that it ... substantiates rather than refutes the phallic interpretation.... Indeed, there is evidence to show that the spires of our churches owe their existence to the uprights or obelisks outside the temples of former ages."[72]

Echoing the same sentiment, Lillian Eichler says in her book entitled *The Customs of Mankind:* "There are still in existence today remarkable specimens of original phallic symbols steeples ... on the churches ... and obelisks ... all show the influence of our Phallus-worshipping ancestors. ... We know now that Christianity did not flash upon the world in a finished state, but grew up step by step in the process of evolution and adapted itself from many forms of worship. Many of its sacred symbols were borrowed from pagan peoples."[73]

1855 Catholic Church   1925 Methodist Church
[Reproduction of churches in downtown Marysville, California.]

Notice the sun symbol of the circular window above the entrances of the above illustrated Catholic and Methodist churches. The circular window that is so commonly used above entrances to churches is sometimes called a 'wheel' window. In antiquity, sun-worshipers believed the wheel design to be a symbol of a *chariot.* They saw the sun as a great *chariot,* which the Sun-god drove across the heavens with arrival of each new day, and passed through the underworld each night. When the ancient

Israelites blended their worship of God with the worship of Moloch, they had dedicated *"chariots* of the sun with fire" (2 Kings 23:4-11).

The horned Sun-god riding a chariot pulled by two horned bulls.

1816 C.E.   Pope Pius VII denounced Bibles as "pestilences".

1844 C.E.   Pope Gregory XVIII condemned Bible societies and ordered priests to tear up all the Bibles they could find.

1854 C.E.   The Immaculate Conception of the Virgin Mary is instituted.

1864 C.E.   Mary is declared to be sinless.

1870 C.E.   The doctrine of Papal Infallibility is instituted.

During the Vatican Council of 1870, on January 9, it was decreed: "The Pope is Christ in office, Christ in jurisdiction and power... we bow down before thy voice, O Pius, as before the voice of Christ, the God of truth; in clinging to thee, we cling to Christ."

1922 C.E.   The Pope is proclaimed to be Jesus Christ.

[The above Catholic dogma is taken from the Catholic Encyclopedia.]

Chapter 8

THE INTERPRETATION
OF SCRIPTURE

*Simply stated, the task of interpreters of the Bible is to find out
the meaning of a statement (command, question) for the author
and for the first hearers or readers, and thereupon to transmit the
meaning to modern readers.*

A. Berkeley Mickelsen

The primary problem that arises with an analysis of the Scriptures
is that previous analysis have generally ignored the use of Replacement
Theology as a factor in the transmission of one Greek manuscript to
another. Such analysis ignore the fact that Christian scribes and translators
have subtracted words, added words, and even changed the tenses of words
in the ancient Greek manuscripts. Many of these changes were human
errors made during the transmission of one manuscript to another. Others,
however, were deliberate changes made to bring passages of Scripture in
harmony with the doctrines of the Church.

The history of the transmission and translation of the ancient Hebrew
and Greek manuscripts is long and complex, as well as one of the least
understood. For this reason, it behooves the serious student to have a basic
understanding of the history that surrounds the transmission of ancient
biblical manuscripts.

One of the oldest translations of the Scriptures is the *Septuagint,* which
is the term used for the Greek translation of the Hebrew Scriptures. The
word *Septuagint* means "seventy" and refers to the seventy ['or seventy-two']

Jewish translators reputed to have produced a Greek version of the first five books of the Hebrew Scriptures during the time of Ptolemy II Philadelphus (285-246 B.C.E.).

According to tradition, King Ptolemy wanted to enhance his library with a translated Greek copy of the *Torah* of Moses. So he sent ambassadors to Eleazar, the high priest in Jerusalem, requesting him to send a Hebrew copy of the *Torah,* with Jewish scholars who could translate the Hebrew text into Greek. It is said that Eleazar selected six elders from each of the twelve tribes well versed in Jewish law and sent them to Alexandria, Egypt.

Some believe the seventy ['or seventy-two'] Jewish scholars went to Alexandria to translate the *Torah* into Greek because at that time Alexandria was a major Jewish center of Hellenism and many Jews had forgotten their Hebrew language and wanted to understand the *Torah,* on which their faith depended. According to Justin Martyr, who lived in the middle of the second century, the seventy elders not only translated the *Torah* of Moses [*i.e.,* the first five books of the Hebrew Scriptures] into Greek but also the entire Tanakh ['Jewish Bible'].[1]

Tradition holds that Ptolemy feared that the Jewish translators might conspire among themselves not to translate all the sacred text of the *Torah.* So Ptolemy put them in separate cubicles and ordered them each to write a translation of the ancient Scriptures, which were based upon the earliest Hebrew texts that go back about 1,000 years to the Masoretes, who lived in the Galilee area of Israel between the seventh and eleventh centuries. When the translations were completed and read before the king they were found to be identically the same, with the same words and same names, from beginning to end.

In the second century the Greek apologist Irenaeus wrote about it in his treaties entitled *Against Heresies,* saying, "So that even the pagans who were present recognized that the scriptures had been translated through the inspiration of God."[2]

The significance of the translation of Hebrew Scriptures into the Greek *Septuagint* cannot be overstated. From the time of its completion the *Septuagint* became the standard text for Greek speaking Jews and Gentiles of the world, as well as for the Apostles and first century community of Believers. That the *Septuagint* was used by the Apostles is evident from the many passages quoted in their Writings to the different congregations scattered throughout Asia Minor.

By the first century there were several different Greek translations of the *Septuagint,* which had faults much like any other translation. Nevertheless, because many Jewish and Gentile converts spoke Greek and not Hebrew, the *Torah* and, most likely, the Prophets and Writings, beginning with the Psalms, were the primary sources of Scripture upon which their faith was established.

The distinguished textual scholar Bruce Metzger says of this important period:

> By the end of the first century of the Christian era, more and more Jews ceased using the Septuagint because the early Christians had adopted it as their own translation. At an early stage, the belief developed that this translation had been divinely inspired, and hence the way was open for several church fathers to claim that the Septuagint presented the words of God more accurately than the Hebrew Bible. The fact that after the first century very few Christians had any knowledge of the Hebrew language meant that the Septuagint was not only the church's main source of the Old Testament but was, in fact, its only source.[3]

The Historical Development of Ancient Manuscripts

Until the fourth century the writing material in common use was papyrus, made of slices of a water reed that grew abundantly in Egypt. Two slices, one vertical, the other horizontal, were pressed together and polished with a smooth stone. Single sheets were used for short writings. For longer writings, papyrus sheets were fastened side by side to form scrolls. The ink used to write was made of charcoal, gum, and water.

In the early second century Greek manuscripts began to be made in "codex" form, where sheets were folded in the middle, sewing them together to form a book, with numbered pages. The codex could be opened and read one leaf at a time. Whereas the scroll was a long sheet of written papyrus twisted into a roll that had to be unrolled with two hands and held in place with both hands to be read.

Because papyrus sheets were made of dried reeds, they became brittle with age, or rotted with dampness and soon wore out. This problem was compounded by the ink used for writing, which faded and became unreadable with time and use. Within a short period of time all the original *inspired* and *inerrant* Writings of the Apostles were lost because the original papyrus Greek manuscripts were not very durable and wore out.

In the fourth century papyrus was superseded by refining the skins of animals, which were much more durable. This form of writing material continued until the fifteenth century, when printing was invented.

During the first few centuries, when the *Septuagint* was copied by hand, there were so many mistakes, changes, and attempts to harmonize passages that copies soon came to differ with one another. By the third century C.E. (AD), the text became so unreliable that Origin made an attempt to correct the many mistakes and changes in a monumental work called the *"Hexapl"*. Other translations of the Hebrew Scriptures into Greek occurred in the fourth century, one of which is attributed to Lucian, a presbyter at Antioch, who is credited by many scholars as being instrumental in the formation of a much later Greek text called the *Textus Receptus*.

In time, Talmudic rabbis regretted the translation of the Hebrew Scriptures into the *Septuagint,* stating that the translation of the *Torah* into Greek was as much a tragedy for the Jewish faith as the making of the Golden Calf.[4]

The Transmission of Ancient Greek Texts

Although the facts are unknown, scholars believe that it is quite possible that all of today's surviving copies came from a single errorless copy made at the beginning of the original book's use and circulation. As the needs for additional copies multiplied with the addition of new congregations, so did the errors of the untrained copyists.

By the early second century virtually all the Epistles that were eventually accepted as Scripture had been copied and made available to congregations in different regions of Asia Minor. Bruce Metzger writes: "there is good evidence to indicate that in the early decades of transmission numerous changes were made in texts in circulation: as entire words or entire lines came to be left out inadvertently or inadvertently copied twice, stylistic changes were made, words were substituted for one another, evident infelicities or outright mistakes were corrected, and so on."[5] Dr. Metzger goes on to say:

It is a striking feature of our textual record that the earliest copies we have of the various books that became the New Testament vary from one another far more widely than do the later copies, which were made under more controlled circumstances in the Middle Ages. Moreover, the quotations of the New Testament by early church fathers evidence a wide array of textual variation during these earliest stages in the history of transmission.[6]

Addressing this same early period, the Greek textual scholar J. Harold Greenlee, professor of New Testament Language at Asbury Theological Seminary, writes in his book entitled *New Testament Textual Criticism:*

> The early period is likewise the period of the rise of what may be called "local texts," a factor which is inter-related with the multiplication of variants. Copies of the N.T. books were carried to various localities by the Christians, each ms. containing its own characteristic textual variants. These mss. would then be further copied, with the resulting copies tending to contain the characteristic variants of the parent ms. plus some additional errors. In this manner, over a period of time the mss. circulating in a given locality would tend to resemble each other more nearly than they would resemble the mss. of any other locality. Even with one locality, however, virtually no two mss. would be identical; and certain groups of mss., while sharing the common "local text," would resemble other mss. of the same local text. To complicate matters, a mss. of one locality might be compared with a mss. of another locality and corrected by it, producing a "mixed" text.[7]

Some of the human errors that were made in the transmission of manuscripts were caused by faulty eyesight, faulty hearing when the text was being read to copyists, faulty memory when a copyist was looking at a manuscript and trying to remember the precise word he was copying,

Christian Scribe at work.

errors of judgment by copyists who did not properly understand the many variations of Greek grammar, and errors of spelling.[8]

There were also intentional errors, such as harmonistic changes [*i.e.,* the altering of a passage to make it harmonize with other passages], additions, the replacing historical and geographical data with a generalized statement, grammatical and linguistic changes, liturgical changes, the incorporation of two passages given differently in two or more manuscripts into one copy, and intentional doctrinal changes.[9]

Scholars agree that most of the human and intentional errors were left in Jerome's Latin Vulgate. Dr. Metzger says, "In revising the corrupt Old Latin text of the Gospels, Jerome was apprehensive lest he be censured for making even the slightest alteration in the interest of accuracy–a fear that events proved to be well founded!"[10]

During the second half of the second century, at Antioch in Syria, another version of the Greek manuscripts was translated called the Syriac Version. By the end of the second century or early third century Syriac versions began to circulate among Syrian congregations.[11]

Earliest (nearly) complete manuscript of the Epistle of Paul.

For many scholars the Syrian version is considered to be the best among the ancient translated versions. Since the nineth century the Syrian Bible, based on the ancient Syrian text, has been the primary version of the eastern churches. These include the Syrian Orthodox, Church of the East [or Chaldean Believers], Syrian Catholics, Malabar [or St. Thomas], and the Syro-Malankarese Church.[12] It is worthy to note that the Syrian text, also called the Antiochian Text, was used as the basis for the first editions of the early sixteenth century printed Greek New Testament. called the *Textus Receptus.*

In 382 C.E., Pope Damasus I (366-384 C.E.) commissioned Jerome to produce a better Latin translation. Jerome spent fifteen years translating Hebrew and Greek manuscripts into what became the Latin Vulgate Bible, which replaced old Latin manuscripts containing numerous errors and contradictions.[13]

The Christian textual scholar F. W. Farrar says of Jerome's practice of allegorization: "He flatters himself that he succeeded in steering safely between the Scylla of allegory and the Charybdis of literalism, whereas in reality his 'multiple senses' and 'whole forest of spiritual meanings' are not worth one verse of the original."[14]

Nevertheless, Jerome's Latin Vulgate Bible was so popular among Catholic scholars that it became the standard version of the Church for nearly 1,000 years. It later became the basis of the pre-Reformation vernacular versions, such as Wycliffe's English translation of the fourteenth century, as well as the first printed Bibles in German (1466), Italian (1471), Catalan (1478), Czech (1488), and French (1530).[15]

The Different Text Types

Among the Apostolic Writings/New Testament texts there are basically three text-types which have been preserved over the centuries from which all translations are taken: the *Western Text,* the *Alexandrian Text,* and the *Byzantine Text.*

The *Western Text,* found both in Greek manuscripts and in translations into other languages, especially Latin, goes back to around the third century. Dr. Metzger says: "The chief characteristic of Western readings is fondness of paraphrase. Words, clauses, and even whole sentences are freely changed, omitted, or inserted. Sometimes the motive appears to have been harmonization, while at other times it was the enrichment of the narrative by inclusion of traditional or apocryphal material."[16]

The fifth century *Alexandrian Text,* found in most papyri, is thought to have originated in Alexandria, Egypt. The *Alexandrian Text* is also found in the fourth century *Codex Vaticanus* and *Codex Sinaiticus,* which are considered by many scholars to be the oldest, best known, and most valuable manuscripts.

The integrity, however, of both the *Codex Vaticanus* and *Codex Sinaiticus* has been criticized by textual scholars. In the *Codex Vaticanus* words and whole phrases are repeated twice in succession or completely omitted. It is believed that some person or persons have gone over every letter in the manuscript with a pen, making many letters impossible to read.

In much the same manner, the *Sinaiticus,* which was discovered in part ['47 leaves'] in a waste paper basket at the monastery of St. Cathreine on Mount Sinai by Constantin von Tischendorf, in 1844, has been corrected and altered by as many as ten different writers. Yet, in spite of these well known altercations, the *Vaticanus* and *Sinaiticus* have been the basis for many modern versions, such as the New American Standard Version (NASV), the New International Version (NIV), and the 1881 Revised Version of the King James (RSV).[17]

Codex Sinaiticus   *Codex Vaticanus*

The Dean of Chichester Cathedral, John William Burgon (1813-1888), who was one of the most prominent critical scholars of the fourth century *Codex Sinaiticus [Aleph]* and *Vaticanus [Codex B],* writes:

As for the origin of these two curiosities, it can perforce only be divined from their contents. That they exhibit fabricated texts is demonstrable. No amount of honest copying – preserved in for any number of centuries – could by possibility have resulted in two such documents. Separated from one another in actual date by 50, perhaps by 100 years, they must needs have branched off from a common corrupt ancestor, and straightway become exposed to fresh depraving influences. We suspect that these two documents are indebted for their preservation, *solely to their ascertained evil character;* which has occasioned that the one eventually found its way, four centuries ago, to a forgotten shelf in the Vatican Library; while the other, after exercising the ingenuity of several generations of critical Correctors, eventually (viz. in A.D. 1844) got deposited in a wastepaper basket of the Convent at the foot of Mount Sinai.[18]

The *Byzantine Text* [also called the Ecclesiastical Text and Antiochian Text] is also called the Majority Text, simply because it has by far the largest number of surviving manuscripts. Shortly before the fourth century the Roman Empire was divided into two parts, the western Roman Empire and the eastern or Byzantine Empire. Within a century after this division the western Roman Empire came to an end, and western Europe sank into a state of barbarism.

From this point on Latin became the dominate language of Europe. The Byzantine Empire continued on, and for about 1,000 years the Greek language remained its official language. In western monasteries, between 400 C.E.-1453, Latin manuscripts, including the Latin Vulgate, were copied and recopied by the monks.

During this same period, in which the eastern Byzantine Church made its Apostolic See in Antioch, Greek manuscripts continued to be copied and recopied by monks until the invasion of the Byzantine Empire by the barbarians and Muslims. In the course of copying, mistakes were made, and no two manuscripts of the Greek manuscripts were the same. It is said that in order to correct copying errors of the Antiochian Text manuscripts were brought into harmony with one another, and where earlier manuscripts differed the readings were combined.

Shortly after the Edict of Milan, in 313 C.E., when Christianity was granted official religious status and sacred manuscripts no longer needed to be hidden for safety, Constantine ordered fifty new copies of the complete Bible to be made for the churches in Constantinople.

With the rise of Constantinople, as the center of the Greek speaking Church, the local text used became the primary text used throughout the Church. Dr. Greenlee says: "Approximately 95 percent of the existing mss. of the N.T. are from the eighth and later centuries, and very few of these differ appreciably from the Byzantine text."[19]

The next major translation event was the translation of the 1382 and 1388 Wycliffe Bible. John Wycliffe was a strong believer that a translation of the Scriptures should be made available to every person. This belief alone made Wycliffe a powerful enemy of Catholic authorities, who were eventually able to bring him to trial for heresy. At a court hearing held at Blackfriars, London, on May 21, 1382, Wycliffe's sermons and writings were condemned as heretical.

It is doubtful that Wycliffe himself took any direct part in translating the famous Wycliffe Bible. At that particular time Wycliffe's health was poor and he died at Lutterworth of a stroke on December 31, 1384.[20] It is believed that both translations were produced by his colleagues and pupils, John Purvey and Nicholas of Hereford.[21]

Dr. Metzger tells us that the first translation of the Wycliffe Bible produced, in 1382 [Early Version], "was extremely literal, corresponding word for word to the Latin."[22] Whereas the second version, which appeared in 1388 [Later Version], expressed the native English language throughout the text. Both translations were based on Jerome's Latin Vulgate and therefore, included the Vulgate Old Testament aprocryphal/deuterocanonical books.[23]

The *Textus Receptus* [Latin, meaning 'text received'] is the name given to a succession of printed Greek texts of the New Testament. The *Textus Receptus* was based on the vast majority [90%] of the 5,300 surviving Greek manuscripts. The extant Greek manuscripts were brought together between the second and fifteenth centuries by various Catholic theologians and publishers, such as Lucian of Antioch (240-312 C.E.), Desiderius Erasmus (1466 -1536), Robert Estienne (1503-1559), Theodore de Beza (1519-1606), and the Elzevir brothers, Abraham (1592-1652) and Boniventure (1583-1652).

Lucian was best know for his revision of the *Septuagint* and Greek New Testament. It is believed that Lucian contributed much to the Antioch text-type Greek manuscripts, which were the basis for the *Textus Receptus*.

In 1516, the Augustinian Catholic priest Desiderius Erasmus produced the first Greek text of the New Testament. It was followed by another in 1519, which was the primary source used by Martin Luther in his translation of the German Luther Bible (1534), as well as other translations of the Reformation Era.

Among Bible scholars, the *Textus Receptus* is often called the "text of the Reformation" or the "text of the Reformers"[24] and therefore, the foundation on which the Protestant movement was established.

In July of 1515, Erasmus went to Basle in hopes of find Greek manuscripts that were good enough to use as copies for the Greek printed text along with a Latin Vulgate text that he had extensively revised. To

Erasmus' amazement, the only manuscripts available required considerable correcting before they could be used as a printer's copy. Erasmus later wrote:

> But one thing the facts cry out, and it can be clear, as they say, even to a blind man, that often through the translator's clumsiness or inattention the Greek has been wrongly rendered; often the true and genuine reading has been corrupted by ignorant scribes, which we see happen every day, or altered by scribes who are half-taught and half-asleep.[25]

On the basis of these findings, Erasmus drew from only about six Greek manuscripts in his 1516 edition, all of which dated from the tenth century and later, and only one which was not of the Byzantine or Antioch text-type. In some parts of the New Testament he had no Greek manuscripts at all, but simply re-translated from the Latin Vulgate. It is said that when Erasmus was criticized for his reliance on the Greek instead of Latin he protested that he was simply following the Greek text, and challenged his critics to "produce a Greek manuscript that has what is missing in my edition."[26]

Robert Estienne, known as Stefanus, a Catholic printer from Paris, who later converted to Protestantism, published four editions of the Greek New Testament, dating from 1546 through 1549, 1550 and lastly 1551. Dr. Metzger informs us that Stefanus' "third edition (1550) approaches more closely the text of Erasmus' fourth and fifth editions."[27] Interestingly, it was Stefanus' third edition (1550) that was used in the translation of the King James Version (1611).

Theodore Beza published several editions of the Greek New Testament. Five were published in 1565, 1582, 1588-89, and 1598. The Christian textual scholar James R. White writes:

> Beza drew from Stephanus' listing of variant readings and added many more of his own, drawing from important manuscripts in his possession.... While following Stephanus' editions closely, Beza did introduce changes based upon his own textual expertise. Some of these were "conjectural emendations," that is, changes made to the text without any evidence from the manuscripts. A few of these changes made it into the KJV...."[28]

Dr. Metzger informs us that Beza's 1565, 1582, 1588-89, and 1598 editions "contain a certain amount of textual information drawn from several Greek manuscripts that Beza had collected himself, as well as Greek manuscripts collated by Henry Stephanus, the son of Robert Stephanus."[29]

In this respect, Beza's 1588-89 editions differed very little from Stephanus' 1551 edition. The significance of Beza's work is that it popularized the *Textus Receptus,* and in 1611 the King James translators relied heavily upon Beza's editions of 1588-89 and 1598.[30]

In January 1604, King James I convened the Hampton Court Conference for the purpose of commissioning a new English version that would correct the textual problems of earlier translations. King James gave 54 scholars, all of whom were members of the Sun-Day Church of England, "instructions designed to guarantee that the new version would conform to the ecclesiology and reflect the episcopal structure of the Church of England and its beliefs about an ordained clergy."[31]

In 1624 the Elzevir brothers, Abraham and Boniventure, published their first Greek New Testament, which was based on the printed Greek New Testament of Erasmus. As earlier noted, Erasmus' fourth and fifth editions were the basis for Stephanus' 1550-51 editions and Beza's 1588-89 editions.

Building upon these works, in 1633, the Elzevir brothers published a second edition of the Greek New Testament in Holland. In the Latin preface of the 1633 edition, they called their book "the text which is now received by all, in which we give nothing changed or corrupted." This is how the Latin term *Textus Receptus* ['text received'] came to be applied to a particular text of the Greek New Testament.

On the European continent, aside from Great Britain, the first Elzevir edition (1624) was for many years the standard edition of the Greek New Testament. But there was a problem with the popular *Textus Receptus.* It contained numerous errors. The textual scholar James R. White writes in his book entitled *The King James Only Controversy:*

> The amazing thing is that these errors *continue* in the
> *Textus Receptus* to this very day. Why Erasmus did not change
> these errors at a later time, we cannot say.... Even more mind-
> boggling is the fact that these errors then survived the editorial
> labors of Stephanus and Beza, to arrive unchanged in the hands

of the KJV translators, and subsequently ended up in the King James Version.[32]

Addressing the need for a better Greek New Testament, Dr. Metzger writes:

> For almost two centuries scholars ransacked libraries and museums, in Europe as well as the Near East, for witnesses to the text of the New Testament. But almost all of the editors during this period were content to reprint the time-honored but corrupt Textus Receptus....[33]

In 1881, the British Greek scholar Brooke Foss Westcott (1825-1901), and Irish theologian Fenton John Anthony Hort (1828-1892) produced two volumes entitled *The New Testament in the Original Greek.* At that time their work was celebrated as the best Greek Testament ever produced. Bishop Westcott of Durham, who was also a professor of Divinity in the University of Cambridge, and Fenton Hort maintained that the Byzantine or Syrian text-type, on which the *Textus Receptus* is based, is filled with "interpolations" ['insertions of words'], most of them due to harmonistic or other assimilations.[34] At the same time, they defended the *Netural Text,* which includes the fourth century *Codex Sinaiticus [Aleph]* and *Codex Vaticanus [B],* on which their 1881 *New Testament in the Original Greek* was based. Wescott and Hort write:

> It is our belief (1) that the readings of the Aleph B should be accepted as the true readings until strong internal evidence is found to the contrary, and (2) that no readings of Aleph B can safely be rejected absolutely...."[35]

These claims of Westcott and Hort were not without their critics. Dr. Metzger says, "the publication in 1881 of the Revised Version of the King James, or Authorized Version of 1611 aroused Burgon's indignation not only on the score of its unidiomatic English but even more because the revisors had followed an underlying Greek text substantially identical with that of Westcott and Hort."[36]

John Burgon insisted that with the exception of manuscript D, which he considered the most corrupt of all the manuscripts, the *Sinaiticus [Aleph]* and *Vaticanus [B]*, the two manuscripts honored by Westcott and Hort, were by far the most depraved, saying:

> ... without a particle of hesitation, that Aleph B D are
> three of *the most scandalously* corrupt copies extant:– exhibit
> *the most shamefully mutilated* texts which are anywhere to be
> met with:–have become, by whatever process (for their history
> is wholly unknown), the depositions of the largest amount of
> *fabricated readings,* ancient *blunders,* and *intentional perversions
> of Truth,–* which are discoverable in any known copies of the
> Word of God.[37]

So here we see distinguished Christian scholars from both camps, those of the *Textus Receptus* camp, and those of the fourth century *Codex Vaticanus* and *Codex Sinaiticus* camp, vilifying the integrity of each other's choice of Greek manuscripts used to translate the Scriptures into what we know today as the Holy Bible.

The Integrity of the Hebrew Scriptures

When it comes to the integrity of ancient Hebrew manuscripts, on which the Tanakh/Old Testament is based, the integrity of the Scriptures is a whole different matter. As earlier noted, the earliest Hebrew texts go back about 1,000 years to the Masoretic text. When the Dead Sea scrolls were found we then had texts going back to about 200 B.C.E., before the birth of *Yeshua*. Even Christian scholars agree that with very minor exceptions, the Masoretic text and the Dead Sea scrolls are identical.

After some twenty-two hundred years of silence, in 1947, a contemporary witness to the credibility of the Hebrew Scriptures came to light. A Bedouin boy herding goats made one of the greatest discoveries of modern history. One day while in the wilderness at the northwest end of the Dead Sea, he threw a stone after one of his flock that had taken refuge in a cave. Hearing the sound of breaking pottery, the young Bedouin climbed into the cave and found several jars containing manuscripts wrapped in cloth.

Qumran cave 4, in which ninety percent of the scrolls were found.

A portion of the discovered copy of the Isaiah scroll.

According to the report, the young boy took the scrolls to a sheikh in Bethlehem. The sheikh saw that the writing was unfamiliar and sent them to a merchant who could read Syriac. He, in turn, sent them to another friend who recommended them to the archbishop of Jerusalem. The archbishop examined the manuscripts and realized that they were not Syriac but Hebrew, and offered to buy them. After some delay, the archbishop purchased five scrolls. A third Bedouin, who claimed some of them, sold his elsewhere.

The largest and finest of these manuscripts proved to be a copy of Isaiah almost two thousand years older than any previously known. There was also a commentary on Habakkuk, two sections of the *Manual of Discipline* and other writings, one of which proved to be a commentary on Genesis. The interest initiated by the discovery of the Bedouin boy led to multiplied discoveries of ancient Hebrew manuscripts in the caves at Wadi Qumran.

Scholars agree that the consistency of the many copies of the Hebrew Scriptures remains without discrepancy because these Scriptures were copied with a reverent fear by Jewish scribes. Josephus writes:

> We have given practical proof of our reverence for our Scriptures. For, although such long ages have now passed, no one has ventured either to add, or to remove, or to alter a

syllable; and it is an instinct with every Jew, from the day of his birth, to regard them as the decrees of God, to abide by them, and, if need be, cheerfully die for them. Time and again ere now the sight has been witnessed of prisoners enduring tortures and death in every form in the theaters, rather than utter a single word against the laws and the allied documents' (Joseph, *Against Apion* 1.42f.).

In making this statement, Josephus is merely acknowledging the attitude of the biblical writers themselves, which is found in passages as Deut. 4:2: "Do not add to the Word which I command you, and do not take away from it, so as to guard the commands of [YHVH] your Elohim which I am commanding you," and Jer. 26:2: "... speak to all the cities of Yehudah... all the words that I command you to speak. Do not diminish a word" (*The Scriptures*).

For these reasons, over the centuries the purity of the Hebrew text has remained uncorrupted.

The Varient Readings of Greek Manuscripts

Today, there are about 5,300 handwritten Greek manuscripts of the New Testament that were copied from fragments of papyrus scrolls originally dating from the first half of the second century and third century, which a few containing two or three verses to nearly entire Bibles.

Affirming the findings of earlier textual scholars, the Messianic researcher Lew White tells us that every one of these handwritten copies differs from every other one.[38] White goes on to say, "there is not one sentence in the NT in which the manuscript is wholly uniform," which is due to "variants put in them deliberately," and "careless handling of the text," or "many created for theological or dogmatic reasons."[39]

The scholars of *Collier's Encyclopedia* inform us that "the variant readings, which thus originated are very numerous; if each variant in every manuscript is counted, the total is about 200,000."[40] The same writer goes on to say: "over 95 percent of the variants are without material significance in ascertaining the meaning of the text, and that by means of textual criticism scholars are able to determine with more or less probability the original text laying behind the remaining variants."[41]

Westcott and Hort indicate that only about one eighth of the variants had any weight, holding the rest to be "trivialities."[42] Philip Schaff estimates that there were only 400 variants that affected the sense of the NT, and only 50 of these were actually important. Schaff goes on to say that not one affected "an article of faith or a precept of duty which is not abundantly sustained by other and undoubted passages, or by the whole tenor of Scripture teaching."[43]

A. T. Robertson states that the textual variants amounted to but "a thousandth part of the entire text."[44] And the British textual scholar B. B. Warfield maintains that "the great mass of the New Testament, in other words, has been transmitted to us with no, or next to no variations."[45]

The Different Methods of Translating Scripture

For most Bible-translation scholars there are primarily three different methods of translation: (1) the *Formal Equivalency*, which is designed to give as *literal* translation as possible; (2) the *Dynamic Equivalency;* and (3) the *Paraphrase Equivalency*, which attempts to translate the meaning from a Greek manuscript into the English language, even when it involves sacrificing a word-for-word translation in the process. In this respect, the KJV and NASV are *Formal Equivalence* translations. The NIV is a *Dynamic Equivalence* translation. And the Amplified Bible is more of a paraphrase than a formal equivalent or dynamic equivalent approach.

There is a fourth method of translation, however, which has been employed over the centuries that is totally ignored by most theologians when addressing the various methods of translation. This writer calls it the *Replacement Equivalency* method, which either by intentional design or lack of understanding the Jewishness of the Scriptures, or an anti-Jewish bias, sanitizes the original Hebraic meaning of the Greek text and replaces it with another meaning.

How do we know that Catholic and Protestant translators employed the *Replacement Equivalence* method in the translation of Greek manuscripts? When we compare the words and passages in the 1611 KJV, the 1881 RSV, the NASV, and the NIV with the leading editions of the original Greek text as found in the Nestle-Aland *Novum Testamentum Graece* text and *Textus Receptus* text, it becomes evident that Protestant translators relied heavily on the 1388 Wycliffe Version, which was based on Jerome's anti-Jewish Latin Vulgate.

The widely accepted Nestle-Aland *Novum Testamentum Graece* text was prepared for the American Bible Society New York published by Wurttembergische Bibleanstalt (Stuttgart, 1898) and edited by Eberhard Nestle (1851-1913), Erwin Nestle (1883-1972), and Kurt Aland (1915-1994). It's text (since the 3rd ed., 1901) was based on a comparison of the texts edited by Tischendorf (1869-1872), Westcott and Hort (1881), and Bernhard Weiss (1894-1900). Where two of these three editions agreed, this was printed by the Nestle-Aland *Novum Testamentum Graece* Bible.

Dr. Bruce Metzger says of the Nestle-Aland *Novum Testamentum:* "The text of Nestle represented the state of nineteenth century scholarship; its apparatus, however, which is a marvel of condensation, supplies with a high degree of accuracy a great amount of textual information, including many early witnesses that were discovered during the twentieth century. Starting with the 26th edition of the Nestle-Aland *Novum Testamentum Graece* (1979), the text (though not the apparatus) is identical with that found in the *United Bible Societies' Greek New Testament.*"[46] Moreover, the Christian scholar J. B. Phillips states that the Nestle Greek text is "the most accurate Greek that we can arrive at."[47]

As you shall see, when comparing passages in the Latin Vulgate, 1388 Wycliffe Version, 1611 KJV, 1881 RSV, NASV, and NIV with the same passages in the Nestle-Aland *Novum Testamentum Graece,* as well as the *Textus Receptus,* it becomes evident that both Catholic and Protestant translators had a serious lack of understanding of the Jewishness of the Scriptures, as well as a distinct anti-Jewish bias.

The Sanitization of the Sabbath

Acts 20:6-8 is one of the passages often used by Christian theologians to establish that the reference in Acts 20:7 to "the first day of the week" is proof that Sun-Day had been marked by the as a special day for public worship. For example, the Bible expositor A. C. Hervey of the *Pulpit Commentary* writes: "**The first day of the week...** is an important evidence of the keeping of the Lord's day by the Church as a day for their Church assemblies."[48]

But was this what Luke really meant when he recorded this important event? Take a look the following translations of the 1611 KJV, 1881 RSV, NASV, and NIV translations of Acts 20:6-8 and note how similar they are to the 1388 Wycliffe Version, which is based on Jerome's anti-Jewish Latin Vulgate.

Jerome's 405 C.E. Latin Vulgate

English	Latin
But we sailed from Philippi after the days of the azymes and came to them to Troas in five days, where we abode seven days.	nos vero navigavimus post dies azmorum a Philippis et venimus ad eos Troadem in diebus quinque ubi demorati sumus diebus septem
And <u>on the first day of the week</u>, when we were assembled to break bread, Paul discoursed with them, being to depart on the morrow.	in una autem sabbati cum convenissemus ad frangendum panem Paulus disputabat eis profecturus in crastinum protraxitque
And he continued his speech until midnight. And there were a great number of lamps in the upper chamber where we were assembled.	sermonem usque in kmediam noctem erant autem lampades copiosae in cen cenaculo ubi eramus congregati (Acts of the Apostles XX).[49]

1388 Wycliffe Version

... for we shipped after the days of therf loaves from Philippi, and came to them at Troas in five days, where we dwelled seven days.

And <u>in the first day of the week</u> when we came to break bread, Paul disputed with them and should go forth in the morrow, and he drew along the sermon into midnight. And many lamps were in the solar where we were gathered together ("The Deeds of Apostles XX").[50]

1611 King James Version (KJV)

6 And we sailed away from Philippi after the days of unleavened bread, and came unto them to Troas in five days; where we abode seven days.

7 And <u>upon the first day of the week</u>, when the disciples came together to break bread, Paul preached unto them, ready to depart on the morrow; and continued his speech until midnight.

8 And there were many lights in the upper chamber, where they were gathered together (Acts 20:6-8).[51]

1881 Revised King James Version (RSV)

6 but we sailed away from Philippi after the days of Unleavened Bread, and in five days we came unto them at Troas, where we stayed for seven days.

7 <u>On the first *day* of the week</u>, when we were gathered together to break bread, Paul talked with them, intending to depart on the morrow; and he prolonged his speech until midnight.

8 There were many lights in the upper chamber, where we were gathered (Acts 20:6-8).[52]

New American Standard Version (NASV)

6 We sailed from Philippi to them at Troas within five days; and there we stayed seven days.

7 <u>On the first day of the week</u>, when we gathered together to break bread, Paul *began* talking with them, intending to leave the next day, and he prolonged his message until midnight.

8 There were many lamps in the upper room where we were gathered together (Acts 20:6-8).

New International Version (NIV)

> 6 But we sailed from Philippi after the Feast of Unleavened Bread, and five days later joined the others at Troas, where we stayed seven days.
>
> 7 <u>On the first day of the week</u>, we came together to break bread. Paul spoke to the people and, because he intended to leave the next day, kept on talking until midnight. 8 There were many lamps in the upstairs room where we were meeting (Acts 20:6-8).

Notice that in each of the above versions Luke states that both he and Paul sailed from Philippi *after* the Feast of Unleavened Bread (v. 6). Why is this particular reference important? Because it establishes that both Luke and Paul were *Torah* observant. They waited until *after* the Feast of Unleavened Bread before traveling on to Troas.

Also, in each of the above versions, Paul's visit with the Troas Nazarenes is recorded as saying, "on the first day of the week we came together to break bread. In the Greek manuscripts, however, this passage says: *"en de tn mia twn saBBatwn"* (v. 7).

So what is the correct translation of the Greek text? The Christian Greek scholar Alfred Marshall translates this passage in his *Interlinear Greek-English New Testament* as found in the Nestle-Aland Greek text: "And on the one (first) of the sabbaths" (Acts 20:7).[53] And the Christian scholar Jay P. Green, Sr. translates the same Greek words as found in the *Textus Receptus, "en de <u>tn mia</u> twn saBBatwn"* (v. 7), as meaning: "And on <u>the one</u> of the sabbaths" (Acts 20:7).[54]

Addressing the meaning of the Greek term *mia,* the Greek scholars Arndt and Gingrich inform us that the Greek words *eis, mia, ev, evos, mias, evos* mean: "numeral one. **1.–a.** in contrast to more than one... **B.** noun w. partitive gen. (Jos., Vi. 204) Mt. 5:19; 6:29; 18:6; Mk. 9:42; Lk. 12:27; 17:2, 22; 23:39; J 19:34."[55]

Equally significant, in each of these verses the Greek terms *eis, mia, ev, evos, mias,* or *evos* are translated by both Dr. Marshall and Dr. Green, Sr. as meaning "one," as "on one of the Sabbaths" (pl.).

Why is this understanding of the Greek text significant? Because it establishes the Jewishness of the above passages; that the Nazarene Believers in Philippi and Troas, including Paul and Luke, observed the appointed festival of Unleavened Bread and seven Sabbath count of the Omer.

The Greek Language of New Testament

Although the Konie Greek of the New Testament is a precise language, with many different rules of grammar, it was never intended to be a literary document. Rather, it was meant to be a conversational document, written in the common language of that day. Thus the message of the Apostles could be understood by the many different peoples throughout the Greek-speaking world, including the Jews of the Dispersion.

According to the Greek language scholar, J. Gresham Machen, professor of New Testament Greek in Westminister Theological Seminary, in Philadelphia, the Konie Greek used by the Jewish writers of the New Testament is much more than a conversational document. Dr. Machen writes:

> Undoubtedly the language of the New Testament is no artificial language of books, and no Jewish-Greek jargon, but the natural, living language of the period. But the Semitic influence should not be underestimated. The New Testament writers were nearly all Jews, and all of them were strongly influenced by the Old Testament. In particular, they were influenced, so far as language is concerned, by the Septuagint, and the Septuagint was influenced, as most ancient translations were, by the language of the original. The Septuagint had gone far toward producing a Greek vocabulary to express the deepest things of the religion of Israel. And this vocabulary was profoundly influential in the New Testament.[56]

With this understanding we should not be surprised that Hebrew parallelisms are found throughout the Greek text of the Apostolic Writings. This is especially true of the term *saBBaton,* meaning "Sabbath".

Arndt and Gingrich tell us that the Greek word *saBBatov* is the Hebrew equivalent of the Hebrew word *Shabbath.*[57] The same Hebrew parallelism can be found in the *Septuagint,* as well as the writings of the great Alexandrian philosopher Philo and Josephus.[58]

The Greek grammar scholars Dana and Mantey tell us that not only has the vocabulary of the New Testament been profoundly influenced by Hebraic thought, but the syntax used to convey the meanings of that Hebraic vocabulary were steeped in Hebraic parallelisms. No where is this use of Hebraic thought more apparent than in Acts 20:7, where Luke employs the *genitive* case to the Greek words *"en de tn mia twn saBBatwn"*.

Why is this use of the *genitive* case important to what Luke is saying in Acts 20:7? Dana and Mantey write: "... the genitive limits as to kind... the genitive reduces the range of reference possible to an idea, and confines its application within specific limits."[59]

This is especially true when a Greek word written in the *genitive* case is preceded by a *definite article*. Dana and Mantey go on to say:

> Nothing is more indigenous to the Greek language than its use of the article. Moulton finds that in the New Testament "its use is in agreement with Attic" (Classical Greek), a feature in which the New Testament is more literary than the papyri (Konie Greek).... The function of the article is to point out an object or to draw attention to it. Its use with a word makes the word stand out distinctly. ... The basal function of the Greek article is to point out *individual identity.*[60]

Thus when Luke employed the definite article *"twn,"* written in the *genitive* case, preceding the noun *"saBBatwn"* (pl.), he was pointing out the Hebraic idea of a limited *type* of Sabbaths (pl.), *not* a generic concept, such as "the first day of the week". To miss the significance of this Hebraic concept is to miss what Luke was saying about Paul's farewell visit to the Nazarene Believers in Philippi and Troas.

Equally significant, because the word *"saBBatwn"* is written in the plural, it is evident that the words *"twn saBBatwn"* ['the sabbaths'] were meant to *identify* a particular group of Sabbaths, which in this case were the seven Sabbaths between the "Day of Unleavened Bread" (v. 6) and the "Day of the Festival of Weeks/ Pentecost" (v. 16).

Affirming this meaning of the Greek word *saBBatwn*, Arndt and Gingrich tell us that the Greek word *saBBatwn* (pl.) is a Hebrew parallelism of the Hebrew word *Shabbaths* (pl.), which is used as a direct reference to the appointed Sabbath festivals in 2 Chronicles 31:3 and Ezek. 46:3, as well as in the writings of Josephus (*Jewish Antiquities,* XIII. 252).[61]

In Jewish thought, the festival of Unleavened Bread [Matza] is an appointed seven day festival that is to be observed by abstaining from eating bread made with leaven for the entire seven day period. It is a High Sabbath and is set to occur in the Spring on the 15th day of the first moon (Lev. 23), the day following Passover. The beginning of the "count" to the next High Sabbath, Shavuot [Weeks]/Pentecost [Fifty], is determined by counting "seven complete Sabbaths," after the weekly Sabbath of the High Sabbath of Unleavened Bread: "And from the morrow after the Sabbath, from the day that you brought the sheaf of the wave offering, you shall count for yourselves: seven complete Sabbaths. Until the morrow after the Sabbath you count fifty days, then you shall bring a new grain offering to [YHVH]" (Lev. 23:15-16; *The Scriptures*).

Why is this appointed time important in the Jewish calendar? Because the fifty days of counting the "Omer" following the weekly Sabbath of the High Sabbath of Unleavened Bread commemorates the giving of the *Torah* on Mount Sinai and the giving of the *Ruach HaKodesh* on Mount Moriah, which is celebrated on the High Sabbath of Shavuot/Pentecost. The daily count of the Omer is meant to bring to rememberance the *journey* from the deliverance of bondage to the *time* of receiving the *Torah/Ruach HaKodesh* on Shavuot/Pentecost.

Luke records that with the arrival of *sunset* the Troas Nazarenes came together to break bread *ev de tn mia twn saBBatwn* ['and on the one of the sabbaths']. Luke states that Paul's teaching extended well into the night ['midnight'], which in Jewish thought would be the beginning of the "first day of the week".

Apparently, because Paul was scheduled to leave the following day ['the first day of the week'], he wanted to teach the Troas Nazarenes as much as he could before departing. This was a common practice of first century rabbinic teaching. Even today, both Jewish and Messianic congregations continue their teachings well after Shabbat has ended, which takes them into the "first day of the week".

Why is this understanding of the appointed seven Sabbaths (pl.) of the Omer count significant? Because it tells us that those first century Troas Nazarenes, including Paul and Luke, not only observed the weekly Sabbath but also *"twn sabbatwn"* ['the Sabbaths' (pl.)] between the appointed High Sabbaths of Unleavened Bread and Shavuot/Pentecost.

Luke also records that there were "many lamps in the upper room where they were assembled" (v. 8). Addressing this ancient Jewish custom, the Messianic researcher Dean Wheelock writes:

> Some claim that it was the smoke from the many lamps which caused Eutychus to become drowsy and fall from the balcony. However, this expression can also be a Hebrew idiom for the traditional *Havdalah* ceremony, which is used to close the Sabbath after sundown. In *Havdalah,* a multi-wick candle is extinguished in a cup or saucer of wine once three stars are visible in the sky. Then each person present lights a candle, or lamp, to create a sea of light. The fact that there were "many lamps" indicates there were a large number of people present for this evening teaching.
>
> ... it is clear that the meeting took place after the close of the Sabbath on what we would call Saturday night, which is the beginning of the first day of the week. Jewish Believers in *Y'shua* would not have found it at all unusual to spend Saturday night in further fellowship following the day of rest. Such Sabbath evening fellowship and study is still part of Jewish tradition.[62]

The Tomb Visit

Since the second century, Christian theologians and apologists have used the Gospel accounts of the Tomb visit as proof that it was on the "first day of the week" that the young Rabbi from Nazareth was resurrected, and from this event came the special day Sun-Day marked out by the first century followers of the young Rabbi from Nazareth as the public day for worship.

For example, the Bible expositor H. R. Renolds of the *Pulpit Commentary* addresses the Tomb visit of John 20:1, saying: "*twn saBBtwn, saBBata,* in the plural, is used for the whole of the week, *sabbaton* including in itself the various days that intervened between sabbath and sabbath, the first, second, third, etc.... All the evangelists agree about the day of the week, which thenceforward became the new beginning of weeks, 'the Lord's day'".[63]

But is this what all four Gospel writers meant when they recorded the Tomb visit? Take a look at the following 1611 KJV, 1881 RSV, NASV, NIV, and 1388 Wycliffe versions of the Tomb account in Matthew, Mark, Luke, and John, and note how similar they are to Jerome's anti-Jewish Latin Vulgate.

Jerome's 405 C.E. Latin Vulgate

English	Latin
And in the end of the sabbath, when it began to dawn <u>towards the first day of the week</u>, came Mary Magdalene and the other Mary, to see the sepulcher.	vespere autem sabbati quae lucescit in primam sabbati venit Maria Magdalene et altera Maria videre sepulchrum (Matthew XXXVIII).[64]
And when sabbath was past, Mary Magdalene and the other Mary the mother of James and Salome brought sweet spices, that coming, they might anoint Jesus	et cum transisset sabbatum Maria Magdalene et Maria Iacobi et Salome emerunt aromata ut venietes urgurent cum
And very early in the morning, <u>the first day of the week</u>, they come to the sepulchre, the sun being now risen.	et valde mane una sabbatorum veniunt ad momumentum orto iam sole (Mark XVI).[65]
And <u>on the first day of the week</u>, very early in the morning, they came to the sepulchre, bring the spices, which they had prepared	una autem sabbati valde diluculo venerunt monumentum portantes quae paraverant aromata (Luke XXIV).[66]
And <u>on the first day of the week</u>, Mary Magdalene commeth early, when it was yet dark, unto the sepulchre: and she saw the stone taken away from the sepulcher.	una autem sabbati Maria Magdalene venit manc cum adhu tenebrae essent ad monumentum et videt lapidem sublatum a monumento (John XX).[67]

1388 Wycliffe Version

But in the eventide of the Sabbath that begins to shine <u>in the first day of the week</u>, Mary Magdalene came, and another Mary, to see the sepulchre (Matthew XXVIII).[68]

And full early <u>in one of the week days</u>, they came to the sepulchre when the sun was risen (Mark XVI).[69]

But <u>in one day of the week</u>, full early, they came to the grave and brought sweet smelling spices that they had arrayed (Luke XXIV).[70]

And <u>in one day of the week</u>, Mary Magdalene came early to the grave when it was yet dark. And she saw the stone moved away from the grave (John XX).[71]

1611 King James Version (KJV)

28 In the end of the Sabbath, as it began to dawn <u>toward the first *day* of the week</u>, came Mary Magdalene and the other Mary to see the sepulchre (Matthew 28:1).[72]

2 And very early in the morning, <u>the first *day* of the week</u>, they came unto the sepulchre at the rising of the sun (Mark 16:2).[73]

24 Now <u>upon the first *day* of the week</u>, very early in the morning, they came unto the sepulchre, bringing the spices which they had prepared, and certain *others* with them (Luke 24:1).[74]

20 <u>The first *day* of the week</u> cometh Mary Magdalene early, when it was yet dark, unto the sepulchre, and seeth the stone taken away from the sepulchre (John 20:1).[75]

1881 King James Revised Version (RSV)

28 Now after the sabbath, <u>toward the dawn of the first day of the week</u>, Mary Magdalene and the other Mary went to see the sepulcher (Matthew 28:1).[76]

2 And very early <u>on the first day of the week</u> they went to the tomb when the sun had risen (Mark 16:2).[77]

24 But <u>on the first day of the week</u>, at early dawn, they went in to the tomb, taking the spices which they had prepared (Luke 24:1).[78]

20 Now <u>on the first day of the week</u> Mary Magdalene came to the tomb early, while it was yet dark, and saw that the stone had been taken away from the tomb unto the sepulcher (John 20:1).[79]

New American Standard Version (NASV)

28 Now after the Sabbath, as it began to dawn <u>toward the first *day* of the week</u>, Mary Magdalene and the other Mary came to look at the grave (Matthew 28:1).

2 Very early <u>on the first day of the week</u>, they came to the tomb when the sun had risen (Mark 16:2).

24 But <u>on the first day of the week</u>, at early dawn, they came to the tomb bringing spices which they had prepared (Luke 24:1).

20 Now <u>on the first *day* of the week</u> Mary Magdalene came early to the tomb, while it was still dark, and saw the stone *already* taken away from the tomb (John 20:1).

New International Version (NIV)

28 After the Sabbath, at dawn <u>on the first day of the week</u>, Mary Magdalene and the other Mary went to look at the tomb (Matthew 28:1).

2 Very early <u>on the first day of the week</u>, just after sunrise, they were on their way to the tomb (Mark 16:2).

24 <u>On the first day of the week</u>, very early in the morning, the women took the spices they had prepared and went to the tomb (Luke 24:1).

20 Early <u>on the first day of the week</u>, while it was still dark, Mary Magdalene went to the tomb and saw that the stone had been removed from the entrance (John 20:1).

Notice that in each of the above versions the Tomb visit is recorded as taking place "on the first day of the week". According to the best manuscripts of the Nestle-Aland Greek text, however, Matthew's Greek text plainly states *"eis mian saBBtwn"* (pl.). Mark 16:1 says, *"mia twn saBBtwn"* (pl.). Luke 24:1 writes: *"tn de mia twn saBBatwn"* (pl.). And John 20:1 records the words: *"tn de mia twn saBBatwn"* (pl.).

Why is this agreement of all four Gospel accounts of the Tomb visit significant? Because each account is written the the plural tense, as well as the *genitive* case, which is the case of "definition or description". In other words, the Greek words *mia twn saBBatwn* is a Hebraic concept that parallels the following Hebrew Scripture: "And from the morrow after the Sabbath, from the day that you brought the sheaf of the wave offering, you shall count for yourselves: seven complete Sabbaths. Until the morrow after the Sabbath you shall count fifty days, then you shall bring a new grain offering to [YHVH]" (Lev. 23:15-16; *The Scriptures*).

Matthew records that Mary Magdalene and the other Mary came to the Tomb "in the end of the sabbath, as it began to dawn toward the first *day* of the week" (Matt. 28:1). Arndt and Gingrich inform us that the Greek word *epiphwskousn,* translated "dawn," can also be interpreted as meaning *"to draw on."*[80]

Affirming this meaning, the Christian scholars of *Strong's Exhaustive Concordance* tell us that the Greek word *epiphwskousn* means *"to draw on"* (#2020). Dr. Alfred Marshall translates the Greek words *"ope de saBBatwn tn epiphwskousn ies mian saBBtwn, nltev Mariam n Magdalene kai n alln Maria Tewpnsai ton tapov"* as follows: "But late of [the] sabbaths, at the drawing on toward one of [the] sabbaths, came Mary the Magdalene and the other Mary to view the grave" (Matt. 28:1).[81]

Think about that for a moment! When the women arrived at the Tomb it was "late of [the] sabbaths, at the drawing on toward one of [the] sabbaths."

Why is this time-factor important? In Jewish thought, the Sabbath ends at *sunset*. This means that when Mary Magdalene and the other Mary arrived at the Tomb it was "late Sabbath," which would have been shortly after *sunset*.

According to John's Tomb account, Mary Magdalene's first visit took place in *skotias* ['darkness,' Jhn. 20:1]. Arndt and Gingrich tell us that the Greek word *skotias* is the same word used in the *Septuagint* to describe the earth at the beginning of creation.[82] The Genesis account states:

> 1 In the beginning God created the heaven and the earth.
>
> 2 And the earth was without form, and void; and **darkness** [Gk. *skotias*] *was* upon the face of the waters.
>
> 3 And God said, Let there be light: and there was light.
>
> 4 And God saw the light, that it *was* good: and God divided the light from the **darkness** [*skotias*].
>
> 5 And God called the light Day, and the **darkness** [*skotias*] he called Night. And the evening and the morning were the first day (Gen. 1:1-4; AKJV).

Here we see that at the beginning of creation there was nothing but **darkness** ['*skotias*']; that when the LORD created the light and separated it from the **darkness** ['*skotias*'], He called the **darkness** ['*skotias*'] "night".

In much the same manner, John records that when Mary first arrived at the Tomb there was *"skoitas"* – **darkness,** meaning "night".

Mark and Luke, however, indicate an early morning first day of the week Tomb visit, "at the rising of the sun" (Mk. 16:1), and "very early in the morning" (Lk. 24:1). These early Tomb accounts cannot be denied. But it also cannot be denied that there were at least two Tomb visits, and possibly three. Dr. Reynolds says: "There were probably other women with these two, or perhaps there were two separate bands of women who early in the morning visited the sepulcher."[83]

Addressing the early morning Tomb visit recorded in Mark 16:2, the Bible expositor E. Bickersteth says: "They brought the spices that they needed on the Saturday evening, after the sabbath was past; and then set out early the next morning, reaching the tomb when the sun was risen."[84]

Commenting on the Tomb visit recorded in Luke 24:1, Dr. H. D. Spence says: "In the foregoing general note on the Resurrection, the probability has been discussed of the holy women having been divided into two companies who separately came to the sepulcher. St. Luke's notice here refers to the party who arrived second at the tomb."[85]

Again, addressing the Tomb visit recorded in John 20:1, Dr. Spence writes: "judging from the synoptists, she [Mary Magdalene] must have been accompanied by other women. This is implied in the *oidamen* of ver. 2....... It is probable that Mary Magdalene had preceded the other women, driven by the intensity of her adoring love and abounding grief...."[86]

Here we have at least two different accounts of the Tomb visit, and at least two groups of women visiting the Tomb at different times, with the first group arriving "late of [the] sabbaths, at the <u>drawing on</u> toward one of [the] sabbaths" (Matt. 28:1), "when it was yet *skotias* ['dark']" (Jhn. 20:1).

What did this first group of women find when they arrived at the Tomb? Matthew states:

> 2 And, behold there was a great earthquake: for the angel of the Lord descended from heaven, and came and rolled back the stone from the door, and sat upon it.
>
> 3 His countenance was like lightening, and his raiment white as snow.
>
> 4 And for fear of him the keepers did shake, and became as dead men.
>
> 5 And the angel answered and said unto the women, Fear not ye: for I know that ye seek Jesus, which was crucified.
>
> 6 He is not here: for he is risen, as he said. Come, see the place where the Lord lay (Matt. 28:2-6; AKJV).

Right! When the first group of women arrived at the Tomb, "at the end of the one of the Sabbaths, being *skotias* ['dark']," they merely *discovered* the empty Tomb! *Yeshua's* resurrection had already taken place!

Keep in mind that *Yeshua's* body had been placed in the Tomb just *before sunset* on Wednesday. Three days and three nights later brings us precisely to *sunset* on "one of the Sabbaths," which followed Passover and the High Sabbath of Unleavened Bread.

Unfortunately, most Christians have never been taught this account of the death and resurrection of *Yeshua.* By the fourth century, Catholic Church authorities had purged everything Jewish from the Christian faith.

When viewed from a Jewish perspective, however, the above rendering of the Tomb visit perfectly fits the Messianic fulfillment of the appointed times of the LORD, who told the people of Israel: "When you come into the land which I give you, and shall reap of its harvest, then you shall bring a sheaf of the first-fruits of your harvest to the priest. And he shall wave the sheaf before [YHVH], for your acceptance. On the morrow after the Sabbath the priest waves it." (Lev, 23:10-11; *The Scriptures.*)

The Wave Sheaf

In ancient Israel, it was at this appointed time when the first-fruits Wave Sheaf was cut, marking the beginning of the barley grain harvest. During Temple times, each time the Wave Sheaf [*i.e.,* first cut of the barley harvest] was cut and brought to the Temple and waved before the LORD by the High Priest, the bodily resurrection of the Messiah from the earth was being rehearsed. Paul alluded to this Messianic symbolism when he wrote to the Corinth Nazarene Believers, saying: "But now Messiah has been raised from the dead, and has become the *first-fruit* of those having fallen asleep" (1 Cor. 15:20; *The Scriptures*).

The cutting of the first-fruits Wave Sheaf was done precisely at *sunset* on "the first of the seven Sabbaths" (pl.), and was commemorated with a ceremony that was witnessed by others who had gathered in the field around the elders. According to Jewish custom, the barley that was first cut down grew in the Ashes Valley across the Kidron. The spot where the first sheaf was to be reaped was marked out by tying the barley together in a bundle while still standing. When the time for the cutting of the sheaf had arrived, Dr. Alfred Edersheim writes:

> ... just as the sun went down, three men, each with a sickle and basket, set to work. Clearly to bring out what was distinctive in the ceremony, they first asked the bystanders three times each of these questions: "Has the sun gone down?" "With this sickle?" "Into this basket?" "On this Sabbath?"... and lastly, "Shall I reap?" Having each time been answered in the affirmative, they cut down barley to the amount of one ephah,...."[87]

Notice the two key questions that were asked by the reapers and affirmed by the witnessing bystanders. Question: "Has the sun gone down?" Reply: "Yes". Question: "On the Sabbath?" Reply: "Yes".

The importance of these two questions accompanied by the affirmation of the witnesses cannot be overstated. Because the affirmative answer to both questions emphasizes two important facts about the Wave Sheaf ceremony: (1) the Wave Sheaf ceremony took place immediately after the sun had gone down; and (2) it was still the Sabbath when the first-fruits Wave Sheaf was cut.

For many, these two simultaneous occurring statements appear to be contradictory. But in Hebraic thought both statements make perfect sense. According to Jewish law, the Sabbath does not end *until* a ceremony called *Havdalah* is held. And *Havdalah* cannot begin *until* three stars are visible in the night sky, which could be as much as an hour *after sunset,* especially when the moon is full during Passover week.

"Good Friday"

Another Jewish observance used by theologians as proof to support the idea that the special day Sun-Day replaced the Sabbath is the notion that the day of preparation in Scripture always means Friday, the day before the weekly Sabbath. Dr. Reynolds writes: "the day before the Sabbath (Jhn. 19:31; Mk. 15:42). ... This note of time certainly blends both the synoptists and John in the assurance that the crucifixion took place on Friday."[88]

From a Christian perspective, Dr. Reynolds' statement sounds well and good *until* we learn that in Jewish thought the day of preparation addressed in all four Tomb accounts (Matt. 27:62; Mk. 15:42; Lk. 23:54; Jhn. 19:31) is the day before the High Sabbath of Unleavened Bread. This annual day of preparation occurs on the 14th of Aviv [Nissan] of every first moon and therefore, is a movable time period on the Jewish calendar.

Confirming this special day of preparation John's employment of the Greek term *megas,* meaning "high" (Jhn. 19:31), establishes that the young Rabbi from Nazareth was executed on the day of preparation before the *megas* ['high'] Sabbath of Unleavened Bread, *not* on Friday, the day of preparation before the weekly Sabbath.

Although there are several theories regarding the date of Rabbi *Yeshua's* execution, a Wednesday Passover is the only day of the week that works with all four Gospel accounts. While many hold to a 30 C.E. Passover date for *Yeshua's* death, the astronomical data obtained from the U.S. Naval Observatory Astronomical Applications Department indicates that Passover on the 14th day of Nizzan, in the year 29 C.E. (A.D.), fell on the second day of the week [our Monday, April 18].[89] In the year 30 C.E., Nissan 14 fell on the sixth day of the week [our Friday, April 7].[90] In the year 31 C.E., Nissan 14 fell on the fourth day of the week [our Wednesday, April 25].[91] Each of these years are noted with the year, day, and hour of the Vernal Equinox and Astronomical New Moon Conjunction, and include the first evening of the visible crescent, the date of the first Nissan, and the 14th day of Nissan.[92]

Contrary to the misconception of many, the evidence establishes a Nissan 14 fourth day of the week date for *Yeshua's* execution [our Wednesday], which means that on the third day [Tuesday] at twilight [the beginning of Nissan 14] *Yeshua* held a Passover Seder with His disciples. Later that night, beginning the fourth day, the young Rabbi was arrested while in the Garden of Gethsemane with His disciples, and by the 3rd hour [our 9 A.M., Wednesday], His hands and feet were pierced by nails as He hung upright on a Roman stake. At the 6th hour [our "noon"], darkness fell over the land until the 9th hour [our 3 P.M.] when *Yeshua* cried out with a loud voice and gave up His Spirit.

According to the Gospel accounts, our Passover Lamb was slain at the exact time [the 9th hour = our 3 P.M.] the High Priest sacrificed the very first Passover lamb slain in the Temple, which was offered for the entire nation of Israel, on Nissan 14. As the High Priest drew the knife across the throat of the lamb, he was required by Jewish law to make a statement. That statement is the exact same statement *Yeshua* made when He bowed His head and gave up His Spirit, saying: "IT IS FINISHED!" (Jhn. 19:30).

Affirming *Yeshua's* execution date of Nissan 14, Dr. E. W. Bullinger writes: "The Four Gospels agree in stating the Lord was *laid in the Sepulcher on the Preparation Day,* which was Nisan 14th, immediately before 'the High Sabbath', Nisan 15th (Matt. 27. 62, Mark 15. 42, Luke 23. 54, John 19. 31, 42). Therefore, He must have been crucified on Wednesday, 14th of Nisan."[93]

Equally significant, Jewish scholars agree that Nissan 14 was indeed the date of *Yeshua's* death. [See Sanhedrin 43a uncensored version.]

According to the Gospel account, shortly after *Yeshua* expired Joseph of Arimathaea went to Pilate and asked for His body. For *Torah* observant Jews and followers of the young Rabbi, the going down of the sun on Wednesday signaled the arrival of the first day of the High Sabbath of Unleavened Bread, the 15th of Nissan.

According to Jewish law, because of the arrival of the High Sabbath of Unleavened Bread, *Yeshua's* body had to be sealed in the earth *before sunset* on Wednesday. On this point there is abundant evidence (Matt. 27:57-58; Mk. 15:42-43; Lk. 23:50-54; and Jhn. 19:38).

Mark notes that "it was the Preparation Day, which is, *o estiv prosaBBatov* ['the day before the Sabbath']" (Mk. 15:42). Luke states that "it was *nmera nv paraskeuns* ['the day of Preparation'], and the Sabbath was approaching" (Lk. 23:54). In the Greek text both writers employ the *definite article* before the word *paraskeun* ['preparation'], emphasizing the importance of this High Sabbath day.

All four Gospel writers tell us that Pilate ordered *Yeshua's* body to be handed over to Joseph of Arimathaea as requested, which would have been that same afternoon [our Wednesday] just *before* the setting of the sun and the beginning of the High Sabbath of Unleavened Bread

Now count *three days* and *three nights,* starting just *before sunset* on Wednesday. The count comes to just *before sunset* on "the first of the Sabbaths," or shortly thereafter, during the ceremony of the cutting of the first-fruits Wave Sheaf. I repeat: the count comes to just *before sunset* on "the first of the Sabbaths," or shortly thereafter, during the ceremony of the cutting of the first-fruits Wave Sheaf.

Many will argue that in the Roman world, because any part of the day and night could be counted as one day and one night, *Yeshua's* death on

Friday and His resurrection on Sun-Day morning perfectly fits this ancient Roman custom, as well as the Jewish custom, of reckoning of time. But there is a problem with this Roman understanding of *three days* and *three nights* referred to in the Gospel accounts. Dr. Bullinger writes:

> The fact that "three days" is used by Hebrew idiom for any part of three days and three nights is not disputed; because that was the common way of reckoning, just as when it was used of years. Three or any number of years was used inclusively of any part of those years, as may be seen in the reckoning of the reigns of any of the kings of Israel and Judah.
>
> But, when the number of "nights" is stated as well as the number of "days", then the expression ceases to be an idiom, and becomes a literal statement of fact.
>
> Moreover, as the Hebrew day began at sunset the day was reckoned from one sunset to another, the "twelve hours in the day" (John 11.9) being reckoned from sunrise, and the twelve of night from sunset. An evening-morning was thus used for a whole day of twenty-four hours, as in the first chapter of Genesis. Hence the expression "a night and a day" in 2 Cor. 11.25 denotes a complete day (Gk. *nucthemeron*).
>
> When Esther says (Est. 4. 16) "fast ye for me, and neither eat nor drink three days", she defines her meaning as being three complete days, because she adds (being a Jewess) "night or day". And when it is written that the fast ended on "the third day" (5.1), "the third day" must have succeeded and included the third night.
>
> In like manner the sacred record states that the young man (in 1 Sam. 30:12) "had eaten no bread nor drank any water, three days and three nights". Hence, when the young man explains the reason, he says, "because three days agone I fell sick". He means therefore three complete days and nights, because, being an *Egyptian* (*vs.* 11, 13) he naturally reckoned his day as beginning at sunrise according to the Egyptian manner (see *Encycl. Brit.*, 11ᵗʰ (Cambridge) ed., vol. xi, p. 77). His "three days agone" refers to the beginning of his sickness, and includes the whole period, giving reason for his having gone without food during the whole period stated.

Hence, when it says that "Jonah was in the belly of the fish three days and three nights" (Jonah 1. 17) it means exactly what it says, and that this can be the only meaning of the expression in Matt. 12. 40; 16. 4.[94]

Addressing this same *three days* and *three nights,* Dr. Brooke Foss Westcott writes:

> Since so far as the balance of evidence goes the Crucifixion was on Friday, and the Resurrection on Sunday, the actual time between them was only one clear day and two parts of days and two whole nights. The reckoning, therefore, here is, strictly speaking, inaccurate. The words are perhaps a mere adaptation of the phrase in Jonah, and are here used only to roughly mark the time of our Lord's stay in the grave. Observe, however, that the addition of "nights" tends to emphasize the reality of our Lord's stay there. It was a matter of days and nights; he spent both kinds of earthly time "in the earth" (cf. ch. iv. 2. note).[95]

Moreover, given the fact that Matthew wrote his Gospel account to a predominately *Torah* observant Jewish audience, and given the fact that those *three days* and *three nights* took place during the holy week of Passover, which was observed from *sunset* to *sunset,* there can be little doubt that the people of that day would have understood those *three nights* and *three days* to mean from *sunset* to *sunset.*

The LORD's Day

According to most theologians, John's statement, "I was in the Spirit on the LORD's day" (Rev. 1:10), is another passage that proves Sun-Day was the day marked by the Apostles for Christian worship. For example, the Bible expositor A. Plummer writes: "The expression occurs only in the New Testament, and beyond all reasonable doubt it means 'on Sunday.'"[96]

But was this what John really meant when he wrote about being in the Spirit on the LORD's day? Again, take a look at the following 1611 KJV, 1881 RSV, NASV, and NIV translations of Revelation 1:10 and note how similar they are to the 1388 Wycliffe Version, which was based on Jermoe's anti-Jewish Latin Vulgate.

Jerome's 405 C.E. Latin Vulgate

English   Latin

I was in the spirit on the Lord's   fui in spiritu in dominica die...
day....   (Apocalypse I).[97]

1388 Wycliffe Version

I was in the Spirit in the Lord's day...
(Apocalypse I).[98]

1611 King James Version (KJV)

10 I was in the Spirit on the Lord's day...
(Rev. 1:10).[99]

1881 King James Revised Version (RSV)

10 I was in the Spirit on the Lord's day...
(Rev. 1:10).[100]

New American Standard Version (NASV)

10 I was in the Spirit on the Lord's day...
(Rev. 1:10).

New International Version (NIV)

10 "On the Lord's Day I was in the Spirit..."
(Rev. 1:10).

For most theologians, John's employment of the words "I was [Gk. *ginomai*] in the Spirit on the LORD's day" is proof that John received his vision of the last days while he was in the Spirit on the "LORD's day," [*i.e.,* 'the first day of the week']. According to Arndt and Gingrich, however, the Greek verb *ginoami* means "*to be born* or *begotten...* of persons and things which change their nature, to indicate their entering a new condition: *becoming something.*"[101]

Affirming this same understanding, Dr.Alfred Marshall and Dr. Jay P. Green, Sr. interpret *ginoami* as meaning "I came to be... (v. 10)."[102]

Equally significant, in the Greek text the words "*tn kuriakn nmera*" ['the LORD's day'] are preceded by the *definite article "tn"*. As earlier noted, the *definite article* always serves to emphasize the person or thing it modifies, which in the above passage are the words "the LORD," *not* the word "day".

Since Latin has no *definite article,* Jerome's Latin Vulgate would not help us in deciding whether to emphasize the nouns "LORD" or "day". And while the English language does have a *definite article,* it serves merely to particularize, to refer to a particular object. In Greek, however, the *definite article* is meant to draw attention to the person or thing being emphasized, such as with the Greek words "*tn kuriakn nmera,*" meaning "the LORD's day."

Moreover, the Greek words "*tn kuriakn nmera*" are written in the *dative case.* Dana and Mantey inform us that the "[*dative* case] is sometimes used of things, but of things personified," having "a distinctive personal touch.... It is personal interest particularized to the point of ownership."[103] In other words, John's employment of the *dative* in the Greek words "*tn kuriakn nmera*" establishes that the particular day being addressed *belongs* to the LORD Himself.

In Jewish thought, the words "the LORD's day" or "day of the LORD" is a common latter day Hebraic concept used throughout the Bible to address a particular time period that *belongs* to the LORD Himself. For example, Peter employed this same latter day Hebrew concept when he wrote to the Nazarene Believers of Asia Minor, saying:

> 10 But the day of the LORD will come like a thief, in which the heavens will pass away with a roar and the elements will be destroyed with intense heat, and the earth and its works will be burned up (2 Pet. 3:10; NASV).

Employing this same latter day Hebrew concept, Paul wrote to the Nazarene Believers in Thessalonica, saying:

> 2 Now we request you, brethren, with regard to the coming of our LORD Jesus Christ and our gathering together to Him,
>
> 2 that you not be quickly shaken from your composure or be disturbed either by a spirit or a message or a letter as if from us, to the effect that the <u>day of the LORD</u> has come (2 Thess. 2:1-2; NASV).

Hundreds of years earlier, the prophet Isaiah spoke about this same latter day Hebrew concept, except he employed the words "that day," saying:

> 2 In <u>that day</u> the Branch of the LORD will be beautiful and glorious, and the fruit of the earth *will be* the pride and the adornment of the survivors of Israel (Isa. 4:2; NASV).

Clearly, these passages establish the idea that the Hebrew concept "the LORD's day" has the same meaning as "the day of judgment," "the last day," "that day," and "the great day of the LORD," which always refers to the physical millennial reign of the Messiah on earth (Matt. 7:22; Lk. 10:12; 2 Thess. 1:10; 2 Tim. 1:18; 4:8).

Not surprisingly, this same latter day Hebrew concept can be found 30 times in the Scriptures, and is referred to in 300 similar passages throughout the Bible.

Equally significant, some of Christianity's most respected nineteenth century scholars, such as J. J. Wettstein, G. A. Deissmann, F. J. A. Hort, and J. B. Lightfoot, reject the idea that the Greek words *"tn kuriakn nmepa"*(Rev. 1:10) mean "the first day of the week".[104]

"On the First Day of the Week"

For most theologians, 1 Corthians 16:1-2f. is proof that the first century followers of the young Rabbi from Nazareth set aside the first day of the week, Sun-Day, as the day for public worship. For example, the Bible expositor G. Findlay of the *Expositor's Greek Testament* writes: "This earliest mention of this Christian day, going to show that the First Day, not the Sabbath, was already the Sacred Day of the Church."[105]

But was this what Paul really meant when he wrote those words? Again, take a look at the following 1388 Wycliffe, 1611 KJV, 1881 RSV, NASV, and NIV translations of 1 Cor. 16:1-2, and note how similar they are to Jerome's anti-Jewish Latin Vulgate.

Jerome's 405 C.E. Latin Vulgate

English	Latin
Now concerning the collections that are made for the saints: as I have given order to the churches of Galatia, so do ye also. <u>On the first day of the week</u>, let every one of you put apart with himself, laying up what it shall well please him: that when I come, the collections be not then to be made.	de collectis autem quae fiunt in sanctos sicut ordinavi ecclesiis Galantiac ita et vos facite per unam sabbati unusquisque vestrum apud se ponat recondens quod ei bene-placuerit ut non cum vencro tune collectae fiant (Corinthians 1:XVI).[106]

1388 Wycliffe Version

But of the gathering of money that are made into saints as I ordained in the churches of Galatia, so also do ye <u>one day of the week</u>. Each of you keep at himself, keeping that pleases to him, that when I come, the gatherings are not made (Corinthians 1:XVI).[107]

1611 King James Version (KJV)

16 Now concerning the collection for the saints, as I have given order to the churches of Galatia, even so do ye. 2 <u>Upon the first *day* of the week</u> let every one of you lay by him in store, as *God* hath prospered him, that there be no gatherings when I come (1 Cor. 16:1-2).[108]

1881 King James Revised Version (RSV)

16 Now concerning the contribution for the saints: as I directed the churches of Galatia, so you also are to do. 2 <u>On the first *day* of the week</u>, each of you is to put something aside and store it up, as he may prosper, so that contributions need not be made when I come (1 Cor. 16:1-2).[109]

New American Standard Version (NASV)

16 Now concerning the collection for the saints, as I directed the churches of Galatia, so do you also. 2 <u>On the first day of every week</u> each one of you is to put aside and save, as he may prosper, so that no collections be made when I come (1 Cor. 16:1-2).

New International Version (NIV)

16 Now about the collection for God's people: Do what I told the Galatian churches to do. 2 <u>On the first day of every week</u>, each one of you should set aside a sum of money in keeping with his income, saving it up, so that when I come no collections will have to be made (1 Cor. 16:1-2).

Notice that the generic word "week" has been added by both Catholic and Protestant translators. In the best Greek manuscripts of the *Textus Receptus,* however, verse 2 says, *"kata mian saBBatwn"* (pl.), meaning "on one of [the] Sabbaths".

As earlier noted, this same Hebraic expression, "on one of the Sabbaths," was employed by all four writers of the Gospels (Matt. 28:1; Mk. 16:2; Lk. 24:1; Jhn. 20:1), which can be traced to the term "sabbath festivals" in the Hebrew Scriptures (2 Chron. 31:3; Ezek. 46:3; Num. 28, 29), as well as in the writings of Josephus (*Jewish Antiquities,* xiii. 252).

Equally significant, Arndt and Gingrich inform us that when the Greek word *mian* is used with a noun written in the *genitive* case, it is translated as a numerical "one".[110]

Nevertheless, since the time of Jerome's revised Latin Vulgate the Greek words *kata mian saBBatwn* (pl.), translated "on the first day of the week," has been proof that Sun-Day was already being kept by the first century followers of *Yeshua* as a sacred day of worship and is, therefore, the appropriate day for collecting tithes and offerings for deeds of worship and charity.

But when the Greek words *kata mian saBBatwn* (pl.) are translated without subtracting or adding words to the text it becomes evident that Paul was admonishing the Nazarene Believers at Corinth to set aside a *one-time* offering "on one of the Sabbaths" (pl.) of the seven weekly Sabbath count between the appointed High Sabbaths of Unleavened Bread and Shavuot/Pentecost.

Why did Paul make his request at this particular time? Luke's account in Acts 16:3 informs us that Paul was making plans to return to Jerusalem. What was the occasion? Paul wanted to be in Jerusalem to celebrate the appointed festival of Shavuot/Pentecost (v. 8), and he wanted to take a *one time* offering from the Gentile Believers in Asia Minor to give to the poor Jewish saints in Jerusalem (v. 3).

The Sanitization of the Health Food Laws

According to most theologians the Old Testament dietary health laws were *done away* with the coming of *Yeshua* and therefore, are no longer relevant to New Testament Believers. One of the passages often used to support this view is Colossians 2:16-17, which is translated in the AKJV as follows:

> 16 Let no man therefore judge you in meat, or in drink, or in respect of a holy day, or of the new moon, or of the sabbath *days:*
>
> 17 Which are a shadow of things to come; but the body *is* of Christ (Col. 2:16-17).

Addressing this same passage, Professor Findlay writes:

> The yearly *feasts,* the monthly *new moon,* and the weekly *sabbath* cover the whole round of Jewish sacred seasons.

These the Colossian Gentile Christians, disciples of St. Paul through Epaphras, had not hitherto observed.... With St. Paul, they shadow forth prophetically *concrete facts of the Christian revelation,* and therefore are displaced by its advent.... Nothing is said here to discountenance positive Christian institutions, or the observance of the Lord's day in particular, unless enforced in a Judaistic spirit."[111]

But is this what Paul really meant when he wrote to the Nazarene Believers at Colossi? Again, take a look at the following 1611 KJV, 1881 RSV, NASV, and NIV translations of this passage, and note how similar they are to the 1388 Wycliffe, which is based on Jerome's anti-Jewish Latin Vulgate.

Jerome's 405 C.E. Latin Vulgate

English	Latin
Let no man therefore judge you in meat or in drink or in respect of a festival day or of the new moon or of the sabbaths, which are a shadow of the things to come: but the body is of Christ.	nemo ergo vos ludicet in cibo aut in potu aut in parte diei festi aut neomeniac aut sabbatorum quac sunt umbra futurorum corpus autem Christi (Colossians II).[112]

1388 Wycliffe Version

Therefore no man judge you in meat or in drink, or in part of feast day, or of neomeny, or of Sabbaths, which are shadow of things to coming, for the body is of Christ (Colossians II).[113]

1611 King James Version (KJV)

16 Let no man therefore judge you in meat, or in drink, or in respect of a holyday, or of the new moon, or of the sabbath *days:* 17 which are a shadow of things to come; but the body *is* of Christ (Col. 2:16-17).[114]

1881 King James Revised Version (RSV)

16 Therefore let no one pass judgment on you in question of food and drink or with regard to a festival or a new moon or a sabbath.

17 These are only a shadow of what is to come <u>but the substance belongs to Christ</u> (Col. 2:16-17).[115]

New American Standard Version (NASV)

16 Therefore no one is to act as your judge in regard to food or drink or in respect to a festival or a new moon or a Sabbath day– 17 things which are a *mere* shadow of what is to come; <u>but the substance belongs to Christ</u> (Col. 2:16-17).

New International Version (NIV)

16 Therefore do not let anyone judge you by what you eat or drink, or with regard to a religious festival, a New Moon celebration or a Sabbath day. 17 These are a shadow of the things that were to come; <u>the reality, however, is found in Christ</u> (Col. 2:16-17).

The first thing to note in this passage is that Paul places the observance of the appointed Sabbaths, holy days, and new moons on the same footing as the eating of food and drink, just as in the *Torah*.

More important, however, is the addition of the italicized verb *"is,"* which has been added to the text (v. 17). Search the best manuscripts in the Nestle-Aland New Testament and *Textus Receptus*. Nowhere can the verb *"is"* be found. It was added by the translators and, as such, gives an entirely different meaning to what Paul was telling those first century Colossi Nazarenes.

Some will argue that in Greek the verb "to be" is often left out but is implied in this text and therefore, should be added, as in Matthew 22:20, 36, 39: "And he saith unto them, whose *is* this image... which *is* the great commandment in the law ... and the second *is* like unto it...."

But there is a problem with this argument. In each of these passages it is clear from the context that the verb "to be" was meant to be added.

When we look at Colossians 2:17 in the context of verses 20-23, however, it is evident that the verb "to be" was never meant to be added. Because Paul says, "… why as living in the world are you subject to its decrees … according to the injunctions and teachings of men?" (vs. 20-23).

Here we see that Paul was addressing the *decrees of men*, which *Yeshua* Himself often addressed when confronted by the rules and regulations of the Pharisees.

Now look at Dr. Alfred Marshall's translation of Colossians 2:16-17, as found in his *Interlinear Greek-English New Testament:*

16 Not therefore anyone you let judge in eating and in drinking or in respect of a feast or of a new moon or of sabbaths, 17 which things is (are) a shadow of things coming, <u>but the body [is] - of Christ.</u>[116]

Notice that Dr. Marshall bracketed the above verb "[is]," indicating that the verb "is" is *not* in the Greek text. Nevertheless, since the time of Jerome's anti-Jewish Latin Vulgate, Christian translators have added the verb "is," making it appear as though Paul was affirming the doctrine of Christian Liberty as opposed to the instruction of *Torah*.

But when verses 16-17 are read in the context of verses 20-23, it becomes evident that Paul was telling the Nazarene Believers at Colossi that there was only *one* authority for rightly judging matters of *Torah* -- "the body of Messiah" (v. 17).

The Cleansing of "All Foods"

For most theologians the words of *Yeshua* in Mark 7:18-19 are proof that the young Rabbi from Nazareth declared "all foods to be clean". Not surprisingly, this same argument was made by Origin and Chrysostom.[117]

But is this what *Yeshua* really meant when He addressed the eating of foods in Mark 7:18-19? Again, take a look at the following 1611 KJV, 1881 RSV, NASV, and NIV translations of Mark 7:18-19, and note how similar they are to the 1388 Wycliffe Version, which is based on Jerome's anti-Jewish Latin Vulgate.

Jerome's 405 C.E. Latin Vulgate

English	Latin
And he saith to them: So are you also without knowledge? Understand you not that every thing from without entering into a man cannot defile him: because it entereth not into his heart but goeth into his belly and goeth out into the privy, <u>purging all meats</u>?	et ait illis sic et vos inprudentes estis non intellegitis quia omne extrinsecus introiens in hominem non potest eum communicare quia non introit in cor eius sed in ventrem et in secessum exit purgans omes escas (Mark VII).[118]

1388 Wycliffe Version

And he said to them, Ye be unwise also? Understand ye not that all thing withoutforth that enters into a man may not defoul him? For it has not entered into his heart, but into the womb, and beneath it goes out, <u>purging all meats</u>. (Mark VII)[119]

1611 King James Version (KJV)

18 And he saith unto them, Are ye so without understanding also? Do ye not perceive, that whatsoever thing from without entereth into the man, *it* cannot defile him; 19 because it entereth not into his heart, but into the belly, and goeth out into the draught, <u>purging all meats</u>? (Mk. 7:18-19)[120]

1881 King James Revised Version (RSV)

18 And he said to them, "Then are you also without understanding? Do you not see that whatever goes into from outside cannot defile him, 19 since it enters, not his heart but his stomach, and so passes on?" [<u>Thus he declared all foods clean.</u>] (Mk. 7:18-19)[121]

New American Standard Version (NASV)

18 And he said to them, "Are you so lacking in understanding also? Do you not understand that whatever goes into the man from outside cannot defile him, 19 because it does not go into his heart, but into his stomach, and is eliminated?" [_Thus He declared all foods clean._] (Mk. 7:18-19)

New International Version (NIV)

18 "Are you so dull?" he asked. "Don't you see that nothing that enters a man from the outside can make him 'unclean'? 19 For it doesn't go into his heart but into his stomach, and then out of his body." [In saying this, _Jesus declared all foods "clean."_] (Mk. 7: 18-19)

The first thing to note about the above translations is that none of the best manuscripts of the Nestle-Aland Greek New Testament and *Textus Receptus* say "all meats" or "all foods". There is, however, a *definite article* before the word "meats," as in *"katarizwv pavta ta Brwmata,"* meaning "purging all _the_ meats".

Why is this employment of the *definite article* important? As earlier noted, in Greek the *definite article* is used to identify the person or thing it modifies. Dana and Mantey tell us that the *definite article* does more than merely ascribe definiteness. It is used "to mark a specific object of thought."[122]

Affirming the importance of the *definite article* in verse 19, Dr. Jay P. Green Sr. interprets the Greek words *"katarizwv pavta ta Brwmata"* as meaning "purging all _the_ foods".[123]

Why is this Hebraic understanding of the Greek words _ta Brwmata_ significant? Because it tells us that the young Rabbi from Nazareth was *not* making a *general* statement about "all foods". Had *Yeshua* been addressing "all foods" generally there would have been no need for Mark to employ the *definite article "ta"* before the Greek word *"Brwmata"*.

By employing the *definite article* before the word *Brwmata*, Mark was using a common form of communication known to the people of that day, which assumed that the foods *Yeshua* was addressing were known to his audience.

Nevertheless, by interpreting the Greek words *"katarizwv pavta ta Brwmata"* to mean "purging all meats" and "declaring all foods clean," Catholic and Protestant translators changed the Hebraic meaning of the Greek text. In doing so, they redirected people's thought process away from the fact that *Yeshua* was a *Torah* observant Jewish Rabbi, who ate *only* kosher foods, and was speaking to *Torah* observant Jewish people, who also ate *only* kosher foods.

By teaching on the washing of one's hands before eating, *Yeshua* made a much larger point about honoring the decrees and traditions of men while breaking the much more important commands of *Torah,* and believing they were worshiping God by keeping the traditions of men.

Making His point, *Yeshua* quoted the prophet Isaiah, saying: "Well hath Isaiah prophesied of you hypocrites, as it is written, This people honoreth me with *their* lips, but their heart is far from me. Howbeit in vain do they worship me, teaching *for* doctrines the commandments of men" (Mk. 7:6-7; AKJV).

The Significance of the Word "For"

For most theologians, 1 Timothy 4:1-5 is another passage that proves that the dietary laws of Leviticus 11 are irrelevant to New Testament Believers.

But is this what Paul really taught? Again, take a careful look at the words Paul wrote to Timothy, saying:

> 1 But the Spirit distinctly says that in latter times some shall fall away from the belief, paying attention to misleading spirits, and teachings of demons,
>
> 2 speaking lies in hypocrisy, having been branded on their own conscience,
>
> 3 forbidding to marry, *saying* to abstain from foods which Elohim created to be received with thanksgiving by those who believe and know the truth.
>
> 4 Because every creature of Elohim is good, and none is to be rejected if it is received with thanksgiving,
>
> 5 for it is set apart by the Word of Elohim and prayer (1 Tim. 4:1-5; *The Scriptures*).

For many, the above passage appears that Paul is telling Timothy that lobsters, shrimp, crab, oysters, clams, catfish, swine, rabbit, bats, lizards, rattlesnake, snails, turtles, etc., are now "clean". A close examination of the text, however, reveals that Paul is saying the exact opposite.

One of the problems of citing this passage as proof that the dietary health food laws of Liviticus 11 are no longer relevant to New Testament Believers is that most Christians stop at verse 4. The problem with stopping at verse 4 is that Paul's teaching doesn't end at verse 4. It continues on through verse 5, saying: "**for** it is set apart by the Word of Elohim and prayer."

Equally significant, they ignore the operative word "**for**" in verse 5, which is the primitive Greek particle *gar,* meaning the "assigning a *reason*" to what has already been stated in the preceding verses.

The point Paul makes in verse 5 is that no food is "to be rejected if it is received with thanksgiving, **for** it is set apart by the Word of Elohim and prayer" (vs. 4-5).

Rather than negating the dietary laws, Paul was affirming their validity. Because everything Paul previously said in verses 1-4 was based upon his employment of the primitive Greek particle "**for**" -- food that is "set apart by the Word of Elohim," as in the dietary health food laws of Leviticus 11 and Deuteronomy 14.

American's Health Crisis

In the Book of Genesis we are told that many of God's people lived hundreds of years, with some living to 900 years of age (Gen. 5:5, 27). Older women were able to conceive and give birth to children, and men were still virile at 100 years of age (Gen. 21:1-8). Moses died at the age of 120, yet "his eyes were not weak nor his strength gone" (Deut. 34:7).

Today, medical doctors and health nutritionists agree that America's current health problems are largely due to processed foods and unhealthy eating habits. America now spends $1 trillion each year on the maintenance of health care. In fact, America spends twice as much per capita for health care as any other nation on earth. Yet, our health as a nation is still worse than the health of most other nations.

The following U.S. health data establishes the reasons the health problems of the American people are among the worst in the world.

* 58 million Americans have high blood pressure;
* half of us die from heart disease and one fourth from cancer, with tobacco use causing 180,000 yearly deaths and 3,000 yearly cases of lung cancer caused by second- hand smoke, and 48,000 yearly deaths caused by colon cancer;
* a 20-year study has found that red meat, pork, and processed meat consumption, such as salami and pastrami [at least 3 oz. every day for men and 2 oz. every day for women], is associated with a 50% increased risk for cancer of the lower colon;
* 20 million people have type 2 diabetes, putting them at risk for serious complications as blindness, kidney failure, heart disease, nerve damage and circulatory failure leading to amputation;
* 41 million have pre-diabetes, which can turn into full-blown diabetes;
* 750,000 suffer strokes each year, in which about 160,000 of these people die, and approximately 200,000 people live with lasting disability;
* half of all Americans have a health problem that requires taking a drug prescription every week;
* 100 million have high cholesterol;
* 24 million have insomnia;
* 50 million have regular headaches;
* 55 billion aspirins are consumed yearly;
* 9 million are alcoholics;
* 40% are overweight;
* 40 million have mental illness;
* 9.6 million older adults each year suffer drug-induced side effects, including 659,000 hospitalizations and 163,000 with memory loss.

Unfortunately, many of the above life-threatening diseases can be often be traced to the ignoring of the dietary health food laws of Scripture.

As a Christian, this writer has known several well-meaning Christians who were afflicted with life-threatening diseases, but would never admit that a personal choice of foods they ate had anything to do with the loss of their health.

Although many years have now passed, I can still hear one minister telling his congregation: "I know why God made pigs!" He then shouted: "Barbecue!" To which the people shouted back: "Amen!"

For most of my life, I too loved to eat barbecued ribs, ham, bacon, roasts beef with brown gravy, catfish, shrimp, processed foods, fastfoods, white flour breads, sodas, pastries, and ice cream. Little did I know that my day of reckoning was on the horizon.

On July 3, 2008, I cut my left thumb on a table saw while cutting a piece of wood. I had foolishly removed the saw-blade guard and the wood kicked out as I pushed it through the saw blade. Instantly, I had a deep gash across the middle of my left thumb, almost cutting it off.

After two trips to the hospital emergency room over a period of three weeks, two different rounds of antibiotics, and an infected thumb that wasn't healing properly, I made the decision to see a family doctor [MD].

On the first visit my new MD ordered a blood test and found that I was anemic. He then ordered a colon exam as a follow-up. Two weeks later, when I awoke from the colon exam the doctor informed my wife and I that I had a malignant tumor in my lower colon. Three days later, I was in a surgeon's office being prepared for surgery.

The following Monday morning I had a four stage tumor [about the size of an apple] removed from my colon. One month later, I began chemo treatment.

It has now been five years since my bout with cancer. I just completed another check-up with my cancer doctor, and was pronounced to be "doing well".

Today, as I look back on that experience the most unsettling part was not knowing that I had a silent killer gowing in my body. My only symptom was fatigue.

I shall never forget my first follow-up visit with my primary MD. He looked at me and said: "Let me get this right. You cut your finger on a saw and you thought that was bad?" I smiled and said: "That's right!"

Needless to say, my eating habits have changed dramatically. I now eat plenty of fresh fruits, berries, almonds, fresh vegetables, beans and brown rice. Every morning, with the exception of Sun-Day, my breakfast consists of a Power Health Shake that is filled with anti-cancer nutrients, such as carrot, kale, garlic, soy protein powder, wheat germ, a banana, and apple juice. Sound boring? It did to me *until* I was treated for colon cancer!

Looking back on my life, I now believe the root-cause of my bout with cancer was *spiritual,* not physical. I had violated God's dietary health laws and almost paid the ultimate price. Today, I eat very little meat, no pork, no scavenger fish or shell fish, sodas, or ice cream. In addition, I've cut way back on my consumption of sugar and sweets.

From my pre-surgery cancer condition to this present day, I have lost 30 pounds, approximately 15% of my body fat, without being on a diet or exercise program. As a result, I now have much more energy, and my body requires less sleep. But most important, I am cancer free!

Unfortunately, it took a life-threatening bout with cancer before I learned the error of my ways.

America's Food Enhancers

For about half of our existence as a nation, until the early 1900s, the American diet was relatively free of food enhancers. People were basically self-sufficient, growing their own vegetables, fruits, grains, and raising their own chickens and animal stock. Today, with the commercialization of food products that early American lifestyle is almost a thing of the past.

Since the early 1900s food conglomerants have converted the American people's taste for food into a multi-billion dollar industry. Giant food corporations now have laboratories where highly paid "food technicians" are constantly developing new food products, snacks, and drinks for the purpose of capturing a greater share of an ever expanding consumer market.

The increase of processed foods has also been accompanied with a growing list of ingredients now listed on food-product labels, which can easily include as many as twenty-five to thirty ingredients for one item.

In the past, little was ever said by medical doctors or politicians about the highly toxic ingredients now used in our processed foods and beverages. Today, however, medical doctors are beginning to confront our government's indifference to the ongoing contamination of America's food and beverage supply.

One of the deadly food enhancers used in most processed foods, such as breads, ketchup, pastries, cereals, sodas, sport drinks, syrups, etc., as well as baby foods, is *High-Fructose Corn Syrup.* Interestingly, *High-Fructose*

Corn Syrup was developed by the Japanese in the 1970s, and is often referred to in the medical profession as "Japan's revenge". It was so named because of America's dropping of the atom bomb on the cities of Hiroshima and Nagasaki, which ended the war in the Pacific.

One of the ingredients of *High-Fructose Corn Syrup* is *amaldehyde*. Ever heard of *formaldehyde?* Its what they use to embalm the dead. According to recent medical journals, *amaldehyde* is a poison which attacks the internal organs of the body, as well as the nervous system. *Amaldehyde* has been tested on mice and found to be a major factor in blocking the signal from the stomach that tells the brain when to stop eating, leading scientists to believe there is a direct link between the American people's consumption of *High-Fructose Corn Syrup* and obesity. In addition, nutritional research scientists at the University of California Davis have discovered that *High-Fructose Corn Syrup* is linked to heart disease and strokes.[124]

According to Dr. Robert Lustig, a University California of San Francisco [USCF] pediatric neuroendocrinologist, over the past three decades Americans have increased their fructose consumption from 15 grams per day to 75 grams per day or more.[125]

Remarkably, the average American now consume 130 pounds of fructose every year.[126] That's about 5 oz. of fructose every day!

Another little known fact the food and beverage conglomerates don't want the American people to know about is the toxic poisons in "Diet" and "Sugar Free" food and drink products found in artificial sweeteners, such as *Aspartame, Splenda* (Sucralose), and *Saccharin.*[127]

The same is true of the artificial food enhancer called *Monosodium Glutamate* [MSG]. MSG is a universally used flavor enhancer that permeates our processed, packaged, and frozen food products. It can be found in baby foods, bacon, bacon bits, baking supplies, barbecue sauce, canned tomato sauce, chili sauce, gravy mixes, beef stock, breads, canned soups, ketchup, salad dressings, seasoned croutons, spices and seasonings, hot dogs, cured meats, Chinese foods, restaurant food buffets, delicatessen foods, diet foods, snack foods, cans of tuna, and injected turkeys.

MSG is used in most dine-in and fastfood restaurants, and is served to our children in school cafeterias on a daily basis. MSG can cause migraine headaches and balance difficulties; precipitate severe shortness of breath, asthma attacks and heart irregularities; cause disabling arthritis, and even serious depressions. Medical science has linked it to inducing disruptive behavior problems in children, as well as Alzheimer's and other nerve-degenerative diseases. Interestingly, MSG is another highly toxic food enhancer that was developed by the Japanese.[128]

America's High Sodium Diet

Equally troubling is the high level of sodium found in processed food and beverages. There is some sodium in all foods, with higher concentrations in animal meat. But the highest levels of sodium are found in processed foods.

Yet in spite of the medical dangers caused by high sodium diets, such as high blood pressure, strokes, cordio-vascular disease, and increase cancer incidence and metastasis, Americans consume 10 times more sodium than their forefathers.

According to the Mayo Clinic "Dietary Guidelines," the recommended daily intake of sodium is not to exceed 2,300 mg. If a person has high blood pressure, kidney disease or diabetes, or is middle-aged or older, or black, however, the recommended daily intake of sodium is not to exceed 1,500 mg per day.[129]

Nevertheless, today, high levels of sodium have become a normal part of the American diet. For most Americans, its taste that counts! And that's exactly what the processed food executives are counting on.

This is precisely the reason we have included the following list of processed food items and their sodium content per serving as found on the "Nutrition Facts" label.

Salt – 2, 325mg per serv. = 1 tbsp.
Ketchup – 190mg per serv. = 1 tbsp.
Potato Chips – 180mg per serv. = 1 oz (15 chips).
Barbeque Chips – 250mg per serv. = 10z (15 chips).
Tortilla Chips – 125mg per serv. = 1oz (10 chips).
Salted Nuts – 120mg per serv. = ¼ cup.
Butter Flavor Popcorn – 520mg per serv. = 1 bag.
Pepperoni Pizza – 1080mg per serv. = 1/5 pizza.
Salad Dressing – 150mg per serv. = 2 tbsp.
Barbecue Sauce – 370mg per serv. = t tbsp.
Pasta Sauce – 600mg per serv. = ½ cup.
Soy Sauce (less sodium) – 575mg per serv. = 1 tbsp.

Soy Sauce (regular) – 920mg per serv. = 1 tbsp.

Teriyaki Marinade – 600mg per serv. = 1 tbsp.

Olives – 260mg per serv. = 5 olives.

Bread & Butter Pickles – 170mg per serv. = 1oz (3 chips).

Sodium Crackers – 190mg per serv. = 5 crackers.

White Bread – 220mg per serv. = 1 slice.

Whole Wheat Bread – 210mg per serv. = 1 slice.

Oatmeal Cookies (plain) – 120mg per serv. = 2 cookies.

Oatmeal Cookies (iced) – 190mg per serv. = 2 cookies.

Angel Food Cake (plain) – 440mg per serv. = 1/8th of cake.

Chocolate Wheat Chex (cereal) – 240mg per serv. = ¾ cup.

Rice Krispies – 220mg per serv. = 1¼ cup.

Raisin Bran – 350mg per serv. = 1 cup.

18 oz can Chunky Vegetable soup – 770mg per serv. = 1 cup.

18 oz can Tomato soup – 408mg per serv. = 1 cup.

14 oz can Tomatoes – 250mg per serv. = ½ cup.

15 oz can Corn – 360mg per serv. = ½ cup.

15 oz can Green Beans – 340mg per serv. = ½ cup.

16 oz can Beans – 470mg per serv. = ½ cup.

16 oz can Chili Beans – 530mg per serv. = ½ cup.

Cheese – 170mg per serv. = 1oz.

Low Fat Cottage Cheese – 450mg per serv. = ½ cup.

Boneless Ham Steak – 690mg per serv. = 2oz.

Bone-in Ham Roast – 840mg per serv. = 3oz.

Smoked Pork Chops – 900mg per serv. = 3oz,

Bacon – 330mg per serv. = 2 slices.

Pork Ribs (with BBQ sauce) – 580mg per serv. = 4oz (2 ribs).

Pork Ribs (without BBQ sauce) – 210mg per serv. = 4oz (2 ribs).

Italian Sausage – 450mg per serv. = 2oz.

Franks (hotdog) – 480mg per serv. = 1 link.

Smoked Sausage Links – 520mg per serv. = ½ link.

Beef Balogna – 310mg per serv. = 1 slice.

BBQ Chicken Wings – 380mg per serv. = 3oz (2 wings).

Chicken (no salt added) – 80mg per serv. = 4oz.

Chicken (12% solution added) – 210mg per serv. = 4 oz.

Turkey (no salt added) – 80mg per serv. = 4oz.

Turkey (15% solution added) – 710mg per serv. = 4oz.

Rib-eye Steak – 200mg per serv. = 4oz.

Chuck Roast – 180mg per serv. = 4oz.
Corned Beef Brisket – 960mg per serv. = 4oz.

(Sodium contents may vary with different companies.)

America's High Fat Diet

Today, America has the greatest number of overweight and obese people of any country in the world. On May 29, 2014, the *Wall Street Journal* reported that a study conducted by the Institute for Health Metrics and Evaluation [IHME] at the University of Washington, between 1980 and 2013, found that obese and overweight kids have increased 50 percent.

As of 2013, 22 percent of girls and 24 percent of boys are overweight or obese. Among men, 37 percent are overweight or obese, and 38 percent of women are overweight or obese. As to the reason, the study found that between processed and fastfoods there is greater consumer access, and prices are cheaper than ever before. Today, the average American consumes three hamburgers and four orders of fries per week. Even though fastfood chains are now taking steps to remove deadly trans fats from their cooking process, a major problem is the killer fats their food products contain.

Just one thigh of Original Kentucky Fried Chicken contains 20 grams of fat. Extra Crispy increases the fat content to 27 grams. Add mashed potatoes, gravy, a biscuit and the fat content is now at 40 grams and 660 calories for one serving.

A Big Mac at McDonald's has 29 grams of fat. Add another 19 grams of fat for french fries and a single meal contains 48 grams of fat, including 920 calories.

A Whopper at Burger King contains 39 grams of fat. Add cheese and the total fat intake is 47 grams. Make it a combo with medium fries and the fat intake is 59 grams. Add a medium soft drink and the fat intake jumps to 67 grams, along with 1,330 calories.

A Baconator at Wendy's has 51 grams of fat. Add an order of medium fries and a medium chocolate Frosty and a single meal has become 81 grams of fat, with 1,670 calories.

A simple grilled Burrito with beef at Taco Bell has 30 grams of fat and 640 calories. For under $10 at Taco Bell a person can get up to 6,000 calories. The same is true for most other fastfood restaurants.

Sugar is another killer. Reportedly, it should be no more than 5 percent of a person's daily diet. Today with kids, its up to 30 percent.

In 1970, Americans spent approximately $6 billion on fastfood. In 2000, we spent more than $110 billion. Today, in spite of repeated warnings from a host of various health organizations, Americans spend more money on fastfood than they spend on personal items, such as computers, new cars, and higher education combined.

America's Nutrition Labels

On January 1, 2006, all processed foods sold in the U.S. were required to list ingredients contained in packaged food and bottled beverages, such as saturated fat, trans fat, cholesterol, sodium, protein, etc. Since that time, many health conscious Americans have relied on the "Nutritional Facts" labels provided on the packaged foods and beverages.

But there is a little known problem with these labels. The U.S. Food and Drug Administration (FDA) ruling on the listing of trans fats states: "if the serving contains less than 0.5 gram, the content, when declared, shall be expressed as zero."

This means that a person could buy a package of cookies, with each cookie containing 0.4 grams of trans fat, and end up eating several grams of trans fats even though the label lists the cookies as having zero trans fats. For most Americans, this is a minor discrepancy, and just not that important. For some, however, it could make a major difference in the quality and longevity of life. A recent fourteen-year study found that just a 2 percent increase in trans fats elevated a person's risk of heart disease by 36 percent.[130]

Another example of misleading "Nutrition Facts" labels is that daily value percentage of fat or sodium is based on a 2,000 calorie diet with a suggested sodium intake of 2,400mg. According to the Mayo Clinic sodium intake guidelines, the 2,400mg daily intake of sodium is acceptable only *if* a person is under 40 years of age and in good health.

As earlier noted, existing "Nutrition Facts" labels make no mention of limiting sodium intake to 1,500mg for mid-aged and older people, especially among those who have high blood pressure, kidney disease or diabetes, or black.

Does anyone know the number of this middle-age and older consumer group that is being kept in the dark about not exceeding the daily sodium limit of 1,500mg? Certainly not this writer. But most certainly, its a large number -- millions of Americans.

America's Ingredient Labels

Another example of misleading information on America's processed food products can be found on the "Ingredients" labels. Under the FDA's current regulation for listing "ingredients" companies are allowed to hide the toxic food enhancer MSG under a number of misleading names, such as "Natural Flavors," "Flavors," "Hydrolyzed Vegetable Protein," "Accents," etc.

The Federal Code of Regulations Section 101.22, defining natural flavorings, states that "natural flavoring" be applied to: "the essential oil, oleoresin, essence or extractive, protein hydrolysate, distillate or any product of roasting, heating or enzymolysis which contains the flavoring constitutents derived from a spice, fruit or fruit juice, vegetable or vegetable juice, edible yeast, herb, bark, root, leaf or similar plant material, meat, seafood, poultry, eggs, dairy products or fermentation products thereof whose significant function in food is flavoring rather than nutritional."[131]

Unfortunately, this defininition opens the door for processed food conglomerates to label *protein hydrolysate* as "natural flavoring," a designation intended to hide the highly toxic ingredient MSG.

The Selling of America's Health

Today in America, we are hearing a lot about the lobbying of Congress by special interest groups. American food conglomerantes such as Kraft, General Mills, Kellog's, Coca Cola, PepsiCo, and others, sell products that make up 60 percent of the American diet. Many of these products contain toxic ingredients such as sugars, salts, trans fats, food colorings, and preservatives labeled as fructose, sucralose, hydrogenated oil, sodium benzoate, potassium benzoate, dodium nitrates, blue, green, red, and yellow, and MSG.

What many Americans want is to be informed about what they are consuming, and whether or not it is healthy. But the food conglomerantes aggrerssively oppose their effort to know becasuse it would adversely affect their profit, which is in the billions. For example, in 2012, the food industry and biotech groups, such as Monsanto and Du Pont, spent $46 million – more than $8 million of which came from Mansanto – to oppose labeling initiatives.[132]

In 2013, top food conglomerantes donated massive amounts of cash to defeat the American consumer's right to know. For example, PepsiCo donated close to $2.5 million, Kraft more than $2 million, Coca Cola $1.7 million, etc.[133]

Add political influence to the millions in cash, and it makes the food conglomerantes one of the most potent forces in America. In 2013, Grocery Manufacturing Association [GMA], whose members include the nations largest food makers, 29 out of 35 GMA's lobbyists were what is called "revolvers" because they previously held government jobs.[134]

Equally troubling, biotech groups, such as Monsanto and Du Pont, are now spending millions to gain approval from the Food and Drug Administration for genetically engineered foods.[135]

But this is nothing new. Since the early 1900s elected politicians, medical doctors, and government officials have been selling the health of the American people to the powerful food and beverage conglomerates for financial and political gain. If you want to know the real story behind America's health problems, as well as the self-serving medical doctors, elected politicians, and government officials who cater to the lobbying interests of America's powerful food and beverage corporations, read Dr. T. Colin Campbell's book entitled *The China Study.*

The Sanitization of Christianity's Hebraic Roots

For most theologians, the great debate about the revelance of the *Torah* to Christian Believers forever ended with the ruling of the Jerusalem Council of Messianic Believers in Jerusalem, which was stated by it spiritual leader James, saying: "Wherefore my sentence is that we trouble not them, which from among the Gentiles are turned to God: but that we write unto them that they abstain from pollutions of idols, and *from* fornication, and *from* things strangled, and *from* blood" (Acts 15:19-20; AKJV).

Dr. G. Campbell Morgan says that this "summing up by James is characterized by wisdom, and his finding was that Gentiles should not be troubled with anything that was purely Jewish. The difficulty cleared away, the discussion ceased."[136]

But was this what James was really saying when he made that important pronouncement about Gentile conduct?

According to Luke's account, the great debate of Acts 15 involved much more than that which is claimed by Christian theologians. For example, in Acts 15:5, Luke writes: "And some of the believers who belonged to the sect of the Pharisees, rose up, saying, 'It is necessary to circumcise them, and to command them to keep the Torah of Mosheh'" (Acts 15:5; *The Scriptures*).

Notice that Luke addresses this particular group of Pharisees as "the sect of Pharisees," who were "Believers". The fact that these Pharisee Believers were calling for the circumcision of Gentile converts suggests that they belonged to the sect of Shammai Pharisees, who held to the strict interpretation of both the *Written* and *Oral Torahs*.

At this point, Luke records that Peter rose up and said:

> 7... Men *and* brethren, ye know how that a good while ago God made choice among us, that the Gentiles by my mouth should hear the word of the gospel, and believe.
>
> 8 And God, which knoweth the hearts, bare them witness, Giving them the Holy Ghost, even as *he did* unto us;
>
> 9 And put no difference between us and them, purifying their hearts by faith.
>
> 10 Now therefore why tempt ye God, to put a yoke upon the neck of the disciples, which neither our fathers nor we were able to bear? (Acts 15:7-10; AKJV).

It is significant for us to understand that in Jewish thought the term "yoke" (v. 10) often means *Torah* [Law]. So here is the great question: Why did Peter say that if Gentile converts were circumcised it would be the same as putting a "yoke" upon their necks?

To an orthodox Jew, the answer was quite obvious. Peter knew that if Gentile converts were made to be circumcised then they too would be obligated to observe the hundreds of man-made rules and traditions of the *Oral Torah*.

Josephus states that this was one of the major issues of that day, saying: "The Pharisees have imposed upon the people many laws taken from the tradition of the fathers, which are not written in the law of Moses" (*Jewish Antiquities,* XIII. 10. 6).

Also, the Messianic researcher Dean Wheelock writes:

> The final outcome of the continuing development of *Pharisaic Oral Tradition* was the development of a full blown *Oral Torah* or law. Thus, there came to be two *Torot,* the *Oral Torah* with its traditions and Rabbinic rulings, now made into law, and the *Written Torah* (God's Law) as found in the first five books of our printed Scriptures.... The intended purpose of the Rabbinic *Oral Torah* was so that all Judaism would have a similar interpretation of the *Written Torah,* thereby providing a sense of unity to all Jews no matter where they lived – certainly a worthy goal. However, the end result was that the *Oral Torah* became a law book unto itself, whose rules could take precedence over the *Written Torah* when the two disagreed.[137]

The Four "Gentile Requirements" of Acts 15

Clearly, Peter's argument was central to the Jerusalem Council's ruling. Because after Peter spoke the Council rejected the idea of requiring Gentile converts to be circumcised, which would have required them to observe both the *Written* and *Oral Torahs.* Instead, the Council agreed to place upon Gentile Believers seeking acceptance into the Jewish Messianic community four requirements: abstaining from idolatry, the eating of things strangled, eating blood, and sexual immorality (v. 19).

Contrary to the misconception of many, these four requirements were neither new or unique to Gentile converts. Rather, they were the very same requirements the patriarchs and children of Israel were commanded to observe, going all the way back to Noah (Gen. 9:4) and Moses (Lev. 3:17; 7:26; 17:10; 19:26; Deut. 12:16).

Affirming the importance of these four requirements, the prophet Ezekiel states that the reason God allowed the people of Judah to be taken into Babylonian captivity was because they did "eat blood, and lifted up their eyes to idols, shed blood, and defiled everyone his neighbor's wife" (Ezk. 33:25-26).

The problem with citing the four requirements of Acts 15:19-20 as being "Gentile requirements" is that most Bible teachers stop at verse 20. The problem with stopping at verse 20 is that James' explanation of the Council's ruling doesn't end at verse 20. It continues on through verse 21, which begins with the primitive Greek particle *gar* ['**for**'], meaning the assigning the *reason* for everything previously said.[138]

What was that *reason* given by the Jerusalem Council for acceptance of Gentile converts into the Jewish community of Believers? James says:

> 21 "<u>For</u> from ancient generations Mosheh has in every city, those proclaiming him – being read in the congregations every Sabbath" (Acts 15:21; *The Scriptures*).

The importance of verse 21 cannot be overstated. Because it is in this verse that James makes his case for the acceptance of *Torah* observant Gentile Believers into the Messianic Jewish community.

Why did James need to explain the *reason* for the Council's ruling? Because at that particular time Gentile converts were attending synagogues on the Sabbath to hear the instruction of *Torah*. Why did those first century Gentile converts go to the synagogue on Shabbat to hear the instruction of *Torah?* Because at that particular time there were few who could read or write, and because scrolls of the Hebrew Scriptures were not readily available.

Some would contradict this statement and say non-Jews were not allowed in synagogues. But this is not true. At the time of *Yeshua,* non-Jews were allowed to sit in the visitor or Gentile section. Even the Temple Mount had an Outer Court where Gentiles could assemble.

There was also a practical matter. The Council's ruling was meant to resolve the day-to-day relationship between Jewish Believers and Gentile converts. At that particular time Messianic congregations were predominately Jewish. Most certainly, *Torah* observant Jewish Believers did not want biblically illiterate Gentile converts, who were steeped in paganism, joining their fellowship and insist on observing their former pagan beliefs and customs.

Nevertheless, as the number of Gentile converts increased, history concurs that this is precisely what happened.

The Character of First Century Worship

In seeking to establish a model for first century worship, perhaps no other passage in the Apostolic Writings has been misrepresented as has James 2:1-4. For example, the Bible expositor E. C. Gibson writes: "Observe the insight which this passage gives us into the character of the assemblies of the early Christians.... Notice (the Greek word) *suvagwgn* used here, and here only in the New Testament, of a Christian assembly for worship (cf. Ignatius, 'Ad Polyc.,' c. iv., *Pukvoterov suvagwgai givestwsan*)."[139]

But is this what James really meant when he employed the Greek word *suvagwgn?* Again, take a look at the following 1611 KJV, 1881 RSV, NASV, and NIV translations of James 2:1-2, and note how similar they are to the 1388 Wycliffe Version, which was based on Jerome's anti-Jewish Latin Vulgate.

Jerome's 405 C.E. Latin Vulgate

English

Latin

My brethren, have not the faith of our Lord Jesus Christ of glory, with respect of persons. For if there shall come into your assembly a man having a golden ring, in fine apparel; and there shall come in also a poor man in mean attire:

fratres mei nolite in personarum acceptione habere fidem Domini nostri Iesu Christi gloriae etenim si introierit inconventu vestro vir aureum anulum habens in veste candida introierit autemet pauper in sordido habitu (James II).[140]

1388 Wycliffe Version

My brethren, nil ye have the faith of our Lord Jesus Christ of glory, in acception of persons. For if a man that has a golden ring and in a fair clothing, comes into your company, and a poor man enters in a foul clothing,... (James II).[141]

1611 King James Version (KJV)

2 My brethren, have not the faith of our LORD Jesus Christ, *the LORD* of glory, with respect of persons. 2 For if there come unto your <u>assembly</u> a man with a gold ring, in goodly apparel, and there come in also a poor man in vile raiment;... (James 2:1-2).[142]

1881 King James Revised Version (RSV)

2 My brethren, show no partiality as you hold the faith of our LORD Jesus Christ, the Lord of glory. 2 For if a man with gold rings and in fine clothing comes into your <u>assembly</u>, and a poor man with shabby clothing also comes in,... (James 2:1-2).[143]

New American Standard Version (NASV)

2 My brethren, do not hold your faith in our glorious LORD Jesus Christ with an *attitude* of personal favoritism. 2 For if a man comes into your <u>assembly</u> with a gold ring and dressed in fine clothes, and there also comes in a poor man in dirty clothes,... (James 2:1-2).

New International Version (NIV)

2 My brothers, as believers in our glorious LORD Jesus Christ, don't show favoritism. 2 Suppose a man comes into your <u>meeting</u> wearing a gold ring and fine clothes, and a poor man in shabby clothes also comes in... (James 2:1-2).

Notice in each of the above versions the underlined English words "assembly," "company," and "meeting" are exactly like Jerome's anti-Jewish Latin Vulgate. According to Arndt and Gingrich, however, the primary meaning of the Greek word *suvagwgn* means "*place of assembly* – **a.** of the Jewish *synagogue.*"[144]

Affirming this understanding Dr. Alfred Marshall and Dr. Jay P. Green, Sr. translate the Greek word *suvagwgn* as meaning "synagogue."[145]

And the Jewish historian Emil Shurer writes:

> ... it is necessary for of all to remark, that the *main object* of these Sabbath assemblages in the synagogue was not for public worship in its stricter sense, *i.e.* not devotion, but religious instruction, and this for an Israelite was above all *instruction in the law.* Josephus rightly views the matter in this light: "Not once or twice or more frequently did our lawgiver command us to hear the law, but to come together weekly, with the cessation of other work, to hear the law and to learn it accurately." Nor was Philo in the wrong, when he called the synagogues "houses of instruction," in which "the native philosophy" was studied and every kind of virtue taught.[146]

Why is this historical understanding of the synagogue assembly of first century Nazarene Believers important? Because in Jewish thought, the instruction of the *Torah* is the highest form of worship.

Contrary to the misconception of many, this is precisely the reason James employed the Hebrew term *"suvagowgn"*. Because it was in the *synagogue* that the first century *ekklesia* ['called out ones'] assembled every Shabbat to be instructed in the *Torah.*

It is also the reason that the Greek term *ekklesia* is a Hebrew parallelism found in the *Septuagint,* which was employed when Israelites gathered for religious purposes (Deut. 31:30), especially to be instructed in the *Torah* (Deut. 4:10; 9:10; 18:16).[147]

It is also the reason James' explanation of the Jerusalem Council's Gentile ruling ended with the the following summary: "<u>For</u> Moses of old time hath in every city them that preach him, being read in the synagogues [Gk. *suvagwgn*] every sabbath day" (Acts 15:21; AKJV).

It is also the reason Paul wrote to the Nazarenes at Thessalonia, saying: "But of the times and seasons, brethren, ye have no need that I write unto you" (1 Thess. 5:1; AKJV).

Why did Paul say that there was there no need for those Nazarenes Believers at Thessalonica to be instructed on the appointed times and seasons? Because Paul knew they had already learned about "the times and <u>seasons</u>," [Gk. *kairwn,* a Hebrew parallel found in the *Septuagint,* meaning *"festal seasons,"* Ex. 23:14, 17; Lev. 23:4].[148]

Where had they learned about the appointed *festal seasons?* Obviously, they had learned about them at the *synagogue,* during the observance of the appointed Spring and Fall festivals.

But even more important, it was the reason Luke recorded the custom of those first century followers of the young Rabbi from Nazareth -- to meet at the *synagogue* on Shabbat. Quoting Paul's own words, Luke writes:

> 17 And it came to pass, that when I was come again to Jerusalem, even while I prayed in the temple, I was in a trance;
>
> 18 And saw him saying unto me, Make haste, and get thee quickly out of Jerusalem: for they will not receive thy testimony concerning me.
>
> 19 And I said, LORD, they know that I imprisoned and beat in every synagogue them that believed on thee.... (Acts 22: 17-19; AKJV).

The significance of this account is that those first century Jewish and Gentile followers of the young Rabbi from Nazareth were still meeting in the *synagogues* in the 60s to be instructed in the *Torah* -- well over thirty years *after* the *Ruach HaKodesh* had been given to those first Jewish Believers on that historic Shavuot/Pentecost day in Jerusalem.

The "Legalistic" Propagandists

For most theologians, Paul's Epistle to the Galatians is the "Magna Charta" of Christian liberty, and Galatians 3:10-13 is proof that those who observe *Torah* are "under the works of the law". The Bible expositor Dr. E. Huxtable writes:

> Withdrawing from the category of those who were of faith, they were preparing to join those who were of the works of the Levitical Law.... the prominent notion of their condition is that they are in a state of slavery, that the dispensation they are under is spiritually an enslaving one, a yoke of bondage.... He (Paul) means, not precisely that a curse has already been definitely pronounced upon them so they now stand there condemned, but that the *threatening* of a curse is always sounding in their

ears, filling them with uneasiness, with constant apprehension that they shall themselves fall under it."[149]

But was this what Paul really meant when he wrote to the new converts of Galatia about the works of *Torah?* Take a look at the following 1611 KJV, 1881 RSV, NASV, and NIV translations, and note how similar they are to the 1388 Wycliffe Version, which is based on Jerome's anti-Jewish Latin Vulgate.

Jerome's 405 C.E. Latin Vulgate

English	Latin
For as many as are of the works of the law are under a curse. For it is written: Cursed is every one that abideth, not in all things which are written in the book of the law to do them. But that in the law no man is justified with God, it is manifest: because the just man liveth by faith. But the law is not of faith; but he that doeth those things shall live in them. Christ hath redeemed us from the curse of the law, being made a curse for us (for it is written: Cursed is every one that hangeth on a tree)	quicumque enim ex operibus legis sunt sub maledicto sunt scriptum est enim maledictus omnis qui non permanserit in omnibus quae scripta sunt in libro legis ut faciat ea quoniam autem in lege nemo iustificatur apud Deum manifestum est quia iustus ex fide vivit lex autem non est ex fide sed qui fecerit ea vivet in illis Christus nos redemit de maledicto legis factus pro nobis maledictum quia scriptum est maledictus omnis qui pendet in ligno (Galatians III).[150]

1388 Wycliffe Version

For all that are of the works of the law, are under curse, for it is written, Each man is cursed that abides not in all things that are written in the book of the law, to do those things. And that no man is justified in the law before God, it is open, for a rightful man lives of belief.

But the law is not of belief. But he that does those things of the law, shall live in them. But Christ again-bought us from the curse of the law, and was made accursed for us. For it is written, Each man is cursed that hangs in the tree ... (Galatians III).[151]

1611 King James Version (KNV)

10 <u>For as many as are of the works of the law are under the curse</u>: for it is written, Cursed *is* every one that continueth not in all things which are written in the book of the law to do them.

11 But that no man is justified by the law in the sight of God, *it is* evident: for, The just shall live by faith. 12 And the law is not of faith: but The man that doeth them shall live in them. 13 Christ hath redeemed us from the curse of the law, being made a curse for us: for it is written, Cursed *is* every one that hangeth on a tree... (Gal. 3:10-13).[152]

1881 King James Revised Version (RSV)

10 <u>For all who rely on works of the law are under a curse;</u> for it is written, "Crused be everyone who does not abide by all things written in the book of the law, and do them." 11 Now it is evident that no man is justified before God by the law; for

"He who through faith is righteous shall live"; 12 but the law does not rest on faith, for "He who does them shall live by them." 13 Christ redeemed us from the curse of the law, having become a curse for us–for it is written, "Cursed be every one who hangs on a tree"... (Gal. 3:10-13).[153]

New American Standard Version (NASV)

10 <u>For as many as of the works of the Law are under a curse</u>; for it is written, CURSED IS EVERYONE WHO DOES NOT ABIDE BY ALL THINGS WRITTEN IN THE BOOK OF THE LAW, TO PERFORM THEM." 11 Now that no one is justified by the Law before God is evident; for, "THE RIGHTEOUS MAN SHALL LIVE BY FAITH." 12

However, the Law is not of faith; on the contrary, "HE WHO PRACTICES THEM SHALL LIVE BY THEM." 13 Christ redeemed us from the curse of the Law, having become a curse for us–for it is written, "CURSED IS EVERYONE WHO HANGS ON A TREE"... (Gal. 3:10-13).

New International Version (NIV)

10 <u>All who rely on observing the law are under a curse</u>, for it is written: Cursed is everyone who does not continue to do everything written in the Book of the Law.

11 Clearly no-one is justified before God by the law, because, The righteous will live by faith.

12 The law is not based on faith; on the contrary, The man who does these things will live by them.

13 Christ redeemed us from the curse of the law by becoming a curse for us, for it is written: Cursed is everyone who is hung on a tree... (Gal. 3:10-13).

Notice that each of the above versions interpret the words of Paul as meaning "all" who live within the framework of the *Torah* are "under a curse" (v. 10). But if this is what Paul meant then Rabbi *Yeshua,* the tens of thousands of Jew and Gentile first century *Torah* observant Believers, including Paul himself, were living under a curse. Because it can easily be established that the young Rabbi from Nazareth was *Torah* observant. Likewise, it can be established that Jewish Believers were meeting daily in the Temple some thirty years after the death and resurrection of *Yeshua* (Acts 2:46). It can easily be established that these same Jewish believers were "... all zealous for the *Torah*" (Acts 21:18-20). And it can easily be established that Paul was a practicing *Torah* observant Pharisee.

Luke records that some thirty years after Paul's conversion experience he told members of a Sanhedrin: "I am a Pharisee, the son of a Pharisee" (Acts 23:6).

What was a Pharisee? The scholars of *Unger's Bible Dictionary* tell us that the term "Pharisee" means "one who associates himself with the law in order to observe it strictly in opposition to the encroachments of Hellenism."[154]

Contrary to the misconception of many, when Paul employed the Greek preposition *"ek,"* in Galatians 3:10, he was *not* addressing *all* who live within the framework of the *Torah*. The Greek grammar scholars Dana and Mantey inform us that the Greek preposition *ek,* meaning "out of, from within," is employed "to add a new idea to the word or modify or even intensify the meaning of that particular word."[155]

Thus when Paul wrote the Greek words *"Osoi gar ek ergwn vomou eisiv, upo katarav"* (v. 10), "For as many as are *ek* [*lit.,* 'out of, from within'] works of law are under a curse," he was intensifying the meaning of what he was saying about the dependency on the works of the *Torah* for salvation.

Affirming this very same emphasis, Dr. Jay P. Green, Sr. translates the Greek preposition *"ek,"* as meaning: "For as many as are *ek* ['out of']works of law are under a curse" (Gal. 3:10).[156]

As earlier noted, the practice of the first century Jewish Believers was to first bring Gentiles to faith in *Yeshua* and then instruct them in the *Torah*. However, it is evident from Paul's letter that a zealous group of Pharisee propagandists had reversed this order, teaching that the Galatian converts had to first observe the *Torah* before they could be justified with God.

Ironically, for the past nineteen hundred years this very same misconception has been taught in the Christian camp, except in reverse. Christian propagandists have been telling Believers that anyone who observes *Torah* ['Law'] is "under a curse".

The most interesting part of this story is that Paul's message to the new Galatian converts refutes both views. Because Paul goes on to say, "Messiah redeemed us from the curse of the Torah, having become a curse for us..." (v. 13).

That, my friend, is precisely what Jewish and Christian propagandists do not want you to know. Because with this Pauline understanding, like the new Galatian converts, you too can observe the *Torah* and fulfill the righteous commands of God with high confidence that you are *not* "under the curse of the *Torah*". Because "Messiah redeemed us from the curse of the Torah, having become a curse for us" (v. 13; *The Scriptures*).

"Making Void the Law"

For most theologians the words "having abolished in his flesh the enmity, *even* the law of commandments" (**Eph. 2:14-15**), is another passage that proves the *Torah* is no longer relevant to New Testament Believers.

But is this what Paul really meant when he wrote those words? Again, take a look at the following 1611 KJV, 1881 RSV, NASV, and NIV translations of Ephesians 2:14-15, and note how similar they are to the 1388 Wycliffe Version, which is based on Jerome's anti-Jewish Lantin Vulgate.

Jerome's 405 C.E. Latin Vulgate

English	Latin
For he is our peace, who hath made both one, and breaking down the middle wall of partition, <u>the enmities in his flesh</u>: <u>making void the law of commandments contained in decrees</u>: that he might make the two in himself into one new man, making peace	Ipse est enim pax nostra qui fecit utraque unum et medium parietem maceriae solvens inimicitiam in carne legem mandatorum decretis evacuans ut duos condat in semet ipsum in unum novum hominem faciens pacem (Ephesians II).[157]

1388 Wycliffe

For he is our peace that made both one, and unbinding the middle wal of a wall without mortar, <u>enmities in His flesh, and voided the law of commandments</u> by dooms, that He make twain in Himself into a new man, making peace... (Ephesians II).[158]

1611 King James Version (KJV)

14 For he is our peace, who hath made both one, and hath broken down the middle wall of partition *between us;*
15 having <u>abolished in his flesh the enmity, *even* the law of</u>

commandments <u>*contained*</u> in ordinances; for to make in himself of twain one new man, *so* making peace... (Eph. 2:14-15).[159]

1881 King James Revised Version (RSV)

14 For he is our peace, who has made us both one, and has broken down the dividing wall of hostility, 15 by <u>abolishing in his flesh the law of commandments and ordinances</u>, that he might create in himself one new man in place of two, so making peace... (Eph. 2:14-15).[160]

New American Standard Version (NASV)

14 For He Himself is our peace, who made both *groujps into* one and broke down the barrier of the dividing wall, 15 by <u>abolishing in His flesh the enmity, *which is* the Law of commandments *contained* in ordinances</u>, so that in Himself He might make the two into one new man, *thus* establishing peace... (Eph. 2:14-15).

New International Version (NIV)

14 For he himself is our peace, who has made the two one and has destroyed the barrier, the dividing wall of hostility, 15 by <u>abolishing in his flesh the law with its commandments and regulations</u>. His purpose was to create in himself one new man out of the two, thus making peace... (Eph. 2:14-15).

Once again, when the above versions are compared with the best Greek manuscripts of both the Nestle-Aland and *Textus Receptus* Greek texts it becomes evident that translators sanitized the meaning of the Greek text by subtracting and adding words.

Dr. Alfred Marshall and Dr. Jay P. Green, Sr., however, translate the Greek words *"tov vomov twn evtolwv ev dogmasiv katargnsas"* as meaning "the law of the commandments in decrees having abolished..." (v. 15).[161]

Nevertheless, for most theologians the words "the law of commandments *contained* in ordinances" are proof that "the enmity" *Yeshua* abolished in

His flesh was the *Torah*. But when these words are understood in the context of what Paul was saying, nothing could be further from the truth.

For example, Paul says to the Gentile Believers in Ephesus: "... remember that you were without Messiah, excluded from the citizenship of Yisra'el and strangers from the covenants of promise, having no expectation and without Elohim in the world" (Eph. 2:12; *The Scriptures*).

Addressing this very passage, S. D. Salmond of the *Expositor's Greek Testament* writes: "So the sense is—'who in His crucified flesh (*i.e.,* by His death on the cross) broke down the middle-wall of the partition, to wit the enmity' (*i.e.,* the hostile feeling between Jew and Gentile)."[162]

Unknown to most Christians, but well known within rabbinic Judaism is the fact that for most of the first century the enmity and hostile feelings between Jews and Gentiles were caused by the anti-Gentile ordinances of the ruling Shammai Pharisees, who were intensely pro-Jewish. During this period the Shammai decrees opposed all approach to, and by, non-Jews, and they dealt harshly with non-Jewish proselytes, even the most distinguished.

Dr. Alfred Edersheim informs us that the Shammai decrees were passed into Jewish law by first executing the murder of a number of Hillelite Pharisees, about 20 C.E., who had come to the deliberative assembly of *eighteen decrees,* of which the objective was to prevent all intercourse with Gentiles and furnish the Shammai leaders of the national movement.[163]

The first twelve *ordinances* forbade the purchase of the most necessary articles of diet from Gentiles; the next five forbade the learning of their language, declared their testimony invalid, and their offerings unlawful, and prohibited all intercourse with them; while the last referred to firstfruits.[164] The Shammai Pharisees held that no Gentile merited a share in the World to Come, no matter how pious or righteous he might be (Sanhedrin 105A; Tosefta, Sanhedrin ch 13).[165]

Thus instead of the "enmity" being the *Torah* of Moses, it was the *eighteen decrees* of the first century Shammai Pharisee dominated Sanhedrin that Messiah *Yeshua* abolished in His flesh, with which Paul was well acquainted.

"The End of the Law is Christ"

Although there are many more passages which have been sanitized of their Hebraic significance, we shall note one more passage that is often used by Christian theologians to prove that the *Torah* was *done away* with the coming of *Yeshua* and, therefore, no longer relevant to New Testament Believers. It is found in **Romans 10:4**.

Once again, take a look at the following 1611 KJV, 1881 RSV, NASV, and NIV translations of Romans 10:4, and note how similar they are to the 1388 Wycliffe Version, which is based on Jerome's anti-Jewish Latin Vulgate.

Jerome's 405 C.E. Latin Vulgate

English | Latin

For the end of the law is Christ: unto justice to every one that believeth.

finis enim legis Christus ad iustitiam omni credenti (Romans X).[166]

1388 Wycliffe Version

4 For the end [Gk. *telos*] of the law is Christ, to Righteousness to each man that believes (Romans X).[167]

1611 King James Version (KJV)

4 For Christ *is* the end [Gk. *telos*] of the law for Righteousness to every one that believeth (Rom. 10:4).[168]

1881 King James Revised Version (RSV)

4 For Christ is the end [Gk. *telos*] of the law, that every one who has faith may be justified (Rom. 10:4).[169]

New American Standard Version (NASV)

4 For Christ is the end [Gk. *telos*] of the law for righteousness to everyone who believes (Rom. 10:4).

New International Version (NIV)

4 <u>Christ is the end [Gk. *telos*] of the law</u> so that there may
be righteousness for everyone who believes (Rom. 10:4).

Notice that in each of the above versions Christian interpreters have translated the Greek word *telos* exactly as Jerome's anti-Jewish Latin Vulgate, meaning "end".

Affirming the same interpretation of the Greek word *telos,* the Bible expositor Dr. J. Barmby writes: "For Christ is law's end, etc. The sense required – a sense which the words very naturally yield – that is with Christ in the field of law as a means of attaining righteousness has ceased and determined. The moment a man sees Christ and understands what He is and what He has done, he feels that legal religion is a thing of the past; the way to righteousness is not the observance of statutes, no matter though they have been promulgated by God Himself...."[170]

And Dr. G. Campbell Morgan writes: "The great statement is made in the words, 'Christ is the end of the law unto righteousness to everyone that believeth."[171]

There is a problem with these claims. Because if Christ is indeed the "end" of the *Torah,* why did Paul tell the Believers at Rome that "the law is holy and the commandment holy, and just, and good" (Rom. 7:12; AKJV)? If Christ is the "end" of the Law, why did James ask Paul to take four Jewish Believers, who had taken a Nazarite vow, to the Temple "... and be cleansed with them, and pay their expenses" (v. 24)? If Christ is the "end" of the Law, why did Paul comply with James' request? And if Christ is the "end" of the "end" of the Law, why did Paul tell a Jewish Sanhedrin some thirty years after his conversion to *Yeshua:* "... <u>I am</u> [Gk. 'Present tense'] a Pharisee, the son of a Pharisee" (Acts 23:6)?

Once again, the central idea of this book bears repeating: The key to understanding the Apostolic Writings is to see them from a first century Jewish perspective, *not* from a twentieth or twenty-first century Christian perspective. Because in Jewish thought the Messiah has always been the *goal,* as well as the *purpose* of the *Torah.*

Affirming this Hebraic understanding, the Messianic Jewish scholar David Stern says:

> … most theologians understand the verse to say that Yeshua terminated the *Torah*. But the Greek word translated "ends" is *telos, f*rom which English gets the word "teleology," defined in Webster's Third International Dictionary as "the philosophlical study of the evidences of design in nature ;… the fact or the character of being directed toward an end or shaped by a purpose—used of… nature … conceived as determined … by the design of a divine Providence…." The normal meaning of *telos* in Greek – which is also its meaning here – is "goal, purpose, consummation," not "termination." The Messiah did not and does not bring the *Torah* to an end. Rather, attention to and faith in the Messiah is the goal and purpose toward which the *Torah* aims, the logical consequence, result and consummation of observing *Torah* out of genuine faith, as opposed to trying to observe it out of legalism. This, not the termination of *Torah*, is Sha'ul's point, as can be seen from the context, Romans 9:30-10:11.[172]

Hopefully, these few examples of misconceptions, mistranslations and changes of the best manuscripts in the Nestle-Aland *Novum Testamentum Graece* and *Textus Receptus* Greek texts will help us understand the powerful hold this anti-Jewish spirit has had on Christianity for the past nineteen hundred years.

As seekers of truth, we need to understand that had Paul lived twice a thousand years he would have never contradicted his beloved Rabbi and Master, *Yeshua HaMashiach,* who told the people of His day: **"Think not that I am come to destroy the law, or the prophets: I am not come to destroy, but to fulfill. For I say unto you, till heaven and earth pass, one jot or one tittle shall in no wise pass from the law, till all be fulfilled. Whosoever therefore shall break one of these least commandments, and shall teach men so, he shall be called least in the kingdom of heaven: but whosoever shall do and teach** *them* **shall be called great in the kingdom of heaven"** (Matt. 5:17; AKJV).

Chapter 9

"TAKE MY YOKE UPON YOU AND LEARN OF ME"

Perhaps no other passage in the New Testament has been used more by theologians to affirm Christianity's New Covenant Theology than the often quoted words of the young Rabbi from Nazareth: "… take my yoke upon you and learn of Me …. For My yoke is easy and My burden is light" (Matt. 11:29-30).

According to the Scottish theologian William Barclay, the primary meaning of this passage is to be found in the word "easy," because when Jesus said: "'My yoke is easy,' He meant it to fit well."[1]

In ancient Israel most of the heavy work was done by oxen that pulled heavy loads with a yoke around their necks. For this reason it was important to have the yoke custom fitted to the animal's neck by a skilled carpenter so that its skin would not be torn when pulling heavy loads. Using the analogy of the custom fitted yoke, Dr. Barclay says, "So Jesus says, 'My yoke fits well…. the life I give you to live is not a burden to gall you; your task, your life, is made to measure to fit you.'"[2]

For most theologians, the heavy burdens *Yeshua* came to remove were the negative commands of the *Torah* -- "Thou shalt not". But for those who understand the first century meaning of the term "yoke," nothing could be further from the truth.

Professor George Foote Moore tells us that within Judaism the saying of the Rabbi R. Nehuniah ben ha-kanah [end of the first century] is familiar: "Everyone who takes upon himself the yoke of the Law is liberated from the yoke of the empire (the burden of foreign government) and from the yoke of the way of the world, but whoever throws off the yoke of the Law is subjected to both of these."[3] Likewise, in the reciting of the first sentence of the Sh'ma (Deut. 6:4f), the Rabbi M. Berakot says that the people are told in the following verses to take upon themselves the specific commandments.[4]

In contrast, the throwing off the yoke of God was understood by the Sages as throwing off the yoke of *Torah,* which meant the deliberate rejection of God's rule and dominion.[5] Thus the aim of the rabbis is to lead more and more people to "take upon themselves the *yoke* of the *Torah.*" And according to the Mishnah, to "make many disciples" of *Torah* is the highest calling of a rabbi (M. Avot 1:1).

As earlier noted, since the time of the Greek and Latin Church Fathers most theologians have focused their attention on the New Testament. Today, however, there is renewed interest in understanding the Hebrew origins of Greek New Testament vocabulary.

Addressing *Yeshua's* use of the Greek term *zugos* ['yoke'], the Christian language scholar David Bivin says:

> How would Jesus' first listeners have heard his words about taking on his yoke? Learning what a "yoke" meant in the writings and culture of Jesus' time will greatly clarify his words. In a rabbi-disciple relationship, the disciple was expected to place himself in a position of total obedience and dedication to his rabbi and his philosophy. It was his desire to become just like him. This was said to be taking on the "yoke" of the rabbi.
>
> Certainly the impression of a "yoke" (of oxen for example) comes immediately to mind as burdensome. But in the proper context, taking on the rabbi's yoke was not negative. When one's desire is to pull the same load as his teacher, the best way to do it is to willingly bind oneself to his yoke and cart.
>
> ... It is important to note that when Jesus said: "Take my yoke upon you," he spoke of the keeping of commandments. Jesus might have been speaking as only God speaks. By calling this yoke "my yoke" (and the burden "my burden"), Jesus

could have been making a shocking statement. The keeping of commandments was referred to as a "yoke," but it is unlikely that a rabbi would have made the claim that this yoke was "his."[6]

The Two Schools of First Century Judaism

At the time of *Yeshua,* Jewish theology had basically two schools of thought regarding the observance of the *Torah* of Moses: the *Halakhah* and the *Haggadah.*

Dr. Alfred Edersheim informs us that the *Halakhah,* which was the school of the Rabbi Hillel, "was so to speak, the Rule of the Spiritual Road, and, when fixed, had even greater authority than the Scriptures of the Old Testament, since it explained and applied them."[7]

The *Haggadah,* which was the second school and was of the Rabbi Shammai, "was only the personal saying of the teacher, more or less valuable according to his learning a popularity, or the authorities which he could quote in his support."[8]

Unlike the *Halakhah,* the *Haggadah* had no absolute authority, either as to doctrine, practice, or exegesis. Thus "all the greater was its influence, and all the more dangerous was its doctrinal license.[9] ... almost all of the doctrinal teaching of the Synagogue is derived from the *Haggadah,*[10] says Dr. Edersheim.

At the head of these two branches of Jewish theology were the Scribes, who were regarded as the chief rabbis of the day. The study of the Scribes focused on the *Midrash,* which pointed to Scriptural investigation. The *Halakhah* focused on what was to be observed, and the *Haggadah* dealt with the *oral* teaching in the broadest possible sense.[11] Included in this study was the "traditions of the Elders," which had a major influence on Israel. Dr. Edersheim writes:

> The first place must here be assigned to those legal determinations, which traditionalism declared absolutely binding on all-not only of equal, but even greater obligation than Scripture itself. And this not illogically, since tradition was equally Divine origin with Holy Scripture, and authoritatively explained its meaning; supplemented it; gave it application to cases not expressly provided for, perhaps not even foreseen in

Biblical times; and generally guarded its sanctity by extending and adding to its provisions, drawing 'a hedge' around its 'garden enclosed.' Thus, in new and dangerous circumstances would the full meaning of God's Law, to its every tittle and iota, be elicited and obeyed. Thus also would their feet be arrested, who might stray from within, or break it from without. Accordingly, so important was tradition, that the greatest merit a Rabbi could claim was the strictest adherence to the traditions, which he had received from his teacher. Nor might one Sanhedrin annul, or set aside, the decrees of its predecessors. To such length did they go in this worship of the letter, that the great Hillel was actually wont to mispronounce a word, because his teacher before him had done so.

These traditional ordinances, as already stated, bear the general name of the *Halakhah,* as indicating alike the way in which the fathers had walked, and that which their children were bound to follow. These *Halakhoth* were either simply the laws laid down in Scripture; or else derived from, or traced to it by some ingenious and artificial method of exegesis; or added to it, by way of amplification and for safety's sake; or, finally, legalised (sic) customs. They provided for every possible and impossible case, entered into every detail of private, family, and public life; and with iron logic, unbending rigor, and most minute analysis pursued and dominated man, turn whither he might, laying on him a yoke which was truly unbearable.[12]

Now we know why the young Rabbi from Nazareth told the people of His day: "Come to Me, all you who labor and are burdened, and I shall give you rest. Take My yoke upon you and learn of Me…. For My yoke is easy and My burden is light" (Matt. 11:28-30).

Now we know why the young Rabbi warned His disciples about the leaven of the Pharisees (Matt. 16:6). He wasn't condemning the observance of the *Torah.* Rather, He was restoring the true meaning of *Torah* by condemning the false teaching that the rigid outward observance of the letter of *Torah* made a person right with God.

Now we know why *Yeshua* told His disciples that the Pharisees "bind heavy burdens and grievous to be born, and lay them on men's shoulders" (Matt. 23:4). He wasn't condemning the observance of *Torah.* Rather, He was restoring the correct meaning of *Torah* by condemning their rigid observance of the hundreds of man-made rules the Scribes and Pharisees had added to *Torah*.

Now we know why the young Rabbi called the Pharisees hypocrites for rejecting the weighter measures of *Torah*, such as "justice, mercy, and faith" (Matt. 23:23). He wasn't condemning their observance of *Torah*. Rather, He restoring the true meaning of *Torah* by condeming the rigid teachings of the Pharisees on the letter of *Torah* as opposed to the Spirit of *Torah*.

And now we know why Matthew was compelled to write so much about the young Rabbi's encounters with the Scribes and Pharisees [more than any other Gospel writer]. Matthew wanted his predominately Jewish audience to understand that not only did *Yeshua* fulfill every Messianic type in the *Torah*, but that a major portion of His ministry was devoted to restoring the Rule of the Spirit of *Torah*.

The Shammai Pharisees

For most theologians the above passages of Scripture are proof that *Yeshua* came to *do away* with the *Torah* and start a new religion called "Christianity". But for those who understand the powerful influence the Shammai Pharisees had on the Jewish thought of that day, nothing could be further from the truth.

Like the two party system in American politics, the Democrats and Republicans, who have two opposing views of the Constitution, the House of Hillel and the House of Shammai had two opposing views of the *Torah*. And like the two party system of America, when one party is in control of the country it is that party which makes the rules by which the people must obey.

History concurs that for most of the first century the Shammai Pharisees were in control of the Sanhedrin. Jewish scholars agree that it was the House of Shammai which made "eighteen measures" ['edicts'] that were to be observed by the Jewish people for most of the first century. According to the Talmud (Shabbat 17A), the day the House of Shammai gained control of the Sanhedrin and passed the "eighteen measures," it was as troublesome for Israel as the day the Golden Calf was built.

Matthew records that the young Rabbi from Nazareth addressed this very issue, saying: "The scribes and the Pharisees sit in Moses' seat ['the

Sanhedrin']: all therefore whatsoever they bid you to observe, *that* observe and do; but do not ye after their works: for they say and do not. For they bind heavy burdens and grievous to be borne, and lay *them* on men's shoulders; but they *themselves* will not move them with one of their fingers" (Matt. 23:2-4; AKJV).

For most theologians, the "works" *Yeshua* addressed in the above passage were the commandments of *Torah*. But when we understand the historical context of that day, it becomes evident that the young Rabbi was speaking against the "eighteen measures," and the ruling party of His day -- the Scribes and Pharisees of Bet Shammai.

Contrary to the misconception of many, it was Caiaphas' Sanhedrin that was controlled by the Shammai Pharisees. It was Caiaphas' Sanhedrin of Shammai Pharisees that dominated the Jewish life of that day. It was Caiaphas' Sanhedrin of Shammai's strict teaching of *Torah* that the young Rabbi challenged when He told the people: "My yoke is easy, and My burden is light" (Matt. 11:30). And it was Caiaphas' Sanhedrin of Shammai Pharisees that plotted the death of the young Rabbi from Nazareth *after* He called the dead body of Lazareth to come forth from the grave (Jhn. 11:47-53).

Matthew, Mark, and Luke record that it was the chief priests and the whole <u>council</u> [Gk. *suvedriov,* meaning "high council, Sanhedrin"[13]] that sought false witnesses against *Yeshua* so that they might put Him to death (Matt. 26:59; Mk. 14:55; Lk. 22:66).

Some will argue that this was not the case. But in the best Greek manuscripts of Nestle-Aland and the *Textus Receptus,* John noted the distinctiveness of these chief Shammai members of the Sanhedrin when he employed the *definite article,* designating them as *"oi arxiereis kai oi Parisaioi,"* meaning "<u>the</u> chief priests and <u>the</u> Pharisees" (Jhn. 11:47).

Once again, the rule governing the function of the *definite article* is worth repeating: the *definite article* does more than mark the object being addressed, it points out *individual identity.*[14]

Thus we know that when John employed the *definite article* before the nouns "chief priests" and "Pharisees" of Caiaphas' Sanhedrin he was identifying a particular group of Pharisees. And make no mistake, the people of that day were well acquainted with the decrees of the Shammai Pharisees.

So here is the great question: Have Christian scholars known about the existence of the Shammai Pharisees who ruled during the time of *Yeshua* and Paul? Indeed they have! The orthodox Rabbi Harvey Falk writes:

> It is widely known to students of Talmud that two opposing schools of Pharisees–Bet Shammai and Bet Hillel–existed from about 30 B.C.E. until approximately 70 C.E. The available evidence indicates that the former usually constituted a majority of the Pharisees until the latter half of the first century C.E. Following the destruction of the Temple in 70 C.E., the center of Jewish scholarship and seat of the Sanhedrin was relocated to Yavneh, where Ben Hillel's authority grew progressively.
>
> ... I have found that certain Christian scholars too have taken note of Bet Shammai's dominate position in Jesus' time. W. D. Davies, in his *Paul and Rabbinic Judaism* (p. 9), quotes from B. H. Branscomb, *Jesus and the Law of Moses*, p. 54: "Apparently then during the lifetime of Jesus the party of Hillel was not yet in control.... It means that an active and rapidly growing party within the ranks of the scholars was at the time in vigorous protest against the currently accepted interpretation of the Torah." How unfortunate that such a seeker of truth was not able to delve any further into what the "vigorous protest" consisted of. Davies himself (*ibid.*) writes, "It is clear that it was Pharisaism, and that of the Shammaite kind, that dominated first century Judaism." But instead of pursuing the matter, he abruptly declares, "Here we shall not attempt any exhaustive survey of Judaism in the first century." It would seem that such men were on the correct trail, but simply lacked the tools they were seeking.
>
> Davies also... furnishes much scholarly evidence that Paul personally observed the 613 Commandments of Judaism through-out his lifetime (pp. 69-70).
>
> ... Yet another Christian scholar who takes note of Bet Shammai's dominate position is George Foot Moore, who writes "... it was perhaps only after the fall of Jerusalem that the Hillelites gained the ascendance" (*Judaism in the First Centuries of the Christian Era*, 1:81).

... Ample evidence exists to demonstrate that both the Scribes and the Hasidim (pious ones) had their origins as far back as the time of Moses, while the term "Pharisee" first appears shortly before the Common Era. It was apparently not before the first century B.C.E. that the hostility between these groups surfaced. It was at the turn of this era that "the Torah became as two Torahs" (Sanhedrin 88B). And it was during this critical period that Bet Shammai came to dominate the "Scribes and Pharisees."[15]

"Learn of Me"

For the past eighteen hundred years the New Testament has been the primary source of knowledge for the historic Rabbi from Nazareth among both Christians and Jews. But for the peoples of the first and second centuries this was not the case. Simple because the New Testament did not exist at that time.

So when *Yeshua* told the people of His day to "learn of Me" (Matt. 11:29), what did He mean? According to the Bible expositor A. Lukyn Williams of the *Pulpit Commentary* "the 'of' is slightly ambiguous, and may refer to Christ as the Example from which they may draw the lesson for themselves, or as the Teacher who will himself instruct them (Col. 1:7)."[16]

Dr. Alexander Bruce of the *Expositor's Greek Testament* says, "This is to be taken metaphorically. The kind of people Jesus expects to become 'disciples indeed' are men who have sought long, earnestly, but in vain, for the *summum bonum,* the knowledge of God.... In coming thence to Christ's school they would find rest by passing from letter to spirit, from form to reality, from hearsay to certainty, from traditions of the past to the present voice of God."[17]

For many, the above comments appear to be biblically sound. But is this what the young Rabbi from Nazareth meant when He told the people of that day to "learn of Me"?

Unknown to most Christians but widely known among the Jewish people, the *Written Torah* is known as *The Book of Knowledge.* Primarily because the first five books of Moses inform us not only about Creation and God's redemptive plan for mankind, but also about the one true Creator of heaven and earth. This understanding is affirmed in the first line of the Sh'ma which plainly says, "The LORD is our God, the LORD is One."

Addressing this divine designation; that the LORD is "One," the Messianic Rabbi Michael Silver says: "The Hebrew word for "one" is *echad* and denotes a composite, *not* an absolute oneness. At the same time while there is but one God, His Name *Elohim* is a *plural* word."[18]

The Hebrew scholar H. C. Leupold writes: "The hortative 'Let us make' (*na'aseh*), is particularly striking because it is plural. Though almost all commentators of our day reject the view ... the truth of the Trinity explains this passage."[19]

Even more important, however, Moses established the significance of the *plurality* of God in the act of Creation when he wrote the Name *Elohim* in the original Hebrew text, stating:

> 3 "And *Elohim said,* 'Let light come to be ....'"
>
> 6 "And *Elohim said,* 'Let an expanse come to be in the waters.'"
>
> 9 "And *Elohim said,* 'Let the waters under the heavens be gathered together into one place, and let the dry land appear.'"
>
> 11 "And *Elohim said,* 'Let the earth bring forth grass, the plant that yields seed, and the fruit tree that yields fruit according to its kind, whose seed is in itself, on the earth.'"
>
> 14 "And *Elohim said,* 'Let lights come to be in the expanse of the heavens to separate the day and night: and let them be for signs and appointed times, and for days, and for years.'"
>
> 20 "And *Elohim said,* 'Let the waters teem with shoals of living creatures, and let the birds fly above the earth on the face of the expanse of the heavens.'"
>
> 24 "And *Elohim said,* 'Let the earth bring forth the living creature according to its kind: livestock and creeping creatures and beasts of the earth, according to its kind.'"
>
> 26 "And *Elohim said,* 'Let *Us* make man in *Our* image, according to *Our* likeness ... (Gen. 1, 3, 6, 9, 11, 14, 20, 24, 26; *The Scriptures*). (Emphasis added.)

Did the first century followers of the young Rabbi from Nazareth understand the significance of the *plurality* of the Name *Elohim* in the Scriptures? Indeed they did! When John began his prologue about the resurrected *Mashiach Yeshua* he employed the strongest Greek term possible to address *Yeshua's* pre-existence with the Triune God-Head personified as the eternal creative *Logos* ['Word'], saying:

> **1** In the beginning was <u>the Word</u> [Gk. *'O Logos*], and <u>the Word</u> [*'O Logos*] was with *Elohim,* and <u>the Word</u> [*'O Logos*] was *Elohim.*
>
> 2 He was in the beginning with *Elohim.*
>
> 3 All came to be through Him, and without Him not even one came to be that came to be (Jhn. 1:1-3).

This first century understanding of the *plurality* of the name *Elohim* cannot be overstated. Because it establishes that the young Rabbi knew that when the people of that day studied the *Book of Knowledge* they would learn of Him, whom John wrote "was with *Elohim,* and was *Elohim*" (v. 1).

Addressing the significance of John's employment of the Greek term *'O Logos,* the scholars of Kittel's *Theological Dictionary of the New Testament* write:

> In Rabbinic discussions *naghadh* "utterance" is a tt. for the giving of the Law and for the commandments. But the statements concerning the pre-existence and majesty of the Torah are not intentionally heaped upon the *logos.* It was in the beginning. It was with God. It was God, or divine. All things were made by it. In it was life. It was the light of men. In the Rabbis these are all sayings about the Torah. But they are now statements about Christ. In Him the eternal Word of Creation, the Word of Law, is not just passed on but enacted. Christ is not just a teacher and transmitter of the Torah, He is Himself the Torah.[20]

Why was this *Torah* understanding of the young Rabbi from Nazareth important to the people of that day? Because when *Yeshua* told the people of His day to "take My yoke upon you and learn of Me," He knew that it was in *The Book of Knowledge* where they would come to know Him best.

What was the payoff? *Yeshua* told the people: "I am meek and lowly in heart: and you shall find rest unto your souls" (Matt. 11:29).

Arndt and Gingrinch inform us that the Greek word *Yeshua* used for "rest" [Gk. *anarausw*] is a Hebrew parallelism of the Greek word employed in the *Septuagint* for the Hebrew word *"shavath"*.

Equally significant, the Christian scholars of *Strongs Exhaustive Concordance* tell us that the Hebrew word *shavath* means "to desist (from exertion), cease, leave off, rest, to come to an end; to keep or celebrate the Sabbath."[21]

Why is this Hebraic understanding significant to the people of that day? Because they were well acquainted with the Hebrew word *"shavath"*. *Shavath* is the Hebrew word used in the commandment to keep the seventh day Sabbath: "Six days thou shalt do thy work, and on the seventh day thou shalt *shavath* (rest)...." (Ex. 23:12; AKJV).[22]

Did the followers of *Yeshua* understand this Hebraic concept? Indeed they did. One classic example of *Yeshua* giving His disciples "rest" from the burdensome rules of the Pharisees is recorded as follows:

> 23 And it came to pass, that he went through the corn fields on the sabbath day; and his disciples began, as they went, to pluck the ears of corn.
>
> 24 And the Pharisees said unto him, Behold, why do they on the sabbath day that which is not lawful?
>
> 25 And he said unto them, Have ye never read what David did, when he had need, and was hungry, he, and they that were with him?
>
> 26 How he went into the house of God in the days of Abiathar the high priest, and did eat the showbread, which is not lawful to eat but for the priests, and gave also to them which were with him?
>
> 27 And he said to them, The sabbath was made for man, and not the Sabbath:
>
> 28 Therefore the Son of Man is LORD also of the sabbath (Mk. 2:23-28; AKJV).

Notice that Mark begins his account by saying that the young Rabbi led His disciples through the corn fields on the Sabbath day. On any other day the Pharisees would have no argument with *Yeshua's* disciples plucking corn from the field to eat (Ex. 23:24). But this event took place on the Sabbath, and was strickly forbidden in rabbinic law as "work".

According to the laws of the Scribes and Pharisees, "work" was classified under thirty-nine different headings, and four of these heading were titled "reaping," "winnowing," "threshing," and "preparing a meal." According to these definitions, the disciples had broken all four laws and, therefore, were considered to be in violation of the great command: "Thou shalt not do any work on the seventh day."

Yeshua responded to the Pharisee's claim by citing the account of David (1 Samuel 21:1-6), reminding them that when David was fleeing for his life and came to the Tabernacle in Nob, he was famished and needed to eat. But there was none available except for the Tabernacle shewbread, which was placed as an offering to the LORD in front of the Holy of Holies.

The shewbread was changed once each week, and then, according to *Torah,* was allowed to be eaten only by the priests (Lev. 24:9). *Yeshua* pointed out that in David's time of need he ate the shewbread that was meant for the priests alone, saying: "The Sabbath was made for man and not man for the Sabbath. Therefore, the Son of man is LORD also of the Sabbath."

Here we see the young Rabbi not only affirming the validity of the Sabbath, but told the Pharisees that they had failed to understand the Rule of the Spirit of the *Torah.*

Even more important, however, the Pharisees had failed to understand the purpose of the young Rabbi's ministry. As "LORD of the Sabbath," *HaMashiach Yeshua* had come to restore the original meaning of *Torah* as it was understood by David, who began his beloved Psalms, saying:

> **1** Blessed is the man who shall not walk in the counsel of the wrong, and shall not stand in the path of sinners, and shall not sit in the seat of scoffers,
>
> 2 But his delight is in the Torah of [YHVH], and he meditates in His Torah day and night.
>
> 3 For he shall be like a tree planted by the rivers of water, that yields its fruit in its season, and whose leaf does not wither, and whatsoever he does prospers (Ps. 1:1-2; *The Scriptures*).

This passage hardly sounds as though David believed the *Torah* was a burdensome Law filled with hundreds of legalistic "thou shalt not" commandments. Nor does it sound as though David wanted the *Torah* to be *done away* with and replaced with a *Torahless* religion.

Did the people of that day understand that the Messiah of Israel would restore the original meaning of *Torah* as understood and taught by David? Indeed they did!

Matthew, Mark, and Luke record that on several occasions, as the young Rabbi went from village to village teaching David's understanding of *Torah,* the people cried out, saying: "Thou Son of David!" "Thou Son of David!" "Thou Son of David!" (Mt. 9:27; 12:23; 15:22; 20:30-31; 21:9-15; 22:42; Mk. 10:47-48; 11:10; Lk. 18:39.)

"Study To Show Thyself Approved Unto God"

Of all the ancient documents which affirm the *Torah* observance of those first century followers of the young Rabbi from Nazareth, none are more critical to our understanding than the Catholic Church's establishment of the Apostolic Writings as sacred Scripture. Because for the first century, and most of the second century, the *Septuagint* was not only the primary source for the study of God's Word, it was the only source.[23]

The Church historian Williston Walker tells us that even though Clement of Rome (93-97 C.E.) was constantly quoting the Hebrew Scriptures as the Word of God, he freely used the words of the New Testament, but nowhere in his writings did he ascribe to them divine authority.[24]

The earliest passages from the Gospels that were designated as Scripture was used as a quotation from Paul, about 110-117 C.E., by Polycarp, and later, about 131 C.E., by Barnabas. Scholars agree that it wasn't until the second century that there is a clear instance of the Apostolic Writings being elevated to the status of Scripture beside the *Septuagint* in the sermon called *II Clement.*[25]

At the time of Justin (153 C.E.), the Gospels were read in Rome, together with the Hebrew Scriptures, which indicates that the Gospels were the first to gain acceptance as inspired Scripture.

By about 200 C.E., according to the witness of the Muratorian fragment, Western Christianity had a New Testament canon which included *Matthew, Mark, Luke, John, Acts, 1ˢᵗ & 2ⁿᵈ Corinthians, Ephesians, Philippians, Colossians, Galatians, 1ˢᵗ & 2ⁿᵈ Thessalonians, Romans, Philemon, Titus, 1ˢᵗ & 2ⁿᵈ Timothy, Jude, 1ˢᵗ & 2ⁿᵈ John, Revelation,* and the so-called *Apocalypse of Peter.*[26]

Thus when Paul wrote to Timothy from prison in Rome, near the end of 66 C.E., saying, "Study to show thyself approved unto God, a workman that needeth not be ashamed, rightly dividing the word of truth" (2 Tim. 2:15; AKJV), he was exhorting Timothy to study the *Written Torah* [*i.e.,* the first five books of Moses].

Likewise, when Peter wrote his first Epistle, sometime in the 60s, to the new Gentile converts in Asia Minor and admonished them to "desire the sincere milk of the word, that ye may grow thereby" (1ˢᵗ Pet. 2:2), he too was exhorting Believers to study the *Written Torah.*

In the same manner, about 62 C.E., when James wrote his Epistle to the Believers in Asia Minor and told them to "become doers of the Word, and not hearers only" (Js. 1:22-25), he too was exhorting Believers to obey the *Written Torah.*

And, about 60-64 C.E., when Paul wrote to the Nazarene Believers at Ephesus and exhorted them to "put on the whole armor of God, that you may be able to stand against the wiles of the devil" (Eph. 6:11-18), he too was admonishing Believers to equip themselves with the armor of the *Written Torah.* In fact, Paul specifically refers to "the breastplate of righteousness [Gk. *dikaisuvns*]" as being one of Believers most important pieces of armor (v. 14). Why was this piece of armor so important?

Arndt and Gingrich inform us that the term *dikaiosuvns* means "*uprightness, righteousness,* in a moral and religious sense; the characteristic required of men by God. **a.** *righteousness* in the sense of fulfilling the divine statutes Mt. 3:15."[27]

Thus, by admonishing the Believers at Ephesus to put on "the breastplate of *dikaisuvns,*" it is clear that he was addressing the need for them to be *Torah* observant. Why was this important? Paul says, "... wherewith ye shall be able to quinch all the fiery darts of the wicked" (v. 15).

The significance of Paul's employment of this Hebraic concept cannot be overstated. Because in ancient Rome the breastplate of the Roman soldier not only protected his heart and vital organs from deadly wounds that could be made by a sword, arrow, or spear, it gave him confidence to take the battle to his enemies and be victorious. Edward Gibbon writes:

> The relaxation of discipline, and the disuse of exercise, rendered the soldiers less able and less willing, to support the fatigues of the service; they complained of the weight of the armor, which they seldom wore; and they successively obtained

the permission of laying aside both their cuirasses [breastplates] and their helmets. The heavy weapons of their ancestors, the short sword, and the formidable *pilum*, which had subdued the world, insensibly dropped from their feeble hands. As the use of the shield is incompatible with that of the bow, they reluctantly marched into the field; condemned to suffer either the pain of wounds or the ignominy of flight, and always disposed to prefer the more shameful alternative. The calvary of the Goths, the Huns, and the Alani, had felt the benefits, and adopted the use of defensive armor; and, as they excelled in the management of missile weapons, they easily overwhelmed the naked and trembling legions, whose hands and breasts were exposed, without defense, to the arrows of the Barbarians. The loss of armies, the destruction of cities, and the dishonor of the Roman name, ineffectually solicited the successors of Gratian to restore the helmets and cuirasses [breastplates] of the infantry. The enervated soldiers abandoned their own and public defence (sic); and their pusillanimous indolence may be considered as the immediate cause of the downfall of the empire.[28]

Therefore, my friend, like the first century Nazarene Believers, reject the idea of building your faith on the philosophies and traditions of men. Rather, put on the "beastplate of *dikaiosuv*" [*lit.,* the armor of the *Written Torah*] that you may be able to "quench all the fiery darts of the wicked."

Begin by setting aside a time each day for personal *Torah* study. In Hebrew, a *Torah* study session is called "Shiur," which means a "measure". For different people the measure can be the study of a certain word, a sentence, a paragraph, a page, several pages, a chapter or more. The amount of time spent in study will differ according to a person's available time: from a few minutes to an hour or more. What is important is that each person gets his or her daily portion of spiritual food.

A good way to begin is by purchasing a few good reference books that will help you understand the Scriptures, the people, the culture, and customs of those days. There are many good reference books available today. *The Complete Word Study New Testament* and *The Complete Word Study Old Testament* are excellent reference books [both include lexical aids that explain the meaning of Hebrew and Greek words and tenses]. *The New Unger's Bible Dictionary* [the best single volume available], *The*

Illustrated Bible Dictionary [Tyndale series, the best Bible dictionary published], *Gesenius' Hebrew-Chaldee Lexicon to the Old Testament* [Hebrew words are numerically coded to Strong's Concordance], *Strong's Exhaustive Concordance* and *The Holeman Bible Atlas* are excellent reference books.

Jewish reference works, such as the *Encyclopedia Judaica,* which can be found in most public and college libraries. The *Jewish Encyclopedia* can be accessed free of charge on the internet.

A good literal translation of the Hebrew and Greek Scriptures will prove to be invaluable in your quest to better understand the original words of Scripture. The following works are excellent study Bibles: *The Interlinear Greek-English New Testament* [Alfred Marshall], *The Interlinear Greek-English New Testament* [Jay P. Green, Sr.], *The Hebrew-Greek Key Study Bible* [the best complete study Bible available], *The Jewish New Testament* and *Complete Jewish Bible* [David H. Stern], *The Interlinear Hebrew-English Old Testament* [Jay P. Green, Sr.], and *The Scriptures* [a literal translation of the Hebrew and Greek that restores the original Names of the Creator].

Equally important is the need for music that celebrates your rich Hebraic heritage as a son or daughter of *HaMashiach Yeshua.* Bathe your mind and spirit in music that is about the God of Abraham, Isaac, and Jacob. Fall in love with the Jewish Messiah of Israel!

When Moses and the children of Israel ascended from the Sea of Reeds, after it opened for them to pass through to the other side, they sang a song of praise and gratitude to the LORD (Ex. 15). As you pass from your own "Sea of Reeds" fill your mind and heart with inspiring Messianic music, which can often be purchased at most local Christian book stores.

If possible, seek out a Messianic congregation in your area, where you can fellowship with like-minded Believers. If there are no Messianic congregations in your area then tap into the growing number of Messianic internet ministries.*

With helps such as these you will soon be able to gain a new understanding of the *Torah* observant faith of those first century followers of the young Rabbi from Nazareth. Before long the people, words, and events of Scripture will take on a whole new meaning. Very soon, you too will begin to see the Scriptures through Jewish eyes.

---

*   See Ministry Resources.

As you study the *Torah,* read all of Exodus 20, Leviticus 11, 19 & 23, and Deuteronomy 16, understanding that you are about to enter into a new covenant relationship with the God of Abraham, Isaac, and Jacob.

Seek to understand the ways of God and how to please Him, as a bride seeks to please her husband. Take to heart Paul's admonition to the Nazarene Believers in Rome, when he said:

> 12 I beseech you therefore, brethren, by the mercies of God, that ye present your bodies a living sacrifice, holy, acceptable unto God, *which is* your reasonable service.
>
> 2 And be not conformed to this world: but be ye transformed by the renewing of your mind, that ye may prove what *is* that good and acceptable, and perfect will of God (Rom. 12:1-2; AKJV).

In doing so, be wise as a serpent and as harmless as a dove. Realize that there are many voices trying to capture your thoughts and allegiance. Like the wise Nazarenes of Berea, examine their teachings in the light of the *Written Torah.* Test them in the holy light of God's Word to prove whether or not they are teaching *Torah* observant faith of those first century followers of the young Rabbi from Nazareth.

Above all, refuse to compromise the truth, no matter how eloquent the argument or distinguished the teacher. Reject the false teaching that the *Torah* belongs only to the Jews. Begin to see the Scriptures from Genesis to Revelation as one complete inspired Word of God, without the man-made divisive terms "Old Testament" and "New Testament".

As you seek the truth, ask the LORD to lead you in His paths of righteousness. Allow the *Ruach HaKodesh* a few days, a week, and even months, to show you what it is that He wants to teach you. In doing this, your Teacher will honor your request and begin to renew your mind. Very soon you too will be able to discern what is worthy and acceptable in the sight of God, as aptly stated by the prophet Isaiah:

> 20 Though [YHVH] gave you bread of adversity and water of affliction, your Teacher shall no longer be hidden. But your eyes shall see your Teacher,

21 and your ears hear a word behind you, saying, "This is the Way, walk in it," whenever you turn to the right, or whenever you turn to the left.

22 And you shall defile the covering of your graven images of silver, and the plating of your molded images of gold. You shall throw them away as a menstrual cloth and say to them, "Be gone!" (Isa. 30:20-22; *The Scriptures*).

Having said this, be prepared for criticism. Remember what *Yeshua* said to those who would follow Him:

34 "Do not think that I have come to bring peace on earth. I did not come to bring peace but a sword,

35 for I have come to bring division, a man against his father, a daughter against her mother, and a daughter-in-law against her mother-in-law –

36 and a man's enemies are those of his own household.

37 "He who loves father or mother more than Me is not worthy of Me, and he who loves son or daughter more than Me is not worthy of Me.

38 "And he who does not take up his stake and follow after Me is not worthy of Me.

39 "He who has found his life shall lose it, and he that has lost his life for My sake shall find it" (Matt. 10:34-39; *The Scriptures*).

A Lesson Finally Learned

Although many years have now passed, I can still remember an early morning Bible study I attended with a small group of seminary students. It took place in the office of Dr. Robert E. Coleman, professor of the Department of Evangelism. That particular morning we were studying Paul's second letter to Timothy. After an initial greeting, Dr. Coleman began by reading Paul's words to Timothy, saying:

10 But thou has fully known my doctrine, manner of life, purpose, faith, longsuffering, charity, patience,

> 11 persecutions, afflictions, which came unto me at Antioch, at Iconium, at Lystra; what persecutions I endured: but of *them* all the LORD delivered me.
>
> 12 Yea, and all that will live godly in Christ Jesus shall suffer persecutions (2 Tim. 3:10-12; AKJV).

After reading Paul's words, Dr. Coleman looked at those of gathered in the room and said: "This passage bothers me more than any other passage in the Bible. Because it says that *all* who live godly in Christ Jesus will suffer persecution. As I measure those words of Paul with my own life, I must confess that my life does not match up to this passage."

I can still hear the silence in the room after our esteemed professor shared with us his concern about Paul's words to Timothy. Everyone sat speechless. We knew Dr. Coleman to be a devoted professor, family man, and devout Christian. Some of us had personally traveled with Dr. Coleman when he was invited to speak a different churches. In fact, at Dr. Coleman's invitation, I had stayed at his home one summer while he and his family were on the road teaching and preaching at different camp meetings and churches.

Dr. Coleman was not only a highly sought-after speaker, he was a well known author who had written several books. His most popular is still the widely read book entitled *The Master Plan of Evangelism,* with a "Foreword" by Billy Graham. It has now sold over 3.5 million copies.

By every account, Dr. Coleman was an outstanding Christian. Yet that morning, Dr. Coleman told us that his life did not match up with those words of Paul to Timothy, saying: "… **all** that will live godly in Christ Jesus shall suffer persecution" (v. 12).

The most troubling part of this story was that each seminary student in the room had the same problem. We too had to admit that our lives failed to match up with Paul's words: "… **all** that will live godly in Christ Jesus shall suffer persecution."

As we discussed Paul's statement, one student suggested that perhaps the reason there was no persecution in our lives was because we lived in a Christian nation. But the suggestion was quickly dismissed. We concluded that Paul never said that those who followed Christ would suffer persecution *unless* they lived in a Christian country. Paul clearly said: "… **all** that will live godly in Christ Jesus shall suffer persecution."

When the Bible study concluded, none of us knew the reason for the lack of persecution in our lives, including our esteemed professor.

For myself, it would not be until forty years later that I would learn the meaning of Paul's profound, yet simple, statement: "… **all** that will live godly in Christ Jesus shall suffer persecutions."

When I finally discovered my Hebraic roots, I knew that that the lack of persecution in my own life had not been due to my lack of commitment to Christ. Nor was it due to a lack of commitment to the Church. As a Christian, not once was I ever criticized for going to church on Sun-Day, or witnessing to my Christian faith. Not once was I ever ridiculed for celebrating Christ's birthday on Christmas. Not once was I ever embarrassed or treated with disrespect for honoring Christ's death on Good Friday, or celebrating the resurrection on Easter Sun-Day.

But when I stopped going to church on Sun-Day; when I stopped observing Christian holidays, such as Christmas, Good Friday, and Easter Sun-Day; when I told my Christian friends that I now observed the seventh day Sabbath, the appointed Spring and Fall festivals, and the dietary food laws of Scripture, I was called a "Jew," a "Judaizer," "legalistic," "living under the law," and given the subtle "I'll pray for you brother" treatment.

The most troubling part of those remarks was that they came from people who belonged to the same religious institution I had belonged to for forty years -- the Christian Church! But I couldn't fault them for their feelings then, nor can I today. Because during those forty years, which I now like to refer to as my forty years of wandering in the wilderness, I too harbored those same anti-Jewish sentiments.

Now, all that has changed. Today, whenever I am criticized for observing the Sabbath, the appointed Spring and Fall festivals, and the dietary food laws of *Torah,* I think back to the time when I attended that early morning Bible study in Dr. Coleman's office, when none of us seminary boys, including our esteemed professor, had a clue as to why there was no persecution in our lives for our Christian faith.

Needless to say, what use to be my most troubling passage in Scripture has become my most cherished: "Indeed, **all** who desire to live godly in Christ Jesus will be persecuted" (2 Tim. 3:12; NASV).

Chapter 10

"LET NO MAN BEGUILE YOU OF YOUR REWARD"

While eternal life is an unmerited gift of God's grace, the Scriptures teach that there is a future judgment in which all Believers must appear before the judgment seat of the LORD and give an account of the works we have done while alive. Today, little said or written about this highly important subject. In the first century, however, such was not the case. The doctrine of works and rewards was a major Apostolic teaching.

For example, about 53 C.E., Paul addressed the doctrine of works and rewards in his first letter to the Believers at Corinth, saying:

> 10 According to the favour of Elohim which was given to me, as a wise master builder I have laid the foundation, and another builds on it. But each one should look how he builds on it.
>
> 11 For no one is able to lay any other foundation except that which is laid, which is [Yeshua] Messiah.
>
> 12 And if anyone builds on this foundation with gold, silver, precious stones, wood, hay, straw,
>
> 13 each one's <u>work</u> [Gk. *"to ergov"*] shall be revealed, for the day shall show it up, because it is revealed by fire. And the fire shall prove the work of each one, what sort it is.

14 If anyone's <u>work</u> [Gk. "*to ergov*"] remains, which he has built on, he shall receive a reward.

15 If anyone's <u>work</u> [Gk. "*to ergov*"] is burned, he shall suffer loss, but he himself shall be saved, but so as through fire (1 Corin. 3: 10-15; *The Scriptures*).

Notice that in the above passage the English word "work" is preceded in the Greek text with the *definite article,* written as "*to ergov,*" meaning "<u>the</u> work". As earlier noted, in Greek the *definite article* serves "to emphasize and identify" the person or thing it modifies.

For example, the Greek name *Iwavns* ['John'] may denote any number of individuals. But when *Iwavns* is preceded with the *definite article,* as in *o' Iwavns* ['<u>the</u> John'], people knew the writer was referring to a particular John, whom the writer assumed to be known by his audience.[1] The same is true for the term "law," which could denote any number of laws. But when the Greek term *vomos* ['law'] is preceded with the *definite article,* as in <u>o</u> *vomos* ['<u>the</u> law'] (*i.e.,* Gk. tx., Rom. 7:1, 4, 6, 7), the people of that day knew the writer was referring to the Law of Moses.

In the same manner, when the Greek term *ergov* ['work'] is preceded with the *definite article,* as in the above passage, "*to ergov,*" the Believers at Corinth knew that Paul was referring to fulfilling the righteous *ergov* ['work'] of *Torah.*

Addressing the origins of the Pauline concept "*to ergov*" ['<u>the</u> work'], the Christian scholars of Kittle's *Theological Dictionary Of The New Testament* write:

> In its concern for the righteousness of works Judaism often appeals to examples of Scripture. Legends concerning the patriarchs Adam, Enoch, Abraham, etc. afford instances of the works demanded by God. Thus we find in Jn. 8:39 the formula <u>*ta*</u> *erga* <u>*tou*</u> *Abraham.* The assumption is that the patriarch knew the Law even though it was not written down, and that they fully performed the works of the commandments. The works of the commandments correspond to what Paul calls the *erga nomou* ['work of law']. Their fulfillment is the fulfillment of the will of God, and the eschatological expectation is ... that God Himself will write the *erga nomou* on fleshly tables of the heart (Jer. 31:33).[2]

Again, about 55 C.E., in a second letter to the Believers at Corinth, Paul addressed that great future day of accountability, saying:

> 9 So we also make it our aim to be well-pleasing to Him, whether being at home, or being away from home.
>
> 10 For we all have to appear before the judgment seat of Messiah, in order for each one to receive according to what he has done in the body, whether good or evil (2 Corin. 5: 9-10; *The Scriptures*).

Again, the scholars of Kittle's *Theological Dictionary* write:

> In later Judaism the developed doctrine of the righteousness of works emerged with the thought of reward which in itself is natural to man. A plain conviction of all biblical piety is that God recompenses man according to his works. Yet in the Bible the decisive point is not the anthropocentric thought of reward but the theological concept of God's power and justice. God knows all the acts of men. The thought of recompense is based on the fact that God recompenses each according to his works.[3]

About 59 C.E., Paul wrote to the Believers at Rome and addressed the Divine Standard by which Gentiles will be judged on that great future day of accountability, saying:

> 11 For there is no partiality with Elohim.
>
> 12 For as many as have sinned without Torah shall also perish without Torah, and as many as have sinned in Torah shall be judged by the Torah.
>
> 13 For not the hearers of the Torah are righteous in the sight of Elohim, but the doers of the law shall be declared right (Rom. 2:11-13).

For most theologians, the doctrine of "works" and "recompense" is a New Testament teaching that began with *Yeshua* and Paul and, therefore, is predominately Christian in nature, such as being a faithful witness for Christ and furthering the works of the Church. But for those who understand the Hebrew Scriptures, it is more. Much more!

Simply because the Hebrew Scriptures abound with examples and teachings on the doctrine of "works" and "recompense". One of the most famous is found in the first book of *Torah* – the Genesis account of Jacob and Esau

"The Man Who Sold His Birthright For a Bowl of His Brother's Red Lentil Stew"

One of the saddest narratives in the Bible is the story of the man who was the rightful heir to the prized Covenant blessing but lost it all because he sold his birthright for a bowl of his brother's "red lentil stew". We know his name. It has lived down through the ages in infamy -- Esau!

As the firstborn, Esau was the heir to the family birthright, which was a prized possession of the peoples of that day. The birthright of the firstborn secured certain immunities and privileges, such as headship of the family, both spiritual and temporal, a double portion of the family estate, and, most important, the right to carry on the prized Covenant blessing of the family patriarchs (Gen. 27:28-29, 33-36). Accompanying the promised blessings of the birthright were certain responsibilities, which included its forfeiture either by a serious offense or by selling it.

In the narrative account, we are told that Esau was a skillful hunter and favorite son of his father, Isaac, who loved the wild game Esau killed and prepared for him to eat. But even more important, Esau was a man who loved excitement, change and freedom.

Jacob, on the other hand, was just the opposite. Jacob was a herdsman who liked stability, prosperity and family. According to the narrative, Jacob was the favorite son of his mother, Rebekah, who understood that it was Jacob who would carry on the family line of the prized Covenant blessing.

Although Jacob obtained Esau's birthright with what many have called an "act of deception," it is clear from the narrative that Jacob was spiritually minded. Unlike Esau, Jacob had spiritual values, and a distinct spiritual ambition, especially when it came to carrying on the Covenant blessing of his family. Professor H. C. Leupold writes:

> It appears, namely that the subject of the birthright (*bekhorah* = "firstbornness," "primogeniture," then the *right* of the first, i.e., birthright.") had been under consideration

between the brothers on a previous occasion. It would also seem that Esau had made some derogatory remarks about its value, or had even spoken about his own readiness to part with the privilege. Otherwise we can hardly believe that Jacob would have made this special request without further motivation, or that Esau would have consented to the bargain without more ado. This, indeed, puts Jacob into a more favorable light, but so does our text (v. 34). Indeed, there is left on Jacob's part a measure of shrewd calculation in so timing his request that catches Esau at a disadvantage, a form of cunning which we must condemn without reservation. Yet the act does not call for such strong criticism as: he was "ruthlessly taking advantage of his brother, watching and waiting till he was sure of his victim".[4]

In the narrative, Jacob's plan to obtain the family birthright begins with Esau coming home after hunting for wild game and finds Jacob making a pot of his favorite stew, stating:

> 30 And Esau said to Jacob, Feed me, I pray thee, with that same red *pottage;* for I am faint: therefore was his name called Edom.
> 31 And Jacob said, Sell me this day thy birthright.
> 32 And Esau said, Behold, I *am* at the point to die; and what profit shall this birthright do to me?
> 33 And Jacob said, Swear to me this day; and he swore unto him: and he sold his birthright unto Jacob.
> 34 Then Jacob gave Esau bread and pottage of lentils; and he did eat and drink, and rose up, and went his way; thus Esau despised *his* birthright (Gen. 25:30-34; AKJV).

What a sad commentary on the life of a man who was the rightful heir to the family birthright. Apparently, Esau was pleased with his decision to sell his birthright. The narrative says, "... Esau did eat and drink, and rose up, and went his way; thus Esau despised his birthright."

Even more astonishing is the account of Esau's attitude *after* he sold his birthright. Because Esau continued to act as though he was still the rightful heir!

Perhaps it was because Esau didn't take the selling of his birthright seriously. Or, maybe it was because Esau continued to enjoy the same family privileges *after* selling his birthright that he enjoyed *before* he sold it. Then again, it could have been that Esau believed his father favored him over Jacob because of the special wild game he killed and prepared for him to eat. The facts are uncertain.

Nevertheless, everything changed the day Esau stood before his father to receive the prized Covenant blessing. The narrative says: "[Isaac] trembled exceedingly, and said, 'Who was it then who hunted wild game and brought it to me? And I ate all of it before you came, and I have blessed him. Yea, he is blessed'" (v. 33).

Immediately, Esau blamed Jacob, saying to his father: "Is not he rightly named Jacob? For he hath supplanted me these two times: he took away my birthright; and, behold, now he hath taken away my blessing" (v. 36).

But at that point it really didn't matter that Esau was the rightful heir to the promised Covenant blessing. It didn't matter that Jacob took advantage of Esau by enticing him to sell his birthright for a bowl of red lentil stew. Nor did it matter that Jacob had tricked his father into giving him the Covenant blessing instead of Esau. The only thing that mattered was Isaac's declaration: "I have blessed him. Yea, he is blessed."

The real tragedy of the Esau narrative is that it wasn't *until* Esau stood before his father that he realized he had lost the prized Covenant blessing. Gone were Esau's privileges of the firstborn. Gone was his double portion of the family estate. And gone was his right to carry on the prized Covenant blessing of the family patriarchs, Abraham and Isaac.

Suddenly, the responsibilities of Esau's birthright, which were previously unimportant, now became a matter of great importance. But it was too late. The writer of Hebrews says, "... when he wished to inherit the blessing, he was rejected; for he found no place for repentance, though he sought it with tears" (Heb. 12:17).

The Deeper Lesson of Esau

The importance of the Esau narrative of the firstborn cannot be overstated. Because the word "firstborn" in Hebrew, *bekira* means the same as "first-fruits".[5]

During the first century one of the major doctrines of the Apostolic Writings was the teaching on "first-fruits". For example, James wrote to the Believers in Asia Minor, saying: "Having purposed it, He brought us forth by the Word of truth, for us to be a kind of first-fruits of His creatures" (James 1:18).

Paul wrote to the Believers in Rome, saying: "... but even we ourselves who have the first-fruit of the Spirit, we ourselves groan within ourselves, eagerly awaiting for the adoption, the redemption of our body" (Rom. 8:23). And writing to the new Gentile converts in Galatia, Paul said: "... if you are of Messiah, then you are seed of Abraham, and heirs according to promise" (Gal. 3:29).

Contrary to the misconception of many, the Jacob and Esau narrative is not just a story about Divine election [*i.e.,* God choosing Jacob over Esau]. Rather, the narrative of Jacob and Esau was written in the ancient form of figurative language to impress upon its readers a much greater lesson.

In the ancient world one of the most powerful forms of teaching was the employment of the figure Word-Picture. Dr. E. W. Bullinger writes:

> The name [Hypotyposis; or, Word-Picture] is given to this figure because it describes an action, event, person, condition, passion, etc., in a lively and forcible manner, giving a vivid representation of it. ... *Hypotyposis* is employed whenever anything is so described as to present it forcibly and vividly to the mind.[6]

Clearly, the obvious interpretation of the Jacob and Esau Word-Picture points to a future time of division and strife between two ancient Peoples, the descendants of Jacob, the Israelites, and the descendants of Esau, the Edomites. But in Jewish thought there is a much deeper meaning to the vivid and forceful Word-Picture narrative of Jacob and Esau.

In Jewish thought there is the obvious meaning of Scripture, and then the deeper meanings, which are viewed as an onion with its many individual layers that can be peeled off one layer at a time. The Word-Picture narrative about Jacob and Esau is such a passage.

Once again, the importance of seeing the Scriptures from a Jewish perspective cannot be overstated. Because in the Hebrew Scriptures the descendants of Edom are equated with the descendants of Rome. For example, the Psalmist prayed: "Remember, O [YHVH], against the sons of

Edom, the day of Yerushalayim, who said, 'Lay it bare, to its foundation!'" (Ps. 137:7; *The Scriptures*).

The Sages taught that verse 7 is the turning of the Psalmist's attention from the exiles of the Babylonian captivity to a future time, in which the second Temple would be destroyed by "the sons of Edom" [*i.e.,* the Roman soldiers under Titus].[7]

In the Book of Lamentations there is a similar allusion to the Roman destruction of the second Temple. While addressing the Babylonian siege of Jerusalem, Jeremiah turns to lament the future destruction of the second Temple, addressing its destroyers, the descendants of Edom, [*i.e.,* the Roman soldiers under Titus], saying: "Rejoice and be glad, O daughter of Edom, you who dwell in the land of Uz! The cup is to pass over to you too, so that you become drunk and make yourself naked" (Lam. 4:21).

Why is this understanding of Jewish history important? Because in the campaign of Nebuchadnezzar against Jerusalem, in 586 B.C.E., the first Temple's wood roof was set afire by the Babylonian soldiers, leaving the Temple's massive stone walls, at some places eighteen feet thick, standing on the Temple Mount foundation.

The destruction of the second Temple by the Romans was much more complete. In 70 C.E., the Roman General Titus took military action against Jerusalem with the aim of purging the Temple worship of the Jews from the face of the earth. This is evidenced by Titus' final assault, which took place on the Temple Mount, when the massive stone walls were razed to their very foundation.

The Bible historian Warner Keller says: "Caesar ordered the whole city and the Temple to be razed to the ground. He left standing only the towers of Phasael, Hippicus, and Mariamne and part of the city wall on the west side."[8]

Over the centuries, given the acts of torture, plunder, murder and exile of the Jewish people during the Catholic crusades and Inquisition, we should not be surprised that Jewish writers have equated the peoples of Rome and Christianity with the descendants of Edom. The scholars of the *Jewish Encyclopedia* write:

> The name "Edom" is used by the Talmudists for the Roman empire, and they applied to Rome every passage of the Bible referring to Edom or to Esau. In Leviticus Rabbah (xiii.) Rome, under the name "Edom," is compared to "Seir" was used by the

poets of the Middle Ages not only for Rome (comp. Ecclus. 1. 26, Hebr.), but also for Christianity (Zunz, "Literaturgesch," p. 620).[9]

Expanding on this ancient use of the name "Rome" for Edom/Esau, the scholars of the *Encyclopedia Judaica* state:

> The intense hatred of Rome after the cruel crushing of the revolt of the Diaspora in the time of Trajan and still more after the harsh suppression of the Bar Kokhba revolt and the decrees of persecution in Hadrian's days; the fact that Rome, like Edom, had destroyed the Temple; the similarity of Edom, compared to a pig, with Rome, for whom the pig (or, more correctly, the sow) was a most important symbol; the allusions to Edom dwelling on high like an eagle and the fact that the eagle, too, was an important Roman symbol; and perhaps finally even the similarity to the name Rome and Romans in several verses that speak of Edom, Seir, and Esau – all these apparently combined to cause the application to Rome of the biblical references to Edom, the eternal enemy of Israel.[10]

With this understanding, here is the great question: What major religion came out of Rome in the fourth century under the reign Constantine and the Roman Catholic Church? History concurs that it was Christianity.

The Priesthood of Rome

Under the old Roman monarchical system the office of the king included religious as well as secular functions. The Roman ruler was both king and priest. As priest, he held the title "Pontifex Maximus" [*lit.*, 'keeper of the Mysteries of Mithraism']. The term "pontiff" comes from the word *pons,* meaning "bridge".[11] The implication of the term "Pontiff Maximus" being that the king or emperor was a "bridge-builder" between this life and the next.

The temporal needs of the priests, who served the "Pontiff Maximus" ['king'], were provided for by funds from the treasury of Rome. Some of them were furnished with residences. And because they served the "Pontiff Maximus," they were also exempted from civil and military duties.

The scholars of *Harper's Dictionary of Classical Literature and Antiquities* (1896) tell us that one of these groups of priests who served the "Pontiff Maximus" were known as *"flamens,"* which comes from the word *"flare,"* meaning one who kindles or keeps the sacred fires.[12] And the scholars of *Hastings Encyclopedia of Religion and Ethics* inform us that the insignia of the *flamens*, besides the *toga praetexta* ['outer garment'], were the *laena*, a short *red* cloak worn over the *toga*, and especially the *pileus* or *galerus*, a conical cap.[13]

Thus it was no coincidence that the color *red* was the official color of the Roman Empire. Nor is it a coincidence that *red* is a sacred color of the Roman Catholic Church. Nor is it a coincidence that the color *red* is worn today by the bishops, priests and deacons, who directly serve the Pontiff Maximus ['Pope'].

Nor was it a coincidence that the anti-Jewish Greek and Latin Church Fathers and fourth century Catholic Church authorities condemned everything Jewish and set out to establish a new religion called "Christianity" – void of its Hebraic roots.

Some will argue that this doesn't prove that Christianity is identified with either Edom or Esau. They're right. It doesn't!

So here is the great question: Did the young Rabbi from Nazareth teach the "Lesson of Esau" to the people His day? Indeed He did!

"Many Will Say To Me In That Day LORD, LORD"

Addressing this great future day of accountability, Matthew records that the young Rabbi from Nazareth said:

> 21 Not everyone that saith unto me, LORD, LORD, shall enter into the kingdom of heaven; but he that doeth the will of my Father which is in heaven.
>
> 22 Many will say to me in that day, Lord, Lord, have we not prophesied in thy name? And in thy name have cast out devils? And in thy name done many wonderful works?
>
> 23 And then I will profess unto them, I never knew you: depart from me, ye that work iniquity (Matt. 7:21-23; AKJV).

According to most theologians, the above passage is addressing what is commonly called "false disciples" in Christianity. For example, Dr. H. D. Spence of the *Pulpit Commentary* writes:

> Ver. 22—**Many will say to me in that day.** The great day. Notice Christ's claim, so early as this, to be the future Judge of the world. **Lord, Lord** (cf. Hos. viii. 2). In ver. 21 a profession of service, *i.e.* as regards work; here, as regards wages. **Have we not prophesied.** Revised Version, *did,* etc.? The thought is not of abiding effect, but merely historical facts. **In thy name? and in thy name have cast out devils? and in thy name done many wonderful works?** Revised Version, by *thy name.* An important difference, for "in" implies some vital connexion (sic). But in this case the revelation (ch. vi. 9, note) of Christ was merely the instrument by which these men proclaimed Divine truths, cast out demons, and wrought miracles. With him, or even with it, they had no real union. Ver. 23—(Cf. Luke xiii. 27.) **And then will I profess unto them.** Openly in the face of all men (cf. ch. x. 32). **I never knew you.** Even when you did all these miracles, etc., I had not that personal knowledge of you which is only the result of heart-sympathy. There was never anything in common between you and me.[14]

Notice that Dr. Spence argues that the words "I never knew you" means that there never was a "personal knowledge" [*i.e.,* relationship with Christ] of those standing before the LORD on that great day of accountability. The problem with stopping with the words "I never knew you" is that the young Rabbi's teaching doesn't end with the words "I never knew you". *Yeshua* goes on to say: "you who work *tnv anomiav* ['the iniquity']. Again, the importance of the *definite article* before the word *anomiav* ['iniquity'] cannot be overstated. The Christian Greek scholars Arndt and Gingrich inform us that the Greek word *avomian* means *"lawlessness, lawless deeds, transgression of the law."*[15]

Expanding on Christ's employment of the term *tnv animiav,* Dr. Brooke Foss Westcott writes:

> **Iniquity.** The assurance of the psalmist becomes the verdict of the Judge. Observe that at this, the end of his discourse,

our Lord speaks not of sin generally (*tnv amartiav*), but of lawlessness (*tnv avomiav*). He has throughout been insisting upon obedience to the Law in its final meaning as essentially necessary for his followers (most recently ver. 12). So that instead of saying, "ye that work sin," he uses the correlative (1 John iii. 4) for sin is neglect of or opposition to the perfect Law of God in three spheres that regards – self, the world, and God (cf. Bishop Westcott, on 1 John iii. 4).[16]

"Depart from Me"

For most Christians, *Yeshua's* words "depart from Me" are a *sentence of doom.* Arndt and Gingrich, however, tell us that the Greek word *apoxwpeite* means "go away, leave, withdraw."[17]

It is significant for us to understand that in Hebrew the word for "depart", *sur* means "to turn aside, to go away, to depart, especially when *drawing near* to a person."[18] In the *Septuagint* the same Hebraic concept of "going away, leaving, withdrawing" is reproduced in the translation of Psalm 6:8, stating: "Depart from me, all you workers of iniquity...."

Notice that neither the Greek term *apoxwpeite* or Hebrew parallelism *sur* convey the idea of a *sentence of doom,* or "to disown totally". But they do convey the idea of *removal* from a person's presence.

Why is this Hebraic concept important to our understanding of *Yeshua's* words: "Depart from Me"? Because we find this same Hebraic expression employed by the young Rabbi when teaching on the Great Wedding Banquet.

The Great Wedding Banquet

Among the parables *Yeshua* taught on that great day of accountability, such as in Matthew 8:11-12; 22:2-14; 25:14-30; 31-46, none are more vivid and forceful than His teaching on the future Great Wedding Banquet. Quoting the young Rabbi's own words, Matthew writes:

> 11 And when the king came in to see the guests, he saw there a man which had not on a wedding garment:

12 And he saith unto him, Friend, how camest thou in
hither not having a wedding garment? And he was speechless.

13 Then said the king to the servants, Bind him hand and
foot, and take him away, and cast *him* into outer darkness; there
shall be weeping and gnashing of teeth.

14 For many are called, but few are chosen (Matt. 22:11-
14; AKJV).

Notice that in the above passage, the "man" (v. 11) cast into "outer
darkness" is called "Friend" (v. 12).

For many, *Yeshua's* use of the term "Friend" was merely a common
courtesy extended to a stranger. But for those who understand the meaning
of the Greek word "Friend," *etaipos,* it means much more. According to
Arndt and Gingrich, *etaipos* establishes the idea of an existing "relationship,"
meaning *"comrade, companion, friend* of one's neighbor ... of playmates ...
of Jesus' disciples."[19]

In the *Septuagint,* the Greek word *etaipos* is a parallel of the Hebrew
word for "friend," *rea,* meaning *"a companion, a friend,* with whom one
has intercourse."[20]

Equally significant, addressing the significance of the "wedding
garment," Dr. Spence writes: *"ouk evedumevov evduma gamou: not garbed
in wedding garment,* the genitive expressing the particular character or
quality of the garment."[21]

Among the peoples of the Orient, it was the custom to present each
guest invited to a royal feast with a festive robe to be worn for that special
occasion. At the time of *Yeshua,* the Romans also had such a custom, the
robes being called "cenatoria".[22] The point Dr. Spence makes about the
young Rabbi's employment of the term "wedding garment," written in
the genitive ['the case of limitation, definition or description'[23]], is that
it signified a certain quality of character required for admission to, and
enjoyment of, the Great Wedding Banquet.[24]

What did *Yeshua* mean when He ordered the man not wearing a
"wedding garment" to be "cast into outer darkness" (v. 13)? Some say that
"outer darkness" is a reference to "unbelievers," who are cast into *geehvva*
['Geehnna'], the "place of burning" (Matt. 5:29; 10:28; 18:9; 23:33; Mk.
9:45, 47; Lk. 12:5). According to Arndt and Gingrich, however, in Jewish
thought *geehvva* [*i.e.,* the place of punishment in the next life, *hell*] is
reserved for the "Last Judgment"[25] (Rev. 20:12f.).

In contrast, the Christian scholars of *The Illustrated Bible Dictionary* tell us that the judgment of Believers on that great day of accountability will take place at Christ's return, at the beginning of His millennial reign on earth from Jerusalem (Matt. 25:14-30; 31-46; 1 Cor. 3:12-15; 2 Cor. 5:10; 1 Pet. 1:17).[26]

Moreover, the Christian scholars of *The Complete Word Study Testament* inform us that a Believer's faithfulness to obey God is considered of such paramount importance that the metaphor "to be case into outer darkness" was used by Christ to emphasize the loss of reward for the Believer who does not walk in the path the LORD has commanded (Matt. 5:3-12; 7:21-23; 10:15; Lk. 6:20-26; 12:47, 48; Acts 10:4, 31; Rom. 2:1-16; 14:10-23; 1 Cor. 3:13; 4:5; 2 Cor. 5:10; 1 Jhn. 4:17; Rev. 20:11-15).[27]

What will that "outer darkness" be? In this writer's opinion the answer can be found in *Yeshua's* words: "… depart from Me" (Matt. 7:23), meaning "to go away" or "to be removed from His presence".

Since John's prologue states that *Yeshua* is "the true Light, which lighteth every man that cometh into the world" (Jhn. 1:8), to be *removed* from His presence at that great future Wedding Banquet would indeed be a sentence of being sent into "outer darkness".

The "Wise Man" and "Foolish Man"

The young Rabbi from Nazareth concluded His teaching on that great future day of accountability with a lesson on the very different lives of "two men," which may have been an allusion to the most famous brothers in Jewish history – Jacob and Esau. Quoting the very words of *Yeshua,* Matthew writes:

> 24 Therefore whosoever heareth these sayings of mine, and doeth [Gk. *poios*] them, I will liken unto a wise man, which built his house upon a rock;
>
> 25 And the rain descended, and the floods came, and the winds blew, and beat upon that house; and it fell not; for it was founded upon a rock.
>
> 26 And every one that heareth these sayings of mine, and doeth [Gk. *poios*] them not, shall be likened unto a foolish man, which built his house upon the same.

27 And the rain descended, and the floods came, and the
winds blew, and beat upon that house; and it fell; and great was
the fall of it (Matt. 7:24-27; AKJV).

For most Christians, the primary emphasis of the above passage is the
"wise man" [*i.e.*, the New Testament Believer], who built his life upon
Jesus Christ [*i.e.*, the rock], as opposed to the "foolish man" [*i.e.*, the non-
Believer], who built his life upon the sand [*i.e.*, a Christless religion].

But there is a problem with this claim. Because the primary emphasis
of *Yeshua's* teaching in this passage is the action verb "doeth" [Gk. *poios*],
which the young Rabbi repeats twice (vs. 24, 26).

Why is the action verb *poios* important to our understanding of what
Yeshua was saying? Arndt and Gingrich inform us that the primary meaning
of the Greek verb *poios* used in this particular sense means as follows: "*do,
keep, carry out, practice, commit*—**a.** *do, keep* the will or law obediently *to
tilnma tou Teou* Mt 7:21; 12:50; Mk 3:35; Jhn 4:34; 6:38; 7:17; 9:31; Eph
6:6; Hb 10:7, 9 (Ps 40:8 'I delight to do thy will, O my God: yea, thy
law is within my heart');--*tov vomou* [*lit.*, 'the law'] Jhn 7:19; Gal 5:3; Mt
5:19; Ro 2:14; Gal 3:10 (Dt. 27:26); vs. 12 (cf. Lev 18:5)—Mt 7:24, 26,
Lk 6:46; Jhn 2:5; 8:44...."[28]

Thus the point the young Rabbi made was that when the storms in
life come the *Torah* observant "wise man" will be blessed by God in this
life and the Age to Come. Whereas the *Torahless* "foolish man," who builds
his life on the "sand" [*i.e.*, the shifting doctrines and traditions of men],
will suffer great loss when the storms of life come in this life, as well as the
Age to Come.

"Little Children, Let No Man Deceive You"

By 90 C.E., the Apostolic Era was about to end. The world John
knew as a young disciple of *Yeshua* was now much different. The Temple
in Jerusalem had been destroyed. Both the Jewish people and Nazarene
Believers had been dispersed among the nations. Gentile converts were
increasing in numbers. And the *Torah* observant faith of those first followers
of the young Rabbi from Nazareth was now being replaced with a *Torahless*
gospel.

Dr. David Smith of *The Expositor's Greek Testament* tells us that it was because of the heresy of Antinomianism, represented by the Nicolaitans, that John was compelled to write to the Believers in Asia Minor.[29] He writes:

> It is said that the Nicolaitans were the followers of Nicolas, one of the seven deacons (Acts vi. 5), and this strange story is told of him by Clement of Alexandria: "He had, they say, a beautiful wife, and after the Ascension of the Saviour, being taunted by the Apostles with jealousy, he brought the woman forward and gave who would permission to marry her. This, they say, is in accordance with that expression of his: 'We must abuse the flesh'. And indeed the adherents of his sect follow up the incident and the saying absolutely and unquestioningly and commit fornication without restraint'. Clement proceeds to attest the moral purity of Nicolas and explain his action as inculcation of ascetic self-restraint, but certainly the sect which bore his name was given over to licentiousness. Clement says elsewhere that they were "dissolute as he-goats," and others bear like testimony. They were Antinomians, disowning moral obligation, *nullam differentiam esse docents in moechando et idoloothy ton edere;* herein being the forerunners of the Gnostics and justifying Tertullian's classification of them with the Cainites. This heresy was rampant among the churches of Asia Minor in St. John's day (*cf.* Rev. ii. 6, 14, 15), and he deals with it in our Epistle. See I, 5-ii. 6, 15-17, iii. 3-10.[30]

Thus it was that John was compelled to write a letter to his "little children". Not surprisingly, John addressed the biblical definition of sin, saying:

> 4 Whosoever committeth sin transgresseth also the law [Gk. *tnv amaptiav*]; for sin is the transgression of the law [*n avomia*].
>
> 5 And ye know that he was manifested to take away our sins and in him is no sin.

6 Whosoever <u>abideth</u> [*lit.,* 'continuous action'] in him sinneth not: whosoever sinneth hath not seen him, neither known him.

7 Little children, let no man deceive you: he that doeth *tnv dikaiosuvnv* ['<u>the</u> righteousness,' *lit.,* "righteousness in the sense of fulfilling the divine statues"[31]] is *dikaios* [*lit.,* 'righteous'], even as he is *dikaios* ['righteous'] (1 John 3:4-7; AKJV).

Addressing John's definition of sin, the Christian theologian Dr. Brooke Foss Westcott writes:

> ... *n amartia estin n avomia, peccatum est iniquitas* V., *sin is lawlessness.* Sin and lawlessness are convertible terms. Sin is not an arbitrary conception. It is the assertion of the selfish will against a paramount authority. He who sins breaks not only by accident or in an isolated detail, but essential the 'law' which he was created to fulfill.[32]

Why was this understanding of the doctrine of sin important to those Gentile Believers in Asia Minor? Because the Antinomians did *not* believe they were commiting sin when they transgressed the Law of Moses.

Over the centuries, little has changed. Today most Christians ignore 1 John 3:4-7 as the New Testament definition of sin. Instead, sin is often defined as follows: Dr. A. Plummer of the *Pulpit Commentary* defines sin as the "transgression of God's will".[33] The Christian professors Ralph Earl, Harvey Blaney and Carl Hanson, tell us that sin is "the transgression of the law of love".[34] And Dr. G. Campbell Morgan says that sin is simply "rebellion against God".[35]

Clearly, these definitions address the sin issue. But they are also highly general in nature, and have often led to definitions of sin rooted in subjective analysis and ecclestialcal bias. For example, in the second, third and fourth centuries, the Greek and Latin Church Fathers, and Catholic Church authorities decreed everything Jewish to be heretical.

During the Middle Ages, Catholic authorities believed it to be a sin to read or own a Bible, or criticize the tenets of the Church. The Inquisition was established to silence all who refused to accept Catholic doctrine and Church policy.

In July 1633, Galileo, the "Father of modern science," was found guilty of heresy by a Roman Catholic Inquisition Court for holding the view that the Sun remained motionless at the center of the universe and the Earth is not at its center, and moves.

More recently, some churches and denominations hold sin to be "drinking coffee," "wearing jewelry," "long hair on men," and so on. At the other extreme, Christians and churches, Jews and synagogues, are now embracing the latest sexual revolution -- homosexuality and Same-sex marriage.

Among the first century followers of the young Rabbi from Nazareth, such was not the case. In the *Septuagint,* which was the primary Bible for Greek speaking Believers, *amartia* ['sin'] was used for the Hebrew word *chatta'ah* ['sin'] 238 times,[36] and was always used with respect to the transgression of *Torah.*

Why did John want the Believers in Asia Minor to understand that sin is the transgression of *Torah?* The answer is quite simple: the definition of sin in *Torah* specifically addresses man's relationship with God, an orderly society, toward one's own self and other people. For example, on loving and treatment of others there are 14 commandments; on marriage, divorce and family there are 23 commandments; on forbidden sexual relations there are 25 commandments; on the times and seasons there are 36 commandments; on dietary laws there are 27 commandments; on business practices there are 14 commandments; on employee and servants there are 19 commandments; on court and judicial procedures there are 36 commandments; on injuries and damages there are 4 commandments; on property and property rights there are 11 commandments; on criminal laws there are 7 commandments; on punishment and restitution there are 23 commandments; on idolatry and idolatrous practices there are 45 commandments; on agriculture and animal husbandry there are 7 commandments.*

"If We Confess our Sin"

Accompanying the definition of sin, John included God's instruction for sin's remedy. As a member of the House of Israel, John knew it well. Thus he wrote to his "little children," saying: "If we confess [Gk. *Present Active Tense,* 'referring to *continuous* or *repeated* action'], our *tas amartias*

---

* See Ministry Resources: Judaism 101.

[*lit.,* 'our sin against *Torah*'], He is faithful and just to forgive us our *tas amartias* ['our sin against *Torah*'], and to cleanse us from all unrighteousness [Gk. *adikia* – the opposite of *dikaiosuvn*,[37] "*righteousness* in the sense of fulfilling the divine statues"[38]] (1 Jhn. 1:9).

Notice John's use of the pronoun "we," exhorting his "little children" to participate with him in the repeated act of "confessing *tas amaptias* [*lit.,* 'the sin against *Torah*'].

Think about that for a moment! Here we have this elderly Apostle, who was well acquainted with the Temple sacrificial offerings that were accompanied with the "confession of *tas amaptias* [*lit.,* 'the sin against *Torah*'], exhorting his "little children" to participate with him in one of the most profound, yet simple acts of redemption – the act of "confessing *tas amaptias*".

According to the Christian scholars of *Strong's Exhaustive Concordance*, the Greek word for "confess," *emologwmen* means "to assent, *i.e.,* covenant, acknowledge, profess, confess, promise."[39] Why did John use the Greek word *emologwmen*? Because in Jewish thought the *verbal* confession of *tas amaptias* is inseparable from *teshuvah* ['repentance']. For example, in Numbers 5:6-7, the commandment to repent for transgressions against the *Torah* makes an explicit mention of "confession" [Heb. *yadhah,* meaning "to speak out, to confess"].

This hardly sounds as though John believed that the *Torah* had been *done away* with the coming of *Yeshua*. Nor does it sound as though John believed that the young Rabbi from Nazareth had fulfilled the commandments for him, making them "out dated" and no longer relevant to the Believer.

For John, the confession of sin was the most important act of faith his "little children" could preform. As a young boy growing up in Israel, John had been taught the importance of this sacred act by his rabbi. This is precisely the reason we have included the the following teaching on the confession of sin by Rabbi S. R. Hirsch, who says:

> If you have recognized that you have sinned, then step into the presence of God and say: "O God, I have erred and sinned. I have been disobedient before You, I have done so-and-so (I am sorry and I am ashamed of what I have done, and will never do it again) ... Feel in yourself how every sin you have committed, however small, even in the mind and heart, immediately brings with it a curse, namely, that it makes you less capable of doing

good, and further inclined to sin; and when you have recognized this, then you can lay the future of your inner and outer life in the just and forgiving hand of God, and as you see yourself in spirit, so confess in word, in order that the picture of your self-abasement may become external to you and stand before you, making it not a passing emotion but a permanent mood and frame of mind which can bear fruit in practical conduct.[40]

"I Have Kept the Faith"

Knowing that his time on earth was short, Paul wrote to Timothy from a Roman prison about his imminent death, saying: "I have fought a good fight. I have finished my course. I have kept the faith. Henceforth, there is laid up for me a crown of righteousness, which the LORD, the righteous Judge, shall give me at that day" (2 Tim. 4:7-8).

According to most theologians, Paul is addressing the keeping of his faith in Christ. For example, the Bible expositor Dr. A. C. Hervey writes:

> Through his long eventful course, in spite of all the difficulties, Conflicts, dangers, and temptations, he had kept the faith of Jesus Christ committed to him, inviolable, unadulterated, whole, and Complete. He had not shrunk from confessing it when death stared Him in the face; he had not corrupted it to meet the views of Jews Or Gentiles; with courage and resolution and perseverance he had Kept it to the end. Oh! Let Timothy do the same.[41]

But is what Paul was really meant when he wrote those words to Timothy about having "kept the faith"? Not according to the best Greek manuscripts, which record Paul as having employed the Greek words *tetnrnka tnv pistiv* [*lit.,* 'I have kept the faith'].

Arndt and Gingrich inform us that the Greek verb Paul employed for "kept," comes from the root word *tereo* and means "to keep, observe, fulfill, especially the Law."[42]

According to Matthew, the Greek verb *tereo* is the same word the *Yeshua* used when He told His disciples to go to the nations of the world "teaching them to *tereo* ['keep'] all that I have commanded you" (Matt.

19:17; AKJV). *Tereo* was also the word *Yeshua* used when He responded to the rich young ruler who asked: "What shall I do to have everlasting life?" *Yeshua* replied: "If thou wilt enter life, *tereo* ['keep'] the commandments" (Matt. 19:17).

According to John, the Greek verb *tereo* is the same word *Yeshua* used when He told His disciples the following: "If you love me, *tereo* ['keep'] My commandments" (Jhn.14:15). *Tereo* is the same word *Yeshua* used when He told His disciples: "If you *tereo* ['keep'] my commandments, you shall abide in My love" (Jhn. 15:10). And *tereo* is the same word *Yeshua* used when He said: "... even as I have *tereo* ['kept'] My Father's commandments and abide in His love" (Jhn. 15:10).

The problem with the claim that Paul had *tereo* ['kept'] his faith in Jesus Christ is that the Bible clearly teaches that salvation is a *gift* that cannot be earned, compensated for, or "kept" by personal effort.

According to *The Original Webster's Unabridged Dictionary* (1901), the term "gift" is defined as follows: "A present; any thing given or bestowed; any thing, the property of which is voluntarily transferred by one person to another without compensation."[43]

Clearly, with this understanding, if one can boast about "keeping" his faith in Christ, then salvation is no longer a *gift*. Rather, it has become something earned by personal effort. And Paul taught that salvation is a *gift* of God, "not of *ergov* ['works'] lest any man should boast" (Eph. 2:8-9).

Since salvation is a *gift* that cannot be *tereo* ['kept'] by personal effort, Paul's employment of the words "I have *tereo* ['kept'] the faith" can mean only one thing: in spite of all the suffering, rejection and hardships Paul had to endure, he *tereo* ['kept'] his *Torah* observant faith in *Yeshua*.

As a ringleader of Nazarene Believers scattered throughout Asia Minor, Paul was hated by Jews, and held to be an insurrectionist by the Romans. Even among Believers, Paul was viewed with skeptcism (2 Corin. 10:8-18; 11:1-32).

Apparently, Paul's physical appearance was such that it did not commend himself to either Jews or Gentiles. A second century apocryphal description of Paul states: "He was a man little of stature, partly bald, with crooked legs, of vigorous physique, with eyes set close together and nose, somewhat hooked."[44]

Nevertheless for Paul, faith in *Yeshua* was not a blind leap of faith based on the teachings and traditions of men. As a *Torah* observant Pharisee (Acts 23:6), even when traveling abroad Paul *tereo* ['kept'] the Sabbath

(Acts 13:14-16, 26, 39, 42-44), and *tereo* ['kept'] the appointed festivals (20:6-8). Likewise, when in Jerusalem, despite strong adversity, Paul *tereo* ['kept'] the appointed festivals (1 Corin. 16:8-9), and *tereo* ['kept'] Temple observances (21:17-26).

Consequently, at the end of life, Paul could say with a high degree of confidence: "I have fought a good fight. I have *tereo* ['kept'] the faith: Henceforth, there is laid up for me a crown of righteousness [Gk. *dikaiosuvns,* "**a.** *righteousness* in the sense of fulfilling the divine statutes Mt. 3:15=ISm 1:1; Mt. 5:20 [45]], which the LORD, the righteous [Gk. *dikaios,* "*upright, just, righteous*"[46]] shall give me at that day, and not to me only, but unto all them also that love His appearing" (2 Tim. 4:8).

What Shall We Then Say?

In conclusion, here is the great question: Should non-Jews try to become Jews? Not according to the Acts 15 debate of the first century Jerusalem Council. But it can be established that the Apostles taught non-Jewish Believers the Judaic concept of *tas amartia* ['the sin'] to be the transgression of *Torah.* It can be established that the Apostles and first century Nazarene Believers *tereo* ['kept'] the seventh day Sabbath, the appointed Spring and Fall festivals, and the dietary health food laws. It can be established that the Apostles made a clear distinction between *justification,* which comes by faith in *Yeshua,* and faith in *ta ergov* ['the works'] of *Torah.* It can be established that God is no respecter between Jews and Gentiles when it comes to the hearing and *poios* ['doing'] the *ergov* of *Torah.* It can be established that first century Gentile converts joined themselves to the Commonwealth of Israel by attending synagogues on Shabbat to be instructed in the *Torah* of Moses. And it can be established that the sanitization of the Jewishness of *Yeshua,* the Apostles, the first century Believers, as well as the Apostolic Writings, began with the Replacement Theology of the Heretic Marcion, the second century Greek and Latin Church Fathers, the sun worshiping Roman Emperor Constantine, and fourth century Roman Catholic Church authorities.

Having said this, it is important for us to understand that there is no one who observes all the applicable *mitzvot* ['commandments'] perfectly, which is to say we are all a "work in progress". It is also important to not let the fact that we will never be able to perfectly observe the LORD's commandments stop us from stepping out in faith and begin walking in the path of *Torah* observance, as we understand it at this time.

Be assured, once you enter into a new covenant relationship with the LORD and begin your own personal journey of *Torah* observance, He has promised to lead you into all truth and guide you on the path of righteousness. As you walk in His light of *Torah* [*lit.,* meaning 'Instruction'] that light will become brighter and brighter. Before long, you will know that you too are walking in faith of those first century *Torah* observant followers of the young Rabbi from Nazareth.

Therefore, my friend, be extremely careful and wise. Reject the false teaching that the *Torah* was *done away* with the coming of *Yeshua* and therefore, is no longer relevant to Believers. Take heed to the warning Paul gave to the Nazarene Believers at Colossi, when he wrote: **"Beware, lest any man spoil you through philosophy or vain deceit, after the traditions of men.... Let no man beguile you of your reward"** (Col. 2:8, 18; AKJV).

Glossary of Terms

Adoration of the Wafer Host: The adoration of the sun-shaped wafer which is transformed into the actual body of *Yeshua*.

Affusion: The act of pouring water upon or sprinkling. When baptism by immersion was changed to affusion.

Anti-Nomianism: [*lit.*, "against law"] – A term coined by Martin Luther defined as holding that under the new order of grace neither moral or religious law is of use or obligation because faith alone is necessary for salvation.

Apostolic Writings: The writings of the Apostles, commonly known in the Bible as the New Testament.

Anti-Semitism: The attitude of hostility toward Jewish people and everything Jewish.

Aviv: [*lit.*, "Spring"] – The first month of the Jewish calendar, also called "Nissan".

B.C.E.: Before Common Era, commonly known as B.C.

Baal: An idol among the ancient Chaldeans and Syrians, representing the sun. The word Baal means "lord" or "commander." The sun-god Baal was worshiped by different nations at different times.

Baptism of the Bells: A ceremony of baptizing the bells to ward off demons and to call the elect to vespers when blessed bells are rung.

C.E.: Common Era, commonly known in Christianity as A.D.

Chag HaMatzot: The appointed seven day biblical Spring festival of Unleavened Bread follows Passover, commemorating the removal of sin from our lives for the purpose of drawing close to God.

Chag HaBikkurim: The appointed biblical Spring festival of First Fruits, commemorating the first cut of the barley harvest, which represents the bodily resurrection of *Yeshua* from the earth.

Commonwealth of Israel: The people of ancient Israel, who were united under the Covenant of the God of Abraham, Isaac, and Jacob.

Communion: The act of administering the sacrament of the eucharist; the participation of Christians in the LORD's Supper.

Co-Redemptrix: The Catholic Church's institution of Mary as Co-Redeemer with Christ.

Covenant: The covenant of commands, prohibitions, and promises of God contained in both the oral and written contract of God, and agreed to by the patriarchs and first Commonwealth of Israel.

Cultivated Olive Tree: An olive tree that has been nurtured with labor and management from a seed to reach its full potential as a mature fruit-bearing tree.

Decalogue: The Ten Commandments given to Moses on Mount Sinai.

Didache: A Church manual of the second century C.E. known as *The Teaching of the Twelve Apostles.*

Ecclesia: The Greek word meaning the "the called-out ones," who are called of God to be a separate and peculiar people, commonly called "the Church" in Christianity.

Eucharist: The sacrament of commemorating the sacrificial death of *Yeshua* by transferring the emblems of bread and wine into the actual flesh and blood of Christ.

Extreme Unction: The rite of anointing in ones' last hours; or the application of sacred oil to the head, the hands, and feet, of a dying person.

Gnostic: An adherent or advocate of Gnosticism; an ancient Greek and Oriental philosophy based on secret superior knowledge modified by the synthesis of Gostic and Christian doctrine.

God-fearers: A name used to describe non-Jews in ancient times who believed in the God of Israel, attended synagogue Sabbath worship, and observed the appointed festivals, dietary health food laws, and instruction in the *Torah* of Moses.

Halakhah: The collective body of Jewish religious instruction, including biblical instruction [the 613 mitzvot] and later Talmudic and Rabbinic instruction, as well as customs and traditions.

Hillel the Elder: (110 B.C.E. – 10 C.E.) – Hillel was one of the most important rabbis of Jewish history. He was the founder of the House of Hillel school for *Tannaim* [Sages of the *Mishnah*].

Hellelites: Those who did not hold to a strict literal interpretation of the *Written Torah* of Moses as taught in the Second Temple school of Hillel.

Havdalah: A ceremony conducted after sunset on Shabbat that closes out the Sabbath and ushers in the new week.

Immaculate Conception: The doctrine that Mary the Virgin, by special grace and privilege, was kept free from all stain of original sin from the first moment of the conception.

Indulgences: The Roman Catholic remission of punishment due to sins,. granted by the Pope or church, and supposed to save the sinner from purgatory; absolution from the censures of the church and from all transgressions.

Judaism: The religious doctrines and rites of the Jewish people as set forth by the *Torah* of Moses.

Law: The Law [*Torah*] of Moses as distinguished from the Christian gospel.

Legalism: The doctrine of salvation by works.

Lent: The observance of fasting by Roman Catholics and other churches before Easter. It begins at Ash-Wednesday, and continues to Easter.

Manichaeism: The belief that there are two supreme principles, the one good, the other evil, which produce all the happiness and calamities in the world. The first principle, "light," was held to be the author of all good; the second, "darkness," was the author of evil. For Christian Manicheans, Christ was the revelation of the "good God," and the God of the Old Testament the revelation of the "lesser God."

Masoretes: A group of Jewish scholars whose purpose was to safeguard the integrity of the Hebrew Scriptures and facilitate its study. Over the years they established a variety of rules with which they protected the correct text.

Matza: Bread baked without yeast.

Mishnah: A textbook giving the essence of the *Oral Torah,* which according to Jewish tradition, was handed down to Moses along with the *Written Torah* at Mount Sinai. The *Oral Torah,* or Mishna, describes how to do what is commanded in the *Written Torah.*

Mithraism: The worship of the Roman sun-god Mithra.

Muratorian fragment: A copy of perhaps the oldest known list of books of the New Testament.

Oral Torah: [*lit.,* "oral instruction"] – According to Rabbinic Judaism, the *Oral Torah* was given by God orally to Moses in conjunction with the

Written Torah after which it was passed down orally through the ages. Later, it was codified and written in the *Talmud.*

Passover: An appointed biblical festival instituted by God to commemorate His deliverance of the ancient Israelites from bondage in Egypt. In the first century Passover was observed by both Jewish and non-Jewish Believers in *Yeshua,* commemorating their deliverance from the bondage of sin.

Pharisees: A sect of Judaism that existed during the second Temple period beginning under the Hasmonean dynasty (140-37 B.C.E.). They believed that the *Oral Torah* was meant to elaborate and explain what was in the *Written Torah.* Moreover, they held that the *Oral Torah,* which was given at Sinai by God to Moses along with the *Written Torah,* was not a fixed text. Rather, it was to be viewed as an ongoing process of analysis and argument in which God continued to be actively involved, and that by participating in this process they were actively participating in God's ongoing revelation to the people of Israel.

Proselytes: Non-Jews who converted to Judaism. The word "proselyte" comes from the Hebrew word *ger,* meaning "a foreigner, a stranger".

Replacement Theology: An anti-Jewish doctrine that emerged from the second century teachings of the Greek and Latin Church Fathers, who taught that the Church had replaced the physical people of Israel as God's chosen people.

Rosh Chodesh: The New Moon, which commemorates the beginning of the new month, the new year, and the appointed Spring and Fall festivals of the LORD.

Rosh HaShanah: The appointed festival which begins the Fall festivals. Also called "Yom Teruah" [Day of the Awakening Blast]. It is also called "Yom Hadin" [Day of Judgment] and marks the beginning of the Ten Days of Teshuvah ['repentence'], which climaxes on Yom Kippur [Day of Atonement].

Sanhedrin: An assembly of judges in every city in the ancient Land of Israel. The Great Sanhedrin of the High Priest was made up of 71 members.

Saturnalia: An ancient Roman festival in honor of the deity Saturn, originally celebrated December 17 through December 23.

Seder: A Hebrew word meaning "order" or "sequence," and is used for Passover, as well as an annual or weekly cycle for the reading of the *Torah.*

Septuagint: The Greek version of the Hebrew Scriptures, especially the first five books of Moses, the *Torah.*

Shabbat: The seventh day Sabbath.

Shammai: (50 B.C.E. – 30 C.E.) – Shammai was the founder of the school known as the House of Shammai. He was the foremost opponent of Hillel, taking a strict position on the interpretation of Jewish law versus Hillel's more liberal interpretation on many matters.

Shammai Pharisee: One who held to the strict view of the letter of the *Torah* of Moses, as taught in the Second Temple school of Shammai.

Shavuot: The appointed Spring festival that commemorates the giving of the *Torah* on Mount Sinai. Also called the festival of "Weeks" and "Pentecost," meaning "fifty," representing the fifty days it took the children of Israel to walk from Egypt to Mount Sinai.

Sh'mini Atzeret: The appointed Fall festival that follows Sukkot. Also called "the Eighth Day of Assembly," commemorating God's eternal grace and mercy that has been bestowed upon His people during the preceding Yamin Tovim [High Holidays].

Sh'ma: "Hear, [O] Israel" are the first two words of the *Torah* that is the centerpiece of morning and evening Jewish prayers: "Hear, O Israel the LORD is our God, the LORD is one" (Deut. 6:4).

Sukkot: The appointed Fall festival that commemorates the Divine protection of the LORD during Israel's journey to the Promised Land. Also called the festival of "Booths" and "Tabernacles".

Talmud: [*lit.,* "instruction, learning"] – A record of rabbinic discussions pertaining to Jewish law, ethics, philosophy, custom and history.

Tosafists: Medieval rabbis from France and Germany who wrote critical and explanatory notes, interpretations, and rulings on the Talmud.

Trans-substantiation: The rite of transforming the bread and wine into the actual body and blood of Christ.

Wave Sheaf: The first cut of the Spring barley harvest, commemorating the beginning of the Spring harvest.

Written Torah: [*lit.,* "written instruction") – The first five books of Moses as found in the Tanakh/Jewish Bible and Old Testament/Christian Bible.

Yehudim: The Greek name for "Jews"; also a title given to first century *Torah* observant Gentile Believers (Rev. 2:9; 3:9); *The Expositor's Greek Testament,* Vol. 5, p. 367.

Yom Kippur: The appointed Fall festival which climaxes the Ten Days of Teshuvah ['repentence']. Also called "Day of Atonement," when atonement was made for the national sins of Israel. On this day only, the High Priest entered the Holy of Holies in the Temple and sprinkled the blood of a goat on the mercy seat, the top covering of the Ark of the Covenant.

Endnotes

Preface

1. *Holy Land, The,* "The Olive Tree," http://www.christus.org.
2. J. D. Douglas, gen. ed., *The Illustrated Bible Dictionary,* (Wheaton, IL: Tyndale House Publishing, 1980), Vol. 1, p. 1114.
3. David Bivin & Roy Blizzard, Jr., *Understanding The Difficult Words Of Jesus,* (Shippensburg, PA: Destiny Image Publishers, 1994), pp. 5, 22-23.
4. Ibid.
5. Merrill C. Tenney, *New Testament Times,* (Grand Rapids, MI: William B. Eerdmans Publishing Co., 1965), p. v.

Chapter 1 *The Great Misconception of Matthew 5:17*

1. Karl Barth, *The Christian Life: Church Dogmatics,* Geoffery W. Bromiley, trans., (Edinburgh, SCT: T & T Publishers, 1956), p. 511.
2. Michael Silver, *The Torah Is Valid,* (Organ, NM: Tree of Life Publications, 2004), p. 187.
3. Philip Schaff, *History Of The Christian Church,* (Grand Rapids, MI: William B. Eerdmans Publishing Company, 1910), Vol. 1, pp. 210-211.
4. Elgin Moyer, *The Wycliffe Biographical Dictionary Of The Church,* (Chicago, IL: Moody Press, 1982), p. 263.
5. E. C. Blackman, *Marcion and His Influence,* (London, 1948), p. 50.

6.   William Barclay, *The Daily Study Bible,* "The Gospel of Matthew," (Philadelphia, PN: Westminister Press, 1956), Vol. 1, pp. 126-128.

7.   Ibid., p. 129.

8.   H. C. Leupold, *Exposition Of Genesis,* (Columbus, OH: The Wartburg Press, 1942), pp. 719-720.

9.   Gerhard Kittel, gen. ed., *The Theological Dictionary Of The New Testament,* Geoffrey W. Bromiley, trans., (Grand Rapids, MI: William B. Eerdmans Publishing Company, 1967), Vol. IV, p. 1062.

10.   David Bivin, *New Light On The Difficult Words Of Jesus: Insights From His Jewish Context,* (Holland, MI: En-Gedi Resource Center, Inc., 2007), p. 10..

11.   Harvey Falk, *Jesus The Pharisee: A New Look At The Jewishness of Jesus,* (Mahwah, NJ: Paulist Press, 1985), pp. 84-85.

12.   H. E. Dana & Julius R. Mantey, *A Manual Grammar Of The Greek New Testament,* (New York, NY: The Macmillian Company, 1927), pp. 181-182.

13.   Merrill F. Unger, *The New Unger's Bible Dictionary,* R. K. Harrison, gen. ed., (Chicago, IL: Moody Press, 1988), p. 997.

14.   *Encyclopedia Judaica,* "Pharisees," CD-Rom Version.

15.   Joseph Good, *Rosh HaShannah and The Messianic Kingdom To Come,* (Nederland, TX: Hatikva Ministries, 1998), p. 12.

16.   Schaff, *History Of The Christian Church,* Vol. 1, pp. 225-226.

17.   Joseph Good, *Prophecies In The Book Of Esther,* (Port Arthur, TX: Hatikva Ministries, 1995), p. 77.

18.   Herbert Lockyer, *All The Men Of The Bible,* (Grand Rapids, MI: Zondervan Publishing House, 1962), p. 269.

19.   C. E. B. Cranfield, *International Critical Commentary,* "Romans," (Edinburgh, SCT: T. & T. Clark, Ltd., 1981), Vol. 2, pp. 853.

20.   Edward H. Sugden, gen. ed., *Wesley's Standard Sermons,* "The Original Nature, Property, and Use of the Law," (London: The Epworth Press, 1964, orig. pub. 1921), Vol. II, pp. 55-56.

21.   Kittel, *Theological Dictionary of the New Testament,* Vol. IV, p. 1046.

22   Dana & Mantey, p. 137.

23.   William F. Arndt & F. Wilbur Gingrich, *A Greek-English Lexicon Of The New Testament and Other Early Christian Literature,* (Chicago, IL: The University of Chicago Press, 1957), pp. 544-545.

24. Barclay, "The Gospel of Matthew," Vol. 1, pp. 124-125.
25. Ibid., p. 125.
26. Ibid., pp. 125-126.
27. George Foote Moore, *Judaism In The First Centuries Of The Christian Era,* (Peabody, MA: Hindrickson Publishers, reprint 1997, orig. pub. 1927), Vol. 1, p. 263.
28. Arndt & Gingrich, #1-c, p. 415.
29. Ibid., #3, p. 677.
30. Spiros Zodhiates, gen. ed., *The Complete Word Study New Testament,* (Chattanooga, TN: AGM Publishers, 1992), Lexical Aids to the New Testament, #4137, p. 931.
31. W. Robertson Nicoll, gen. ed., *The Expositor's Greek Testament,* "The Gospel Of Matthew," Alexander Balmain Bruce, expos., (Grand Rapids, MI: William B. Eerdmans Publishing Company, 1940), Vol. 1, p. 104.

Chapter 2 *The Roots of Replacement Theology*

1. Tenney, pp. 321-322.
2. Robert Louis Wilken, *John Chrysostom and The Jews: Rhetoric and Reality In The Late Fourth Century,* (Berkeley, CA: University of California Press, 1983), p. xv.
3. Ibid.
4. Rodeny Stark, *The Rise of Christianity: How The Obscure, Marginal Jesus Movement Became The Dominant Religious Force In The Western World In A Few Centuries,* (Princeton, NJ: Princeton University Press, 1997), pp. 66-67.
5. Walter Laqueur, *The Changing Face Of Antisemitism: From Ancient Times To The Present Day,* (England: Oxford University Press, 2006), p. 48.
6. Benjamin Field, *The Handbook of Christian Theology:* cited by D. Shelby Corlett, *The Christian Sabbath*, pp. 5-6.
7. D. Shelby Corlett, *The Christian Sabbath,* (Kansas City, MO: Beacon Hill Press, nd), p. 9.
8. Judaeus Philo of Alexandria, Egypt, *Life Of Moses II,* Vol. IV, pp. 19-20.
9. Flavius Josephus, *Against Apion.* ii. 39.

10. Schaff, *History Of The Christian Church,* Vol. 2, p. 203.
11. Ibid.
12. Ibid.
13. Ibid., p. 204.
14. Ibid.
15. Ibid., p. 205.
16. Ibid., Vol. 3, pp. 383-384.
17. Ibid.
18. Ibid.
19. Ibid.
20. Ibid.
21. Ibid.
22. Ibid.
23. Ibid.
24. Ibid.
25. Paul J. Glenn, *The History Of Philosophy,* (St. Louis, MO: B. Herder Book Co., 1929), p. 151.
26. Ibid., p. 152.
27. Constantine quote – *Venerable Day Of The Sun* – 321 C.E.: Cod Justin. Bk. III. Tif. XII.3 (de feriss); also quoted by Philip Schaff, *History Of The Christian Church,* Vol. 3, pp. 105-106.
28. Schaff, *History Of The Christian Church,* Vol. 2, p. 201.
29. Will Durant, *The Story Of Civilization, Caesar and Christ,* (New York, NY: Simon & Schuster, 1944), Vol. 3, pp. 655-656.
30. W. T. Jones, *A History Of Western Philosophy,* (New York, NY: Harcourt, Brace & World, Inc., 1952), Vol. I, pp. 344-345.
31. *Catholic Encyclopedia, The,* "Constantine," (New York, NY: Robert Appleton Company, 1911), Vol. 4, p. 300.
32. Schaff, *History Of The Christian Church,* Vol. 3, pp. 14-15.
33. Edward Gibbon, *The Decline and Fall of the Roman Empire,* (New York, NY: Peter Fenelon Collier & Son, MCMI), Vol. II, pp. 182-183.
34. Durant, Vol. 3, p. 66.
35. *Catholic Encyclopedia,* (1911), Vol. 4, p. 300.
36. Gibbon, Vol. II, pp. 180-181.
37. Moore, Vol. I, p. 236.
38. *Catholic Encyclopedia,* (1911), Vol. 13, p. 611.

39. Philip Schaff, gen. ed., *The Post-Nicene Fathers, Libronix Digital Library Systems 1 Od; Church History Collections,* quoted by MS Windows XP, (Garland, TX: Ga.axie Software, 2002).

40. Dale W. Jacobs, gen. ed., *World Book Encyclopedia,* (Chicago, IL: World Book, Inc., 2001), Vol. 3, p. 666.

41. W. E. Vine, *An Expository Dictionary of New Testament Words,* (Westwood, NJ: Revell Publishers, 1940), p. 256.

42. *Catholic Encyclopedia,* (1911), Vol. 3, p. 656.

43. Alexander Hislop, *The Two Babylons,* (England: A & C Black, 1916), p. 93.

44. Louis Shores, gen. ed., *Collier's Encyclopedia,* (New York, NY: P. F. Collier, 1993), Vol. 6, p. 403.

45. *Encyclopedia Britannica, The,* (Chicago, IL: Encyclopedia Britannica, Inc., 1991), Vol. 3, p. 283.

46. George Rines, gen. ed., *Encyclopedia Americana,* (Danbury, CT: Grolier Inc., 1994), Vol. 6, p. 528.

47. Kenneth Barker, gen. ed., *The NIV Study Bible,* (Grand Rapids, MI: Zondervan Publishing House, 1995), p. 1613.

48. Charles Foster Kent, *A History Of The Jewish People,* (London: John Murry, 1927), pp. 339- 340.

49. Lew White, *Fossilized Customs,* (Louisville, KY: Strawberry Island Messianic Publishing Institute for Scripture Research, nd.), p. 31.

50. James Hastings, gen. ed., *Hastings Encyclopedia Of Religion and Ethics,* "Mithraism," (New York, NY: Charles Scribner's Sons, 1928), Vol. VIII, pp. 753, 754, 755, 759.

51. Jones, Vol. I, p. 295.

52. Unger, *Unger's Bible Dictionary,* p. 227.

53. Tenney, p. 120.

54. Ibid.

55. Susan E. Richards, *Holidays & Holy Days,* (Ann Arbor, MI: Vine Books, 2001), p. 119.

56. White, Lew, p. 55.

57. Hislop, pp. 162-163.

58. Jones, Vol. I, pp. 294-295.

59. White, Lew, p. 31.

60. Schaff, *History Of The Christian Church,* Vol. 2, pp. 623-624, 630.

61. Ibid.

62. From the Letter of the Emperor Constantine (Eusebius, "Life of Constantine," Vol. III, Ch. XVIII).

63. Schaff, *Post Nicean Fathers.*

64. Schaff, *History Of The Christian Church,* Vol. 2, p. 208.

65. Richardson, pp. 58-59.

66. Lillian Eichler, *The Customs Of Mankind,* (Garden City, NY: Nelson Doubleday, Inc., 1924), pp. 421-422.

67. Noah Webster, *The Original Webster's Unabridged Dictionary,* rev. by Chauncey A. Goodrich, (USA: The Dictionary Publishing Co., second ed., 1901), p. 377.

68. Hislop, p. 110.

69. E. W. Bullinger, *Figures Of Speech Used In The Bible,* (Grand Rapids, MI: Baker Book House, reprint 1968, orig. pub. 1898), p. xvi.

70. Schaff, *History Of The Christian Church,* Vol. 2, pp. 241-244.

71. Ibid., Vol. 5, pp. 714-715.

72. Ibid.

73. Ibid.

74. Ibid.

75. Ibid.

76. Ibid.

77. Ibid.

78. Durant, Vol. 3, p. 741.

79. Hastings, *Hastings Encyclopedia Of Religion and Ethics,* "Sacraments," Vol. X, pp. 897-902.

80. Ibid., p. 902.

81. Ibid.

82. *Catholic Encyclopedia,* (1911), Vol. 10, p. 404.

83. White, Lew, p. 31.

84. *Wikipedia.Com,* "Biblical Law in Christianity"; http://www.wikipedia.com/biblical-law-in-christianity.htm

85. Ron Moseley, *Yeshua: A Guide to the Real Jesus and the Original Church,* (Clarksville, MD: Messianic Jewish Publishers, 1966), p. 70.

86. Webster, *The Original Webster's Unabridged Dictionary,* p. 750.

87. Zodhiates, *Complete Word Study New Testament,* Lexical Aids To The N.T. # 2537, p. 912.

88. Arndt & Gingrich, pp. 537-538.

89. Webster, *The Original Webster's Unabridged Dictionary,* p. 1140.
90. *Companion Bible,* "Appendix Notes," by E. W. Bullinger, (Grand Rapids, MI: Kregel Publications, orig. pub. 1922), #95, pp. 137-138.

Chapter 3 *The Sect of the Nazarenes*

1. Douglas, *Illustrated Bible Dictionary,* Vol. 1, p. 266.
2. Samual Tobias Lachs, *A Rabbinic Commentary on the New Testament,* (Hoboken, NJ: KTAV Publishing House, Inc., 1973), p. 112.
3. Alfred Edersheim, *The Temple in Jesus' Day,* (Grand Rapids, MI: William B. Eerdmans Publishing Company, 1986), p. 49.
4. Arndt & Gingrich, p. 240.
5. Ibid.
6. *Exploring The New Testament,* Ralph Earle, ed., (Kansas City, MO: Beacon Hill Press, 1955), p. 227.
7. Williston Walker, *A History of the Christian Church,* (New York, NY: Charles Scribner's Sons, 1918), p. 21.
8. H. D. M. Spence & Joseph S. Exell, gen. eds., *The Pulpit Commentary,* "The Acts Of The Apostles," A. C. Hervey, expos., (Grand Rapids, MI: William B. Eerdmans Publishing Company, 1950), Vol. 18, p. 55.
9. Ibid.
10. Moseley, p. 107.
11. Unger, *Unger's Bible Dictionary,* p. 906.
12. Douglas, *Illustrated Bible Dictionary,* Vol. 2, pp. 1060, 1063.
13. Unger, *Unger's Bible Dictionary,* p. 907.
14. Ibid.
15. Douglas, *Illustrated Bible Dictionary,* Vol. 2, p. 1011.
16. Jay P. Green, Sr., gen. ed., *The Interlinear Hebrew-English Old Testament,* "Leviticus & Numbers," (Lafayette, IN: Authors For Christ, Inc., 1996), Vol. 1, #5139, p. 328 (Lev. 25:5, 12).
17. James Strong, *Strong's Exhaustive Concordance of the Bible,* (Iowa Falls, IA: World Bible Publishers, reprint 1989), Hebrew-Chaldee Dictionary of the Old Testament, #5139, p. 102.
18. Arndt & Gingrich, p. 173.

19. Strong, Hebrew-Chaldee Dictionary of the O.T., #7522, p. 146.
20. Arndt & Gingrich, #2, p. 574.
21. Webster, *Original Webster's Unabridged Dictionary,* p. 742.
22. Marcus Dodd, gen. ed., *The Expositor's Greek Testament,* "The Gospel Of Saint John," (Grand Rapids, MI: William B. Eerdmans Publishing Company, 1967), Vol. 1, p. 478.
23. James Orr, gen. ed., *The International Standard Bible Encyclopedia,* "Nazarene," (Grand Rapids, MI: William B. Eerdmans Publishing Company, 1939), Vol. IV, p. 2123.
24. Douglas, *Illustrated Bible Dictionary,* Vol. 1, p. 246.
25. Schaff, *History of the Christian Church,* Vol. 2, p. 431.
26. Charles Buck, *A Theological Dictionary,* (London: Printed by William Clowes, MDCCCXXXIII—1833), pp. 659-660.
27. Moore, Vol. III, p. 244.
28. Spence & Exell, *Pulpit Commentary,* "Acts of the Apostles," Vol. 18, p. 231.
29. Gibbon, Vol. II, p. 228.
30. Ibid., Vol. III. pp. 20, 21, 26, 27, 32, 33.
31. From uncertain Eastern origin, attached to the *Clementine Recognitions:* From P. G., I, p. 1456, as cited by James Parkes, *The Conflict of the Church and the Synagogue* (New York, NY: Atheneum, 1974), pp. 398-400.
32. Kenneth S. Wuest, *Wuest's Word Studies From the Greek New Testament,* "The Day of Christ," (Grand Rapids, MI: William B. Eerdmans Publishing Company, 1961), Vol. 3, pp. 35-43.
33. Ibid.
34. Arndt & Gingrich, p. 114.
35. *New Testament King James Version 1611,* "The Second Epistle of Paul the Apostle to the Thessalonians," (New York, NY: American Bible Society, nd.), p. 457.

Chapter 4 *The Grafting-In to the "Olive Tree"*

1. Spence & Exell, *Pulpit Commentary,* "The Epistle of Paul to the Romans," Vol. 18, p. 322.
2. Douglas, *Illustrated Bible Dictionary,* Vol. 2, p. 1114.

3. Spence & Excell, *Pulpit Commentary,* "The Epistle of Paul to the Romans," Vol. 18, p. 322.

4. Cranfield, Vol. 2, p. 565.

5. David H. Stern, *Messianic Jewish Manifesto,* (Jerusalem: Jewish New Testament Publications, 1991), p. 49.

6. Bivin & Blizzard, Jr., pp. 145, 151-152.

7. Steve Wohlberg, *Exploding the Israel Deception,* (Roseville, CA: Amazing Facts, 2006), p. 59.

8. Karl Barth, *The Christian Life: Church Dogmatics,* Geoffrey W. Bromiley, trans., (Grand Rapids, MI: Willaim B. Eerdmans Publishing Company, 1981); cited by Dean Wheelock, "Replacement Theology," issue 09-2; Vol. 14, No. 1, p. 5.

9. *Wikipedia.Com.,* "People of God".

10. Ibid.

11. *Arutz Sheva,* "1964-2014; two Popes and the Temple Mount," February 4, 2014; http://www.israelnationalnews.com/article/1964-2014/two-popes-and-the-temple mount.htm

12. *BBC News,* "Flashback: 1964 Papal visit," March 21, 2000.

13. *Wikipedia.Com.,* "Fundamental Agreement Between the Holy See and the State of Israel."

14. *Angelfire.Com.,* "Vatican Agenda".

15. *Arutz Sheva,* "1964-2014; two Popes and the Temple Mount," February 4, 2014.

16. Ibid., "Abbas Accuses Israel of Judaizing Jerusalem at Papal Meeting," May 25, 2014.

17. *The Times of Israel,* "How the Pope triumphed over the Israeli-Palestinian Conflict," May 29, 2014.

18. *Arutz Sheva,* "Israel Unhappy with Papal-Palestinian 'Propaganda Stunt,'" May 25, 2014.

19. Ibid., "Abbas Accuses Israel of Judaizing Jerusalem at Papal Meeting," May 25, 2014.

20. *The Times of Israel.Com.,* "Pope Francis wades into Mideast peacemaking," June 8, 2014.

21. Ibid.

22. Wohlberg, p. 53.

23. Strong, Hebrew & Chaldee Dictionary of the O.T, #2318, p. 48.

24. Zodhiates, *Complete Word Study New Testament,* Lexical Aids To The N.T., #2537, p. 912.

25. Rick Lastrapes, "New Covenant,"(Albuquerque, NM: Letter to R. Rhoades, April 2010).

26. *Jewish Encyclopedia.Com.*, "Day of the Lord," Emil G. Hirsch; http://www.jewishenyclopedia.com/day-of-the-lord.htm

27. Roy Schoeman, *Salvation Is From the Jews: The Role Of Judaism In Salvation History From Abraham To The Second Coming,* (San Francisco, CA: Ignatius Press, 2003), p. 351; Barry Yeoman, "Evangelical Movement on the Rise," Jewish Telegraph Agency, November 15, 2007.

28. Tim McGirk, *Time World,* "Israel's Messianic Jews Under Attack," June 6, 2008.

29. Matthew Wagner, *The Jerusalem Post,* "Messianic Jews to Protest Discrimination," June 26, 2006.

Chapter 5 *The Replacement of the "Olive Tree"*

1. Walker, p. 54.
2. Glenn, p. 153.
3. Ibid., p. 154.
4. Ibid.
5. Ibid., pp. 153-154.
6. A. Berkeley Mickelsen, *Interpreting The Bible,* (Grand Rapids, MI: William B. Eerdmans Publishing Company, 1963), p. 34.
7. Moseley, p. 40.
8. Walker, p. 163.
9. Kittel, *Theological Dictionary Of The New Testament,* Vol. IV, p. 1032.
10. Bernard Ramm, *Varieties Of Christian Apologetics,* (Grand Rapids, MI: Baker Book House, 1965), p. 147.
11. Robert F. Davidson, *Philosophies Men Live By,* (New York, NY: Holt, Rinehart & Winston, Inc., 1952), p. 325.
12. Ramm, p. 150.
13. Ibid., p. 154.
14. Walker, p. 167.
15. Glenn, p. 165.
16. Plato, *Republic,* Benjamin Jowett, trans., (London: Oxford University Press, 1892), Vol. II, pp. 379C, 380C.

17. Glenn, pp. 149-150.

18. Ibid.

19. Ibid.

20. Ibid.

21. Ibid.

22. Ibid.

23. *Wikipedia.Com,* "John Wycliffe: Basal Positions in Philosophy".

24. Cecil Roth & Geoffrey Wigoder, chf. eds., *Encyclopedia Judaica,* "Martin Luther," (Israel: Keter Publishing House Jerusalem Ltd., 1996), Vol. 3, p. 103.

25. Robert Michael, *Holy Hatred: Christianity, Antisemitism, and The Holocaust,* (New York, NY: Palgrave Macmillan, 2006), p. 109.

26. Ibid.

27. Ibid.

28. Graham Noble, "Martin Luther and German anti-Semitism," *History Review* (2002), No. 42, pp. 1-2.

29. Michael, p. 110.

30. Ibid., p. 111.

31. Ibid., p. 112.

32. Ibid., p. 113.

33. Ibid., p. 117.

34. Ibid.

35. Richard Grunberger, *The 12-Year Reich: A Social History Of Nazi Germany 1933- 1945,* (NP: Holt, Rinehart & Winston, 1971), p. 465.

36. Marc H. Ellis, *Hitler and The Holocaust: Christian Anti-Semitism,* (NP: Baylor University Center for American and Jewish Studies, Spring 2004), Slide 14.

37. Ibid.

38. Adolf Hitler, *Mein Kampf,* Ralph Manheim, trans., (Boston, MA: Houghton Mifflin Company, 1971), p. 65.

39. *History.Com.,* "The Rise of the Third Reich".

40. Ibid.

41. *History.Com.,* "The Fall of the Third Reich".

42. Ibid.

43. Ibid.

44. Draper, *Science and Religion,* (New York, NY: 1876), p. 48; cited by Lew White, *Fossilized Customs,* p. 103.

45. Taylor, *Diegesis,* nd., p. 50; cited by Lew White, *Fossilized Customs,* p. 103.
46. White, Lew, p. 103.
47. Ibid.
48. Ibid., p. 48.
49. Jones, Vol. I, p. 318.

Chapter 6 *Admissions About the Sabbath*

1. James Parkes, *The Conflict of the Church and the Synagogue: A Study in the Origins of Antisemitism,* (New York, NY: Atheneum, 1977), p. 96.
2. John G. Shae, *American Catholic Quarterly Review,* "The Observance of Sunday and Civil Laws for It's Enforcement," January 1883, pp. 139, 149, 152; cited by *National Sunday Law Crisis,* (Altamont, TN: Harvestime Books, 1989), pp. 37, 58-59.
3. Peter Geiermann, C. SS. R., *The Convert's Catechism Of Catholic Doctrine,* (St. Louis, MO: B. Herder Book Company, 1930), pp. 50-51.
4. *Oxford Dictionary Of The Christian Church,* "Pope," (Oxford University Press, 2005); cited by *Wikipedia.Com.,* "Roman Catholic Popes".

Chapter 7 *The Apostolic/Church Timelines*

1. Dean & Susan Wheelock, *Hebrew Roots,* (Minneapolis, MN: Hebrew Roots Press, May/June/July, 2008), Issue 08-2, Vol. 13, No. 1, p. 13.
2. Walker, p. 22.
3. Henry H. Halley, *Halley's Bible Handbook,* (Minneapolis, MN: Grason Company, 1927), p. 459.
4. Unger, *Unger's Bible Dictionary,* p. 827.
5. Good, *Rosh HaShannah and The Messianic Kingdom To Come,* pp. iv-v.
6. Nicoll, *Expositor's Greek New Testament,* "Romans," James Denny," expos., Vol. 2, p. 854.

7. Zodhiates, *Complete Word Study New Testament,* Lexical Aids Of The N.T., #5546, p. 946.
8. Arndt & Gingrich, p. 71.
9. Ibid.
10. Alfred Marshall, trans., *The Interlinear Greek-English New Testament: The Nestle Greek Text With A New Literal English Translation,* "II Peter," (Grand Rapids, MI: Zondervan Publishing House, 1958), "II Peter," p. 926.
11. Schaff, *History of the Christian Church,* Vol. 1, p. 398.
12. Ibid., p. 402.
13. Tenney, pp. 321-322.
14. Douglas, *Illustrated Bible Dictionary,* Vol. 1, p. 1085.
15. Ibid., p. 788.
16. Shores, *Colliers Encyclopedia,* Vol. 6, p. 403.
17. Emil Schurer, *A History of the Jewish People in the Time of Jesus Christ,* (Peabody, MA: Hendrickson Publishers, reprint 2010, orig. pub. 1890), Vol. II, p. 256.
18. Ibid., pp. 256-257.
19. Ibid., p. 232.
20. Ibid., p. 260.
21. Good, *Rosh HaShannah and The Messianic Kingdom To Come,* p. 14.
22. Schaff, *History Of The Christian Church,* Vol. 2, p. 203.
23. *Epistle To Diognetus,* Chapters iii and vi (abridged); P.G., II, p. 1174; cited by James Parkes, p. 101.
24. Schaff, *History Of The Christian Church,* Vol. 2, p. 203.
25. Ibid., p. 204.
26. Parkes, 98.
27. Glenn, p. 153.
28. Schaff, *History Of The Christian Church,* Vol. 2, p. 204.
29. Glenn, p. 154.
30. Parkes, pp. 161-162.
31. Glenn, p. 155.
32. Parkes, pp. 166-167.
33. Ibid., pp. 165-166.
34. Schaff, *History Of The Christian Church,* Vol. 3, p. 389.
35. Parkes, p. 160.
36. Ibid.

37. Glenn, p. 157.
38. Schaff, *History Of The Christian Church*, Vol. 3, p. 384.
39. Ibid.
40. Parkes, p. 154.
41. Ibid., pp. 174-175.
42. Ibid., p. 175.
43. Ibid. p. 176.
44. Ibid., pp. 382-386.
45. Ibid., p. 244.
46. Ibid.
47. Ibid.
48. Ibid.
49. Theophanes the Confessor, *The Chronicle;* cited by Michael Whithy, *The Ecclesiastical History of Evagrius Scholasticus,* (England: Liverpool University Press, 2000), p. 164.
50. Ibid.
51. Ibid.
52. Letters 28, 40, 75 & 82 in the Edition of Augustine's correspondence with Jerome by Marcus Dodds, or P.L., XXXIII, same numbers; cited by James Parkes, p. 96.
53. Schaff, *History Of The Christian Church*, Vol. 2, p. 484.
54. Walker, p. 61.
55. Halley, p. 488.
56. Durant, Vol. 3, p. 654.
57. Walker, p. 155.
58. Schaff, *History Of The Christian Church*, Vol. 7, pp. 737-738.
59. Halley, p. 590.
60. Schaff, *History Of The Christian Church*, Vol. 3, p. 630.
61. Ibid., Vol. 7, p. 492.
62. Jones, Vol. II, p. 584.
63. Schaff, *History Of The Christian Church*, Vol. 7, p. 493.
64. Ibid.
65. Walker, p. 351.
66. Spence & Excell, *Pulpit Commentary,* "Romans," Vol. 18, p. 323.
67. Schaff, *History Of The Christian Church*, Vol. 8, p. 806.
68. Ibid., Vol. 7, pp. 737-738.
69. *Catholic Encyclopedia,* "Theology," (1911), Vol. 14, p. 586.
70. Ibid., "Mass, Sacrifice of," Vol. 10, p. 6.

71. C. I. Scofield, *Scofield Reference Bible,* (New York, NY: Oxford University Press, 1917), p. 847.

72. Sanger Brown II, *Sex Worship and Symbolism Of Primitive Races,* (Boston, MA: The Gorham Press, orig. pub. 1916, Sec. Ed., 1922), p. 39.

73. Eichler, p. 55.

Chapter 8 *The Interpretation of Scripture*

1. Bruce M. Metzger, *The Bible In Translation: Ancient And English Versions,* (Grand Rapids, MI: Baker Academic, 2001), p. 15.

2. Ibid., p. 16.

3. Ibid., p. 18.

4. Ibid., p. 20.

5. Bruce M. Metzger & Bart D. Ehrman, *The Text Of The New Testament,* (New York, NY: Oxford University Press, 1964), p. 275.

6. Ibid.

7. J. Harold Greenlee, *Introduction To New Testament Textual Criticism,* (Grand Rapids, MI: William B. Eerdmans Publishing Company, 1964), "Matthew," pp. 60-61.

8. Ibid., pp. 63-65.

9. Ibid., pp. 66-68.

10. Metzger & Ehrman, *Text Of The New Testament,* p. 266.

11. Metzger, *Bible In Translation,* p. 26.

12. Ibid., p. 28.

13. Greenlee, p. 47.

14. Mickelsen, pp. 53-54.

15. Metzger, *Bible In Translation,* p. 35.

16. Metzger & Ehrman, *Text Of The New Testament,* p. 277.

17. James R. White, *The King James Only Controversy,* (Minneapolis, MN: Bethany House Publishers, 1995), p. 33.

18. David Otis Fuller, *Which Bible?,* (Grand Rapids, MI: International Publications, 1971), pp. 56-57.

19. Greenlee, pp. 61-62.

20. Metzger, *Bible In Translation,* p. 57.

21. Ibid.

22. Ibid.

23. Ibid.
24. White, James, p. 69.
25. Desiderius Erasmus, *Collected Works Of Erasmus,* Epistle 337; cited by *Wikipedia.Com.,* "Desiderius Erasmus".
26. White, James, p. 69.
27. Metzger, *Text Of The New Testament,* p. 150.
28. White, James, p. 65.
29. Metzger, *Text Of The New Testament,* p. 151.
30. Ibid., pp. 151-152.
31. *Wikipedia.Com.,* "Authorized King James".
32. White, James, p. 65.
33. Metzger, *Text Of The New Testament,* pp. 152-153.
34. Ibid., p. 177.
35. Ibid., p. 179.
36. Ibid., p. 181.
37. Ibid., p. 182.
38. White, Lew, p. 20.
39. Ibid.
40. Shores, *Collier's Encyclopedia,* Vol. 17, p. 466.
41. Ibid.
42. Brooke Foss Westcott & Fenton John Anthony Hort, *Introduction To The New Testament In The Original Greek,* (Harper & Brothers, 1882), p. 2.
43. Philip Schaff, *Companion To The Greek Testament and The English Version,* (Harper, 1883), p. 177.
44. A. T. Robertson, *An Introduction To The Textual Criticism Of The New Testament,* (Broadman; 1925), p. 22.
45. B. B. Warfield, *An Introduction To The Textual Criticism Of The New Testament,* (London: 1886), p. 14.
46. Metzger, *Text Of The New Testament,* pp. 190-191.
47. Marshall, *The International Greek-English New Testament* p. ii.
48. Spence & Excell, *Pulpit Commentary,* "The Acts Of The Apostles," Vol. 18, p. 143.
49. *Latin Vulgate.Com.,* "New Testament: Acts 20:6-8".
50. W. R. Cooper, trans., *Wycliffe New Testament 1388,* "The Deeds of the Apostles," (London: The British Library, 2002), pp. 440-441.
51. *New Testament King James Version 1611,* "Acts," p. 317.

52. *The New Testament In Four Versions: King James, Revised Standard, Phillips Modern English, New English Bible*, "Acts," (New York, NY: The Iverson-Ford Associates, 1963), pp. 415-416.

53. Marshall, *Interlinear Greek-English New Testament*, "Acts," p. 559.

54. Green, Sr., *The Interlinear Greek-English New Testament*, "Acts," p. 385.

55. Arndt & Gingrich, pp. 229-230.

56. J. Gresham Machen, *New Testament Greek For Beginners*, (New York, NY: The Macmillian Company, 1923), pp. 5-6.

57. Arndt & Gingrich, p. 746.

58. Ibid.

59. Dana & Mantey, p. 73.

60. Ibid., p. 137.

61. Arndt & Gingrich, p. 746.

62. Wheelock, p. 17.

63. Spence & Excell, *Pulpit Commentary*, "The Gospel According to St. John The Divine," Vol. 17, p. 462.

64. *Latin Vulgate.Com.*, "New Testament: Matthew 28:1".

65. Ibid., "Mark 16:2".

66. Ibid., "Luke 24:1".

67. Ibid., "John 20:1".

68. Cooper, *Wycliffe New Testament 1388*, "The Book Of Matthew," p. 69.

69. Ibid., "The Book Of Mark," p. 112.

70. Ibid., "The Book Of Luke," p. 183.

71. Ibid., "The Book Of John," p. 236.

72. *New Testament King James Version 1611*, "Matthew," p. 75.

73. Ibid., "Mark," p. 124.

74. Ibid., "Luke," p. 205.

75. Ibid., "John," p. 261.

76. *New Testament In Four Versions*, "Matthew," p. 94.

77. Ibid., "Mark," p. 158.

78. Ibid., "Luke," p. 262.

79. Ibid., "John," p. 334.

80. Arndt & Gingrich, p. 304.

81. Marshall, *Interlinear Greek-English New Testament*, "Matthew," p. 134.

82. Arndt & Gingrich, pp. 764-765.

83. Spence & Excell, *Pulpit Commentary*, "The Gospel According To St. Matthew," Vol. 15, p. 639.

84. Ibid., "The Gospel According To St. Mark," Vol. 16, p. 346.

85. Ibid., "The Gospel According To St. Luke," Vol. 16, p. 268.

86. Ibid., "The Gospel According To St. John The Divine," Vol. 17, p. 462.

87. Alfred Edersheim, *The Life And Times Of Jesus The Messiah*, (New York, NY: Longmans, Green, and Company, 1899), Vol. II, Book IV, p. 619.

88. Spence & Excell, *Pulpit Commentary*, "The Gospel According To St. John The Divine," Vol. 17, p. 432.

89. *Passover Dates 26-34 A.D.*, "Crucifixion Passover Dates"; http://www.judaismvschristianity.com/passover-dates-26-34-a.d.; http:..usno.navymil/USNO/astronomical-applications/data-services/spring-phenomena-25-b.c.e.-to-38- c.e.htm

90. Ibid.

91. Ibid.

92. Ibid.

93. E. W. Bullinger, *Companion Bible*, "Appendix Notes," #165, p. 188.

94. Ibid. #144, p. 170.

95. Spence & Excell, *Pulpit Commentary*, "The Gospel According St. Matthew," (Bishop Westcott, "Introduction," p. 344, edit., 1872), Vol. 15, p. 494.

96. Spence & Excell, *Pulpit Commentary*, "The Revelation Of St. John The Divine," Vol. 22, p. 5.

97. *Latin Vulgate.Com.* "Revelation 1:10".

98. Cooper, *Wycliffe New Testament 1388*, "The Apocalypse," p. 496.

99. *New Testament King James Version 1611*, "The Revelation Of St. John The Divine," p. 538.

100. *New Testament In Four Versions*, "Revelation," p. 780.

101. Arndt & Gingrich, #1, #4, pp. 157-158.

102. Marshall, *Interlinear Greek-English New Testament*, "Revelation," p. 957; Green, Sr., *Interlinear Greek-English New Testament*, "Revelation," p. 657.

103. Dana & Mantey, pp. 84-85.

104. Douglas, *Illustrated Bible Dictionary*, Vol. 2, p. 909.

105. Nicoll, *Expositor's Greek Testament,* "The First Epistle Of Paul To The Corinthians," Vol. 2, p. 945.

106. *Latin Vulgate.Com.,* "1 Corinthians 16:1-2".

107. Cooper, *Wycliffe New Testament 1388,* "The Epistle To The Corinthians I," p. 295.

108. *New Testament King James Version 1611,* "The First Epistle Of Paul The Apostle To The Corinthians," pp. 395-396.

109. *New Testament In Four Versions,* p. 542.

110. Arndt & Gingrich, pp. 229-230.

111. Spence & Excell, *Pulpit Commentary,* "Epistle Of Paul The Apostle To The Colossians," Vol. 20, p. 92.

112. *Latin Vulgate.Com.,* "Colossians 2:16-17".

113. Cooper, *Wycliffe New Testament 1388,* "Colossians," p. 340.

114. *New Testament King James Version 1611,* "Epistle Of Paul The Apostle To The Colossians," p. 446.

115. *New Testament In Four Versions,* "Colossians," p. 626.

116. Marshall, *Interlinear Greek-English New Testament,* "Colossians," p. 795.

117. Spence & Excell, *Pulpit Commentary,* "The Gospel According To St. Mark," Vol. 16, p. 294.

118. *Latin Vulgate.Com.,* "Mark 7:16-17".

119. Cooper, *Wycliffe New Testament 1388,* "The Gospel Of Mark," p. 87.

120. *New Testament King James Version 1611,* "The Gospel According To St. Mark," p. 96.

121. *New Testament In Four Versions,* "Acts," p. 376.

122. Dana & Mantey, p. 137.

123. Green, Sr., *Interlinear Greek-English New Testament,* "Mark," p. 115.

124. *60 Minutes,* "America's Sugar Consumption," (Google: Robert Lustig, "Sugar is a Poison," 6/25/09).

125. Ibid.

126. Ibid.

127. *Fructose.Com.,* "The Dangers of High Fructose Corn Syrup"; http:// www.diabeteshealth.com; *Natural News.Com.,* "Feature Articles on Artificial Sweeteners," http://www.naturalnews.com/artificial sweeteners; *Natural Choice Chiropractic,* "The Secret Dangers of Splenda (Sucralose), an Artificial Sweetener," http://www.

naturalchoicechiro.com; *The Douglas Report.Com.,* "Aspartame: The Sweet Deception," http://www.douglasreport.com.

128. George R. Schwartz, M.D., *In Bad Taste: The MSG Syndrome,* (Santa Fe, NM: Health Press, 1988), pp. 1-4.

129. *Mayo Clinc.Com.,* "Nutrition and Healthy Eating," Mayo Clinic Staff; http://www.mayoclinic.com/health/sodium.htm

130. *Ban trans Fats.Com.,* "New Labeling".

131. Schwartz, p. 53.

132. *Eat Drink Politics.Com.,* "Are Junk Food Corporations Hiding Behind Lobbyists to stop GE Food Labeling in Washington State?," September 17, 2013.

133. Ibid.

134. Ibid.

135. Ibid.

136. G. Campbell Morgan, *An Exposition of the Whole Bible,* "Acts," (Westwood, NJ: Fleming H. Revell Company, 1959), p. 455.

137. Dean & Susan Wheelock, "The Other Torah," (Lakewood, WI: Hebrew Roots, January/February/March, 2010), Issue 10-1; Vol. 4, No. 3, p. 14.

138. Arndt & Gingrich, p. 151.

139. Spence & Excell, *Pulpit Commentary,* "The General Epistle Of James," Vol. 21, p. 28.

140. *Latin Vulgate. Com.,* "James 2:1-2".

141. Cooper, *Wycliffe New Testament 1388,* "James," p. 465.

142. *New Testament King James 1611,* "James," pp. 503-504.

143. *New Testament In Four Versions,* "James," p. 722.

144. Arndt & Gingrich, p. 790.

145. Marshall, *Interlinear Greek-English New Testament,* "James," p. 898; Green, Sr., *Interlinear Greek-English New Testament,* "James," p. 615.

146. Schurer, Second Division, Vol. II, p. 54.

147. Arndt & Gingrich, p. 240.

148. Ibid., pp. 395-396.

149. Spence & Excell, *Pulpit Commentary,* "The Epistle Of Paul To The Galatians," Vol. 20, pp. 126-127.

150. *Latin Vulgate.Com.,* "Galatians 3:10-13".

151. Cooper, *Wycliffe New Testament 1388,* "To Galatians," pp. 580, 582.

152. *New Testament King James 1611,* "Epistle of Paul The Apostle To The Galatians," pp. 419-420.

153. *New Testament In Four Versions,* "Galatians," pp. 580, 582.

154. Unger, *Unger's Bible Dictionary,* p. 997.

155. Dana & Mantey, p. 9, 102.

156. Green, Sr., *Interlinear Greek-English New Testament,* "Galatians," p. 511.

157. *Latin Vulgate.Com.,* "Ephesians 2:14-15".

158. Cooper, *Wycliffe New Testament 1388,* "Epistle To The Ephesians," p. 324.

159. *New Testament King James 1611,* "Epistle of Paul The Apostle To The Ephesians," p. 428.

160. *New Testament In Four Versions,* "Ephesians," p. 594.

161. Marshall, *Interlinear Greek-English New Testament,* "Ephesians," p. 763; Green Sr., *Interlinear Greek- English New Testament,* "Ephesians," p. 522.

162. Nicoll, *Expositor's Greek Testament,* "Epistle To The Ephesians," Vol. 3, p. 295.

163. Edersheim, *The Life And Times Of Jesus The Messiah,* Vol. I, Book, p. 239.

164. Ibid.

165. Ibid.

166. *Latin Vulgate.Com.,* "Romans 10:4".

167. Cooper, *Wycliffe New Testament 1388,* "Epistle of Paul To The Romans," p. 259.

168. *New Testament King James 1611,* "Epistle of Paul the Apostle To The Romans," p. 357.

169. *New Testament In Four Versions,* "Romans," p. 478.

170. Nicoll, *Expositor's Greek Testament,* "Paul's Epistle To The Romans," Vol. 2, p. 669.

171. Morgan, p. 466.

172. Stern, pp. 227-228.

Chapter 9 *"Take My Yoke Upon You and Learn of Me"*

1. Barclay, "Matthew," Vol. 2, p. 19.

2. Ibid.

3. Moore, Vol. I, p. 465.
4. Ibid., pp. 465-466.
5. Ibid.
6. Bivin, pp. 23, 29.
7. Edersheim, *The Life And Times Of Jesus The Messiah*, Vol. I, p. 11.
8. Ibid.
9. Ibid., pp. 11-12.
10. Ibid.
11. Ibid., p. 94.
12. Ibid., pp. 97-98.
13. Arndt & Gingrich, pp. 793-794.
14. Dana & Mantey, p. 137.
15. Falk, pp. 93-95, 156.
16. Spence & Excell, *Pulpit Commentary*, "The Gospel According To St. Matthew," Vol. 15, p. 450.
17. Nicoll, *Expositor's Greek Testament*, "The Synoptic Gospels," Vol. 1, p. 180.
18. Silver, p. 269.
19. Leupold, p. 86.
20. Kittel, *Theological Dictionary Of The New Testament*, "The Distinctiveness of the *logos* Saying in John 1:1," Vol. IV, pp. 134-135.
21. Strong, Hebrew & Chaldee Dictionary of the O.T., #7673, p. 148.
22. Arndt & Gingrich, p. 58.
23. Metzger, *Bible In Translation*, p. 18.
24. Walker, pp. 59-60.
25. Ibid.
26. Ibid.
27. Arndt & Gingrich, p. 195
28. Gibbon, Vol. III, p. 74.

Chapter 10 *"Let No Man Beguile You of Your Reward"*

1. Dana & Mantey, p. 143.
2. Kittel, *Theological Dictionary Of The New Testament*, Vol. II, p. 646.
3. Ibid., p. 647.
4. Leupold, pp. 712-713.

5. Douglas, *Illustrated Bible Dictionary,* Vol. 1, p. 507.

6. Bullinger, *Figures Of Speech Used In The Bible,* p. 444.

7. Nosson Scherman & Meir Zlotowitz, gen. eds., *Tehillum,* "The Book of Psalms," The ArtScroll Tanach Series, (Brooklyn, NY: Mesorah Publications, 1995), Vol. 2, pp. 1623-1624.

8. Warner Keller, *The Bible As History,* William Neil, trans., (New York, NY: William Morrow & Company, 1956), p. 407.

9. *Jewish Encyclopedia.Com.,* "Edom: Edox, Idumea; Use of Names".

10. Roth & Wigoder, *Encyclopedia Judaica,* "Edom," Vol. 6, pp. 157-158.

11. Hasting, *Hastings Encyclopedia of Religion and Ethics,* "Priests, Priesthood (Romans)," Vol. X, p. 326.

12. Harry Thursdon Peck, gen. ed., *Harper's Dictionary of Classical Literature and Antiquities,* (New York, NY: Harper & Brothers, 1896), p. 675.

13. Hasting, *Hastings Encyclopedia of Religion and Ethics,* "Priest, Priesthood (Romans)," Vol. X, p. 329.

14. Spence & Excell, *Pulpit Commentary,* "The Gospel According To St. Matthew," Vol. 15, p. 285.

15. Arndt & Gingrich, p. 71.

16. Spence & Excell, *Pulpit Commentary,* "The Gospel According To St. Matthew," Vol. 15, pp. 285-286.

17. Arndt & Gingrich, p. 101.

18. Gesenius, #5493, p. 582.

19. Arndt & Gingrich, p. 314.

20. Gesenius, #7453, p. 772.

21. Spence & Excell, *Pulpit Commentary,* "The Gospel According To St. Matthew," Vol. 15, pp. 358-359.

22. Ibid.

23. Dana & Mantey, pp. 72-73.

24. Spence & Excell, *Pulpit Commentary,* "The Gospel According To St. Matthew," Vol. 15, pp. 358-359.

25. Arndt & Gingrich, p. 152.

26. Douglas, *Illustrated Bible Dictionary,* Vol. 2, p. 838.

27. Zodhiates, *Complete Word Study New Testament,* "Matthew," pp. 24-25.

28. Arndt & Gingrich, pp. 841-842.

29. Nicoll, *Expositor's Greek Testament,* "The Epistles Of John," Vol. 5, p. 184.

30. Ibid., p. 156.

31. Arndt & Gingrich, p. 195.

32. Brooke Foss Westcott, *The Epistles Of St. John,* (Grand Rapids, MI: William B. Eerdmans Publishing Company, orig. pub. 1892, reprint 1960), p. 102.

33. Spence & Excell, *Pulpit Commentary,* "The First Epistle General Of John," Vol. 22, p. 71.

34. Earl, Blaney & Hansen, p. 421.

35. Morgan, p. 527.

36. Kettel, *Theological Dictionary Of The New Testament,* Vol. I, p. 271.

37. Arndt & Gingrich, #2, p. 17.

38. Ibid., p. 195.

39. Strong, Greek Dictionary Of The New Testament, #3670, p. 69.

40. Nosson Scherman & Meir Zlotowitz, *Viduy,* (Brooklyn, NY: The ArtScroll Series, Mesorah Publications, Ltd., 2003), pp. 8-9.

41. Spence & Excell, *Pulpit Commentary,* "The Second Epistle To Timothy," Vol. 21, p. 59.

42. Arndt & Gingrich, p. 822.

43. Webster, *Original* Webster's Unabridged Dictionary, p. 600.

44. Lockyer, p. 270.

45. Arndt & Gingrich, p. 195.

46. Ibid., pp. 194-195.

Bibliography

Arndt, William F., & Gingrich, F. Wilbur, *A Greek-English Lexicon Of The New Testament and Other Early Christian Literature.* Chicago, IL: University of Chicago Press, 1957.

Atlas Of The Bible: An Illustrated Guide To The Holy Land. Pleasantville, NY: The Readers Digest Association, Inc., 1981.

Barclay, William, *The Daily Study Bible.* Philadelphia, PN: Westminister Press, 1956.

Barth, Karl, *The Christian Life: Church Dogmatics.* Grand Rapids, MI: William B. Eerdmans Publishing Company, 1981.

Bivin, David, *New Light On The Difficult Words of Jesus: Insights From His Jewish Context.*Holland, MI: En-Gedi Resource Center, Inc., 2007.

Brown, Francis, S. R. Driver & Charles A. Briggs, *The New Brown-Driver-Briggs- Gesenius Hebrew and English Lexicon.* Peabody, MA: Hendrickson Publishers, 1979.

Blackman, E. C., *Marcion and His Influence.* London, 1948.

Blizzard Jr., Roy & David Bivin, *Understanding the Difficult Words of Jesus.* Shippensburg, PA: Destiny Image Publishers, 1994.

Brown, Sanger, *Sex Worship and Symbolism Of Primitive Races.* Boston, MA: The Gorham Press, 1916.

Buck, Charles, *A Theological Dictionary.* London: Printed by William Clowes, MDCCCXXXIII).

Bullinger, E. W., *Figures of Speech Used In The Bible.* Grand Rapids, MI: Baker Book House, reprint. 1968; orig. pub. 1898.

Campbell, T. Colin, *The China Study.* Dallas, TX: Benbella Books, 2006.

Colbert, Don, *Walking In Divine Health.* Lake Mary, FL: Published by Siloam, 1999.

Cooper, W. R., *The Wycliffe New Testament*. England: The British Library, 2002.

Catholic Encyclopedia, The. New York, NY: Robert Appleton Company, 1911.

Companion Bible, The. Grand Rapids, MI: Kregel Publications, 1922.

Complete Word Study Old Testament, The. Chattanooga, TN: AGM Publishers, 1994.

Corlett, D. Shelby, *The Christian Sabbath*. Kansas City, MO: Beacon Hill Press, nd.

Cranfield, C. E. B., *Romans*. Edinburgh: T. & T. Clark, Ltd., 1981.

Dana, H. E. & Mantey, Julius R., *A Manual Grammar Of The Greek New Testament*. New York, NY: The Macmillian Company, 1927.

Danker, Federick William, *A Greek-English Lexicon Of The New Testament and Other Early Christian Literature*. Chicago, IL: University of Chicago Press, 2000.

Davidson, Robert F., *Philosophies Men Live By*. New York, NY: Holt, Rinehart & Winston, Inc., 1952.

Douglas, J. D., gen. ed., *The Illustrated Bible Dictionary*. Wheaton, IL: Tyndale House Publishing, 1980.

Durant, Will, *The Story Of Civilization, Caesar and Christ*. New York, NY: Simon & Schuster, 1944-1977.

Earl, Ralph, gen. ed., *Exploring the New Testament*. Kansas City, MO: Beacon Hill Press, 1955.

Edersheim, Alfred, *The Life and Times Of Jesus The Messiah*. New York, NY: Longmans, Green, and Company, 1899.

Edersheim, Alfred, *The Temple: Its Ministry and Services*. Peabody, MA: Hendrickson Publishers, Inc., 1994.

Edersheim, Alfred, *The Temple in Jesus' Day*. Grand Rapids, MI: William B. Eerdmans Publishing Company, 1986.

Eichler, Lillian, *The Customs Of Mankind*. Garden City, NY: Nelson Doubleday, Inc., 1924.

Falk, Harvey, *Jesus The Pharisee: A New Look At The Jewishness Of Jesus*. Mahwah, NJ: Paulist Press, 1985.

Feinstein, David, *The Jewish Calendar*. Brooklyn, NY: Mesorah Publications, Ltd., 2004.

Forlong, J. G. R., *Encyclopedia of Religions*. New Hyde Park, NY: University Books, 1964.

Fuller, David Otis, *Which Bible?*. Grand Rapids, MI: Grand Rapids International Publications, 1970.

Geiermann, Peter, *Convert's Caterchism of Catholic Doctrine*. St. Louis, MO: B. Herder Book Company, 1930.

Gesenius, H. W. F., *Gesenius' Hebrew-Chaldee Lexicon To The Old Testament*. Grand Rapids, MI: Baker Book House, 1979.

Gibbon, Edward, *The Decline and Fall of the Roman Empire*. New York, NY: Peter Fenelon Collier & Son, MCMI.

Glenn, Paul J., *A History of Philosophy*. St. Louis, MO: B. Herder Book Company, 1929.

Golden, Hyman E., *A Treasury of Jewish Holidays*. New York, NY: Twayne Publishers, 1952.

Good, Joseph, *Prophecies In The Book Of Esther*. Port Arthur, TX: Hatikva Ministries, 1995.

Good, Joseph, *Rosh HaShannah and The Messianic Kingdom To Come*. Nederland, TX: Hatikva Ministries, 1998.

Green, Sr., Jay P., *The Interlinear Greek-English New Testament*. Grand Rapids, MI: Baker Book House, 1988.

Green, Sr., Jay P., *The Interlinear Hebrew-English Old Testament*. Lafayette, IN: Authors For Christ, Inc., 1989.

Greenlee, J. Harold, *Introduction To New Testament Textual Criticism*. Grand Rapids, MI: William B. Eerdmans Publishing Company, 1964.

Grunberger, Richard, *The 12-Year Reich: A Social History Of Nazi Germany 1933- 1945*. Austin, TX: Holt, Rinehart and Winston, 1971.

Guillemette, Pierre, *The Greek New Testament Analyzed*. Scottdale, PN: Herald Press, 1986.

Halley, Henry H., *Halley's Bible Handbook*. Minneapolis, MN: Zondervan Publishing House, 1927.

Hastings, James, *Hastings Encyclopedia of Religion and Ethics*. New York, NY: Charles Scribner's Sons, 1928.

Hislop, Alexander, *The Two Babylons*. England; A & C Black, 1916.

Hitler, Adolph, *Mein Kampf*. Boston, MA: Houghton Mifflin Company, 1971.

Jones, W. T., *A History Of Western Philosophy*. New York, NY: Harcourt, Bruce & World, Inc., 1952.

Keller, Warner, *The Bible As History*. New York, NY: William Morrow and Company, 1956.

Kent, Charles Foster, *A History Of The Jewish People*. London: John Murray, 1927.

Kittel, Gerhard, gen. ed., *The Theological Dictionary of the New Testament*. Grand Rapids, MI: William B. Eerdmans Publishing *Company*, 1964.

Lachs, Samuel Tobias, *A Rabbinic Commentary on the New Testament*. Hoboken, NJ: KTAV Publishing House, 1973.

Laqueur, Walter, *The Changing Face Of Antisemitism: From Ancient Times To The Present Day*. England: Oxford University Press, 2006.

Lockyer, Herbert, *All The Men Of The Bible*. Grand Rapids, MI: Zondervan Publishing House, 1962.

Loeupold, H. C., *Exposition Of Genesis*. Columbus, OH: The Wartburg Press, 1942.

Maimonides, Moses, *The Mishneh Torah*. Palestine: Azriel Printing Press, 1937.

Marshall, Alfred, *The International Greek-English New Testament: The Nestle- Greek Text With A New Literal Translation*. Grand Rapids, MI: Zondervan Publishing House, 1958.

McKenzie, John L., *The Dictionary Of The Bible*. New York, NY: Macmillan Publishing Company, 1965.

Metford, J. C. J., *Dictionary Of Christian Lore and Legend*. London: Thames & Hudson, 1983.

Metzger, Bruce M., *The Bible in Translation*. Grand Rapids, MI: Baker Academic, 2001.

Metzger, Bruce M. & Bart D. Ehrman, *The Text Of The New Testament*. New York, NY: Oxford University Press, 2005.

Michael, Robert, *Holy Hatred: Christianity, Antisemitism, and the Holocaust*. New York, NY: Palgrave Macmillan, 2006.

Mickelsen, A. Berkeley, *Interpreting The Bible*. Grand Rapids, MI: William B. Eerdmans Publishing Company, 1963.

Moore, George Foote, *Judaism In The First Century Of The Christian Era*. Peabody, MA: Hendrickson Publishers, Vol. I, reprint 1997; orig. pub. 1927.

Moore, George Foote, *Judaism In The First Century Of The Christian Era*. Cambridge, MA: Harvard University Press, Vol. III, 1940.

Moore, George Footel, *Judaism In The First Century Of The Christian Era*. Cambridge, MA: Harvard University Press, Vol. II, 1944.

Morgan, G. Campbell, *An Exposition Of The Whole Bible*. Old Tappan, NJ: Fleming H. Revell Company, 1959.

Mosely, Ron, *Yeshua: A Guide To The Real Jesus And The Original Church.* Baltimore, MD: Lederer Books, 1996.

Moyer, Elgin, *The Wycliffe Biographical Dictionary Of The Church.* Chicago, IL: Moody Press, 1982.

New American Standard Bible. Grand Rapids, MI: Zondervan, 1960.

New Encyclopedia Britannica, The. Chicago, IL: Encyclopedia Britannica Inc., 1991.

Nestle, Eberhard, *Novum Testamentum Graece.* Stuttgart, Germany: Wurttembergische Biblelanstalt, 1960.

New Testament King James 1611. New York, NY: American Bible Society nd.

New Testament In Four Versions: King James, Revised Standard, Phillips Modern English, New English Bible. New York, NY: The Iversen-Ford Associates, 1963.

Nicoll, W. Robertson, *The Expositor's Greek Testament.* Grand Rapids, MI: William B. Eerdmans Publishing Company, 1967.

NIV Study Bible, The. Grand Rapids, MI: Zondervan Publishing House, 1995.

Oberman, Heiko, *Luther: Man Between God and the Devil.* New York, NY: Image Books, 1989.

Orr, James, gen. ed., *The International Standard Bible Encyclopedia.* Grand Rapids, MI: William B. Eerdmans Publishing Company, 1939.

Parkes, James, *The Conflict of the Church and the Synagogue.* New York, NY: Atheneum, 1977.

Plato, *Republic.* London: Oxford University Press, 1892.

Ramm, Bernard, *Varieties Of Christian Apologetics.* Grand Rapids, MI: Baker Book House, 1965.

Richardson, Susan E.,*Holidays & Holy Days.* Ann Arbor, MI: Vine Books, 2001.

Rines, George, gen. ed., *Encyclopedia Americana.* Danbury, CT: Grolier, Inc., 1994.

Roth, Cecil & Geoffery Wigoder, chf. eds., *Encyclopedia Judaica.* Keter Publishing House, 1996.

Schaff, Philip, *The History Of The Christian Church.* Grand Rapids, MI; William B. Eerdmans Publishing Company, 1910.

Schaff, Philip, *The Post-Nicene Fathers.* MS Windows XP, Garland, TX: Software, 2002.

Scherman, Nosson & Meir Zlotowitz, *Tehillim,* "The Book of Psalms," The ArtScroll Series. Brooklyn, NY: Mesorah Publications, 1995.

Schurer, Emil, *A History Of The Jewish People In The Time Of Jesus Christ.* Peabody, MA: Hendrickson Publishers, reprint 2010; orig. pub. 1890.

Schwartz, George, *In Bad Taste: The MSG Syndrome.* Santa Fe, NM: Health Press, 1988.

Scofield, C. I., *Scofield Reference Bible.* New York, NY: Oxford University Press, 1917.

Scriptures, The. Northriding, S. Africa: Institute For Scripture Research, 2006.

Shores, Louis, gen. ed., *Colliers Encyclopedia.* New York, NY: C. F. Collier, 1993.

Silver, Michael "Mordechai," *The Torah Is Valid.* Organ, NM: Tree of Life Publications, 2004.

Spence, H. D. M. & Joseph S. Exell, gen. eds., *The Pulpit Commentary.* Grand Rapids, MI: William B. Eerdmans Publishing Company, 1950.

Stark, Rodney, *The Rise Of Christianity: How The Obscure, Marginal Jesus Movement Became The Dominant Religious Force In The Western World.* Princeton, NJ: Princeton University Press, 1997.

Stern, David H., *Messianic Jewish Manifesto.* Jerusalem: Jewish New Testament Publications, 1991.

Strong, James, *Strong's Exhaustive Concordance Of The Bible.* Iowa Falls, IA: World Bible Publishers, reprint 1989; orig. pub. 1890.

Sugden, Edward H., gen. ed., *The Standard Sermons of John Wesley.* London: The Epworth Press, 1921.

Tanakh: A New Translation of The Holy Scriptures According to the Traditional Hebrew Text. Philadelphia, PN: The Jewish Publication Society, 1985.

Tenney, Merrill C., *New Testament Times.* Grand Rapids, MI: William B. Eerdmans Publishing Company, 1965.

Unger, Merrill F., *The New Unger's Bible Dictionary.* Chicago, IL: Moody Press, 1988.

Vine, W. E., *An Expository Dictionary Of New Testament Words.* Westwood, NJ: Revell Publishers, 1940.

Walker, Williston, *A History Of The Christian Church.* New York, NY: Charles Scribner's Sons, 1959; orig. pub. 1918.

Webster, Noah, *The Original Webster's Unabridged Dictionary.* USA: The Dictionary Publishing Company, 1901.

Westcott, Brooke Foss, *The Epistles Of St. John.* Grand Rapids, MI: William B. Eerdmans Publishing Company, reprint 1960; orig. pub. 1883.

White, James, *The King James Controversy.* Minneapolis, MN: Bethany House Publishers, 1995.

White, Lew, *Fossilized Customs: The Pagan Origins Of Popular Customs.* Louisville, KY: Strawberry Islands Messianic Publishing Institute For Scripture Research, nd.

Wilken, Robert Louis, *John Chrysostom and The Jews: Rhetoric and Reality In The Late Fourth Century.* Berkeley, CA: University of California Press, 1983.

Wohlberg, Steve, *Exploding The Israel Deception.* Roseville, CA: Amazing Facts, 2006.

World Book Encyclopedia. Chicago, IL: World Book Publishers, 2001.

Wuest, Kenneth S., *Wuest's Word Studies From the Greek New Testament.* Grand Rapids, MI: William B. Eerdmans Publishing Company, 1961.

Zodhates, Spiros, gen. ed., *The Complete Word Study New Testament.* Chattanooga, TN: AGM Publishers, 1992.

Ministry Resources

We have listed the following resources in hopes that they will be of further help in the growth and maturity of the Beleiver. However, not all the views expressed by these ministries are necessarily the views of this writer. Therefore, it is incumbent upon each person to test the validity of these views in the light of Scripture.

ArtScroll Library: call for free catalogue to order the suggested "Viduy" ['confession of sin'] booklet, Hebrew Bibles, cookbooks for healthy eating, books on parenting, the festivals, crafts, and much more; http://www.artscroll.com.

Azamra: subscribe free to Rabbi Avraham Greenbaum's weekly teachings for Jews and Gentiles from Jerusalem; http://www.azamra.org.

Etz Chayim-Tree of Life Messianic Congregation: offers weekly teachings and materials, such as the Messianic Siddur that can be used by congregations and individuals at home; http://www.etz-chayim.org.

God's Learning Channel: offers 24 hour programing through TV and Internet, exploring the Hebrew Roots of Christianity; http://www.godslearningchannel.com.

First Fruits of Zion: offers written study and CDs that directs the teaching of Torah toward *Yeshua HaMashiach;* http://www.ffoz.org.

Hatikva Ministries: an internet ministry which offers free teachings on Tuesday evenings that focus on the significance of the Temple as it relates to the life of the Believer, at 7:00 pm. CT. Joseph Good also offers DVD teachings on the last days, such as "America in Prophecy," "The False Messiah," "The Days of Awe," etc. http://www.hatikva.org.

Healing Secrets From The Bible; Patrick Quillin, Ph.D., RD., CNS., has written an outstanding book on tips for a healthy and longer life, which can be ordered from most book stores and Amazon; http://www.amazon.com.

Hebrew Roots; subscribe for free periodical issues on subjects such as the Feasts of the Lord, the *Torah* of Truth, Preparing the Bride, Wedding of Messiah, Gentiles and the *Torah,* a Believer's Passover Haggadah [Seder Booklet], including many other written and audio teachings; http://www.HebrewRoots.net.

Jerusalem Perspective: subscribe for free articles highlighting the Hebraic and Jewish nature of *Yeshua's* sayings; http://www.jerusalemperspective.com.

Jewish Encyclopedia.Com.: an excellent Jewish research source that is free on the Internet; http://www.jewishencyclopedia.com.

Jewish Jewels: subscribe for free newsletter. View *Jewish Jewels* on TV and the webb; http://www.jewishjewels.org.

Judaism 101: a list of the 613 mitzvot ['commandments'] as compiled by the Jewish scholar "Rambom," better known as Maimonides; http://www.jewfaq.org/613.htm

Outreach Israel Ministries: an internet ministry which offers free weekly weekly teachings on the Believer's walk in Torah, including booklets on many important questions frequently asked about the Scriptures; http://www.outreachisrael.net.

The China Study: one of the best scientific researched and documented books in today's market on the dangers of eating meats and processed foods. Written by Dr. T. Colin Campbell, *The China Study* can be ordered at most book stores and Amazon; http://www.amazon.com.

The Complete Word Study Old Testament and *The Complete Word Study New Testament* can be ordered at most book stores, as well as www.amazon.com.

The Hebrew-Greek Key Study Bible can be ordered at most book stores and Amazon; http://www.amazon.com.

The Scriptures: A literal translation of Genesis through Revelation, which restores the Name of the Creator and Messiah to the text in each place it occurs in the Scriptures. *The Scriptures* can be ordered at most book stores and Amazon; http://www.amazon.com.

In Divine Health: a book filled with medical research and biblical insights on disease-preventing nutrition, written by Don Colbert, M.D. *In Divine Health* can be ordered in most Christian book stores and Amazon: http://www.amazon.com.

You Tube Messianic Music: on the internet tap into music videos of noted Messianic artists, such as Johathan Settel, Paul, Wilbur, Joel Chernoff, Barry & Batya Segal, etc.

INDEX

J

K

L